Contemporary Conflict Resolution

Second Edition

This book is dedicated to the founders of the field and to the new generation of conflict resolvers from all parts of the world who are carrying on their work

Contemporary Conflict Resolution

The prevention, management and transformation of deadly conflicts

SECOND EDITION

Oliver Ramsbotham,
Tom Woodhouse and Hugh Miall

polity

First published in 2005 by Polity Press

Polity Press
65 Bridge Street
Cambridge CB2 1UR, UK

Polity Press
350 Main Street
Malden, MA 02148, USA

ISBN: 0-7456-3212-2
ISBN: 0-7456-3213-0 (pb)

A catalogue record for this book is available from the British
Library and has been applied for from the Library of Congress.

Typeset in 10.5 on 13pt Swift
by Servis Filmsetting Ltd, Manchester
Printed and bound in Great Britain by MPG Books Ltd, Bodmin, Cornwall

For further information on Polity, visit our website:
www.polity.co.uk

Contents

List of Figures

List of Tables

List of Boxes

List of Maps

Preface

We produced the first edition of this book in order to provide a comprehensive account of the way in which conflict resolution emerged as a field of academic enquiry and how it might be utilized in the effort to manage post-Cold War conflict peacefully. Since the book was published, the conflict landscape has continued to change dynamically. Conflict resolution, conflict prevention and post-conflict peacebuilding techniques and policies have become familiar in the mandates and objectives of a wide range of international organizations and projects in recent years. Indeed, this has been so prevalent that critics have suggested that the effect of this mainstreaming of the conflict resolution agenda has been to re-enforce existing global power structures and to stabilize international relations in favour of the powerful. At the same time, new conflict challenges have emerged in the post-11 September 2001 environment where wars on terror have preoccupied policy-makers and public debate.

In this second edition of the book we have attempted to respond to these issues in two main ways. First, we have aimed to reclaim terms such as conflict resolution and conflict transformation, or conflict prevention and post-conflict peacebuilding, from those who in our view misuse them, by explaining clearly how they are understood within the conflict resolution tradition. As in the case of appeals to freedom and democracy, we argue that those who invoke these concepts should ensure that their purposes and actions are consonant with them – or else stop using such language. We suggest that peace and conflict research is part of an emancipatory discourse and practice which is making a valuable and defining contribution to emerging norms of democratic, just and equitable systems of global governance. We argue that conflict resolution has a role to play in the radical negotiation of these norms, so that international conflict management is grounded in the needs of those who are the victims of conflict and who are frequently marginalized from conventional power structures.

Second, we have tried to engage constructively with the radical agenda of critical theorists and others, who claim that conflict resolution is incapable of serving a truly emancipatory purpose of this kind because it is limited to 'problem-solving' that takes the world as it finds it and seeks to do no more than manage existing structures. In our view this is a misleading caricature of conflict resolution. We aim to show how transformation in the interest of emancipation has been integral to conflict resolution from the start. Our central argument is that the main thrust of critical thinking is illuminating, exciting and entirely in tune with the conflict resolution tradition. But we also think that so far the various critical approaches become abruptly less impressive, if not entirely silent, when it comes to suggesting specific remedies or practical directions ahead. So our second purpose in the book is to bridge this gap by looking carefully at current practice from a conflict resolution perspective with a view to defining the key steps that need to be taken if decisive progress is to be made in the direction sketched out in critical theory.

Part I is a thorough updating of the first edition of the book. Part II is an entirely new addition which aims to define what we call 'cosmopolitan conflict resolution' and which we see as the main task for the next generation of conflict resolvers.

We want to acknowledge the help of many people in the task of revising this book. Most of all, the example of those who founded the field provided much of the inspiration for what we have attempted here. The more we have studied the work of people such as Elise and Kenneth Boulding, of Adam Curle, Johan Galtung, John Burton, and many other pioneers, the more we realized how wise and prescient they were. We would also like to thank our colleagues, and especially our students, at the Centre for Conflict Resolution, Department of Peace Studies, at the University of Bradford, and at the Richardson Institute at the University of Lancaster. They have brought a wealth of experience from all parts of the world to our universities and we have learned from them at least as much as we have imparted. We hope that this book will provide some help to them as they return to their communities and proceed with the work of ridding the world of the scourge of war.

Acknowledgements

The authors and publisher gratefully acknowledge permission to reproduce copyright material.

Addams, Jane, Quotation, Women's International League for Peace and Freedom

Boulding, Kenneth, *The Three Faces of Power*, Sage Publications, 1989, for table 1.3

Boulding, Kenneth, extracts reprinted from *Journal of Conflict Resolution* on publication of first issue, 1957, and in *Journal of Conflict Resolution* 27(1), Sage Publications, 1973

Boulding, Elise, address to the International Sociological Associations Symposium, Bielefeld, July 1994, Women's International League for Peace and Freedom

Brown, M., ed., *The International Dimensions of Internal Conflict*, MIT Press, 1996, for table 4.4

Reproduced with the Permission of Her Majesty the Queen in Right of Canada, Represented by the Minister of Foreign Affairs, 2005, for box 6.2

Erikkson, M. et al., *Journal of Peace Research* 41(5), Sage Publications, 2004, for table 3.1

Francis, D., *People Peace and Power: Conflict Transformation in Action*, Pluto, 2002, for figure 1.11

Freire, P., *Pedagogy of the Oppressed*, Continuum International Publishing Group, 1993

Gleditsch, N., *Regional Distribution of Major Armed Conflicts by Type*, Sage Publications, 2002

Heaney, Seamus, lines from 'The Cure at Troy', reprinted from *The Cure at Troy: A Version of Sophocles' Philoctetes*, copyright © 1990 by Seamus Heaney, by permission of the publishers, Faber & Faber Ltd and Farrar Straus & Giroux, Inc.

Langille, H. P., *Bridging the Commitment Capacity Gap: Existing Arrangements and Options for Enhancing UN Rapid Deployment Capabilities*, Wayne, NJ, Center for UN Reform Education, 2002, for box 6.3

Lederach, J. P., *Preparing for Peace: Conflict transformation Across Cultures*, Syracuse University Press, 1995, for table 9.1

Lederach, J. P., *Building Peace: Sustainable Reconciliation in Divided Societies*, US Institute of Peace, 1997, for figure 1.10

Lewer, N., *International Non-Governmental Organisations and Peace Building Perspectives from Peace Studies and Conflict Resolution*, Working Paper 3, Centre for Conflict Resolution, University of Bradford, 1999, for box 9.1

OSCE, Report by Max van der Stoel

George Papandreou, for box 15.1

Marshall, Donna, *Women in War and Peace*, US Institute of Peace, 2000, for box 12.2

Renner, M., *The Anatomy of Resource Wars*, Worldwatch Institute, Paper 162, 2002, for table 4.2

Reynolds Levy, L., *The Internet and Post Conflict Peace Building*, Centre for Conflict Resolution, University of Bradford, 2004, for figure 9.1

Taheri, A, in *The Times*, 26 May 2003, Times/NI Syndication

Wallensteen, P., *Understanding Conflict Resolution*, Sage Publications, 2002, for box 7.1

Whyte, J, *Interpreting Northern Ireland*, Oxford University Press, 1990, for box 4.1

Every effort has been made to trace all copyright holders, but if any has been inadvertently overlooked, the publishers will be pleased to include any necessary credits in any subsequent reprint or edition.

Boxes and Tables

Cambridge University Press for table 2.1, reprinted from K. Holsti, *Peace and War: Armed Conflicts and International Order 1648–989* (Cambridge University Press, 1991).

Nicole Ball: extract reprinted from 'Rebuilding war-torn societies', in Chester A. Crocker, Fen Osler Hampson, with Pamela Aall (eds), *Managing Global Chaos: Sources of and Responses to International Conflict* (United States Institute of Peace Press, 1996), by permission of the United States Institute of Peace.

List of Abbreviations

ACCORD	African Centre for the Constructive Resolution of Disputes
ADF	Alliance of Democratic Forces (Uganda)
ADR	Alternative Dispute Resolution
AFL	Armed Forces of Liberia
AFRC	Armed Forces Revolutionary Council (Sierra Leone)
AIAI	Al-Ittihad al-Islamiya (Somalia)
AKUF	Arbeitsgemeinschaft Kriegsursachenforschung (work group on war research, Hamburg)
ALiR	L'Armée pour la Liberation du Rwanda
ANC	African National Congress
ARENA	Alianza Republicana Nacionalista (El Salvador)
ARI	Adversarial, Reflexive, Integrative
ARK	Anti-Ratna Kampanja (anti-war campaign, Croatia)
ASEAN	Association of South-East Asian Nations
ASG	Abu Sayaff Group (Philippines)
AU	African Union
CBO	Community-based Organization
CCCRTE	Coordinating Committee for Conflict Resolution Training in Europe
CDS	Conflict Data Service (Northern Ireland)
CECORE	Centre for Conflict Resolution (Uganda)
CEDAW	Convention on the Elimination of All Forms of Discrimination Against Women
CFSP	Common Foreign and Security Policy
CIACG	Coalition Interagency Coordination Group (US/Iraq)
CIDCM	Center for International Development and Conflict Management (Maryland, USA)
CIS	Commonwealth of Independent States
CIVPOL	Civilian Police
CMOC	Civil-Military Operation Centre
CODESA	Convention for a Democratic South Africa
COW	Correlates of War Project
CPA	Coalition Provisional Authority (Iraq)
CPN-M	Communist Party of Nepal-Maoist
CPRU	Conflict Prevention and Reconstruction Unit (World Bank)
CZM	Centar za Mir (Centre for Peace, Croatia)

DDR	Disarmament, Demobilization, Repatriation
DDRRR	Disarmament, Demobilization, Repatriation, Resettlement and Reintegration
DPA	Department of Political Affairs (UN)
DPKO	Department of Peacekeeping Operations (UN)
DRC	Democratic Republic of Congo
DUP	Democratic Unionist Party (Northern Ireland)
ECCP	European Centre for Conflict Prevention
ECHO	European Community Humanitarian Office
ECOMOG	Economic Community of West African States Ceasefire Monitoring Group
ECOWAS	Economic Community of West African States
ECPS	Executive Community on Peace and Security (UN)
ELN	Ejército de Liberación Nacional (Colombia)
EPL	Ejército Popular de Liberación (Colombia)
ETA	Euskadi Ta Askatasuna (Basque Country and Liberty)
ETIM	Eastern Turkestan Islamic Movement (China)
EU	European Union
EZLN	Ejército Zapatista de Liberación Nacional (Mexico)
FAFO	Institute for Applied Social Sciences (Norway)
FARC	Fuerzas Armados Revolucionarias Colombianas
FBH	Federation of Bosnia-Herzegovina
FDLR	Forces Democratiques de Liberation du Rwanda
FIS	Front Islamique du Salut (Algeria)
FMNL	Farabundo Marti Front for National Liberation (El Salvador)
FRELIMO	Frente para a Libertaçâo de Mocambique
FRETILIN	Frente Revolucionario Timorense de Libertacao e Independencia (Timor)
FRY	Federal Republic of Yugoslavia
FSU	Former Soviet Union
FYROM	Former Yugoslav Republic of Macedonia
GAM	Gerakan Aceh Merdeka (free Aceh movement)
GCPP	Global Conflict Prevention Pool (UK)
GDP	Gross Domestic Product
GEDS	Global Event-Data System
GIA	Groupe Islamique Armée (Algeria)
GICM	Moroccan Islamic Combat Group
GRIT	Graduated and Reciprocal Initiatives in Tension Reduction
GRO	Grassroots Organization
GSPC	Group for the Call and Combat (Algeria)
HCNM	High Commissioner for National Minorities
HUJI	Harakat ul-Jihad-Islami (Pakistan)
HUM	Harakat ul-Mujahidin (Pakistan)
IAA	Islamic Army of Aden (Yemen)
ICISS	International Commission on Intervention and State Sovereignty
ICRC	International Committee of the Red Cross
ICT	Information Communications Technology

IDEA	International Institute for Democracy and Electoral Assistance, Stockholm
IDP	Internally Displaced Person
IFI	International Financial Institution
IFOR	Implementation Force (Bosnia)
IG	Al-Gamaa al-Islamiya (Egypt)
IGO	Inter-governmental organization
IISS	International Institute for Strategic Studies
IMAT	International Military Advisory Team (Sierra Leone)
IMF	International Monetary Fund
IMU	Islamic Movement of Uzbekistan
INCORE	Initiative on Conflict Resolution and Ethnicity
INGO	International non-governmental organization
INTERFET	International Force in East Timor
IPA	International Peace Academy
IPRA	International Peace Research Association
IRA	Irish Republican Army
IRW	Intervention, reconstruction, withdrawal (operation)
ISAF	International Security Assistance Force (Afghanistan)
JCR	Journal of Conflict Resolution
JI	Jemaah Islamiya (South-East Asia)
JIACG	Joint Interagency Cooperation Group (US)
JKLF	Jammu and Kashmir Liberation Front (India)
JM	Jaish-e-Mohammed (Pakistan)
JWP	Joint Warfare Publication (UK Ministry of Defence)
KFOR	The NATO-led Kosovo Force
KLA	Kosovo Liberation Army
KLA/KCF	Khalistan Liberation Force/Khalistan Commando Force (India)
KMM	Kumpulan Mujahidin Malaysia
KNU	Karen National Union (Myanmar)
LAS	League of Arab States
LNGO	Local non-governmental organization
LRA	Lord's Resistance Army (Uganda)
LT	Lashkar-e-Yayyiba (Pakistan)
LTTE	Liberation Tigers of Tamil Eelam (Sri Lanka)
MAR	Minorities at Risk program (Maryland)
MCPMR	Mechanism for conflict prevention, management and resolution
MFDC	Democratic Forces of the Casamance (Senegal)
MILF	Moro Islamic Liberation Front (Philippines)
MINUCI	UN Mission in Ivory Coast
MINUGUA	UN Verification Mission in Guatemala
MINUSTAH	UN Stabilization Mission in Haiti
MISAB	Inter-Africa Mission to Monitor the Implementation of the Bangui Agreements
MLC	Mouvement de Liberation Congolais
MNLF	Moro National Liberation Front (Philippines)
MONUA	UN Observer Mission in Angola

MONUC	UN Mission in Democratic Republic of Congo
MPLA	Movimento Popular de Libertacao de Angola
MRTA	Movimento Revolucionario Tupac Amaru (Peru)
NATO	North Atlantic Treaty Organization
NDA	National Democratic Alliance (Sudan)
NGO	Non-governmental organization
NIWC	Northern Ireland Women's Coalition
NLA	National Liberation Army
NP	National Party (South Africa)
NPA	New People's Army
NPT	Non-Proliferation Treaty
NSSR	National Security Strategy Report (US)
OAS	Organization of American States
OAU	Organization of African Union
ODIHR	Office for Democratic Institutions and Human Rights (OSCE)
OECD	Organization for Economic Cooperation and Development
OIC	Organization of the Islamic Conference
OLF	Oromo Liberation Front
ONLF	Ogaden National Liberation Front
ONUB	UN Observer Group in Burundi
ONUC	UN Operation in the Congo
ONUCA	UN Observer Group in Central America
ONUMOZ	UN Operation in Mozambique
ONUSAL	UN Observer Mission in El Salvador
OOTW	Operations Other Than War
ORHA	Office for Reconstruction and Humanitarian Assistance (US/Iraq)
OSCE	Organization for Security and Cooperation in Europe
PBSO	Peacebuilding Support Office
PCF	Post-Conflict Fund (World Bank)
PCIA	Peace and Conflict Impact Assessment
PCRU	Post-Conflict Reconstruction Unit (UK)
PDD	Presidential Decision Directive (US)
PFLP	Popular Front for the Liberation of Palestine
PIOOM	Interdisciplinary Research Program on Causes of Human Rights Violations
PKK	Kurdistan Workers' Party (Turkey)
PLO	Palestine Liberation Army
PNG	Papua New Guinea
POLISARIO	Popular Front for the Liberation of Sanguia, El-Hamra and Rio de Oro (Western Sahara)
PRIO	Peace Research Institute Oslo
PSC	Protracted Social Conflict
PSO	Peace Support Operation
PTSD	Post-traumatic Stress Disorder
PUK	Patriotic Union of Kurdistan (Iraq)
RBH	Republic of Bosnia-Herzegovina

RCD	Rassemblement Congolaises pour la Democratie
RDMHQ	Rapidly Deployable Mission HQ
RENAMO	Resistencia Bacional Mocambicana
RPF	Rwanda Patriotic Front
RS	Republika Srpska (Serb Republic)
RUC	Royal Ulster Constabulary
RUF	Revolutionary United Front (Sierra Leone)
SADC	South African Development Council
SAIRI	Supreme Assembly for the Islamic Revolution in Iraq
SALT	Strategic Arms Limitation Talks
SB	Shanti Bahina (Army of Peace, Bangladesh)
SFOR	Stabilization Force (Bosnia)
SHIRBRIG	Stand-by High Readiness Brigade
SIPRI	Stockholm International Peace Research Institute
SL	Senderoso Luminoso (shining path, Peru)
SPLA	Sudanese People's Liberation Army
SRRC	Somali Reconciliation and Restoration Council
SRSG	Special Representative of the Secretary-General
SSA	Shan State Army
SWAPO	South-West Africa People's Organization (Namibia)
TCC	Troop-Contributing Country
TCG	Tunisian Combat Group
TFF	Transnational Foundation for Peace and Future Research
TRC	Truth and Reconciliation Commission (South Africa)
UCDP	Uppsala Conflict Data Program
UKDFID	UK Department for International Development
UKFCO	UK Foreign and Commonwealth Office
UKMOD	UK Ministry of Defence
ULFA	United Liberation Force of Assam
UNAMA	UN Assistance Mission in Afghanistan
UNAMIR	UN Assistance Mission for Rwanda
UNAMSIL	UN Mission in Sierra Leone
UNAVEM	UN Angola Verification Mission
UNCRO	UN Confidence Restoration Operation (Croatia)
UNCTC	UN Counter-Terrorism Committee (of the Security Council)
UNDP	UN Development Programme
UNDPI	UN Department for Public Information
UNEF	UN Emergency Force (Middle East)
UNESCO	UN Educational, Scientific and Cultural Organization
UNFICYP	UN Peacekeeping Force in Cyprus
UNGA	UN General Assembly
UNHCR	UN High Commissioner for Refugees
UNICEF	UN Children's Fund
UNITA	Uniao Nacional para a Independencia Total de Angola
UNITAF	United Task Force (Somalia)
UNITAR	UN Institute for Training and Research
UNMEE	UN Mission in Eritrea-Ethiopia

UNMIBH	UN Mission in Bosnia and Herzegovina
UNMIK	UN Mission in Kosovo
UNMIL	UN Mission in Liberia
UNMISET	UN Mission in East Timor
UNMOP	UN Mission of Observers in Prevlaka
UNOCI	UN Mission in Ivory Coast
UNOMIL	UN Observer Mission in Liberia
UNOSOM	UN Operation in Somalia
UNPREDEP	UN Preventive Deployment Force (Macedonia)
UNPROFOR	UN Protection Force (former Yugoslavia)
UNPWG	UN Policy Working Group on the UN and Terrorism
UNSAS	UN Stand-by Arrangement System
UNSC(R)	UN Security Council (Resolution)
UNSG	UN Secretary-General
UNTAC	UN Transitional Authority in Cambodia
UNTAES	UN Transitional Administration for Eastern Slavonia, Baranja and Western Sirmium (Croatia)
UNTAET	UN Transitional Administration in East Timor
UNTAG	UN Transition Assistance Group (Namibia)
UPF	United People's Front (Nepal)
USAID	US Agency for International Development
USDOD	US Department of Defense
USIP	US Institute of Peace
UTO	United Tajik Opposition
WILPF	Womens' International League for Peace and Freedom
WMD	Weapons of Mass Destruction
WNBF	West Nile Bank Front (Uganda)
WOMP	World Order Models Project

PART I

CONTEMPORARY CONFLICT RESOLUTION

Introduction to Conflict Resolution: Concepts and Definitions

IN this second edition of our book we bring the survey of the conflict resolution field up to date at the beginning of the twenty-first century. Conflict resolution as a defined specialist field has come of age in the post-Cold War era. It has also come face to face with fundamental new challenges, some of which have come into even sharper focus since the first edition of this book.

Why a Second Edition?

As a defined field of study, conflict resolution started in the 1950s and 1960s. This was at the height of the Cold War, when the development of nuclear weapons and the conflict between the superpowers seemed to threaten human survival. A group of pioneers from different disciplines saw the value of studying conflict as a general phenomenon, with similar properties whether it occurs in international relations, domestic politics, industrial relations, communities, families or between individuals. They saw the potential of applying approaches that were evolving in industrial relations and community mediation settings to conflicts in general, including civil and international conflicts.

A handful of people in North America and Europe began to establish research groups to develop these new ideas. They were not taken very seriously. The international relations profession had its own categories for understanding international conflict, and did not welcome the interlopers. Nor was the combination of analysis and practice implicit in the new ideas easy to reconcile with traditional scholarly institutions or the traditions of practitioners such as diplomats and politicians.

Nevertheless, the new ideas attracted interest, and the field began to grow and spread. Scholarly journals in conflict resolution were created. Institutions to study the field were established, and their number rapidly increased. The field developed its own subdivisions, with different groups studying international crises, internal wars, social conflicts and approaches ranging from negotiation and mediation to experimental games.

By the 1980s, conflict resolution ideas were increasingly making a difference in real conflicts. In South Africa, for example, the Centre for Intergroup Studies was applying the approaches that had emerged in the field to the developing confrontation between apartheid and its challengers, with impressive results. In the Middle East, a peace process was getting under way in which negotiators on both sides had gained experience both of each other and of conflict resolution through problem-solving workshops. In Northern Ireland, groups inspired by the new approach had set up community relations initiatives that were not only reaching across community divides but were also becoming an accepted responsibility of local government. In war-torn regions of Africa and South-East Asia, development workers and humanitarian agencies were seeing the need to take account of conflict and conflict resolution as an integral part of their activities.

By the closing years of the Cold War, the climate for conflict resolution was changing radically. With relations between the superpowers improving, the ideological and military competition that had fuelled many regional conflicts was fading away. Protracted regional conflicts in Southern Africa, Central America, and East Asia moved towards settlements. It seemed that the UN could return to play the role its founders expected.

The dissolution of the Soviet Union brought to a close the long period in which a single international conflict dominated the international system. Instead, internal conflicts, ethnic conflicts, conflicts over secession and power struggles within countries became the norm in the 1990s. These reflected not so much struggles between competing centres of power, of the kind that had characterized international conflict for most of the 350 years since the peace of Westphalia, but the fragmentation and breakdown of state structures, economies and whole societies. At their extreme, in parts of Africa, the new wars witnessed the return of mercenary armies and underpaid militias which preyed on civilian populations in a manner reminiscent of medieval times.

In this new climate, the attention of scholars of international relations and comparative politics turned to exactly the type of conflict that had preoccupied the conflict resolution thinkers for many years. A richer cross-fertilization of ideas developed between conflict resolution and these traditional fields. At the same time, practitioners from various backgrounds were attracted to conflict resolution. International statesmen began to use the language, international organizations set up Conflict Resolution Mechanisms and Conflict Prevention Centres. A former President of the United States, Jimmy Carter, became one of the most active leaders of a conflict resolution non-govermental organization (NGO). The Nyerere Foundation was established with comparable aims for Africa. Development and aid workers, who had earlier tended to see their function as 'non-political', now became interested in linking their expertise to conflict resolution approaches, because so many of the areas they were most concerned with were conflict zones – 'complex humanitarian emergencies' were seen also to be 'complex political emergencies'. A similar cross-fertilization took place with international peacekeepers. Overseas development ministries in several countries set up conflict units and began funding conflict prevention and resolution initiatives on a significant scale. Regional organizations such as the Organization for Security and Cooperation in Europe (OSCE) and the Organization of African Unity (OAU) (now the African Union (AU)), did the same.[1] The UN Secretary-General declared the prevention of violent conflict to be a central goal for the international community in the new millennium. How to achieve a 'peaceful settlement of disputes' between states was a familiar theme in the international relations and strategic studies literature and had always been part of the stock-in-trade of international diplomacy. Less familiar was the challenge to statist international organizations of managing non-state conflicts.

A greater degree of impact, however, also brought greater scrutiny, and the development of searching critiques from different quarters. This second edition of our book has been largely prompted by these. Conflict resolution had always been controversial, both in relation to outside disciplines, and internally amongst its different protagonists and schools. It also drew persistent fire from critics at different points along the political and intellectual spectrum from neo-realists to neo-Marxists. After the high hopes of the early 1990s, three developments in particular took the gloss off what were no doubt often unrealistic expectations of rapid results. First, there were the difficulties that international interveners encountered in chaotic war zones such as in Bosnia (1992–5) and Somalia (1992–3). A number of analysts pointed to the impact of globalization on the weakening of vulnerable states, the provision of cheap weaponry suitable for 'asymmetric war', and the generation of shadow economies that made 'new wars' self-perpetuating and profitable. Conflict resolution was seen to be incapable of addressing this nexus. Second, there was the collapse of the Israeli-Palestinian 'Oslo' peace process with the launch of the second intifada or uprising in September 2000. The Oslo process had been hailed at the time as an example of success for classic conflict resolution approaches. Third came the shock of the destruction of the World Trade Center and the attack on the Pentagon on 11 September 2001, together with the kaleidoscope of events that followed, summed up as the 'war on terror'. What possible answer could conflict resolution have to what was seen as the lethal combination of 'rogue states', globalized crime, the proliferation of weapons of mass destruction, and the fanatical ideologues of international terrorism?

Behind these political challenges lay more precisely focused intellectual challenges. We will look briefly at three of these here in order to clarify what is characteristic of the conflict resolution approach and to explore the scope and limits of the field (Woodhouse, 1999b). These themes will be carried through the rest of the book.

Our first set of critics, exemplified by David Shearer's analysis of 'conflict resolution in Sierra Leone' (1997), question whether a conflict resolution consensus-promoting strategy, based on impartial mediation and negotiation by the international community, is appropriate in cases where war is fuelled by 'greed' rather than 'grievance' (Berdal and Malone, eds, 2000). 'Warlord insurgencies' or clan-based criminal mafias driven by economic motives are unlikely to be amenable to resolution by consent and negotiation. Indeed, pursuit of mediated settlements and the bringing in of humanitarian aid can have the unintended effect of prolonging the conflict and feeding the warring factions, with civilian populations suffering most. Targeted military action, on the other hand, is said to be much more likely to have the effect of foreshortening the conflict by persuading those losing ground to accept a settlement – as demonstrated in Bosnia in 1995. This is a variant of the traditional realist criticism of conflict resolution, in which international politics is seen as a struggle between antagonistic and irreconcilable groups with power and coercion as the only ultimate currency, and 'soft power' approaches of conflict resolution dismissed as ineffective and dangerous. The essence of our response to this criticism is that in the kinds of conflict prevalent since the end of the Cold War a 'quick military fix' is rarely possible. Moreover, as exemplified particularly in chapters 6 and 8, where we describe how military force has been used by international interveners in response to conflicts of this kind, its function has been to create political space for a post-war reconstruction process defined largely in terms of conflict resolution principles.

Our second set of critics, exemplified in Mark Duffield's paper 'Evaluating conflict resolution' (1997; also see 2001), argue that, far from contemporary internal wars being aberrant, irrational and non-productive phenomena, they represent 'the emergence of entirely new types of social formation adapted for survival on the margins of the global economy' (p. 100). Instead of recognizing this, however, the most powerful economies and governments treat these wars as local symptoms of local failures, and therefore expect 'behavioural and attitudinal change' in those countries. The disciplinary norms of 'liberal governance' are imposed from outside. Conflict resolution, described by Duffield as a 'socio-psychological model', together with aid and human development programmes, is seen to have been co-opted into this enterprise – used as an instrument of pacification in unruly border territories so that existing power structures can continue to control the global system. This is a variant of the traditional Marxist criticism, which sees 'liberal' conflict resolution as naive and theoretically uncritical, since it attempts to reconcile interests that should not be reconciled, fails to take sides in unequal and unjust struggles, and lacks an analysis within a properly global perspective of the forces of exploitation and oppression. We will engage with this substantial critique throughout the rest of this book, arguing that what is criticized is a caricature of conflict resolution, not conflict resolution itself, and that from the beginning the field incorporated the imperative of structural change in asymmetric conflict situations – albeit no doubt not in a classic Marxist manner.

In general, in response to both of these criticisms, whereas realist theory and most Marxist theory sees violence as unavoidable and integral to the nature of conflict, such determinism is rejected in conflict resolution. Here there are always seen to be other options, and direct violence is regarded as an avoidable consequence of human choice.

Our third set of critics, exemplified in Paul Salem's 'Critique of western conflict resolution from a non-western perspective' (1993; see also Salem, ed., 1997), argue that the 'western' assumptions on which conflict resolution rests are not applicable universally. Salem questions some of the 'hidden assumptions in the western approach to conflict resolution' from an Arab Muslim perspective and suggests that they are not shared in other parts of the world. These are examples of a wider 'culture critique' that has been much dicussed in the conflict resolution field in recent years and will be looked at again, particularly in chapter 15.

In response to these and other criticisms, this book argues that, on the contrary, the developing tradition of thinking about conflict and conflict resolution is all the more relevant as the fixed structures of sovereignty and governance break down. All over the world, societies are facing stresses from population growth, structural change in the world economy, migration into cities, environmental degradation and rapid social change. Societies with institutions, rules or norms for managing conflict and well-established traditions of governance are generally better able to accommodate peacefully to change; those with weaker governance, fragile social bonds and little consensus on values or traditions are more likely to buckle. Strengthening the capacity of conflict resolution within societies and political institutions, especially preventatively, is a vital part of the response to the phenomena of warlordism and ethnonationalism. We argue that conflict resolution has a role to play, even in war zones, since building peace constituencies and understandings across divided communities is an essential element of humanitarian engagement. We argue that conflict resolution is an integral part of work for development, social justice and social transformation, that aims to tackle the problems of which mercenaries and child soldiers are symptoms. We argue for a broad understanding of conflict resolution, to include not only mediation between the parties but also efforts to address the wider context in which international actors, domestic constituencies and intra-party relationships sustain violent conflicts. We argue that although many of the recent theories and practices of conflict resolution may have been articulated more vociferously in the West, their deep roots reach into far older world traditions from which they draw their inspiration. Indeed, every culture and society has its own version of what is, after all, a general social and political need. The point is not to abandon conflict resolution because it is western, but to find ways to enrich western and non-western traditions through their mutual encounter. And, finally, this applies all the more urgently to the phenomenon of international terrorism. Here, conflict resolution teaches that short-term denial strategies on their own will fail unless accompanied by and embedded within middle-term persuasion strategies, long-term prevention strategies, and international coordination and legitimation strategies. We look at this in more detail in chapter 11.

Conflict Resolution Models

We begin our survey by looking at general framework models that relate the different components of conflict resolution to each other (complementarity) and to the nature and phases of the conflicts being addressed (contingency). We will then give a brief synopsis of some of the classical ideas that have shaped conflict resolution thinking and practice and are still foundations of the field. At the end we will add some more recent models that are also proving influential.

We must at the outset note the current debate within the field between 'conflict resolvers' and 'conflict transformers' – although we will then set it aside. In this book we see conflict transformation as the deepest level of the conflict resolution tradition, rather than as a separate venture as some would prefer (Vayrynen, ed., 1991; Rupesinghe, ed., 1995; Jabri, 1996; Francis, 2002; Lederach, 2003).[2] In our view it does not matter in the end what label is used as the umbrella term (candidates have included 'conflict regulation' and 'conflict management' as well as conflict resolution and conflict transformation), so long as the field is coherent enough to contain the substance of what is being advocated in each case. We believe that the field retains its coherence, that it is best left intact, and that conflict resolvers and conflict transformers are essentially engaged in the same enterprise – as shown in titles of books such as Dukes's 1996 *Resolving Public Conflict: Transforming Community and Governance*. We continue to use conflict resolution as the generic term here for three reasons. First, because it was the earliest term used to define the new field (the 1957 *Journal of Conflict Resolution*). Second, because it is still the most widely used term among analysts and practitioners, as we can see by noting important titles published year by year between the time we began writing the first edition of our book (1995) to the present second edition (2005).[3] Third, because it is the term that is most familiar in the media and among the general public.

Framework Models

We begin by offering a simplified model of Johan Galtung's seminal thinking on the relationship between conflict, violence and peace. As described in chapter 2, Galtung was one of the founders of the field, and the breadth of his understanding of the structural and cultural roots of violence is a corrective to those who caricature conflict resolution as purely relational, symmetrical or psychological.

Galtung's models of conflict, violence and peace

In the late 1960s Johan Galtung (1969; see also 1996: 72) proposed an influential model of conflict that encompasses both symmetric and asymmetric conflicts. He suggested that conflict could be viewed as a triangle, with contradiction (C), attitude (A) and behaviour (B) at its vertices (see figure 1.1). Here the contradiction refers to the underlying conflict situation, which includes the actual or perceived 'incompatibility of goals' between the conflict parties generated by what Mitchell calls a 'mis-match between social values and social structure' (1981: 18). In a symmetric conflict, the contradiction is defined by the parties, their interests and the clash of interests between them. In an asymmetric conflict, it is defined by the parties, their relationship and the conflict of interests inherent in the relationship. Attitude includes

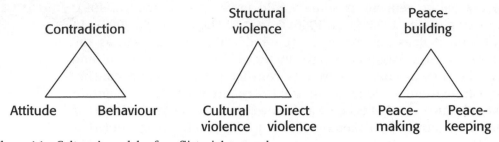

Figure 1.1   Galtung's models of conflict, violence and peace

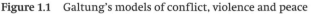

the parties' perceptions and misperceptions of each other and of themselves. These can be positive or negative, but in violent conflicts parties tend to develop demeaning stereotypes of the other, and attitudes are often influenced by emotions such as as fear, anger, bitterness and hatred. Attitude includes emotive (feeling), cognitive (belief) and conative (will) elements. Analysts who emphasize these subjective aspects are said to have an expressive view of the sources of conflict. Behaviour is the third component. It can include cooperation or coercion, gestures signifying conciliation or hostility. Violent conflict behaviour is characterized by threats, coercion and destructive attacks. Analysts who emphasize objective aspects such as structural relationships, competing material interests or behaviours are said to have an 'instrumental' view of the sources of conflict.[4]

Galtung argues that all three components have to be present together in a full conflict. A conflict structure without conflictual attitudes or behaviour is a latent (or structural) one. Galtung sees conflict as a dynamic process in which structure, attitudes and behaviour are constantly changing and influencing one another. As the dynamic develops, it becomes a manifest conflict formation as parties' interests clash or the relationship they are in becomes oppressive. Conflict parties then organize around this structure, to pursue their interests. They develop hostile attitudes and conflictual behaviour. And so the conflict formation starts to grow and intensify. As it does so, it may widen, drawing in other parties, deepen and spread, generating secondary conflicts within the main parties or among outsiders who get sucked in. This often considerably complicates the task of addressing the original, core conflict. Eventually, however, resolving the conflict must involve a set of dynamic changes that involve de-escalation of conflict behaviour, a change in attitudes and transforming the relationships or clashing interests that are at the core of the conflict structure.

A related idea due to Galtung (1990) is the distinction between direct violence (children are murdered), structural violence (children die through poverty) and cultural violence (whatever blinds us to this or seeks to justify it). We end direct violence by changing conflict behaviour, structural violence by removing structural contradictions and injustices, and cultural violence by changing attitudes. These responses relate in turn to broader strategies of peacekeeping, peacebuilding and peacemaking. Galtung defined 'negative peace' as the cessation of direct violence and 'positive peace' as the overcoming of structural and cultural violence as well.

Conflict escalation and de-escalation

The process of conflict escalation is complex and unpredictable. New issues and conflict parties can emerge, internal power struggles can alter tactics and goals, and secondary conflicts and spirals can further complicate the situation. The same is true of de-escalation, with unexpected breakthroughs and setbacks changing the dynamics, with advances in one area or at one level being offset by relapses at others, and with the actions of third parties influencing the outcome in unforeseen ways. Here we offer the simplest model in which escalation phases move along a normal distribution curve from the initial *differences* that are part of all social developments, through the emergence of an original *contradiction* that may or may not remain latent, on up through the process of *polarization* in which antagonistic parties form and the conflict becomes manifest, and culminating in the outbreak of direct *violence* and *war* (see figure 1.2). As we will see in chapter 3, escalation models such as this are popular with those who try to find objective criteria for measuring statistical changes in conflict levels in different countries from year to year. They are also used by those who attempt to match appropriate conflict resolution strategies to them (Glasl, 1982; Fisher and Keashly, 1991).

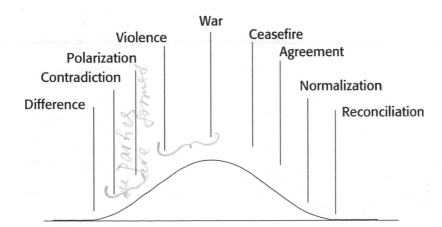

Figure 1.2   Conflict escalation and de-escalation

The hourglass model: a spectrum of conflict resolution responses

Here we combine Galtung's ideas on conflict and violence with escalation/de-escalation phases to produce the 'hourglass' model of conflict resolution responses (Ramsbotham and Woodhouse, 1999). The hourglass represents the narrowing of political space that characterizes conflict escalation, and the widening of political space that characterizes conflict de-escalation. As the space narrows and widens, so different conflict resolution responses become more or less appropriate or possible. This is a contingency and complementarity model, in which 'contingency' refers to the nature and phase of the conflict, and 'complementarity' to the combination of appropriate responses that need to be worked together to maximize chances of success in conflict resolution (see figure 1.3).[5] Conflict transformation is seen to encompass the deepest levels of cultural and structural peacebuilding. Conflict settlement (which many critics wrongly identify with conflict resolution) corresponds to what we call 'elite peacemaking' – in other words, negotiation

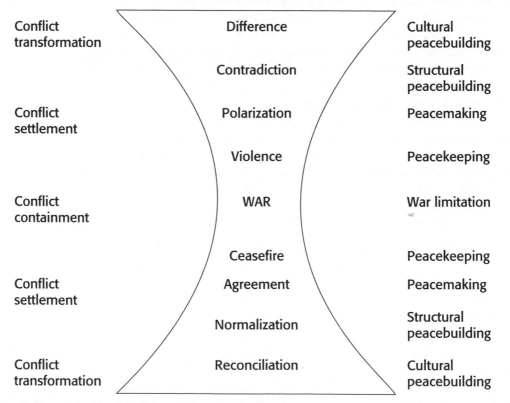

Conflict transformation	Difference	Cultural peacebuilding
	Contradiction	Structural peacebuilding
Conflict settlement	Polarization	Peacemaking
	Violence	Peacekeeping
Conflict containment	WAR	War limitation
	Ceasefire	Peacekeeping
Conflict settlement	Agreement	Peacemaking
	Normalization	Structural peacebuilding
Conflict transformation	Reconciliation	Cultural peacebuilding

Note: in de-escalation phases conflict resolution tasks must be initiated at the same time and are nested. They cannot be undertaken sequentially as may be possible in escalation phases – see chapters 5 and 8. We suggest that what is sometimes called deep peacemaking (which includes reconciliation) is best seen as part of cultural peacebuilding.

Figure 1.3   The hourglass model: conflict containment, conflict settlement and conflict transformation

or mediation among the main protagonists with a view to reaching a mutually acceptable agreement. Conflict containment includes preventive peacekeeping, war limitation and post-ceasefire peacekeeping. War limitation is made up of attempts to constrain the fighting geographically, to mitigate and alleviate its intensity, and to bring about its termination at the earliest possible moment. In this model we distinguish between the elite peacemaking that forms the substance of conflict settlement, and the deeper levels of peacemaking (including reconciliation) that are better seen as part of cultural peacebuilding.

In chapter 5 (Preventing Violent Conflict) we will look at the top half of the hourglass model. In chapter 6 (Peacekeeping) we will look at the conflict containment components. In chapter 7 (Ending Violent Conflict) we will look at the conflict settlement components. And in chapters 8–10 (on post-war peacebuilding) we will look at the bottom half of the hourglass model.

Table 1.1 indicates the range of complementary processes and techniques relevant to the hourglass model of escalation and de-escalation offered in this book, and elaborated in the section below.

Classical Ideas

Conflict is an intrinsic and inevitable aspect of social change. It is an expression of the heterogeneity of interests, values and beliefs that arise as new formations generated by social change come up against inherited constraints. But the way we deal with conflict is a matter of habit and choice. It is possible to change habitual responses and exercise intelligent choices.

Conflict approaches

One typical habit in conflict is to give very high priority to defending one's own interests. If Cain's interests clash with Abel's, Cain is inclined to ignore Abel's interests or actively to damage them. Leaders of nations are expected to defend the national interest and to defeat the interests of others if they come into conflict. But this is not the only possible response.

Figure 1.4 illustrates five approaches to conflict, distinguished by whether concern for Self and concern for Other is high or low. Cain has high concern for Self and low concern for Other: this is a 'contending' style. Another alternative is to yield: this implies more concern for the interests of Other than Self. Another is to avoid conflict and withdraw: this suggests low concern for both Self and Other. Another is to balance concern for the interests of Self and Other, leading to a

Table 1.1 Conflict resolution techniques, complementarity and the hourglass model

Stage of conflict	Strategic response	Examples of tactical response (skills and processes)
Difference	Cultural peacebuilding	Problem-solving Support for indigenous dispute resolution institutions and CR training Fact finding missions and peace commissions
Contradiction	Structural peacebuilding	Development assistance Civil society development Governance training and institution building Human rights training Track II mediation and problem-solving
Polarization	Elite peacemaking	Special envoys and official mediation Negotiation Coercive diplomacy Preventive peacekeeping
Violence	Peacekeeping	Interposition Crisis management and containment
War	War limitation	Peace enforcement Peace support and stabilization
Ceasefire	Peacekeeping	Preventive peacekeeping Disarmament and security sector reform Confidence building and security enhancing measures Security in the community through police training
Agreement	Elite peacemaking	Electoral and constitutional reform Power sharing and de-centralization of power Problem-solving
Normalization	Structural peacebuilding	Collective security and cooperation arrangements Economic resource cooperation and development Alternative defence
Reconciliation	Cultural peacebuilding	Commissions of enquiry/truth and justice commissions Peace media development Peace and conflict awareness education and training Cultural exchanges and initiatives, sport as reconciliation Problem-solving as future imaging

search for accommodation and compromise. And there is a fifth alternative, seen by many in the conflict resolution field as the one to be recommended where possible: high regard for the interests of both Self and Other. This implies strong assertion of one's own interest, but equal awareness of the aspirations and needs of the other, generating energy to search for a creative problem-solving outcome.

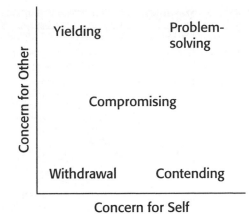

Figure 1.4   Five approaches to conflict

Win–lose, lose–lose, win–win outcomes

What happens when the conflict approaches of two parties are considered together? Parties to conflicts are usually inclined to see their interests as diametrically opposed. The possible outcomes are seen to be win–lose (one wins, the other loses) or compromise (they split their difference). But there is a much more common outcome in violent conflicts: both lose. If neither is able to impose an outcome or is prepared to compromise, the conflictants may impose such massive costs on each other that all of the parties end up worse off than they would have been had another strategy been adopted. In conflict resolution analysis this is found to be a much more common outcome than is generally supposed. When this becomes clear to the parties (often regrettably late in the day), there is a strong motive based on self-interest for moving towards other outcomes, such as compromise or win–win. The spectrum of such outcomes may well be wider than conflictants suppose.

Traditionally, the task of conflict resolution has been seen as helping parties who perceive their situation as zero-sum[6] (Self's gain is Other's loss) to reperceive it as a non-zero-sum conflict (in which both may gain or both may lose), and then to assist parties to move in the positive sum direction. Figure 1.5 shows various possible outcomes of the conflict between Cain and Abel. Any point towards the right is better for Abel, any point towards the top is better for Cain. In the Bible, the prize is the Lord's favour. Cain sees the situation as a zero-sum conflict: at point 1 (his best outcome) he gets the Lord's favour, at 2 (his worst) the Lord favours Abel. All the other possibilities lie on the line from 1 to 2 in which the Lord divides his favour, more or less equally, between the two brothers. Point 3 represents a possible compromise position. But it is the other diagonal, representing the

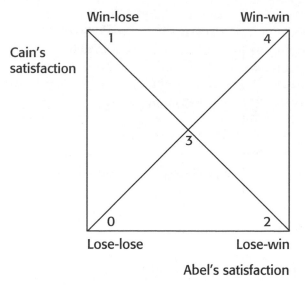

Figure 1.5   Zero-sum and non-zero-sum outcomes

non-zero-sum outcomes, that is the more interesting from a conflict resolution perspective: the mutual loss that actually occurred, at 0, when Abel was slain and Cain lost the Lord's favour, and the mutual gain that they missed, at 4, if each had been his brother's keeper.

Prisoner's Dilemma and the evolution of cooperation

Prisoner's Dilemma is a simple representation in game theory, that clearly illustrates the tendency for contending strategies to end in lose–lose outcomes. Two players (prisoners accused of crime) each have two choices: to cooperate with each other (remain silent) or to defect (inform on the other). The choices must be made in ignorance of what the other will do (they are kept in separate cells). The possible pay-offs are given in table 1.2. It can be seen that, whatever choice the other may make, each player considered singly gains a higher pay-off by choosing to defect (if the other cooperates, defection earns 5 points rather than 3; if the other defects, defection earns 1 point rather than 0). So the only rational course is to defect. But this is not the best

Table 1.2 Prisoner's Dilemma		
	Cooperate	Defect
Cooperate	3, 3	0, 5
Defect	5, 0	1, 1

outcome for either, since, whereas mutual defection earns 1 point each, mutual cooperation would have earned both of them 3 points. So the individually rational choice turns out to deliver a mutual lose–lose outcome. The collectively rational choice is for both to cooperate, reaching the elusive win–win outcome (point 4 in figure 1.5). But if both could communicate and agree to go for mutual cooperation, how can each guarantee that the other will not subsequently defect, tempted by the 5 point prize? In this kind of social trap, self-interested parties can readily get stuck at lose–lose outcomes.

The trap depends on the game being played only once. If each move is part of a sequence of repeated games, there are possibilities for cooperative behaviour to evolve. In a well-known series of experiments, Robert Axelrod (1984) invited experts to submit programs for a Prisoner's Dilemma competition run on computer. A spectrum of 'nice' and 'nasty' strategies was submitted and each was tested in pairs against all the others in repeated interactions. The surprise clear over-all winner was a simple strategy called 'Tit-for-Tat' (submitted by the conflict resolution analyst Anatol Rapaport), which began by cooperating on the first move, and thereafter copied what the other had done on the previous move. The repeated overall success of Tit-for-Tat shows, in Richard Dawkins's phrase, that, contrary to a widely held view about competitive environments of this kind (including Darwinian natural selection), 'nice guys finish first' (Dawkins, 1989: 202–33). Tit-for-Tat is not a push-over. It hits back when the other defects. But, crucially, it initially cooperates (it is 'generous'), and it bears no grudges (it is 'forgiving'). Its responses are also predictable and reliable (it has 'clarity of behaviour'). For the 'evolution of cooperation' to get going in a mêlée of competing strategies, there must be a critical if at first quite small number of initially cooperating strategies, and the 'shadow of the future' must be a long one: interaction must not be confined to just one game (for example, with one player able to wipe out another in one go). But, so long as these conditions operate, even though 'nasty guys' may seem to do well at first, 'nice guys' come out on top in the end.[7] Natural selection favours cooperation.

So taking account of the future relationship (for example, between two communities who will have to live together) is one way out of the trap. Another is to take the social context into account. Imagine, for example, that the prisoners know that there is a gang outside who will punish them if they defect and reward them if they cooperate. This can change their pay-offs and hence the outcome. A similar change occurs if instead of considering only their own interests, the parties also attach value to the interests of each other: social players are not trapped.

Positions, interests and needs

How can the parties reframe their positions if they are diametrically opposed, as they often are? One of the classical ideas in conflict resolution is to distinguish between the positions held by the parties and their underlying interests and needs. For example, Egypt and Israel quarrel over Sinai. Each claims sovereignty and their positions seem incompatible. But in negotiations it turns out that Egypt's main interest is in national territorial integrity and Israel's main interest is in security. So the political space is found for what came to be the Camp David settlement. Interests are often easier to reconcile than positions, since there are usually several positions that might satisfy them. Matters may be more difficult if the conflict is over values (which are often non-negotiable) or relationships, which may need to be changed to resolve the conflict, although the same principle of looking for a deeper level of compatible underlying motives applies. Some analysts take this to the limit by identifying basic human needs (for example, identity, security, survival) as lying at the roots of other motives. Intractable conflicts are seen to result from the denial of such needs, and conflict can only be resolved when such needs are satisfied. But the hopeful argument of these analysts is that, whereas interests may be subject to relative scarcity, basic needs are not (for example, security for one party is reinforced by security for the other). As long as the conflict is translated into the language of needs, an outcome that satisfies both sides' needs can be found (see figure 1.6).

Third-party intervention

Where two parties are reacting to each others' actions, it is easy for a spiral of hostility and escalation to develop through positive feedback. The entry of a third party may change the conflict structure and allow a different pattern of communication, enabling the third party to filter or reflect back the messages, attitudes and behaviour of the conflictants. This intervention may dampen the feedback spiral.

Although all third parties make some difference, 'pure' mediators have traditionally been seen as 'powerless' – their communications are powerful, but they bring to bear no new material resources of their own. In other situations there may also be powerful third parties whose entry alters not only the communication structure but also the power balance. Such third parties may alter the parties' behaviour as well as their communications by judicious use of the carrot and the stick (positive and negative inducement); and they may support one outcome rather than another. Of course, by taking action, powerful third parties may find themselves sucked into the conflict as a full party. Figure 1.7

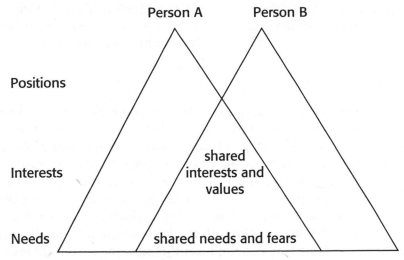

Person A   Person B

Positions

Interests

shared
interests and
values

Needs   shared needs and fears

Source: from Floyer Acland, 1995: 50

Figure 1.6   Positions, interests and needs

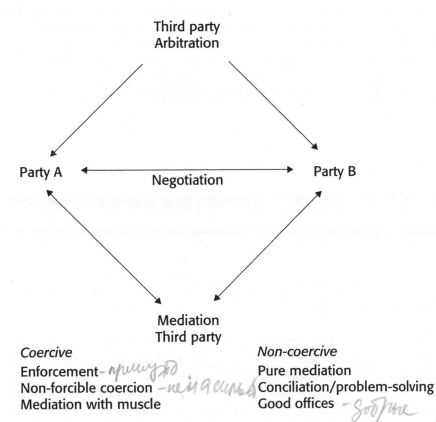

Third party
Arbitration

Party A   Negotiation   Party B

Mediation
Third party

Coercive   *Non-coercive*
Enforcement- *apuuyƭo*   Pure mediation
Non-forcible coercion – *nein a cun6d* Conciliation/problem-solving
Mediation with muscle   Good offices – *soɔpne   yeuyns*

Figure 1.7   Coercive and non-coercive third party intervention

illustrates how third parties may act as arbiters (with or without the consent of the conflict parties), or may try to facilitate negotiations or mediate between the parties (coercively or non-coercively).

Three faces of power

It may seem strange to call "pure mediators" powerless, when they may provide the impetus to resolve the conflict. This is because the term 'power' is ambiguous. On the one hand it means the power to command, order, enforce – coercive or 'hard' power. On the other, it means the power to induce cooperation, to legitimitize, to inspire – persuasive or 'soft' power. Hard power has always been important in violent conflict, but soft power may be more important in conflicts managed peacefully. Kenneth Boulding (1989) calls the former 'threat power' ('do what I want or I will do what you don't want'). Following earlier theorists of management-labour negotiations, he then further distinguishes between two forms of soft power: 'exchange power', associated with bargaining and the compromising approach ('do what I want and I will do what you want'), and 'integrative power', associated with persuasion and transformative long-term problem-solving ('together we can do something that is better for both of us'). This roughly coincides with Joseph Nye's distinction between military, economic and legitimacy power, of which the United States has a huge preponderance of the first, a large share of the second, but only a limited and highly ambiguous measure of the third (Nye, 2002). Nye concludes that soft power is much more important, even from a self-interested perspective, than many unreconstructed realists may suppose. Conflict resolvers try to shift emphasis away from the use of threat power and towards the use of exchange and integrative power (see table 1.3).

Table 1.3 Three faces of power		
Threat power	Exchange power	Integrative power
Destructive	Productive	Creative
productive	destructive	productive
creative	creative	destructive

Source: from Boulding, 1989: 25

Third parties like politicians and governments may use all these forms of power. In terms of third-party intervention (see figure 1.7) it is helpful to distinguish between powerful mediators, or 'mediators with muscle', who bring their power resources to bear, and powerless mediators, whose role is confined to communication and facilitation. Track I diplomacy involves official governmental or intergovernmental representatives, who may use good offices, mediation, and sticks and carrots to seek or force an outcome, typically along the win–lose or 'bargaining' line (between the points 1, 3 and 2 in figure 1.5). Track II diplomacy, in contrast, involves unofficial mediators who do not have carrots or sticks. They work with the parties or their constituencies to facilitate agreements, encouraging the parties to see their predicament as lying along the lose–lose to win–win line (between points 0, 3 and 4 in figure 1.5) and to find mutually satisfactory outcomes.

Symmetric and asymmetric conflicts

So far we have been considering conflicts of interest between relatively similar parties. These are examples of *symmetric* conflicts. Conflict may also arise between dissimilar parties such as between a majority and a minority, an established government and a group of rebels, a master and his servant, an employer and her employees. These are *asymmetric* conflicts. Here the root of the conflict lies not in particular issues or interests that may divide the parties, but in the very structure of who they are and the relationship between them. It may be that this structure of roles and relationships cannot be changed without conflict.

Classical conflict resolution, in some views, applies only to symmetric conflicts. In asymmetric conflicts the structure is such that the top dog always wins, the underdog always loses. The only way to resolve the conflict is to change the structure, but this can never be in the interests of the top dog. So there are no win–win outcomes, and the third party has to join forces with the underdog to bring about a resolution.

From another point of view, however, even asymmetric conflicts impose costs on both parties. It is oppressive to be an oppressor, even if not so oppressive as to be oppressed. There are costs for the top dogs in sustaining themselves in power and keeping the underdogs down. In severe asymmetric conflicts the cost of the relationship becomes unbearable for both sides. This then opens the possibility for conflict resolution through a shift from the existing structure of relationships to another.

The role of the third party is to assist with this transformation, if necessary confronting the top dog. This means transforming what were unpeaceful, unbalanced relationships into peaceful and dynamic ones. Figure 1.8 illustrates how the passage from unpeaceful to peaceful relationships may involve a temporary increase in overt conflict as people become aware of imbalances of power and injustice affecting them (stage 1, education or 'conscientization'), organize themselves and articulate their grievances (stage 2, confrontation), come to terms in a more equal way with those who held a preponderance of power over them (stage 3, negotiation) and finally join in restructuring a more equitable and just relationship (stage 4, resolution). There are

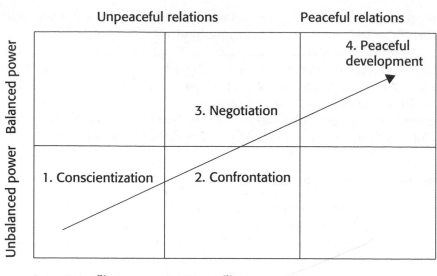

Source: from Curle, 1971 and Lederach, 1995

Figure 1.8   Transforming asymmetric conflicts (I)

many ways in which this can be approached without using coercion. There is the Gandhian tactic of 'speaking truth to power', influencing and persuading the power-holders. Then there are the tactics of mobilizing popular movements, increasing solidarity, making demonstrations of resolve, establishing a demand for change. Raising awareness of the conflict among those who are external or internal supporters of the top dog may start to weaken the regime (as did, for example, the opponents of apartheid in South Africa). The unequal power structure is unbalanced; it is held up by props of various kinds; removing the props may make the unbalanced structure collapse. Another tactic is to strengthen and empower the underdogs. The underdogs may withdraw from the unbalanced relationship and start building anew: the parallel institutions approach. Non-violence uses soft power to move towards a more balanced relationship.

New Developments in Conflict Resolution

The new patterns of major armed conflict that became prominent in the 1990s suggested a more nuanced model of conflict emergence and transformation. This model sees conflict formations arising out of social change, leading to a process of violent or non-violent conflict transformation, and resulting in further social change in which hitherto suppressed or marginalized individuals or groups come to articulate their interests and challenge existing norms and power

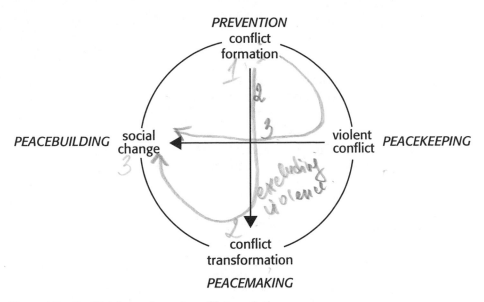

Figure 1.9   Conflict dynamics and conflict resolution

structures. Figure 1.9 shows a schematic illustration of phases of conflict, and forms of intervention that may be feasible at different stages. A schematic life cycle of conflict sees a progression from peaceful social change to conflict formation to violent conflict and then to conflict transformation and back to peaceful social change. But this is not the only path. The sequence can go from conflict formation to conflict transformation and back to social change, avoiding violence. Or it can go from conflict formation to violent conflict back to the creation of fresh conflicts.

In response, there has been a differentiation and broadening in the scope of third-party intervention. Whereas classical conflict resolution was mainly concerned with entry into the conflict itself and with how to enable parties to violent conflict to resolve the issues between them in non-violent ways, the contemporary approach is to take a wider view of the timing and nature of intervention. In the 1990s came Fisher and Keashly's (1991) complementarity and contingency model, mentioned earlier, with its attempt to relate appropriate and coordinated resolution strategies to conflict phases. Lederach's (1997) model of conflict resolution and conflict transformation levels has also been influential, with its emphasis on 'bottom-up' processes and the suggestion that the middle level can serve to link the other two (see figure 1.10). Francis has developed Curle's original asymmetric conflict model, embedding classic conflict resolution strategies within wider strategies for transforming conflicts of this kind (see figure 1.11). Encarnacion et al. (1990) have elaborated models of third-party intervention in order to

Source: from Lederach, 1997

Figure 1.10   Actors and approaches to peacebuilding

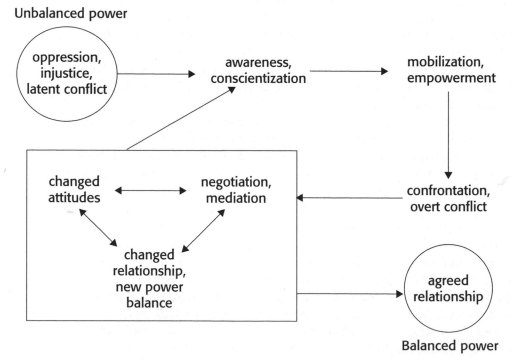

Source: from Francis, 1994

Figure 1.11   Transforming asymmetric conflicts (II)

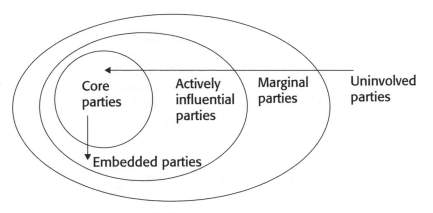

Source: from Encarnacion et al., 1990: 45

Figure 1.12   The gradient of conflict involvement

stress the way external parties may come to be core parties as their level of involvement increases, and to emphasize the importance of 'embedded parties' from inside the conflict who often play key roles in expediting moves to resolution (see figure 1.12). In general there has been a shift from seeing third-party intervention as the primary responsibility of external agencies towards appreciating the role of internal 'third parties' or indigenous peacemakers. Instead of outsiders offering the fora for addressing conflicts in one-shot mediation efforts, the emphasis is on the need to build constituencies and capacity within societies and to learn from domestic cultures how to manage conflicts in a sustained way over time. This suggests a multitrack model in place of the earlier Track I and Track II models mentioned above, in which emphasis is placed on the importance of indigenous resources and local actors, what we might call Track III (see figure 1.13). There is a shift towards seeing conflict in its context (associated sometimes with structuralist, constructivist or discourse-based views of social reality).

Summing up all of this new work, it is helpful to locate contemporary armed conflicts within a framework that encompasses different levels from international level (global, regional, bilateral), through national state level, down to societal level (see figure 1.14).

Most major armed conflicts today are hybrid struggles that spill across the international, state and societal levels. This is what makes them so hard to resolve or transform. The 58-year conflict in Kashmir, for example, is variously interpreted as a conflict between India and Pakistan (international) or as an ethnic/religious identity struggle (social). As such it is simultaneously affected by changes at *international level*, ranging from the global level (e.g. the transition from a bipolar to a unipolar world) and regional level down to bilateral state–state relations, and by changes at *social level*, ranging from top-level elites

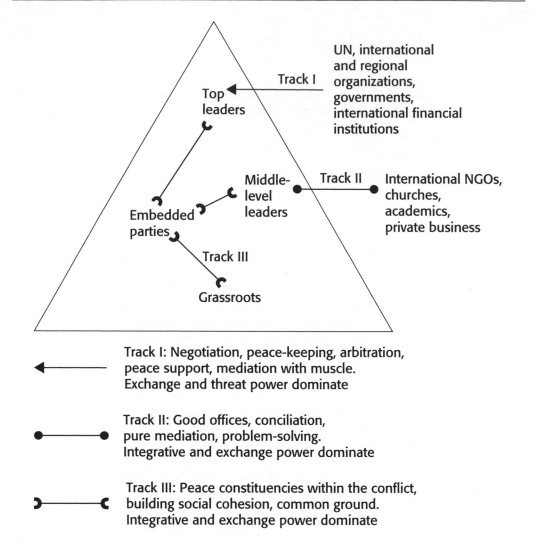

Figure 1.13   Multitrack conflict resolution

through middle-level leadership and down to local and grassroots interests. Figure 1.15 shows the significance of the ambivalent role played by the state at *state level* in all this, at the same time the main actor on the international scene and also (in theory) the main satisfier of internal social needs. Conflict transformation, therefore, needs to operate simultaneously at all these levels, including vertical relations up and down across the levels from the grassroots up to the international, and horizontal relations across and between all the social actors involved. In dynamic terms, depending on the stage the conflict has reached, as illustrated in the hourglass model (figure 1.3), the overall aim is to work to prevent the narrowing of political space associated

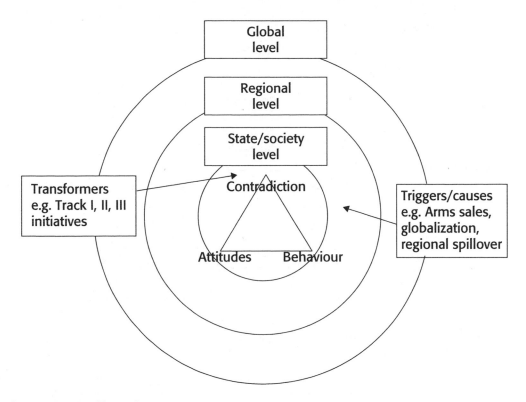

Figure 1.14   Conflict and context

with conflict escalation and to encourage the widening of political space associated with conflict de-escalation and transformation.

Finally, criticisms of gender blindness, cultural insensitivity and lack of critical awareness have prompted responses from the conflict resolution field that we describe below.

Terminology

Although terminology is often confusing, with the same terms used in different ways both within the academic literature and in general usage, we offer the following definitions of how key terms are used in this book.

By *conflict* we mean the pursuit of incompatible goals by different groups. This suggests a broader span of time and a wider class of struggle than armed conflict. We intend our usage here to apply to any political conflict, whether it is pursued by peaceful means or by the use of force. (Some theorists, notably John Burton, have distinguished

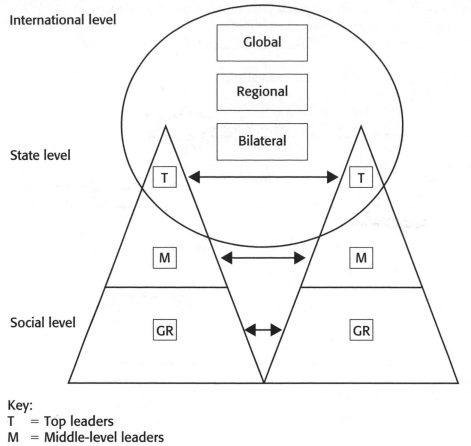

International level

State level

Social level

Key:
T   = Top leaders
M   = Middle-level leaders
GR = Grassroots leaders

Source: Developed with Nick Lewer during a workshop at the National Defense College of Pakistan, Islamabad, February 2005

Figure 1.15   Modelling international–social conflict: a framework for transformation

between disputes about negotiable interests that can be settled by compromise, and more deep-seated conflicts that involve human needs and can only be resolved by removing underlying causes.)

Armed conflict is a narrower category denoting conflicts where parties on both sides resort to the use of force. It is notoriously diffi-cult to define, since it can encompass a continuum of situations rang-ing from a military overflight or an attack on a civilian by a single soldier to an all-out war with massive casualties. The research commu-nity has identified a number of thresholds and rules for deciding what to count. We consider these definitions in chapter 3.

Violent conflict, or *deadly conflict*, is similar to armed conflict, but also includes one-sided violence such as genocides against unarmed civilians. We mean direct, physical violence. We acknowledge the strong argument in peace research for broadening the concept of violence to include exploitative social relations that cause unnecessary suffering, but prefer to use the now well-known term 'structural violence' for this.

Contemporary conflict refers to the prevailing pattern of political and violent conflicts at the beginning of the twenty-first century; *contemporary armed conflicts* refer only those that involve the use of force.

Conflict settlement means the reaching of an agreement between the parties to settle a political conflict, so forestalling or ending an armed conflict. This suggests finality, but in practice conflicts that have reached settlements are often reopened later. Conflict attitudes and underlying structural contradictions may not have been addressed.

Conflict containment incudes peacekeeping and war limitation (geographical constraint, mitigation and alleviation of intensity, and termination at the earliest opportunity).

Conflict management, like the associated term 'conflict regulation', has been used as a generic term to cover the whole gamut of positive conflict handling. Here we understand it to refer in a more limited way to the settlement and containment of violent conflict.

Conflict resolution is a more comprehensive term which implies that the deep-rooted sources of conflict are addressed and transformed. This implies that behaviour is no longer violent, attitudes are no longer hostile, and the structure of the conflict has been changed. It is difficult to avoid ambiguity since the term is used to refer both to the process (or the intention) to bring about these changes, and to the completion of the process. A further ambiguity is that conflict resolution refers to a particular defined specialist field (as in 'conflict resolution journals'), as well as to an activity carried on by people who may or may not use the term or even be aware of it (as in 'conflict resolution in Central America'). Nevertheless, these two senses of the term are tending to merge.

Conflict transformation is a term which for some analysts is a significant step beyond conflict resolution, but which in our view represents its deepest level. As clarified in figure 1.3, it implies a deep transformation in the institutions and discourses that reproduce violence, as well as in the conflict parties themselves and their relationships. It corresponds to the underlying tasks of structural and cultural peacebuilding.

Negotiation is the process whereby the parties within the conflict seek to settle or resolve their conflicts. *Mediation* involves the intervention of a third party; it is a voluntary process in which the parties retain control over the outcome (pure mediation), although it is sometimes combined with positive and negative inducements (mediation with muscle). *Conciliation* or *facilitation* is close in meaning to pure mediation, and refers to intermediary efforts to encourage the parties to move towards negotiations, as does the more minimalist role of providing good offices. *Problem-solving* is a more ambitious undertaking in which conflict parties are invited to reconceptualize the conflict with a view to finding creative, win–win outcomes. *Reconciliation* is a longer-term process of overcoming hostility and mistrust between divided peoples.

We use *peacemaking* in the sense of moving towards settlement of armed conflict, where conflict parties are induced to reach agreement voluntarily, for example as envisaged in Chapter VI of the UN Charter on the 'Pacific Settlement of Disputes' (Article 33). *Peacekeeping* (traditionally with the consent of the conflict parties) refers to the interposition of international armed forces to separate the armed forces of belligerents, often now associated with civil tasks such as monitoring and policing and supporting humanitarian intervention. *Peace-enforcement* is the imposition of a settlement by a powerful third party. *Peacebuilding* underpins the work of peacemaking and peacekeeping by addressing structural issues and the long-term relationships between conflictants. With reference to the conflict triangle (see figure 1.1), it can be suggested that peacemaking aims to change the attitudes of the main protagonists, peacekeeping lowers the level of destructive behaviour, and peacebuilding tries to overcome the contradictions which lie at the root of the conflict (Galtung, 1996: 112).

Finally, it is worth noting that the aim of conflict resolution is not the elimination of conflict, which would be both impossible and, as is made clear in Curle's model of the transformation of asymmetric conflicts (see figure 1.8), sometimes undesirable. Rather, the aim of conflict resolution is to transform actually or potentially violent conflict into peaceful (non-violent) processes of social and political change. This is an unending task as new forms and sources of conflict arise.

Structure of the Book

The structure of the book is based on the idea that, having described the evolution of the conflict resolution field (chapter 2), examined the statistical bases for analysis (chapter 3) and characterized the nature of contemporary conflict (chapter 4), broad distinctions can then be made between the tasks of preventing violent conflict (chapter 5), mitigating or alleviating violent conflict once it has broken out while at the same time searching for ways of terminating it (chapter 6), ending violent conflict (chapter 7), and ensuring that conflict does not subsequently regress to violence but is lastingly transformed into peaceful processes of political and social change (chapter 8), including peacebuilding (chapter 9) and reconciliation (chapter 10). We are not suggesting that conflicts necessarily go through these phases, but think that this is the simplest expository structure to adopt. In addition to a thorough updating of these chapters, this second edition of the book offers a series of additional new chapters in Part II that explore aspects of the field not fully covered in the first edition. This includes terror and global order (chapter 11), gender issues (chapter 12), the ethics of intervention (chapter 13), dialogue, discourse and disagreement (chapter 14), the culture question (chapter 15) and a concluding survey of the state of the field and thoughts on the main tasks for the next generation of conflict resolvers (chapter 16).

Recommended reading

Burton and Dukes, eds (1990); Cheldelin et al., eds (2003); Deutsch and Coleman, eds (2000); Fisher (1997); Jeong, ed. (1999); Kriesberg (1998); Mitchell and Banks (1996); Sandole (1999); Sandole and van der Merwe (1993); Wallensteen (2002b).

Conflict Resolution: Origins, Foundations and Development of the Field

The reasons which have led us to this enterprise may be summed up in two propositions. The first is that by far the most important practical problem facing the world today is that of international relations – more specifically the prevention of global war. The second is that if intellectual progress is to be made in this area, the study of international relations must be made an interdisciplinary enterprise, drawing its discourse from all the social sciences and even further.

Kenneth Boulding on the publication of the first issue of the Journal of Conflict Resolution, 1957

The threat of nuclear holocaust remains with us and may well continue to do so for centuries, but other problems are competing with deterrence and disarmament studies for our attention. The journal must also attend to international conflict over justice, equality and human dignity; problems of conflict resolution for ecological balance and control are within our proper scope and especially suited for interdisciplinary attention.

Journal of Conflict Resolution, 1973, 27(1): 5

THE two extracts from the *Journal of Conflict Resolution* quoted above give a good idea of the way in which conflict resolution, constituted as a distinct field of study through the setting up of formal centres in academic institutions and the publication of professional journals, first defined itself and then expanded its remit during what we are calling its foundational period in the 1950s and 1960s, and its period of further construction and expansion in the 1970s and 1980s. In this chapter we describe the historical evolution of the field, some of whose classic concepts we have already outlined in chapter 1. We present conflict resolution as progressing through five stages of intergenerational development and practice. The first, second and third generations are dealt with in this chapter, looking at the ideas of the precursors up to 1945, the founders between 1945 and 1965, and the consolidators between 1965 and 1985. The rest of the book concerns the work of those we are calling reconstructors between 1985 and 2005, who have had to accommodate the field to the post-Cold War world.

Clearly, these temporal generational categories are not watertight and people and ideas move across them. Many of the founders of the field, and those who followed as 'second generation' consolidators (like Adam Curle for example), continue to work and their ideas are still evolving to the present day. Therefore these generations can also be regarded as temporal-intellectual categories, where those in the first and second generations essentially targeted a state-centric approach to conflict resolution; those in the third generation developed an approach which looked to civil society and used a less state-centric lens; those in the fourth generation then attempted to construct a complex and complementary architecture, which linked levels from civil society to the state and beyond to the regional and international levels. At the end of the book we look ahead to the possible task of the coming fifth generation of conflict resolvers, who will carry the enterprise through the first quarter of the twenty-first century. The fifth generation represents a new wave of conflict resolution theory and action which faces the challenge of continuing to innovate and refine the field so that it is responsive to twenty-first-century conflict. This new generation draws on radical conflict resolution theory and discourse and also on elements of counter hegemonic varieties of critical theory. In this way it will seek to be more sensitive and reflective in developing appropriate context-sensitive strategies which prefigure and embody what we term a cosmopolitan conflict resolution project, by which we mean the emergence of an institutionalized global competence, drawing on an emancipatory ethic, to resolve conflict and sustain peace non-violently.

Despite the apparent diversity of activity throughout this period, in what amounted to a wide-ranging pursuit to define both the methods and concepts of conflict resolution, two main concerns predominated. The first was the effort to identify the conditions for a new world order based on conflict analysis, conflict prevention and problem-solving. The second was the effort to mobilize and inspire ever widening and inclusive peace constituencies based on the promotion of the values of non-violent peacemaking. Putting these two dimensions of activity together, conflict resolution emerged as an enterprise which was normatively associated with the promotion of peace at three levels. First, through a radical reformation of world political systems. Second, through the promotion of an inclusive anti-war and pro-peace politics. Third, through the fashioning of methodologies and processes that provided the opportunity to move beyond the politics of protest towards a proactive peacemaking project. This proactive peacemaking project was concerned to address the behavioural, attitudinal and structural/objective elements of Galtung's conflict triangle (chapter 1, figure 1.1). It also aligned conflict resolution not only with the negative peace goals of preventing war and containing violent conflict, but, crucially, with the even more challenging task of building positive peace by addressing the attitudinal and structural conditions associated with violent conflict behaviours.

Precursors: The First Generation, 1918–1945

The failure of the variety of peace, socialist and liberal internationalist movements to prevent the outbreak of the First World War motivated many people in the years that followed to develop a 'science' of peace which would provide a firmer basis for preventing future wars than what were in some quarters seen as the frequently sentimental and simplistically moral responses of pacifism.

The study of peace and the quest for world order

Although the institutionalization of peace research did not begin until the years after 1945, a related development took place after 1918 – the establishment of international relations (IR) as a distinct academic discipline. The first Chair in International Relations was endowed at the University College of Wales, Aberystwyth, in 1919. The initiative sprung from the same anti-war sentiment that inspired the early advocates of peace research. The sponsor of this Chair was the Welsh industrialist and Liberal MP David Davies, who conceived the initiative as a memorial to students of the college who were killed in the Great War. During the period 1920–45, international relations courses and institutes were established throughout the UK, Europe and North America, many of them initially motivated by the idealist aspiration to promote peace by study and research into the dynamics of international relations (van den Dungen, 1996: 7). One of the sub-themes in this book is the way in which IR subsequently came to be dominated by realist thinking, perhaps in reaction to the inadequacies of the League of Nations and what were seen as failed attempts at appeasing aggression in the 1930s, thus vacating the intellectual ground that would be occupied by conflict resolution after World War II.

As described by van den Dungen (1996), a variety of proposals and initiatives emerged in Europe between 1919 and 1939, which foreshadowed the later institutionalization and development of conflict resolution. Some of these enterprises were associated with an air of optimism surrounding the early years of the League of Nations, such as an International University Federation for the League of Nations formed at Prague in 1924. Another source of influence was from the activities of American internationalists associated with the Carnegie Endowment for International Peace. In 1930 a German Peace Academy was founded, and in 1931 perhaps the first chair of peace research (Chair for the Study of International Institutions for the Organization of Peace) was created in France at the University of Lyons. Many of these initiatives foundered in the rising tide of international violence in the 1930s, and are easy to dismiss as overly idealistic at the time. But powerful ideas endure and prove capable of inspiring future generations when conditions for their implementation are more propitious. Some of the early advocates identified by van den Dungen were natural scientists who were aware and critical of the greater contributions made by science and scientists to the causes of war rather than to the causes of peace. Others were medical professionals who had an understanding of the physical and mental costs of war and were struck by the medical analogy: if war was like a disease, then knowledge of symptoms and aetiology should precede diagnosis and therapy or cure. Many proponents of peace research also shared the view that the causes of war and the problems of creating a durable peace were so complex that only a multidisciplinary approach would be adequate and that academic learning needed to spring from broader humanistic and idealistic motivations. These ideas would be drawn on in the foundation of the future field of conflict resolution.

Meanwhile, although not known to many of those calling for a new science of peace, other important pioneering work was being done which would later enrich conflict resolution. Prominent here was the thinking of Mary Parker Follett (1942) in the field of organizational behaviour and labour-management relations. Advocating a 'mutual gains' approach to negotiation associated with what would be called 'integrative bargaining', as against the traditional concession/convergence approach associated with 'distributive bargaining', she anticipated much of the later problem-solving agenda as outlined in chapter 1. Whereas distributive bargaining assumes concealment, inflated initial demands and zero-sum contexts, the integrative bargaining advocated in the mutual gains approach tries to redefine the negotiation as a shared problem to be resolved. Pooling knowledge and resources and looking to maximize mutual gain is seen to yield greater pay-offs to all parties.

Initiatives in three other fields would also prove of importance to the future interdisciplinary study of conflict resolution – psychology, politics and international studies. For example, in the field of psychology, frustration-aggression theories of human conflict (Dollard et al., 1939) and work on the social psychology of group conflict conducted by

Kurt Lewin (1948) would be influential. Similarly, in the field of political studies, Crane Brinton's approach to the analysis of political revolution (1938) – that revolution takes place when the gap between distributed social power and distributed political power reaches a critical point – can be taken as exemplary of what was to prove another significant strand (carried forward later in Dahrendorf (1957), Gurr (1970) and Tilly (1978)). In international studies, Mitrany's (1943) functionalist approach to overcoming the win–lose dynamic inherent in realist analyses of competitive interstate relations via a progressively denser network of cooperative cross-border frameworks made necessary by the advance of technology – seen by some to have previsaged the evolution of the European Union – would inspire similar ideas for sustaining peace through cross-border institution-building in future conflict resolution circles (complemented by Karl Deutsch's (1957) analysis of the development of 'political community' in the North Atlantic area). Of central significance in all this, and perhaps the critical catalyst in the later emergence of the conflict resolution field, were the early empirical studies of war and conflict conducted in the inter-war years by the Russian Pitirim Sorokin, the Englishman Lewis Fry Richardson and the American, Quincy Wright.[1] Here at last was a proper statistical basis upon which to base analysis – so thought the founders of the conflict resolution field when they came across this work in the 1950s.

Against this background of intellectual research and development, and in the context of the failure to prevent the second major world war of the century, the most significant institutional development in this period of first generation activity came right at the end of the period – with the formation of the United Nations. Representatives of fifty countries met in San Francisco at the United Nations Conference on International Organization to draw up and agree the Charter of the United Nations. The Organization officially came into existence on 24 October 1945.

Although it was itself the outcome of the plans of the great powers for a post-Second World War order, and particularly the powers which were the victors in that war, the UN was not merely the creature of those powers, and its formation marked a significant, even if imperfect, development historically in the evolution of world order. Holsti (1991) has looked at peace agreements and security architectures that have shaped the growth of the international system between 1648 and 1945 with significant milestones after the Thirty Years War (Westphalia 1648), Louis XIV's wars (Utrecht 1713), the Napoleonic Wars (Vienna 1815), World War I (Paris 1919) and World War II (San Francisco 1945) (see table 2.1).

Looking at these epoch-making phases of war and peacemaking, Holsti isolates what he calls eight prerequisites for peace. These are

Table 2.1 The evolution of attempts to create a peaceful post-war international order

Prerequisites for peace	Westphalia	Utrecht	Vienna	Paris	San Francisco
Governance	Yes	Yes	Yes	No*	Yes
Legitimacy	Yes	No	Yes	No	Yes
Assimilation	Yes	Yes	Yes	No	Yes
Deterrence	Yes	No	Yes	No	No**
Conflict resolution	No	No	Yes	Yes	Yes
War as problem	No	No	No	Yes	Yes
Peaceful change	No	No	No	No	No
Future issues	No	No	No	No	No
Conditions satisfied	4/8	2/8	5/8	2/8	5/8

Source: Holsti, 1991: ch.13

* short lived governance mechanism in League of Nations

** failure to develop deterrent capacity such as proposed Military Staff Committee or UN Standing Forces

related to: *governance* (some system of responsibility for regulating behaviour in terms of the conditions of an agreement); *legitimacy* (a new order following war cannot be based on perceived injustice or repression, and principles of justice have to be embodied into the post-war settlement); *assimilation* (linked to legitimacy: the gains of living within a system are greater than the potential advantages of seeking to destroy it); *a deterrent system* (victors should create a coalition strong enough to deter defection, by force if necessary, to protect settlement norms, or to change them by peaceful means); *conflict resolving procedures and institutions* (the system of governance should include provision and capacity for identifying, monitoring, managing and resolving major conflict between members of the system and the norms of the system would include willingness to use such institutions); *consensus on war* (a recognition that war is the fundamental problem, acknowledgement of the need to develop and foster strong norms against use of force and clear guiding principles for the legitimate use of force); *procedures for peaceful change* (the need to review and adapt when agreements no longer relate to the reality of particular situations: peace agreements need to have built-in mechanisms for review and adaption); and *anticipation of future issues* (peacemakers need to incorporate some ability to anticipate what may constitute conflict causes in the future: institutions and system norms should include provision for identifying, monitoring and handling not just the problems that created the last conflict but future conflicts as well).

Holsti's conclusion from this survey is instructive. The least success has come around developing methods of peaceful change and anticipation of conflict-generating future issues. In general, the more criteria that were met in each agreement, the more stable and peaceful was the ensuing period. The San Francisco meeting which established the UN did a great deal to stabilize interstate relations and provides one explanation at least for the decline of interstate conflict. However, it did not anticipate the forces that would generate future conflicts, which, as we have seen, were civil wars with high levels of civilian casualties; nor did it put in place the mechanisms for peaceful system change. A constant failure of those who have been war leaders has been a failure to 'enlarge the shadow of the future' instead of remaining in the shadow of the past. As Holsti puts it:

> it may be asking too much for wartime leaders to cast their minds more to the future. The immediate war settlements are difficult enough. But in so far as the peacemakers were involved not just in settling a past war but also in constructing the foundations of a new international order, foresight is mandatory. The peace system must not only resolve the old issues that gave rise to previous wars; it must anticipate new issues, new actors, and new problems and it must design institutions, norms and procedures that are appropriate to them. (Holsti, 1991: 347)

Somewhat along these lines, the *United Nations Intellectual History Project* has been established to explore the role of the world organization, not as a bureaucratized institution, but as creator and disseminator of ideas, for example around the concept of human security which at the level of international organizations provides a distinctive normative framework to guide future conflict resolution interventions.[2]

Non-violence, pacifism and conflict resolution

Finally, despite the tensions between peace researchers and peace activists noted above, the development of conflict resolution as a distinct field of academic enquiry with a strong praxis also owes much to non-violence and pacifist traditions and to the thinkers whose ideas nourished it.

The work of non-violence theorists such as Gene Sharp (1973), and the persistence of historical traditions and practices of pacifism such as those contained in the beliefs of Quakers and Mennonites, or in the ideas of Gandhi, have cross-fertilized with academic enterprise to enhance understanding of violent political conflict and alternatives to it. The objectives of Gandhi's *satyagraha* ('struggle for truth') were to make latent conflict manifest by challenging social structures which were harmful because they were highly inequitable, but to do this without setting off a spiral of violence – the complementary value was non-violence (*ahimsa*). In the Gandhian model of conflict, which contains within it built-in inhibitors of violence, the objective is not to win, but, through what Bondurant called the Gandhian dialectic, 'to achieve a fresh level of social truth and a healthier relationship between antagonists' (Wehr, 1979: 64). In the teachings of the Buddha (the *Dhamma*), on the other hand, McConnell (1995) has shown how the doctrine of the middle way and the four noble truths locate the deepest roots of conflict in the perceptions, values and attitudes of conflictants. While this does not ignore what Gandhi would have seen as oppressive structures, it does direct the peacemaker to focus on changes in self-awareness and the development of self-knowledge.

Weber (1999, 2001) has made a strong case for seeing Gandhian ideas in particular as integral to the normative framework later adopted within conflict resolution. Strong echoes of *satyagraha* can be discerned, for example, in Burton's analysis of conflict as rooted in the denial of ontological human needs, and in the uses of the problem-solving method by Burton, Kelman, Mitchell and others to achieve mutually acceptable and self-sustaining outcomes as described. The radical and socially transformative objectives of Gandhian social theory are also echoed in the conflict transformation models associated with peacebuilding from below which we deal with in chapter 9 (Woodhouse, 1986). Within the 'emancipatory discourse' of a Gandhian framework, conflict resolution techniques are seen as 'tools for transformation' (Curle, 1990), and the field is located within a wider continuum, which includes world order, human security, and non-violent peacemaking (Woodhouse, 1991).

There is also a measure of creative tension between conflict resolution and non-violent direct action, however. For example, as we have seen, some argue that conflict resolution is problematic in situations of high asymmetry between adversaries, where more committed strategies associated with non-violent direct action can better raise awareness and make asymmetrical relations more balanced, at which point mediation and other forms of third-party intervention become both more legitimate and more effective (Clark, 2000; Dudouet, 2005). Conversely, some activists and advocates of non-violent direct action have recognized that there are 'spaces' in the hourglass model of conflict (chapter 1, figure 1.3), where non-violence may be strategically inappropriate, difficult or counter-productive (Randle, 2002: 11–50).

Foundations: The Second Generation, 1945–1965

The sustained development of peace and conflict research in the form of institutional growth had to wait until the post-1945 world, when the added threat of nuclear weapons added a new urgency. The first institutions of peace and conflict research appeared in the twenty-year period between 1945 and 1965. The Peace Research Laboratory was founded by Theodore F. Lentz at St Louis, Missouri, after the bombing of Hiroshima and Nagasaki in 1945. Science, according to Lentz, 'did increase physical power but science did not increase physical harmony . . . the power-harmony imbalance has been brought about by science in misorder' (Lentz, 1955: 52–3). Lentz argued not only that people had a capacity to live in harmony, but that 'humatriotism' was a value which would emerge from rigorous research into human attitudes and personality. One of the first attempts to follow up this lead was taken by a group of pioneers of the new conflict resolution field at the University of Michigan.

Kenneth Boulding, Michigan and the *Journal of Conflict Resolution*

Kenneth Boulding was born in Liverpool in the north of England in 1910. Motivated personally and spiritually as a member of the Society of Friends (Quakers), and professionally as an economist, he moved to America in 1937, married Elise Bjorn-Hansen in 1941, and began with her a partnership that was to make a seminal contribution to the formation of peace and conflict research. After the war he was appointed as Professor of Economics at the University of Michigan. Here, with a small group of academics, which included the mathematician-biologist Anatol Rapoport, the social psychologist Herbert Kelman and the sociologist Robert Cooley Angell, he initiated the *Journal of Conflict Resolution* (JCR) in 1957, and set up the Center for Research on Conflict Resolution in 1959. Inspirational to what Boulding called the 'Early Church' of the peace research movement (Kerman, 1974: 48) was the work of Lewis Richardson, brought over on microfilm by his son Stephen, and not yet published at that time.

Boulding's publications focused firmly on the issue of preventing war, because, partly as a result of the failures of the discipline of international relations, 'the international system is by far the most pathological and costly segment of the total social system' (Kerman, 1974: 83). *Conflict and Defense* advanced the thesis of the decline or obsolescence of the nation-state, while *Perspectives on the Economics of Peace* argued that conventional prescriptions from international relations were unable even to recognize, let alone analyse, the consequences of this obsolescence. If war was the outcome of inherent characteristics in the sovereign state system, then it might be prevented in Boulding's view by a reform of international organization, and by the development of a research and information capability. From this capability, data collection and processing could enable the advance of scientific knowledge about the build-up of conflicts, to replace the inadequate insights available through standard diplomacy. In the first issue of the JCR in March 1957, Wright had an article proposing a 'project on a world intelligence centre', which showed the influence of Richardson from the past, whilst anticipating what has more recently come to be called early warning and conflict prevention. For Boulding, in these formative years of conflict theory, conflict resolution meant the development of a knowledge base in which 'social data stations' would emerge, forming a system analogous to a network of weather stations which would gather a range of social, political and economic data to produce indicators 'to identify social temperature and pressure and predict cold or warm fronts' (Kerman, 1974: 82).

Johan Galtung and conflict resolution in Northern Europe

While the developments at Michigan and the interest of the Bouldings in peace as well as conflict research provided one polar point for the emergence of peace research, its main elaboration was to be defined in developments in Europe. Lawler (1995) makes a distinction between the more limited agenda of conflict research (seeking to reduce the incidence and extent of war) and the emergence of peace research whose origins were not in North America but in Scandinavia, and most remarkably in the work of Johan Galtung. We have already introduced Galtung's concept of the conflict triangle, and his distinction between direct violence, structural violence and cultural violence, in chapter 1 (figure 1.1). To this can be added his further distinction between negative and positive peace, the former characterized by the absence of direct violence, the latter by the overcoming of structural and cultural violence as well. Negative peace can be associated with the more limited but better defined 'minimalist' agenda of preventing war, and in particular nuclear war, as advocated by what might be called the North American pragmatist school. Positive peace encompasses the broader but vaguer 'maximalist' agenda insisted upon by the European structuralists.

The medical analogy, which seems to have occurred to so many of the peace science pioneers, was also at work in Galtung's background. His father was a physician and Galtung absorbed the ethic, transforming it into the notion of the peace researcher as a 'social physician' guided by a body of scientific knowledge. He studied philosophy, sociology and mathematics. In 1958 he became visiting professor of sociology at Columbia University, returning to Oslo in 1960 to help found a unit for research into conflict and peace, based within the Institute for Social Research at the University of Oslo and the precursor to the

International Peace Research Institute Oslo (PRIO). The further development of peace research institutions in Europe in the 1960s was vigorous: thus, in 1962 the Polemological Institute was formed in Groningen, Holland; in 1966 the Stockholm International Peace Research Institute (SIPRI) was opened to commemorate Sweden's 150 years of peace; and in 1969 the Tampere Peace Research Institute was formed in Finland. Galtung was also the founding editor of the *Journal of Peace Research* which was launched in 1964.

This is not the place to attempt a summary of Galtung's work. His output since the early 1960s has been phenomenal and his influence on the institutionalization and ideas of peace research seminal. He saw the range of peace research reaching out far beyond the enterprise of war prevention to encompass study of the conditions for peaceful relations between the dominant and the exploited, rulers and ruled, men and women, western and non-western cultures, humankind and nature. Central here was the search for positive peace in the form of human empathy, solidarity and community, the priority of addressing 'structural violence' in peace research by unveiling and transforming structures of imperialism and oppression, and the importance of searching for alternative values in non-western cosmologies such as Buddhism.[3]

The struggle between European structuralists and North American pragmatists to define the peace research and conflict resolution agenda was at times hard-hitting. In an article in the *Journal of Peace Research* in 1968, for example, Herman Schmid castigated many of those working in the field for failing to engage critically with issues of social justice. Absence of war on its own (negative peace) can obscure deep injustices which make a mockery of peace, and, if unaddressed, contain the seeds of future violent conflict (pp. 217–32). On the other hand, as Lawler's conclusion to his study of Galtung's ideas suggests, although the constant expansion of the peace research and conflict resolution agenda may be seen as a sign of its dynamism, 'it may also be seen as acquiring the qualities of an intellectual black hole wherein something vital, a praxeological edge or purpose, is lost'. This was a criticism made, among others, by Boulding.[4] The second quotation, from the *Journal of Conflict Resolution* (1973), cited at the head of this chapter may be seen to represent an uneasy compromise between the maximalist and minimalist poles, which has more or less persisted to this day. In our view, the central core of the conflict resolution approach described in this book does represent the 'praxeological edge or purpose' of peace research. As both an analytic and normative field, conflict resolution takes violent or destructive conflict as its topic, and aims to gain an accurate understanding of its nature and aetiology in order to learn how it can best be overcome. This implies not only the treatment of symptoms, but work on conflict causes as well.

While we have organized this account of the history of peace and conflict research into chronologies based on generations, the device is, as noted above, artificial. Most of the key thinkers and activists remain active across the 'generations', none more so than Galtung. The 'Galtungian project' for peace research and action has matured into third-generation activity, especially in the TRANSCEND approach formed in 1993 as a teaching, training and research organization to pursue these ideas. In *Searching for Peace* Galtung and his colleagues define the philosophy and methodologies of TRANSCEND and present an exploration of the case for a new 'forum to address underlying structures and cultures of violence, and the need for new language, dialogue and perspectives such as might offer more creative and viable alternatives for the twenty first century' (Galtung and Jacobsen, 2000: 47; Galtung, 2004).

John Burton and a new paradigm in international studies

At this point we can review the contribution of our third 'founder figure', John Burton. Burton was born in Australia in 1915. He studied at the London School of Economics from 1938, gained a Master's degree and, in 1942, a doctorate. He joined the Australian civil service, attended the foundation conference of the United Nations in San Francisco, served in the Australian Department of External Affairs and as High Commissioner in Ceylon. He was appointed to a post at University College London in 1963, following a period on a research fellowship at the Australian National University in Canberra. His appointment coincided with the formation of the Conflict Research Society in London, of which he became the first Honorary Secretary. An early product of this initiative was the publication of *Conflict in Society* (de Reuck and Knight, eds, 1966) with contributions from Boulding, Rapoport and Burton. Following soon after the appearance of other important studies of social conflict as a generic phenomenon, whether at community, industrial or other levels (Coser, 1956; Coleman, 1957), and coinciding with a rediscovery of Georg Simmel's pioneering work (1902), this represented a significant step in the drawing together of multidisciplinary insights for the study of conflict at international level from a much broader perspective than was current in the formal international relations field. Whereas some earlier social scientists, such as the Chicago School, regarded conflict as dysfunctional and the job of the sociologist to remove it, most analysts in the conflict resolution tradition saw conflict as intrinsic in human relationships so that the task became one of handling it better.

This was linked to attempts to coordinate international study through the formation of an International Peace Research Association (IPRA), which held its first conference at Groningen in Holland in 1965. At the same time, during 1965 and 1966, Burton organized the meetings which were to result in the use of controlled communication, or the problem-solving method, in international conflict, to be outlined further in the next section. These meetings were sufficiently impressive for both the Provost of University College London and the British Social Science Research Council to support and develop the theoretical and applied techniques which Burton and his group were pioneering. The result was the formation in 1966 of the Centre for the Analysis of Conflict established under the directorship of Burton and based at University College London.

Burton later spent a period in the mid-1980s at the University of Maryland, where he assisted Edward Azar with the formation of the Center for International Development and Conflict Management and where he worked on the concept of protracted social conflict, which became an important part of an emerging overall theory of inter-national conflict, combining both domestic-social and international dimensions and focused at a hybrid level between interstate war and purely domestic unrest. This model, described more fully through an outline of Azar's analysis in chapter 4, in our view anticipated much of the revaluation of international relations thinking that has taken place since the end of the Cold War. Burton himself did not hold back from making extravagant claims for this new approach in conflict analysis and conflict resolution, describing it as a decisive paradigm shift.

Burton finished his formal academic career as a professor at the Institute for Conflict Analysis and Resolution at George Mason University in Virginia, and as a fellow at the United States Institute for Peace in the late 1980s. Here he produced four volumes of the Conflict Series (1990), which offer a good summation of his own work and that of colleagues, associates and others working with him in the field.

Early influences on Burton's intellectual journey away from the conventional wisdom of international relations traditions were systems theory as a new vocabulary and set of explanations for the cooperative and competitive behaviour of social organisms, and games theory as a means of analysing the variety of options and orientations available to the conflict parties. The work of Schelling (1960) on irrationality in competitive strategies and Rapoport (Rapoport and Chammah, 1965) on the self-defeating logic of win–lose approaches were influential here. As Rapoport put it: 'the illusion that increasing losses for the other side is equivalent to winning is the reason that the struggles are so prolonged and the conflicting parties play the game to a lose/lose end' (1967: 441). We have introduced some of these ideas in chapter 1.

Another source of inspiration for Burton were the insights drawn from industrial relations, organizational theory and client-centred social work. Here the legacy of Mary Parker Follett's 'mutual gains' approach was being vigorously carried forward (Blake et al., 1963; Walton and McKersie, 1965), and applied further afield in family conciliation work, community mediation and the rapidly expanding arena of alternative dispute resolution (ADR) in general, which sought less costly alternatives to formal litigation (Floyer Acland, 1995). Much of this literature, and related literatures on, for example, race and ethnic relations, was based on studies in social psychology and social identity theory, which examined the dynamics of intergroup cooperation and conflict through field-based surveys and small group experimentation. The work of Kurt Lewin was further developed to show how group affiliation and pressure to gain distinctiveness by comparison with other groups can lead to intergroup conflict, and how positive relations can be restored or new relationships negotiated between groups in conflict. Deutsch was amongst the first to apply this kind of research explicitly to conflict resolution (1949, 1973). Useful recent surveys of a wide field include Fisher (1990) and Larsen, ed. (1993). This research has explored both the negative and positive aspects. Negatively, it has concentrated on processes of selective perception through forms of tunnel vision, prejudice and stereotyping, on malign perceptions of the 'other', on dehumanization and the formation of enemy images, on the displacement of feelings of fear and hostility through suppression and projection. Positively, it has focused on changing attitudes, on developing mutual understanding and trust, on the development of common or 'superordinate goals', and on the general identification of conditions which promote positive intergroup contact (Sherif, 1966; Deutsch, 1973). These insights were at the same time applied to international conflict, as later summed up in Mitchell (1981). Linked to this were studies of 'perception and misperception' among decision-makers in international politics, to borrow Jervis' 1976 title. Burton drew on this material in a series of books published in the late 1960s and early 1970s, including: *Systems, States, Diplomacy and Rules* (1968), *Conflict and Communication* (1969), and *World Society* (1972).

What made it possible to unlock these intractable conflicts for Burton was above all the application of needs theory (Maslow, 1954; Sites, 1990) through a 'controlled communication' or problem-solving approach. As already indicated in chapter 1 (figure 1.6), the positing of a universal drive to satisfy basic needs such as security, identity and recognition provided Burton with the link between causal analysis and modes of resolution precisely because of the differences between interests and needs. Interests, being primarily about material 'goods', can be traded, bargained over and negotiated. Needs, being non-material, cannot be traded or satisfied by power bargaining. However, crucially, non-material human needs are not scarce resources (like territory or oil or minerals might be) and are not necessarily in short supply. With proper understanding, therefore, conflicts based on unsatisfied needs can be resolved. It is possible (in theory) to meet the needs of both parties to a conflict, because 'the more security and recognition one party to a relationship experiences, the more others are likely to experience' (Burton, 1990: 242). For example, although the question of sovereignty in Northern Ireland or Jerusalem may appear to be intractable, if the conflict can be translated into the underlying basic needs of the conflict parties for security, recognition and development, a space is opened up for the possibility of resolution.

But the problem-solving approach was seen as more than a conflict resolution technique by Burton. It was to become a central concept in his idea of the paradigm shift in thinking about behaviour and conflict in general that he believed was essential if humankind was to avoid future disaster. He was again influenced by some of the concepts in general systems theory here, and in particular the idea of first order and second order learning. In systems theory, attention is given to the role of social learning and culture in the way in which social systems change. The theory holds that, although social systems 'learn' through their members who individually adjust their world views according to experience, sociocultural systems also have underlying assumptions which make the system as a whole more resistant to change than their individual members. These underlying assumptions are defined by Rapoport as 'default values', which, because they are so commonly used, become regarded as immutable, and actors in the system tend to forget that they can exercise choices in order to attain goals. When problems occur, they are addressed by reference to the 'default values' and this kind of reaction is termed first order learning. Orderly and creative transformation of social systems, however, depends upon a capacity for second order learning, which requires a willingness and capacity for challenging assumptions. Ideological orientations to social change are regarded as the antithesis of second order learning, because ideologies are claims to ultimate truth achieved with a pre-defined set of ends and means, the challenging of which is seen as heretical. For systems theorists such as Rapoport, 'the critical issue of peace and the need to convert conflict to co-operation demand incorporation of second order learning in social systems, and the most effective way to produce social learning is through a participative design process' (Rapoport, 1986: 442).

This idea of second order learning, or second order change, is further developed by Burton and Dukes in the third volume of the Conflict Series (1990), where it is seen to be essential for human survival. The problem-solving approach, given philosophical depth through Charles Sanders Peirce's 'logic of abduction' (1958), is the means of overcoming blockages to second order learning, thereby becoming a central element in what Burton saw as a new political philosophy, which moves beyond episodic conflict resolution to a new order marked by 'provention' (a neologism that has not been widely adopted): 'conflict provention means deducing from an adequate explanation of the phenomenon of conflict, including its human dimensions, not merely the conditions that create an environment of conflict, and the structural changes required to remove it, but more importantly, the promotion of conditions that create cooperative relationships' (Burton and Dukes, eds, 1990: 2). It connotes, in other words, a proactive capability within societies to predict and avoid destructive conflict by the spread of the problem-solving method and philosophy throughout all relevant institutions, discourses and practices. In sum, we can see how far the Burtonian concept of problem-solving and conflict resolution is from the way it is sometimes caricatured in transformationist critiques, where it is wrongly equated with Cox's different use of the term (1981). Indeed, in our view Burtonian problem-solving, seen as paradigm shift rather than workshop technique, is itself firmly at the transformationist end of the conflict resolution spectrum (see chapter 1).

Consolidation: The Third Generation, 1965–1985

By the late 1960s and early 1970s, as suggested in the second quotation from the *Journal of Conflict Resolution* at the head of this chapter, conflict resolution, drawing from a wide range of disciplines and with a reasonably sound institutional base, had defined its specific subject area in relation to the three great projects of avoiding nuclear war, removing glaring inequalities and injustices in the global system, and achieving ecological balance and control. It was attempting to formulate a theoretical understanding of destructive conflict at three levels, with a view to refining the most appropriate practical responses. First, there was the interstate level, where the main effort went into translating détente between the superpowers into formal win–win agreements. Here the processes which produced the 1963 Limited Test Ban Treaty, and later Strategic Arms Limitation Talks and Non-Proliferation Treaty negotiations were seen to vindicate Osgood's 'graduated and reciprocal initiatives in tension reduction' (GRIT) approach (1962) and to exemplify Axelrod's analysis of the 'evolution of cooperation' described in chapter 1 (table 1.2). Similar work went into the formulation of 'alternative defence' strategies in the early 1980s. The expansion of the European Economic Community and of the North Atlantic security area were seen as further confirmation of the ideas of Mitrany and Karl Deutsch. Second, at the level of domestic politics, a great deal of conflict resolution work, particularly in the United States, went into the building up of expertise in family concili-ation, labour and community mediation, and alternative dispute resolution (ADR). An important new initiative here was in public policy disputes in general (Susskind, 1987). Here the sub-field of public conflict resolution aims to increase participation in democratic deci-sion-making at all levels (Barber, 1984; Dukes, 1996). Third, between the two, and for this book the most significant development in the 1970s and 1980s, was the definition, analysis and prescriptive thinking about what were variously described as 'deep-rooted conflicts' (Burton, 1987), 'intractable conflicts' (Kriesberg et al., eds, 1989) or 'protracted social conflicts' (Azar, 1990), in which the distinction between inter-national and domestic level causes was seen to be elided. Here the emphasis was on defining the elements of 'good governance' at consti-tutional level, and of intergroup relations at community level. Since we will be outlining Edward Azar's thinking about protracted social conflict in chapter 4, we will not elaborate these concepts here. They seem to us to have constituted a significant advance in thinking about what has since become the prevailing pattern of large-scale contem-porary conflict. These levels of analysis were brought together from a conflict resolution perspective in studies such as Kriesberg's *The Sociology of Social Conflicts* (1973) and Mitchell's *The Structure of International Conflict* (1981).

In what follows we select for attention the first systematic attempts to apply the problem-solving approach to real conflicts, and the major advances in the analysis of the negotiation and mediation processes which took place in this period. We end the section by noting the concomitant expansion of the conflict resolution institutional base worldwide, and pay tribute to the role of Elise Boulding, both in encouraging it and in articulating its wider significance.

The Harvard School: problem-solving and principled negotiation

One of the most sustained attempts to wed theory to practice was the attempt to set up 'problem-solving workshops' to tackle the more intractable conflicts of the day. Initially referred to as 'controlled communication', the first attempt to apply the problem-solving method was in two workshops in 1965 and 1966, which were designed to address aspects of the conflict between Malaysia, Singapore and Indonesia, and between the Greek and Turkish communities in Cyprus. The London Group, whose members included Michael Banks, Anthony de Reuck, Chris Mitchell and Michael Nicholson as well as Burton, were joined for the second workshop in 1966 by Herb Kelman and Chad Alger from America. Kelman, who formed at Harvard the Program on International Conflict Analysis and Resolution, and who had already been a significant influence in the emergence of conflict resolution research in the pioneering initiatives at the University of Michigan, went on to become perhaps the leading practitioner-scholar of the problem-solving method over the following thirty years, specializing in the Israeli-Palestinian conflict (Doob, ed., 1970; Kelman, 1996). To anticipate events in the 1990s, Kelman's longstanding 1974–91 'pre-negotiation' Arab-Israeli interactive problem-solving workshops, followed by the 1991–3 'para-negotiation' workshops, and post-1993 'post-negotiation' workshops (fifty-four workshops in all so far), involved many of the chief negotiators of the 1993 agreement on both sides. Participants were influential, but non-official, figures; meetings were held in private academic environments, encouraged by third-party facilitation, but only in an enabling capacity inasmuch as ground rules were explained and a problem-solving agenda followed. Information was shared and participants were encouraged to listen without judging each others' needs, concerns and perspectives; there was then joint exploration of options, joint analysis of likely constraints and a joint search for ways of overcoming those constraints. These were seen as non-binding non-official micro-processes, which, it was hoped, would contribute to macro-level negotiations but in no way substitute for them. One of the chief ways in which they might do this was through the building of new relationships.

As experience developed amongst a growing circle of scholar-practitioners in the 1970s and 1980s, problem-solving workshops were used to pursue a variety of goals – for example, in some cases they performed a research and educational or training role – and it became clear that each workshop had to be designed with some reference to the specific characteristics of the particular conflict. A universal model for the ideal problem-solving process did not emerge. Nevertheless, there now exists a whole cluster of approaches – known variously as interactive conflict resolution, third-party consultation, process-promoting workshops, facilitated dialogues – which use many of the essential characteristics of the problem-solving approach (Fisher, 1997). This is well explained and illustrated in Mitchell and Banks's *Handbook of Conflict Resolution: The Analytical Problem-Solving Approach* (1996). The difficult questions of methodology and evaluation have been much discussed (Mitchell, 1993), with a view to enhancing the process of hypothesis generation, theory testing and theory use.

By the 1980s the study of negotiation in international conflict had also taken on the win–win, problem-solving and mutual gain vocabulary of conflict resolution, particularly through the work of Roger

Fisher and William Ury at the Harvard Program on Negotiation, popularized through their best-selling title *Getting to Yes* (1981), and more recently through the quarterly *Negotiation Journal*. We noted in chapter 1 (figure 1.6) the distinction between positions and interests which is central in the 'principled negotiation' approach. The Harvard Program involves a consortium of academic centres, and, in authentic conflict resolution vein, draws from a range of disciplines including politics, psychology, anthropology, sociology and international relations, as well as labour relations, community negotiations and public planning. A number of systematic analyses and comparative studies of successful and unsuccessful negotiation approaches and styles are now available, including Druckman, ed. (1977), Zartman, ed. (1978), Pruitt (1981), Raiffa (1982), Hall, ed. (1993), Pruitt and Carnevale (1993) and Zartman and Rubin (1996).

Adam Curle: the theory and practice of mediation

The practice of mediation has a long history, traceable to Greek and Roman times in the West. By 1945 there were critical studies of state-level diplomacy and international mediation to complement the day-to-day experience acquired by professional diplomats and negotiators (Mitchell and Webb, eds, 1988). The attempt by the international community to convert this into a more formal institutionalized practice following the call in Chapter VI of the United Nations Charter for agreed mechanisms for the peaceful settlement of disputes inspired studies such as that by Oran Young (1967), which included an assessment of the role of the United Nations and its agencies. Nevertheless, a number of scholars in the conflict resolution tradition in the early 1980s agreed with Pruitt that there was a deficit in critical studies of mediation which still lacked systematic analysis (Pruitt and Rubin, 1986: 237). Since then much of the deficit has been made up. In addition to Mitchell and Webb, the literature now includes Touval and Zartman (1985) and Bercovitch and Rubin (1992), as well as Kressell and Pruitt, eds (1989), Bercovitch, ed. (1996) and a host of individual studies of particular mediations in specific conflicts. Quite sophisticated comparisons are now being made of different types of mediation, with or without 'muscle', by different types of mediator (official and unofficial, from the UN to individual governments, insider-partial or outsider-neutral), and in different types of conflict situation. A special issue of the *Journal of Peace Research* published in February 1991 encouraged critical comparison of the efficacy of new paradigm approaches (non-coercive and based broadly on problem-solving) in relation to power-coercion-reward models. Coming out of this have been attempts to suggest that different types of third-party intervention are effective at different stages of the conflict process, that they can be seen as complementary, and that the type of appropriate intervention is contingent upon the nature and stage of the conflict. As we saw in chapter 1, in one well-known model stages of conflict are related to optimal conflict resolution interventions (Fisher and Keashly, 1991). The argument is that softer forms of intervention are more appropriate when miscommunication and mistrust is high (when the subjective elements are strong), whereas harder forms of intervention are more successful when substantive interests are at the forefront. This is considered more fully in chapter 6, as is, in chapter 7, the question whether there are 'ripe moments' for the resolution of conflicts (Zartman, 1985). Relating all of this to the 'conflict triangle' (chapter 1, figure 1.1), it is possible to see the structural approach exemplified by Galtung as addressing the 'contradiction' apex of the triangle, the 'controlled communications' approach of Burton and Kelman as addressing the 'attitude' apex, and the analytic study of various types of bargaining/negotiation, mediation/conciliation and (less usual) arbitration/adjudication approaches exemplified by Zartman, Bercovitch, Druckman, Pruitt and Rubin as addressing the 'behaviour' apex.

As a complement to the emphasis on Track I mediation in many of the studies noted above, we take Adam Curle as our exemplar for the development of 'soft' mediation in the conflict resolution field, particularly what MacDonald and Bendahmane (1987) christened Track II mediation. Coming from an academic background in anthropology, psychology and development education, Curle moved from Harvard to take up the first Chair of Peace Studies at the University of Bradford, which, together with the Richardson Institute for Conflict and Peace Research at the University of Lancaster and the Centre for the Analysis of Conflict at the University of Kent (a relocation of the original 1966 centre based at University College London) was to become a focal point for conflict resolution in the UK.

Curle's academic interest in peace was a product of front-line experiences of conflict in Pakistan and in Africa, where he not only witnessed the threats to development from the eruption of violent conflicts, but was increasingly drawn into the practice of peacemaking, especially as a mediator. Most importantly, during the intensive and searing experiences of the Biafran War he felt a compelling need to understand more about why these conflicts happened (Curle, 1971, 1986; Yarrow, 1978). Violence, conflict, processes of social change and the goals of development began to be seen as linked themes. *Making Peace* (1971) defines peace and conflict as a set of peaceful and unpeaceful relationships, so that 'the process of peacemaking consists in making changes to relationships so that they may be brought to a point where development can occur'. Given his academic background, it was natural that he should see peace broadly in terms of human development, rather than as a set of 'peace-enforcing' rules and organizations. And the purpose of studying social structures was to identify those that enhanced rather than restrained or even suppressed human potential.

In the Middle (1986) points to the importance of mediation and reconciliation themes in peace research and practice in the conflict-ridden world of the late twentieth century. Curle identified four elements to his mediation process: first, the mediator acts to build, maintain and improve communications; second, to provide information to and between the conflict parties; third, to 'befriend' the conflict parties; and, fourth, to encourage what he refers to as active mediation, that is to say to cultivate a willingness to engage in cooperative negotiation. His philosophy of mediation is essentially a blend of values and experiences from Quaker practice,[5] with the knowledge of humanistic psychology absorbed in his early professional career, with both of these influences tempered and modified by his experiences in the field.

Curle's work is an illustration both of the applied nature of conflict resolution and its stress on the crucial link between academic theory and practice. It also provides one example of an approach to Track II or citizens diplomacy (what Diamond and MacDonald (1996), call multi-track diplomacy because they include business contacts, the churches, etc.), and a number of studies have contributed to a fuller understanding of the methods and approaches of mediation and third-party intervention in conflicts at both official-governmental and unofficial-citizens' diplomacy level activity. A useful book on official diplomacy is Berridge (1995), while a good general account of unofficial diplomacy is provided by Berman and Johnson in the introduction to their 1977 edited book, which includes a definition of citizens' diplomacy and a classification of the types of citizens organizations that conduct it (MacDonald and Bendahmane, 1987; Aall, 1996; Anderson, 1996b). However, it is important to recognize that Curle's thinking and practice did not stay fixed at the point of Track II mediation. During the wars in former Yugoslavia he broadened his concept and practice of peacemaking to include the empowerment of individuals and civil society groups in a wide variety of roles, and developed, along with John Paul Lederach and others, new approaches to peacebuilding from below, based primarily on his work with and support for the Osijek Centre for Peace Nonviolence and Human Rights, which we examine more fully in chapter 9 (Curle, 1994, 1995, 1999).

Elise Boulding: new voices in conflict resolution

During the 1970s and 1980s the number of peace researchers and conflict resolution specialists worldwide continued to grow from a few hundred to perhaps thousands, and the institutional bases for conflict resolution expanded accordingly, mainly in Western Europe, North America and Japan, but also increasingly in other parts of the world (ECCP website, see chapter 3). Notable centres were established in areas of protracted conflict such as South Africa, Northern Ireland, the Spanish Basque country and Sri Lanka. In this section we have taken the work of Elise Boulding as exemplary of this process of expansion and of the development of thinking that has accompanied it.

Elise Boulding trained as a sociologist and was involved in the early work of the Michigan Centre outlined above, serving as Secretary-General of the International Peace Research Association (IPRA) from 1964 and chair of the Women's International League for Peace and Freedom, of which she was subsequently international chair. With the help of UNESCO, the IPRA Newsletter, started by Boulding, developed the network which facilitated the formulation of the Association, and she continued to serve as its editor for a number of years. In order to encourage wider participation in peace and conflict resolution processes, she introduced the idea of 'imaging the future' as a powerful way of enabling people to break out of the defensive private shells into which they retreated, often out of fear of what was happening in the public world, and encouraging them to participate in the construction of a peaceful and tolerant global culture. The use of social imagination and the idea of imaging the future was placed within the context of what she called the '200-year present', that is, the idea that we must understand that we live in a social space which reaches into the past and into the future: 'it is our space, one that we can move around directly in our own lives and indirectly by touching the lives of the young and old around us' (Boulding, E., 1990: 4). She was also an early exponent of the idea of civil society, of opening up new possibilities for a global civic culture which was receptive to the voices of people who were not part of the traditional discourses of nation-state politics, and in this she anticipated many of the preoccupations of conflict resolution workers today. Women and children were obviously excluded groups, but she added to these the idea that globalism and global civic culture needed to accommodate the many culture communities which were not heard in the existing international order. For Elise Boulding, the next half of our '200-year present', that is the next one hundred years from the 1980s, contains within it the basis for a world civic culture and peaceful problem-solving among nations, but also for the possibility of Armageddon. She saw the development of indigenous and international citizens' networks as one way of ensuring that the former prevailed. For her, peacemaking demands specific 'craft and skills', a peace praxis encompassing 'all those activities in which conflict is dealt with in an integrative mode – as choices that lie at the heart of all human interaction' (1990: 140). In the inter-subjective relationships which make up social and political life, as also in the structures and institutions within which they are embedded, the success with which this is inculcated and encouraged will determine whether, in the end, we are peacemakers or warmakers.

Reconstruction: The Fourth Generation, 1985–2005

In this chapter we have noted the diverse nature of the conflict resolution tradition, rooted in different disciplines and encompassing the 'subjectivist' controlled communication and problem-solving approach, the 'objectivist' rational negotiation/mediation approach and the 'structuralist' social justice approach. We have tentatively suggested that these correspond to attempts to address the 'attitude', 'behaviour' and 'contradiction' vertices of the conflict triangle. Nevertheless, despite this diversity, quite a simple central commitment prevails. Having grown in a number of centres through the pioneering work of a small group of individuals, the enterprise of conflict resolution is now conducted across an international network where scholars and practitioners from many countries share in the common objective of formulating, applying and testing structures and practices for preventing, managing, ending and transforming violent and destructive conflict. Conflict resolution does not prescribe specific solutions or end goals for society, beyond a commitment to the core assumption that aggressive win–lose styles of engagement in violent conflict usually incur costs that are not only unacceptably high for the conflict parties, but also for world society in general. This does not mean endorsing the status quo, since unjust and oppressive systems are seen as some of the chief sources of violence and war. What it does entail, as the previous chapter suggests, is a search for ways of transforming actually or potentially violent conflict into peaceful processes of political and social change. Within this search, conflict resolution has emerged as a field of theory and practice which is part of a longer process of evolution towards a global peace culture. The rest of the book looks at the work of the contemporary fourth generation of conflict resolvers which has had to adapt to the changed international scene since the end of the Cold War. In the next two chapters we turn to an examination of the nature and sources of contemporary conflict. This will serve as an analytic foundation for the chapters that follow.

Recommended reading

Dunn (1995); Kriesberg (1997); Lawler (1995); Väyrynen, ed. (1991).

Statistics of Deadly Quarrels

Would it not be wise to endow the science of peace with rich
and strong schools just as one has done for its elder sister, the
science of war?

Raphael Dubois, writing shortly before World War I

Having outlined the history of the conflict resolution field, we move
on to a consideration of contemporary conflict. From the beginning,
the study of conflict resolution has been seen to depend upon
prior analysis of conflict data. We have seen how this was clear in the
original 1957 issue of the *Journal of Conflict Resolution*, where both
Boulding and Wright proposed global conflict data stations to alert
the international community to the early onset of situations likely to
erupt into full-scale violence. In this chapter we will familiarize
ourselves with the 'statistics of deadly quarrels', to borrow the title of
Richardson's posthumously published seminal study that did so much
to excite the interest of the early conflict resolvers (1960b). This will
serve as the basis for the conflict analysis chapter that follows. We will
first establish what statistics suggest about prevalent patterns of large-
scale conflict, and then consider how far comparable statistics about
patterns of terrorism compel us to revise them in the light of events
since 11 September 2001.

The Conflict Domain

What are to count as the relevant conflicts? Conflict resolution
analysts have traditionally included all levels of conflict from intra-
personal conflict through to international conflict, and all stages of
conflict escalation and de-escalation. In this book we restrict our
focus to actual or potentially violent conflicts, ranging from social
conflict situations which threaten to become militarized beyond
the capacity of domestic civil police to control, through to full-scale
interstate war. In line with the idea of the measurable escalation

stages referred to in chapter 1 (figure 1.2), we may note the scale used by the Interdisciplinary Research Program on Causes of Human Rights Violations (PIOOM) at Leiden University, which distinguished five stages of escalation: (1) 'peaceful stable situations', defined as a 'high degree of political stability and regime legitimacy'; (2) 'political tension situations', defined as 'growing levels of systemic strain and increasing social and political cleavages, often along factional lines' (not included in their statistics); (3) 'violent political conflict', where tension has escalated to 'political crisis' inasmuch as there has been 'an erosion of political legitimacy of the national government' and/or a 'rising acceptance of violent factional politics' (quantified as up to 99 people killed in any one calendar year); (4) 'low-intensity conflict', where there is 'open hostility and armed conflict among factional groups, regime repression and insurgency' (100 to 999 people killed in any one year); and (5) 'high-intensity conflict', where there is 'open warfare among rival groups and/or mass destruction and displacement of sectors of the civilian population' (1,000 or more people killed in a year) (Jongman and Schmid, 1997). The striking assumption here is that contemporary conflict will be mainly 'internally' generated and that interstate war of the classic kind can be virtually ignored. Whatever the longer-term prospects for a revival of interstate war, this is in marked contrast to most quantitative studies of major armed conflict and war since 1945, and is an eloquent testimony to the transformation in conflict studies which has taken place in recent years, as discussed further in chapter 4.

Richardson included both international and domestic conflicts in his dataset of 'deadly quarrels' between 1820 and 1949. By deadly quarrel he meant 'any quarrel which caused death to humans. The term thus includes murders, banditries, mutinies, insurrections, and wars small and large' (1960b). Sorokin included revolutions as well as wars in his study (1937).

Most studies since the 1950s in the 'classical' phase of the statistical study of international conflict, however, confined the field to interstate and related wars above a certain measurable threshold. The well-known Correlates of War (COW) Project, for example, initiated at the University of Michigan in the 1960s by Singer and Small, takes its start date from 1816. It covers 'interstate wars', defined as conflicts 'involving at least one member of the interstate system on each side of the war, resulting in a total of 1,000 or more battle-deaths', and 'extra-systemic' wars (e.g. imperial war, colonial war and internationalized civil war), defined as international wars 'in which there was a member of the interstate system on only one side of the war, resulting in an average of 1,000 battle deaths per year for system member participants' (Singer and Small, 1972: 381–2).[1] In Singer's more recent work, however, these restrictive definitions have been progressively relaxed in a partial return to Richardson's original wide canvas, as noted below.

In contrast to this, as Wallensteen explains, is the Hamburg University (AKUF) Project, initiated by Kende and developed by Gantzel (Gantzel and Schwinghammer, 2000). AKUF builds on a post-1945 dataset, and the criterion for inclusion is not battle-related deaths, which are seen as unreliable and unduly restrictive since they do not reflect other kinds of suffering. In contrast to the realist state-centric starting point of COW, AKUF 'relates the onset of war to the development of capitalist societies' and sees conflict as 'a result of the new forms of production, monetarization of the economy and the resulting dissolution of traditional forms of social integration' (Wallensteen, 2002b: 22).

Different again is Wallensteen's own University of Uppsala Conflict Data Project, which uses the concept of 'armed conflict' and approaches the analysis from a more conflict resolution perspective. Unlike COW or AKUF, which are 'satisfied once they have identified the actors and the actions', the Uppsala project 'requires that the conflict should have an issue, an incompatibility' (Wallensteen, 2002b: 24). Major armed conflicts are defined as 'prolonged combat between the military forces of two or more governments, or of one government and at least one organized armed group [thus ruling out spontaneous violence and massacres of unarmed civilians], and incurring the battle-related deaths of at least 1,000 people for the duration of the conflict' (SIPRI Yearbook, 1997: 17). Major armed conflicts are subdivided into 'intermediate conflicts' and 'wars'. A minor armed conflict is one in which overall deaths are fewer than 1,000.

The different results obtained from the COW, AKUF and Uppsala projects can be seen to reflect the differing theoretical presuppositions upon which they are based. This shows how important it is to be clear what those presuppositions are before relying on a particular set of figures. Other datasets used in this chapter are equally disparate. The Minorities at Risk Project at the Center for International Development and Conflict Management (CIDCM) at Maryland University, for example, initiated in 1986, compares data on the political aspirations of some 250 minority communal groups worldwide and includes measures taken, short of the use of armed force. Within this brief, lists are drawn up of 'ethno-nationalist peoples' who have fought 'sustained or recurrent campaigns of armed force aimed at least in part at securing national independence for a communal group, or their unification with kindred groups in adjoining states' between 1945 and the 1990s. Terrorist and guerrilla strategies are also counted (Gurr, 1995: 5; 2000). In contrast, the Humanitarianism and War Project at Brown University is more concerned with data for 'populations at risk' in 'complex humanitarian emergencies' (Weiss and Collins, 1996).

As a result of these variations, the composite list of major deadly conflicts in progress in 2002–3, given in table 3.1, represents a series of compromises between competing datasets.

Table 3.1 Countries with major armed conflicts in progress 2002–3

Location	Inception	Principal conflictants	Deaths
Afghanistan	1978	Taliban, Northern Alliance, regional warlords, US and coalition, Al-Qaida	1–2m
Algeria	1992	Govt vs. FIS, GIA etc. (Islamic)	>60,000
Angola	1975	Govt vs UNITA	>500,000
Burundi	1993	Govt vs Hutu etc. militias	>100,000
Colombia	1978	Govt vs FARC, ELN, EPL	>50,000
Congo-Brazzaville	1993	Govt vs Ntsiloulous, etc.	>10,000
DRC/Zaire	1993	Govt vs RCD, RCD faction, MLC, Rwanda, Uganda	>1.5m
Ethiopia	1998	Ethiopia, Eritrea	>100,000
Ethiopia	1977	Govt vs OLF, ONLF	>2,000
India	1979	Govt vs ULFA (Assam)	>5,000
India	1989	Govt vs JKLF, Pakistan (Kashmir)	>30,000
Indonesia	1999	Govt vs GAM (Aceh)	>2,000
Israel	1948	Govt vs PLO, Hamas, Hezbollah, Islamic Jihad, PFLP, al-Aqsa Martyrs Brigade	>18,000
Myanmar	1948	Govt vs SSA	>100,000
Nepal	1997	CPN-M, UPF	>7,000
Philippines	1969	Govt vs MPA, MILF	>50,000
Russia	1991	Govt vs Chechen rebels	>20,000
Rwanda	1991	Govt vs ALiR and FDLR	>800,000
Senegal	1990	Govt vs MFDC	>3,000
Sierra Leone	1989	Govt vs RUF, AFRC, ECOMOG, Kamajors	>25,000
Somalia	1996	Govt vs SRRC	>400,000
Sri Lanka	1983	Govt vs LTTE	>60,000
Sudan	1983	Govt vs SPLA, NDA	>1.5m
Turkey	1984	Govt vs PKK	>30,000
Uganda	1994	Govt vs LRA, WNBF, ADF	>1,000

Source: This list includes major armed conflicts with a cumulative total of 1,000 or more conflict-related deaths since fighting began. Data was compiled from the list in the first edition of this book and the sources cited there, revised and updated with particular reference to the lists published by the Centre for Systemic Peace (<http://members.aol.com/CSPmgm/warlist.htm>), and the Uppsala Conflict Data Project (Gleditsch et al., 2002; Eriksson, 2002, appendix 1).[2]

Conflict Trends

Data collected by Wallensteen, Gurr and Marshall and others show that the number of armed conflicts rose steadily until the end of the Cold War but fell thereafter. According to the Uppsala University data used by SIPRI, over the period 1989–96 'there was an almost constant decline in the number of major armed conflicts worldwide' (SIPRI Yearbook, 1997: 20). At the same time Wallensteen and Axell reported a 'new pattern of conflict' in the 1990s in which the prime emphasis was on 'challenges to existing state authority', including secessionist movements which threaten the territorial integrity of the state (former Yugoslavia, Chechnya) and challenges to central control which may also end in fragmentation with no one actor in overall command (Liberia, Somalia) (1995: 345). More specifically, in 2003 Peter Wallensteen and his colleagues at the Uppsala Conflict Data Project concluded that:

> A total of 226 armed conflicts have been recorded for the years 1946–2002. Of these, 116 were active in the period 1989–2002, including 31 in 2002. There were five wars in 2002. Both numbers were the lowest for this period. Seven interstate-armed conflicts were recorded in 1989–2002, of which one was still active in 2002. In 2002, a larger proportion of complex major armed conflicts were resolved, compared with new and minor armed conflicts. Although the data on armed conflict presented here suggest that there is a decline in the use of armed force, there is an increased feeling of fear and insecurity in many parts of the world because of terrorism incidents. (Eriksson et al., 2003: 593)

Trend statistics suggested that even 'the number of actions of international terrorism is lower than in previous years' (ibid.: 597) (although equivalent figures for 2003–4, unavaliable at the time of writing, are likely to show a marked increase if attacks in Iraq are included). The data from AKUF (2002) and CIDCM (Marshall and Gurr, 2003) have confirmed this. For example, based on data through to the mid-1990s on 'minorities at risk', Gurr estimated that, although there were eleven 'new ethnonational wars of autonomy and independence' in 1991–3, there were no new ethnonational wars in 1994–6, suggesting that the turbulence following the collapse of the Soviet Union and the end of the Cold War was dying away. Moreover, whereas at the end of each five-year period between 1971 and 1990 there had been between twenty-two and twenty-five ongoing ethnonational wars, in 1996 there were eleven. Of the twenty-four wars ongoing in 1993, eight had been contained or suppressed and five settled through accommodation three years later (Gurr, 1998). In 2000 Gurr concluded that the long-term trend of 'increasing communal-based protest and rebellion' that began in the 1950s had now peaked and was on the wane: 'the number of groups using armed violence has been declining after decades of increase' (2000: 275). Clearly, though, these suggested recent trends may be a poor basis for future prediction. And the incidence of international terrorist attacks, to which the media have been highly sensitized since 11 September 2001, has added further uncertainty (see box 3.1). So has the US reaction announced in President

---

Box 3.1 The threat from Al-Qaida

The Iranian revolution of 1978–9 and the Soviet invasion of Afghanistan in 1979 stimulated the multiplication of transnational Islamist links and focused widespread Muslim frustration into a geopolitical jihad against what were seen as the two main threats from the ungodly against Islam – Soviet communism and western capitalism. The aim of the Al-Qaida 'network of networks' was to provide a global 'base' for this historic effort. The expulsion of the Soviet forces from Afghanistan was seen as a glorious vindication of the enterprise, and efforts were refocused into a concerted assault on the Judaeo-Christian West and in particular its overweening leading power, the United States. Attacks were mounted on the World Trade Center (1993), the Khobar Towers in Saudi Arabia (1996), the Kenya and Tanzania embassies (1998) and USS *Cole* in Yemen (2000). The opinion of experts seems to be divided on the extent to which, since September 2001, Al-Qaida can be seen to be behind particular attacks, or whether fragmented groups affiliate themselves to Al-Qaida in a loose and constantly changing way mainly to qualify for often relatively small amounts of funding (some, indeed, have questioned whether Al-Qaida exists at all). In this way the distinction between international terrorism and other kinds of terrorism (e.g. Chechen separatism) may be blurred. Be that as it may, a number of attacks have been attributed to Al-Qaida:

1 11 September 2001: New York and Washington, 2,826 killed
2 22 December 2001: Richard Reid overpowered on Paris/Miami flight
3 23 January 2002: Daniel Pearl kidnapped and beheaded in Karachi, 12 killed
4 8 September 2002: car bomb in Kabul and attempt to kill Hamid Karzai in Kandahar, 32 killed
5 6 October 2002: French oil-tanker *Limburg* rammed off Al Mukalla, Yemen
6 12 October 2002: Bali nightclub bomb, 202 killed
7 28 October 2002: US diplomat Laurence Foley shot in Amman, Jordan
8 28 November 2002: suicide bombing at Israeli-owned hotel in Mombassa, Kenya, 15 killed (80 injured); shoulder-fired missile narrowly misses Israeli aircraft with 261 passengers
9 5 January 2003: ricin found in flat in Wood Green, London
10 February–April 2003: 32 European tourists missing in Algeria
11 12 May 2003: suicide bombings Riyadh, Saudi Arabia, 29+ killed
16 16 May 2003: suicide bombings in Casablanca, Morocco, 41 killed
17 August 2003: suicide bombings at Marriott Hotel, Jakarta, Indonesia, 12 killed
18 November 2003: explosions in housing compound, Riyadh, Saudi Arabia, 17 killed
19 November 2003: suicide bombings at two synagogues in Istanbul, Turkey, and a bomb at British bank, 25 killed
20 March 2004: coordinated bomb blasts on railway system in Madrid, Spain, 191 killed
21 May 2004: attack on offices of a Saudi oil company in Khobar, Saudi Arabia, and foreign oil workers taken hostage in a nearby residential compound, 22 killed
22 7 July 2005: suicide bombings in London, 56 killed, some 700 injured

Bush's first National Security Strategy Report (NSSR) of 20 September 2002, with its doctrine of 'anticipatory defense' and pre-emptive military action against hostile states and terrorist groups seen to be threats to national and international security (above all where there is a threat that weapons of mass destruction might get into terrorist hands). Nevertheless, for reasons given in the final section of this chapter, most conflict analysts still conclude that their existing analytic models retain credibility and do not need to be substantially altered.

Within all this there have been attempts to find quantitative measures for conflict escalation and de-escalation from year to year (PIOOM have used thirteen variables and SIPRI have used a five-level numerical scale) and to note regional variations and changes in the incidence of different conflict types (see next section).

One major trend, however, shows through in almost all accounts, and that is a decline in the proportion of interstate wars (see figure 3.1). Over a longer-term time frame, according to Holsti, the number of interstate wars per year per state has gone down steadily over the past hundred years, comparing the 1918–41 with the 1945–95 periods (1996: 24). In chapter 4 we will suggest that the key transition here came earlier rather than at the end of the Cold War, but since 1989 the

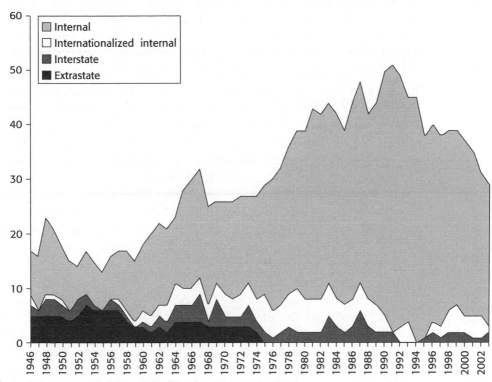

Figure 3.1   Number of armed conflicts by type, 1946–2003

decline in the number of interstate wars has approached its limit. There were no interstate wars in 1993 and 1994, only a minor border altercation between Peru and Ecuador in 1995 and a flare-up in the long-running dispute between India and Pakistan over Kashmir in 1996 (Wallensteen and Sollenberg, 1996; SIPRI Yearbook, 1997: 17). In 2002 there was only one interstate war, together with foreign inter-ventions in Angola, Congo-Brazzaville and Afghanistan (Eriksson et al., 2003: 594–5). Evidently Iraq would be added in 2003. We should no doubt hesitate before celebrating 'the end of international war' – for example, with continuing instability in Kashmir or increased tension between China and Taiwan. Nevertheless, given the data to hand, the main thrust in this book must clearly be to discuss conflict resolution in relation to non-interstate rather than to interstate war.

Conflict Distribution

Many commentators agree that, with the ending of the Cold War, regional patterns of conflict have become all the more significant. There have, therefore, been efforts to compare characteristics of conflict from region to region.[3] At the heart of such studies lies the attempt to provide a reliable statistical basis for distinctions such as those between 'zones of peace' and 'zones of war' (Kacowicz, 1995). There are many variations here. For example, Holsti (1996: ch. 7), following Deutsch (1954), Jervis (1982), Väyrynen (1984) and Buzan (1991), distinguishes 'pluralistic security communities' in which no serious provisions are made for war between member states such as North America, the Antipodes or Western Europe; 'zones of peace' between states such as the Caribbean and the South Pacific; 'no-war zones' such as South-East Asia and (perhaps) East Asia; and 'zones of war' such as Africa, some former Soviet republics, the Middle East, Central America, South Asia and the Balkans.

It is clearly relevant to conflict resolution to understand the distinc-tions between regional 'security regimes' with relatively stable inter-state relations such as the Association of South-East Asian Nations (ASEAN), 'security communities' which avoid large-scale violence as in Western Europe and North America, and more volatile and conflict-prone regions. There are several quite striking regional variations here, such as the surprising absence of interstate war in South America since 1941 despite its famously turbulent past (Holsti, 1996: 150–82). The level of violent conflict in Southern Africa since the 1990s has been going down, but not in the Great Lakes region. Why is this? Setting geographical location aside, is there a quantitative and quali-tative difference in the incidence and nature of armed conflict

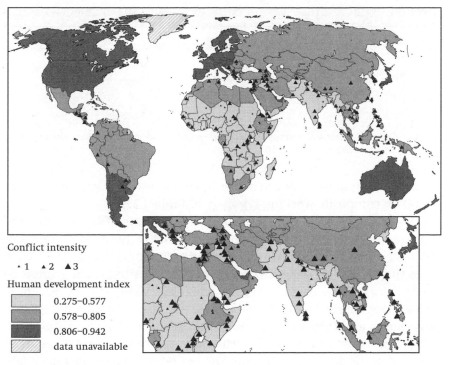

Conflict intensity

• 1   ▲ 2   ▲ 3

Human development index

	0.275–0.577
	0.578–0.805
	0.806–0.942
	data unavailable

Source: O'Loughlin, 2004

Map 3.1   Distribution of armed conflicts, 1946–2000

between and within developed countries in comparison with so-called Third World or postcolonial countries? And do different types of conflict predominate in different regions? (See map 3.1.)

Conflict Types

This leads to one of the most testing questions in conflict analysis. Are there different types of conflict which need to be distinguished from each other if effective and discriminate conflict resolution is to be undertaken? Unfortunately, current conflict typology is in a state of confusion. There are as many typologies as analysts, and the criteria employed not only vary, but are often mutually incompatible. A compilation of some of the different labels used in well-known analyses from the 1990s soon runs to well over a hundred. Some differentiate in terms of conflict parties,[4] others in terms of conflict issues,[5] others in terms of conflict causes,[6] but most in terms of hybrid lists that seem to muddle diverse categories. Some have two types, others run to more than twenty. The field is littered with typologies suggested by particular authors but discarded by others. Nevertheless, based on

Table 3.2 A working conflict typology

Conflict type	Example
Interstate	Gulf War 1991
Non-interstate	
revolution/ideology	Algeria
identity/secession	Sri Lanka
factional	Liberia

a comparison of some of the better-known studies we venture to offer our own composite working typology in table 3.2.

First, it may be helpful to think more in terms of historically and geographically based 'generations' of conflict rather than in terms of blanket typologies. After all, the roots of all major conflicts reach back into the historical past – often several centuries back. Superimposed on this are clusters of 'enduring rivalries', many still unresolved, going back, respectively, to the time of the break-up of the Russian, Austro-Hungarian and Ottoman empires at the end of the First World War (we might add Northern Ireland to this list); the political settlements at the end of the Second World War; the period of decolonization (1950s, 1960s); the postcolonial period (1970s, 1980s); and, finally, the break-up of the Soviet bloc (1990s). Perhaps a new generation of terrorist and anti-terrorist conflicts has now been superimposed.

Second, we would do well to heed Singer's advice that a classificatory system should 'remain as atheoretical as possible' lest, 'by accepting conventional labels of certain armed conflicts, we buy into simplistic interpretations, and ultimately embrace disastrous reactions and responses' – although it is unlikely that we will succeed in finding a typology which is 'logically exhaustive, mutually exclusive, operationally explicit, semantically consistent, and substantively comparable' (1996: 40, 48). Box 3.2 compares Singer's conflict typology with that of Holsti (1996). The two seem more or less to coincide. Omitting Singer's 'extra-systemic wars' and Holsti's 'decolonizing wars' on the grounds that the era of decolonization is all but over, there seems to be rough agreement about a distinction between *interstate conflict*, and two types of non-interstate conflict: *revolution/ideology* conflict (Singer's and Holsti's type (c)), and *identity/secession* conflict (Singer's and Holsti's type (d)). This is also partially mirrored in the Uppsala typology mentioned above (SIPRI Yearbook, 1997: 23), which is based on 'conflict causes', and sees major armed conflict as caused by 'two types of incompatibilities': 'government conflicts', which are contested incompatibilities concerning 'government (type of political system, a change of central government or in its composition)'; and 'territory conflicts', which are

Box 3.2 Conflict typologies: a comparison

Singer's conflict typology (1996: 43–7) is based on the political status of conflict parties. He retains his original distinction between (a) interstate wars and (b) extra-systemic (mainly colonial) wars, but here adds two further classes of non-interstate conflict: (c) 'civil' conflicts, in which, unlike (b), one protagonist may be 'an insurgent or revolutionary group within the recognised territorial boundaries of the state', and (d) the 'increasingly complex intrastate wars' in former colonial states, where the challenge may come from 'culturally defined groups whose members identify with one another and with the group on the basis of shared racial, ethnic, linguistic, religious, or kinship characteristics'. Holsti (1996: 21) has also recently adapted his typology. He earlier categorized international (interstate) conflict up to 1989 in terms of twenty-four issues, grouped into five composite sets: conflict over territory, economics, nation-state creation, ideology, and 'human sympathy' (i.e. ethnicity/religion). He concluded that the incidence of the first two had been declining, but that of the last three was, if anything, increasing (1991: 306–34). He later focuses on non-interstate war and bases his typology on 'types of actors and/or objectives', ending up with four categories of conflict: (a) 'standard state versus state wars (e.g., China and India in 1962) and armed interventions involving significant loss of life (the United States in Vietnam, the Soviet Union in Afghanistan)'; (b) 'decolonizing wars of "national liberation"'; (c) 'internal wars based on ideological goals' (e.g., the Sendero Luminoso in Peru, the Monteneros in Uruguay); and (d) 'state-nation wars including armed resistance by ethnic, language and/or religious groups, often with the purpose of secession or separation from the state' (e.g., the Tamils in Sri Lanka, the Ibos in Nigeria).

contested incompatibilities concerning 'control of territory (interstate conflict), secession or autonomy'. These two types of conflict again coincide quite closely with our revolution/ideology and identity/secession conflicts – except that interstate conflict and non-interstate identity/secession conflict are conflated in the Uppsala typology under the heading 'territory conflict'. A number of other conflict resolution analysts also recognize the distinction between revolution/ideology and identity/secession conflicts.[7]

Finally, we are also tempted to distinguish revolution/ideology and identity/secession conflicts in turn from a third class of non-interstate conflict, *factional conflict*, in which the fighting is not about revolutionary-ideological issues, nor about identity-secessionist issues, but solely about the competing interests or power struggles of political or criminal factions. This may be seen to coincide with a category of 'economic opportunity' conflicts (Collier and Hoeffler, 2001). Holsti implicitly acknowledges a sub-category of factional conflict, inasmuch as the shorthand designation for his type (c) conflicts is 'internal factional/ideological' conflict.

This line of enquiry, therefore, suggests that provisional distinctions may usefully be made between three types of predominantly non-interstate conflict. The term 'non-interstate conflict' should not be misunderstood. All it means is that these are not classic wars between two states. It does not imply that states are not involved either overtly or covertly, or that 'internal wars' do not spill across state borders or draw other states in. The term 'factional conflict' covers *coups d'état*, intra-elite power struggles, brigandage, criminality and warlordism, where the aim is to usurp, seize or retain state power merely to further economic and other interests. The term 'revolution/ideology conflict' includes the more ambitious aim of changing the nature of government in a state, for example by (a) changing the system from capitalist to socialist, or (b) changing the form of government from dictatorship to democracy, or (c) changing the religious orientation of the state from secular to Islamic. In the post-Cold War world it is possible to discern a decline in the incidence of (a) but not in the incidence of (b) and particularly not of (c). The term 'identity/secession conflict' involves the relative status of communities or 'communal groups', however defined, in relation to the state. Depending upon the nature of the group and the contextual situation, this includes struggles for access, for autonomy, for secession or for control (Gurr, 1995: 3–5).[8] In brief, a factional conflict is merely a struggle to control the state or part of the state, a revolution-ideology conflict is in addition a struggle to change the nature of the state, and an identity-secession conflict may well be a threat to the integrity of the state (see table 3.2). We might be tempted to see this as roughly coinciding with Zartman's distinction between greed, creed and need conflicts (Zartman, 2000).

Needless to say, specific conflicts elude neat pigeon-holing of this kind on closer inspection. Scholars disagree about categorization, as seen, for example, in the elaborate attempts by Marxist analysts in the 1960s and 1970s to interpret ethnic conflict as class conflict (Munck, 1986), in contrast to the reverse trend on the part of many analysts in the 1990s. More recently, we have seen attempts to class all non-interstate conflicts as economically motivated 'greed' conflicts (Collier and Hoeffler, 2001). Moreover the conflicts themselves often change character over time, are interpreted in different ways by the conflict parties, and can always be captured and manipulated by unscrupulous power-brokers who subsequently justify their depredations by appeal to principle. For example, the conflict in Afghanistan in the mid-1990s could be interpreted as a revolution/ideology conflict to the extent that it was identified with Taleban's drive to create an Islamic state; or as an identity/secession conflict to the extent that it was seen as a struggle between Pashtuns (Taleban), Uzbeks (Dostum) and Tajiks (Masood); or as a merely factional conflict if the fighting

Table 3.3 Regional distribution of major armed conflicts by type, 1990–2002			
	G	T	Total
Europe	0	6	6
Middle East	3	6	9
Asia	7	12	19
Africa	15	4	19
Americas	5	0	5

G = government (type of political system, change of central government or its composition)

T = territory (control of territory (interstate), secession or autonomy)

Source: Calculated from Uppsala data (Gleditsch et al., 2002). Conflicts included are those with a cumulative total of 1,000 combat deaths. Sub-conflicts involving the same actors are not counted separately.

was seen to be perpetuated simply by the interests of rival war lords and their clients; or even as an interstate conflict by proxy if the war was seen to be little more than the playing out on Afghan soil of what were essentially rivalries between outside states such as Pakistan, Uzbekistan and Iran. For this reason we advise that conflict typologies, essential though they are for effective conflict analysis, should be understood as being permanently under review.

Returning to the question posed at the end of the last section, according to the Uppsala classification system, it is striking that in the Americas there have been no major 'territorial' (identity/secession) conflicts in the early 1990s, whereas in Europe there have been no 'government' (revolution/ideology) conflicts (see table 3.3).

Terrorism and Conflict

In the wake of the 11 September 2001 terrorist attacks in New York and Washington, and the subsequent 'war on terror', do we need to recognize an entirely different set of issues that render previous analysis outmoded? This is the implication of claims heard in some quarters that 9/11 has 'changed everything' (as noted in Booth and Dunne, eds, 2002; Halliday, 2002). To address this question we need to relate what we have seen so far in this chapter to a separate set of statistics: those produced by specialists on terrorism. Terrorism is not a new phenomenon and has its own analysts, who until recently tended to work surprisingly independently of mainstream conflict analysis.

Let us note first how Peter Wallensteen and his colleagues at Uppsala have retained their conflict analysis framework unchanged in their most recent statistics of armed conflict through to 2002

(Eriksson et al., 2003). In an additional section on 'terrorism and armed conflict' (pp. 597–9) they note how terrorism 'has recently been used to cover distinct different actions, such as criminal activities and gang-sterism' as well as more traditional political purposes, and 'is often directed against civilians and symbolic societal targets, as opposed to government targets'. Their overall conclusion, though, is that, just as the incidence of armed conflicts have continued to decline since the early 1990s, so too 'trend statistics suggest that the number of actions of international terrorism is lower than in previous years' (as noted above, this will no doubt change if attacks in Iraq in 2003–4 are included). Four types of terrorism are distinguished according to how closely related they are to the types of armed conflict that the Uppsala project analyses. The first type is the kind of terror that is an unavoid-able aspect of most armed conflicts. The second type is terrorism as a supplementary measure in asymmetric conflicts, particularly to enhance the influence of auxiliary or affiliated groups (Tamil Tigers in Sri Lanka, Hezbollah in Lebanon). These two types of terrorism are seen to be amenable to negotiation and political agreement like normal political conflict. The third type is where terrorism is more important to some groups than other forms of more traditional armed action (for example, the Lord's Resistance Army in Uganda, or the Revolutionary United Front in Sierra Leone). This type of terrorism may be associated more with economic opportunity or greed than with wider political purpose, is harder to accommodate within a peace process, and is therefore likely to require different 'police' responses. Finally, there is the fourth category of groups – notably, but not exclusively, radical Islamists such as Al-Qaida – that operate internationally and have multiple international purposes for which it is harder to mobilize large populations in order to wage guerrilla war. This is the category of dedicated small groups not amenable to political talks or agreements, which must be combated in ways to be explored later in chapter 11. Although this type of terrorism is harder to fit into conventional conflict typologies, it is by no means unprecedented, and is akin to previous generations of left-wing terrorism such as international Bolshevism in the 1920s and 1930s, Che Guevara's strategy for radical global change in the 1960s, and the ambitions for world revolution of Lin Biao in China during the cultural revolution (Eriksson et al., 2003).

With reference to terrorism studies, we will abstract two aspects to guide us. First, however complex and inconsistent definitions of terror-ism are – and notoriously subject to political manipulation – we will follow those who take terrorism to refer to particular actions and strategies rather than to specific actors or distinct political purposes. In other words, individuals, groups, movements and governments may all adopt terrorist tactics at various times in order to further their political or economic purposes – and then abandon them while still pursuing those purposes. There may be groups that only employ terrorist means and whose purpose does not reach beyond terror itself, but these are exceptional. In this book, therefore, terrorism is taken to be a set of actions or strategies adopted by groups for certain purposes, not the identity of those groups or the nature of those purposes.

Box 3.3 Definitions of terrorism

In line with the approach adopted in this book, Wardlow's definition of terrorism is focused on the forms of deliberate violence threatened or used, its targets and its wider audience, not on the perpetrators' identity or political, ideological or criminal purpose:

> [Terrorism is] the use, or threat of use, of violence by an individual or a group, whether acting for or in opposition to established authority, when such an act is designed to create extreme anxiety and/or fear-inducing effects in a target group larger than the immediate victims with the purpose of coercing that group into acceding to the political demands of the perpetrators. (Wardlow, 1982: XX)

After the 9/11 attack, the US government defined terrorism more narrowly by restricting the term to 'subnational groups or clandestine agents' and confining the targets to 'noncombatants':

> The term 'terrorism' means premeditated, politically motivated violence perpetrated against noncombatant targets by subnational or clandestine agents, usually intended to influence an audience.
>   The term 'international terrorism' means terrorism involving citizens or the territory of more than one country.
>   The term 'terrorist group' means any group practising, or that has significant subgroups that practise, international terrorism. (22 USC 2656f(d))

In contrast are the recurrent requests from Islamic and Arab countries (including the League of Arab States, Gulf Cooperation Council and Organization of the Islamic Conference members) for a comprehensive international agreement on 'the definition of terrorism', which clearly includes 'state terrorism' and distinguishes 'between terrorism and the legitimate struggle of nations against foreign occupation' (League of Arab States' submission to the UN Security Council Counter-Terrorism Committee, February 2003).

The UK Terrorism Act 2000 defines terrorism as the use or threat of action where 'the use or threat is designed to influence the government or to intimidate the public or a section of the public' and 'the use or threat is made for the purpose of advancing a political, religious or ideological cause' and the action includes 'serious violence against a person', 'serious damage to property' or 'creating a serious risk to the health or safety of the public or a section of the public'.

In its December 2004 report, *A More Secure World*, the UN High Level Panel defined terrorism as:

> any action . . . that is intended to cause deaths or serious bodily harm to civilians or non-combatants, when the purpose of such an act, by its nature or context, is to intimidate a population or compel a government or an international organisation to do or to abstain from doing something. (p. 49)

Box 3.3 begins with an example of the kind of definition accepted here, and then includes contrasting US and Arab/Islamic definitions to illustrate how politically loaded definitions are (which is why, despite twelve UN conventions, no formal definition of terrorism has yet been agreed), and ends with the definition in the UK Terrorism Act 2000 and the UN High Level Panel 2004 definition.

Second, consistent with Wardlow's definition, we will follow a number of terrorist analysts in recognizing a typology of terrorism that accords closely to our own typology of major armed conflict. This strongly suggests that we should correlate national/separatist terrorism with identity/secession conflict, and that we should see 'social revolutionary terrorism', 'right-wing terrorism' and 'religious fundamentalist terrorism' as three manifestations of revolution/ideology conflict (see box 3.4).

We end up, therefore, with a combined terrorism/major armed conflict typology in which types of terrorism correlate closely to the typology of non-interstate conflicts in table 3.2, so long as, with Martin (2003), we are prepared to recognize a category of 'criminal terrorism' to correlate with factional conflict.[9] There are clear policy implications from this that we will pursue in chapter 11. That leaves two types of terrorism that do not fit our conflict typology.

First, there is 'state terrorism', which includes internal repression as well as external acts of terror and state sponsorship of terrorism. This has historically been by far the largest form of such violence. The 2002 edition of the US State Department's *Patterns of Global Terrorism* report named Cuba, Iran, Iraq, Libya, North Korea, Sudan and Syria as state sponsors of terrorism (with Libya unexpectedly dropping off the

---

Box 3.4 Typologies of terrorism

Schmid and Jongman (1988) distinguish between: (a) national/separatist terrorism (such as the Provisional IRA in Ireland, the Tamil Tigers (LTTE) in Sri Lanka, or ETA in Spain); (b) social revolutionary terrorism (such as the Red Army Faction in Germany, or Sendero Luminoso and MRTA in Peru); (c) right-wing terrorism (such as neo-Nazi, racist and anti-government 'survivalist' groups); and (d) religious fundamentalist terrorism (including Jewish, Christian, Islamic and Sikh groups).

Post et al. (2002) accept the Schmid/Jongman typology, although they suggest a fifth category of 'new religion terrorism' to cover groups like the Japanese-based Aum Shinrikyo in their analysis of 'the five principal types of radical groups' most prone to adopting terrorist methods (pp. 110–12).

Martin (2003) has quite similar categories, including various forms of 'communal (e.g. ethno-nationalist) terrorism', 'the terrorist left', 'the terrorist right' and 'religious terrorism', as well as 'criminal terrorism' (pp. 112–215), but also includes 'state terrorism' (pp. 80–111) and 'international terrorism' (pp. 216–42).

list in 2004). More direct is the terrible toll exacted by totalitarian governments both in pursuit of ideological goals and in terrorizing opposition into submission in order to maintain their grip on power. In this sense, by far the greatest number of terrorist atrocities in the past century has been perpetrated by what Walter Laqueur calls 'terrorism from above' (1999). According to some estimates, well over 160 million of their own citizens were 'intentionally killed' by repressive governments in the twentieth century. Finally, we have already noted how in the Arab-Islamic world 'state terrorism' is a reference to the tactics used by the state of Israel, while western countries in general and the United States in particular are regularly accused of 'state terrorism' in particular cases (for example, the atomic bombing of Hiroshima and Nagasaki). The December 2004 UN High Level Panel report decided not to include state terrorism in its terms of reference on the grounds that 'the legal and normative framework against state violations is far stronger than in the case of non-state actors' so that the argument was not 'compelling' (paragraph 160). (The Panel also recognized the argument about 'the legitimate struggle of nations against occupation', but denied that this legitimized acts of terrorism.)

Table 3.4 A conflict resolution terrorism typology

Terrorism type	Conflict type
State terrorism	
Insurgent terrorism	
Ideological	Revolution/ideology
Social revolutionary (SL, FARC)	
Right wing/survivalist	
Radical religious (GIA)	
Nationalist-separatist (LTTE, ETA, KLA)	Identity/secession
Economic/factional (RUF, LRA)	Factional
International terrorism (Al-Qaida)	

Second there is 'international terrorism'. This does not refer to the international connections that link most terrorism to transborder networks, including diaspora support constituencies, internet communications or criminal supply and money-laundering facilities, but to the relatively small groups of dedicated terrorists who are international in both personnel and purpose and are not rooted in nationally based organizations. In the form of 'Islamic radicalism' this has come to dominate popular perceptions of what terrorism is, often because international *jihadis* are involved in other conflicts, such as separatist struggles for national identity as in Palestine or Chechnya, and may be disproportionately influential thanks to training, experience, media profile and funding. But we think that it is important to retain a clear grip on the different types of terrorism, despite blurred and contested boundaries, because this is essential for clear and effective policy response as discussed in chapter 11 (see table 3.4).

Conflict Costs

Before concluding this chapter we must briefly note human and material costs of contemporary violent conflicts. At least 28 million people have been killed in more than 150 major armed conflicts fought mainly in the Third World since 1945 (IISS, 1997); another estimate puts the total at 40 million civilian and military deaths (Leitenberg, 2003). The proportion of civilian casualties has risen from only 5 per cent of total casualties in the First World War, to 50 per cent by the Second World War, to 80–90 per cent by the end of the century, of whom the majority are women and children (Lake, ed., 1990: 4; Grant, 1992: 26; Collier et al., 2003). This is a reversion to older types of warfare.

Beyond the toll of direct combat-related deaths, civil wars increase infant and adult mortality, as a result of disease, famine, displacement and the collapse of health and other services. The indirect deaths usually outweigh the direct effects of wars (Stewart and Fitzgerald, 2001). In developing countries conflicts frequently cause food shortages and famines, due to either deliberate use of hunger as a weapon or the unplanned effects of fighting on production and distribution (Messer, 1998). The land may be mined, the wells may be poisoned. People are forced to flee their homes and abandon their means of livelihood. At their peak in 2000, internal conflicts generated 21 million refugees and 25 million internally displaced people (Norwegian Refugee Council, 2004). Since then, fortunately, the number of refugees has fallen with the number of internal conflicts, to 17 million at the end of 2003 (UNHCR, 2004). In African countries like Angola, Eritrea, Liberia, Mozambique, Rwanda, Somalia and Sudan, up to half or more of the total population have been forced to flee at some point. In southern Sudan, where one in five people are estimated to have died as a result of the war, 80 per cent of the population was displaced at one time or another. All of this is compounded by the length of time that certain classes of conflict last – in some cases an average of 25 years (Gurr, 1995: 52). Whole generations have no other experience than war. The resultant size of the cumulative death toll is difficult to comprehend, while the overall tally of material destruction, psychological suffering and human misery – what Michael Cranna calls 'the true cost of conflict' (Cranna, ed., 1994) – dwarfs any gains by particular conflict parties.

Conflict has catastrophic effects on the economic development of affected countries, generally leading to falling production, falling exports, greater indebtedness and falling social expenditure (Stewart and Fitzgerald, 2001). The typical civil war puts development into reverse, reducing pre-war incomes in directly affected countries by 15 per cent on average, and reducing growth in neighbouring countries on average by 0.5 per cent per annum (Collier at al., 2003: 2). These effects tend to persist after the fighting is over, and the resulting mal-development and institutional deformation raises the risk of the conflict being renewed.

To take one example of a hard-hit country, Mozambique is estimated to have suffered 1.5 million deaths in the armed conflict that ended in 1992. Half the population were displaced at one time or another. Markets, communications and the capital stock were all damaged and public health suffered badly. The cumulative loss of output is esti-mated at more than US$20bn. When the conflict came to an end, as a result of the end of the Cold War and international and local media-tion (Hume, 1994), the economy began to grow again, but this growth has been uneven and Mozambique remains one of the poorest coun-tries in Southern Africa, still heavily dependent on aid.

Other costs include the opportunity costs involved in diversion of resources to military purposes, and indirect effects such as export of drugs and AIDS (Collier et al., 2003). There are environmental costs resulting from acts of war, as in Saddam Hussein's setting fire to the Kuwaiti oil wells, plunder of natural resources (for example, forests) and indirect effects of fighting and forced migration. Cultural costs arise from deliberate or unintended damage to the cultural heritage, and intergenerational costs include the scars of war, abuse, flight and genocide which continue to traumatize the next generation.

Given human suffering and economic costs on this scale, why is more not done to prevent this suffering and to bring wars to an end once they have started? Despite the widespread social costs, conflicts do have beneficiaries, for whom they can represent a source of livelihood and economic advancement. Warlords, militias, certain sections of governing elites and rebel groups may profit from oppor-tunities to exploit land, labour or resources, and outside arms manufacturers, traders and corporations sometimes harvest rich pick-ings from conflict zones (see below table 4.2). There is, as yet, insuffi-cient effort to regulate such profiteering and to prevent aid from falling into the wrong hands (Stewart and Fitzgerald, 2001). The human and material costs do, however, provide a very strong impe-tus for the central aim of conflict resolution: to find means of recon-ciling differences and achieving social change without the use of violence.

Conflict Mapping and Conflict Tracking

Having concentrated so far on types and patterns of conflict, we conclude the chapter with a brief note on the mapping and tracking of individual conflicts, and identify some of the ways in which conflict analysis can be aided by the wealth of data now available on the internet.

Conflict mapping, in Paul Wehr's words, is 'a first step in intervening to manage a particular conflict. It gives both the intervenor and the conflict parties a clearer understanding of the origins, nature, dynamics and possibilities for resolution of the conflict' (1979: 18). It is a method of presenting a structured analysis of a particular conflict at a particular moment in time. It is used by analysts to give a quick profile of a conflict situation, and is also widely used in conflict resolution workshops to elicit from participants a snapshot of their view of the conflict. Any particular map should be understood to represent the views of the author(s), and, as a schematic, to be indicative rather than comprehensive.

Adapting Wehr's conflict mapping guide (1979: 18–22),[10] we suggest the steps outlined in box 3.5 for preparing an initial profile of a

---

Box 3.5 A conflict mapping guide

A   Background
  1   Map of the area.
  2   Brief description of the country.
  3   Outline history of the conflict.

B   The conflict parties and issues
  1   Who are the core conflict parties?
       What are their internal sub-groups, on what constituencies do they depend?
  2   What are the conflict issues?
       Is it possible to distinguish between positions, interests (material interests, values, relationships) and needs?
  3   What are the relationships between the conflict parties?
       Are there qualitative and quantitative asymmetries?
  4   What are the different perceptions of the causes and nature of the conflict among the conflict parties?
  5   What is the current behaviour of the parties (is the conflict in an 'escalatory' or 'de-escalatory' phase?)?
  6   Who are the leaders of the parties? At the elite/individual level, what are their objectives, policies, interests, and relative strengths and weaknesses?

C   The context: global, regional and state-level factors
  1   At the state level: is the nature of the state contested? How open and accessible is the state apparatus? Are there institutions or fora which could serve as legitimate channels for managing the conflict? How even is economic development and are there economic policies which can have a positive impact?
  2   At the regional level: how do relations with neighbouring states and societies affect the conflict? Do the parties have external regional supporters? Which regional actors might be trusted by the parties?
  3   At the global level: are there outside geopolitical interests in the conflict? What are the external factors that fuel the conflict and what could change them?

conflict. This can be supplemented by a diagram showing the main parties and third parties, the issues and the channels of communication and influence between them (Fisher et al., 2000). Having mapped the structure of the conflict, the next step is to use the information in the map to identify the scope for conflict resolution, preferably with the help of the parties or embedded third parties. Such an analysis would identify: changes in the context which could alter the conflict situation, including the interests and capacities of third parties to influence it; changes within and between the conflict parties, including internal leadership struggles, varying prospects for military success, the readiness of general populations to express support for a settlement; possible ways of redefining goals and finding alternative means of resolving differences, including suggested steps towards settlement and eventual transformation; likely constraints on these; and how these might be overcome. These issues are considered further in the chapters that follow.

A conflict map is an initial snapshot. Analysts may then want to keep updating it by regular 'conflict tracking'. This can now be done increasingly efficiently through the internet. The revolution in communications technology which has occurred over the past ten years or so has already had an impact on conflict resolution and post-conflict peacebuilding (Reynolds Levy and Wessels, 2001; Reynolds Levy, 2004). In particular, high-quality data and information, both quantitative and qualitative in nature, is available on a variety of websites (see box 3.6).

Box 3.6 Sources of information for conflict tracking

International Crisis Group: <www.icg.org>
Based in Brussels, with 100 field analysts on five continents, this organization provides analyses of current conflicts and advocates policy responses. Its 'Crisis Watch' bulletin reports developments in some 70 conflict situations and assesses whether in the past month the situation has significantly improved, deteriorated or remains the same.

European Centre for Conflict Prevention: <www.euconflict.org>
Based in Utrecht in the Netherlands, this programme provides information and surveys covering prevention and peacebuilding efforts in the main violent conflicts in the world, with a primary focus on civil society actors. Presented through a searchable database, surveys of conflicts provide background information, detailed descriptions of ongoing activities to transform the conflicts, and assessments of future prospects for conflict prevention and peacebuilding. The database also provides directories leading to local and international organizations working in the field of conflict prevention and peacebuilding in relation to the conflict being researched.

Box 3.6 Sources of information for conflict tracking – cont'd

INCORE: <www.incore.ulst.ac.uk>
Based at the University of Ulster in Northern Ireland, INCORE offers a Conflict Data Service (CDS) which provides a detailed database on conflicts and conflict-related issues worldwide, offering information on conflicts in specific countries, thematic information as well as interdisciplinary guides on how conflict affects and interacts with other issues and phenomena. The CDS also provides an online database of peace agreements from around the world. INCORE also provides an Ethnic Conflict Research Digest.

Minorities at Risk (MAR): <www.cidcm.umd.edu/inscr/mar/>
The MAR project was initiated by Ted Robert Gurr in 1986 and has been based at the University of Maryland's Center for International Development and Conflict Management (CIDCM) since 1988. MAR tracks 285 politically active ethnic groups throughout the world from 1945 to the present. MAR focuses specifically on ethnopolitical groups, non-state communal groups that have 'political significance', following two criteria: first, the group collectively suffers, or benefits from, systematic discriminatory treatment vis-à-vis other groups in a society; second, the group is the basis for political mobilization and collective action in defence or promotion of its self-defined interests. The centrepiece of the project is a dataset that tracks groups on political, economic and cultural dimensions. The project also maintains analytic summaries of group histories, risk assessments and group chronologies for each group in the dataset.

Uppsala Conflict Data Program (UCDP): <www.pcr.uu.se/research/UCDP/>
For more than 20 years, the Department of Peace and Conflict Research at the University of Uppsala in Sweden has been operating the Uppsala Conflict Data Project (UCDP). The project's dataset is one of the most accurate and well-used datasets on global intra- and interstate armed conflicts in the world. Data on armed conflict is collected on an annual basis (calendar year). Until now, comparable data on armed conflicts have been available for the post-Cold War period, i.e. from 1989 and on. Recently, the data have been expanded to cover the full post-World War II period, 1946–2001, as part of a collaborative project between the Uppsala Conflict Data Project and the International Peace Research Institute, Oslo. Data on armed conflicts have been published yearly in the report series *States in Armed Conflict* (Department of Peace and Conflict Research, Uppsala University) since 1987, in SIPRI *Yearbook* (Oxford University Press: Oxford) since 1988, and in the *Journal of Peace Research* since 1993. The project's website also gives profiles of individual conflicts.

In early 2004 the UCDP launched a web-based Global Conflict Database which in 2003 held information on 117 conflicts between 1989 and 2003. The UCDP also includes links to other significant projects that contain web-based data on conflicts such as: Arbeitsgemeinschaft Kriegsursachenforschung at the University of Hamburg (AKUF) and the MIT CASCON System for Analysing International Conflict. UCDP has also initiated a series of more specialized projects including the Human Security Index; the UN in Armed Conflicts;

Prevention of Violent Conflicts; Reconciliation after Internal Conflict; Conflict Termination; Political and Social Effects of Internal Armed Conflict. Finally, UCDP provides a comprehensive listing of the datasets available to researchers in its Conflict Dataset Catalogue.

Sources: all project descriptions are from the project websites

Recommended reading

Collier et al. (2003); Eriksson et al. (2003); Gantzel and Schwinghammer (2000); Gleditsch et al. (2002); Gurr (2000); Gurr et al. (2001); Marshall and Gurr (2003); Wallensteen (2002b); Wallensteen and Sollenberg (2001).

Understanding Contemporary Conflict

The historian of great events is always oppressed by the difficulty of tracing the silent, subtle influences which in all communities precede and prepare the way for violent outbursts and uprisings.

Winston Churchill, 1898

Having introduced some of the main concepts in conflict resolution theory in chapter 1, described the evolution of the field in chapter 2 and looked at the statistical basis for diagnosis in chapter 3, we begin our survey of conflict resolution in the early twenty-first century by considering the way in which major armed conflict has been analysed within the conflict resolution tradition. Adequate conflict analysis – *polemology*, to borrow the French terminology – has from the start been seen as the essential prerequisite for normative conflict resolution. This chapter, therefore, provides the necessary conceptual basis for those that follow.

Theories and Frameworks

In chapter 1 we introduced some well-known general theories of conflict from the conflict resolution tradition. These models are intended to highlight generic aspects of conflict and conflict resolution. At the other end of the spectrum are specific political and historical explanations of particular conflicts. But at the intermediate level, between generic models and individual explanations, is it possible to find what Vasquez calls a 'unified theory of conflict' (1995: 137), sufficient to account for the prevailing patterns of post-Cold War conflict with which we are concerned?

It seems unlikely on the face of it that a single all-encompassing explanation will be adequate for conflicts of different types in all the countries that were listed in table 3.1 (see p. 58). Apart from anything else, since the time when systematic studies were first undertaken in the conflict resolution field it has been recognized that there are

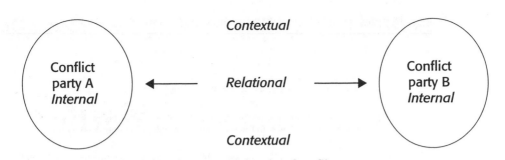

Figure 4.1   Internal, relational and contextual theories of conflict

apparently irreducible discrepancies between major schools of analysis.[1] Using figure 4.1 as a schematic model, it is helpful to see how some of these theories are *internal*, because they locate the sources of conflict mainly *within* the nature of the protagonists (e.g. certain ethological and anthropological theories), some are *relational*, because they look for sources mainly in relations *between* conflict parties (e.g. certain theories in behavioural sociology and social psychology), and some are *contextual*, because they look mainly *outside* to the conditioning contexts that structure the conflict and in some versions also generate the conflict parties themselves (e.g. certain neo-realist and Marxist theories).[2]

This was already evident in the thinking of the European theorists of the early modern period. For Machiavelli, conflict was a result of the human desire for self-preservation and power. For Hobbes, the three 'principal causes of quarrel' in a state of nature were competition for gain, fear of insecurity, and defence of honour. For Hume, the underlying conditions for human conflict were relative scarcity of resources and limited altruism. For Rousseau, the 'state of war' was born from 'the social state' itself.

Moreover, different types of explanation are more often than not politically compromised, whether propounded by conflict protagonists or by third parties. This was the case during the Cold War[3] and is a common feature of post-Cold War conflicts. For example, in box 4.1 we may note the discrepancy between 'third-party' relational interpretations of the Northern Ireland conflict such as the 'internal-conflict' model, and the 'traditional nationalist' and 'traditional unionist' interpretations historically espoused by the main conflict parties. This also shows how 'neutral' outside views, including academic theories of various kinds, can become as politically implicated in the struggle as any others.[4]

Nevertheless, there are explanations of conflict at the intermediate level which offer insight into contemporary conflict and help to situate it in the context of social and international conditions. Here, we will focus on the late Edward Azar's theory of protracted social

---

Box 4.1 Interpretations of the Northern Ireland conflict

1 The traditional nationalist interpretation: Britain v. Ireland
   The Irish people form a single nation and the fault for keeping Ireland divided lies
   with Britain.
2 The traditional unionist interpretation: Southern Ireland v. Northern Ireland
   There are two peoples in Ireland who have an equal right to self-determination,
   Protestant (unionist/loyalist) and Catholic (nationalist/republican), and the fault for
   perpetuating the conflict lies with the refusal of nationalists to recognize this.
3 Marxist interpretations: capitalist v. worker
   The cause of the conflict lies in the combination of an unresolved imperial legacy and the
   attempt by a governing capitalist class to keep the working class repressed and divided.
4 Internal-conflict interpretations: Protestant v. Catholic within Northern Ireland
   The cause of the conflict lies in the incompatibility between the aspirations of the two
   divided communities in Northern Ireland.

Source: from Whyte, 1990: 113–205

---

conflict (PSC) as an example of conflict resolution analysis from the late 1970s and 1980s, which anticipated much of the current preoccupation with the domestic social roots of conflict and failures of governance. We will then bring Azar's ideas up to date by evaluating them in the light of conflict theories that have come to prominence in the years since his death in 1991.

The Context for an Evaluation of Conflict Resolution Theory

Within five years of Azar's death Holsti was writing that wars of the late twentieth century 'are not about foreign policy, security, honor, or status; they are about statehood, governance, and the role and status of nations and communities within states' (1996: 20–1). It may seem strange, therefore, that '[u]ntil recently, international relations theorists and strategic studies analysts paid comparatively little attention to the causes, effects and international implications of ethnic and other forms of communal conflict' (Brown, ed., 1993: vii). By the mid-1990s it had became suddenly fashionable to focus analysis on 'internal conflicts' (Brown, ed., 1996), 'new wars' (Kaldor and Vashee, eds, 1997), 'small wars' (Harding, 1994), 'civil wars' (King, 1997), 'ethnic conflicts' (Stavenhagen, 1996), 'conflict in post-colonial states' (van de Goor et al., eds, 1996) and so on, and for humanitarian and development NGOs and international agencies to refer to 'complex human emergencies' or 'complex political emergencies'. But this had not been the case during Azar's lifetime. Holsti himself, for example, had continued to focus on interstate war in his 1991 study of armed conflict between 1648 and 1989. It was only by 1996 that he had changed his emphasis, diagnosing the status of communities within states and the nature of new and weak states as the 'primary locale of present and future wars' (1996: vii). This may not seem surprising in view of the decline in the relative incidence of interstate as against non-interstate war recorded in annual statistical analyses published in the 1990s, as we saw in the previous chapter. But this trend had been evident long before the 1990s, on some accounts reaching back to 1945,[5] and, although international relations and strategic studies analysts may have paid relatively little attention to the international implications of 'ethnic and other forms of communal conflict' during the Cold War period, a number of scholars in the peace and conflict research field had long been preoccupied with them in their attempts to uncover the sources of what were variously termed 'deep-rooted conflicts' (Burton, 1987), 'intractable conflicts' (Kriesberg et al., eds, 1989) and 'protracted social conflicts'.

It has become popular in recent years for analysts to relate accounts of the evolution of modern warfare to accounts of the evolution of the modern state. The key qualitative turning points are seen to have been, first, the emergence of the so-called sovereign dynastic state in Europe, heralded by Machiavelli, Bodin and Hobbes from the sixteenth and seventeenth centuries; second, the coming of the principle of popular sovereignty and national self-determination from the time of the American and French revolutions; and, third, the bipolar stand-off at great power level after 1945. The first is associated with the domestic monopolization and reorganization of military force by sovereigns and its projection outwards to create the relatively formal patterns of early modern interstate warfare in place of earlier more sporadic, localized and ill-disciplined manifestations of organized violence. The second heralded the transition to mass national armies and 'total war' accompanying the first industrial revolution and the romantic movement and reaching its climax in the First and Second World Wars. The advent of nuclear weapons and the military stand-off between the Soviet and western blocs rendered major interstate war unviable (with a few exceptions at lower levels). Instead, the prevailing patterns of armed conflict in the 1950s and 1960s became wars of national independence associated with decolonization, and those of the 1970s and 1980s were postcolonial civil wars in which the great powers intervened as part of a continuing geopolitical struggle for power and influence (Howard, 1976; Giddens, 1987; Keegan, 1993). For this reason Rice (1988) has called the prevailing pattern of post-1945 wars 'wars of the third kind' (in contrast to the two earlier Clausewitzean phases), a term subsequently endorsed by Holsti (1996) and others. These are wars in which communities seek to create their own states in wars of 'national liberation', or which 'involve resistance by various peoples against domination, exclusion, persecution, or dispossession of lands and resources, by the post-colonial state' (Holsti, 1996: 27).

Some detect a further evolution in prevailing patterns of conflict in the 1990s, as it were a third phase of 'wars of the third kind', namely a pattern of post-Cold War conflict which is seen to bear little resemblance to European wars in the era of the dynastic state or to the 'total wars' of the first half of the twentieth century, if anything resembling earlier medieval wars in their lack of differentiation between state and society, soldier and civilian, internal and external transactions across frontiers, war and organized crime (Van Crefeld, 1991). Kaldor characterizes these 'new wars' in terms of political goals (no longer the foreign policy interests of states, but the consolidation of new forms of power based on ethnic homogeneity); ideologies (no longer universal principles such as democracy, fascism or socialism, but tribalist and communalist identity politics); forms of mobilization (no longer conscription or appeals to patriotism, but fear, corruption, religion, magic and the media); external support (no longer superpowers or ex-colonial powers, but diaspora, foreign mercenaries, criminal mafia, regional powers); mode of warfare (no longer formal and organized campaigns with demarcated front-lines, bases and heavy weapons, but fragmented and dispersed, involving paramilitary and criminal groups, child soldiers, light weapons, and the use of atrocity, famine, rape and siege); and the war economy (no longer funded by taxation and generated by state mobilization, but sustained by outside emergency assistance and the parallel economy, including unofficial export of timber and precious metals, drug-trafficking, criminal rackets, plunder) (Kaldor and Vashee, eds, 1997: 7–19).

In fact, both Kaldor and Holsti follow Rice in suggesting that the key turning point in all this was not so much 1989 or 1990, as 1945. For Kaldor, '[s]ince 1945, there have been very few interstate wars' (1999: 29), while for Holsti:

> The problem is that the Clausewitzean image of war, as well as its theoretical accoutrements, has become increasingly divorced from the characteristics and sources of most armed conflicts since 1945. The key question is: given that most wars since 1945 have been *within* states, of what intellectual and policy relevance are concepts and practices derived from the European and Cold War experiences that diagnosed or prescribed solutions for the problem of war *between* states? (1996: 14; italics in the original)

Does this suggest that the analysis of interstate war, which has dominated international relations since 1945, is largely irrelevant to post-1945 conflict? Entire tracts of quantitative research over the post-war decades have been devoted to the search for 'correlates of interstate war' which might give a clue to its sources and nature. Analysts have sought to align measurable features of interstate and related wars such as its incidence, frequency, duration, magnitude, severity, intensity and costs, with empirically verifiable variables, such as structures (e.g. whether the hegemonic system is unipolar, bipolar, multipolar), relations (e.g. patterns of alliances, distribution of relative capabilities, configurations of power and power transition, arms races), national attributes (e.g. levels of domestic unrest, types of domestic regime, levels of economic development), and other aspects of what Mansbach and Vasquez (1981) call the 'paths to war' (e.g. the positive expected utility for decision-makers in initiating hostilities).[6] This vast enterprise has produced mixed results.[7] But is it possible that, in terms of prevailing patterns of post-1945 conflict, most international relations and strategic studies experts were looking in the wrong direction? Could it be that, mesmerized by the bipolar stand-off at great power level, analysts subsumed both decolonizing wars of national liberation and postcolonial civil wars into traditional Europeanized conceptual categories, failing to notice the qualitative change that had taken place when prevailing patterns of major armed conflict ceased being intra-European interstate wars after 1945? And was it only with the collapse of the Soviet Union that analysts belatedly realized that the 'new' patterns of post-Cold War conflict were in fact not so new, but had been prevalent, albeit under different geopolitical conditions, for nearly half a century?

We do not want to pronounce on these large questions here, beyond noting that this is the context within which Azar's work should be evaluated, because he had been arguing for a radical revision of prevailing Clausewitzean ideas since the 1970s. He was not alone in doing this, of course. He was heavily indebted to other conflict resolution theorists, notably John Burton with whom he co-published, although we will not try to disentangle credit for contributory ideas here. We should also be careful about unhistorical assumptions about 'new' features of warfare, which can in most cases be shown to have a long ancestry (Newman, 2004). Nevertheless, throughout this period there were still 'Clausewitzean' wars going on (between India and Pakistan, Israel and her neighbours, China and Vietnam, Iraq and Iran), 'mixed civil-international wars' were largely structured by Cold War geopolitics, and at great power level the two main alliances were still strenuously preparing for the possibility, if not likelihood, of a thoroughly Clausewitzean military encounter, despite the nuclear stalemate. It was the latter which largely preoccupied international relations and strategic studies analysts at the time, so that the reconceptualization of prevailing patterns of conflict offered by Azar and other conflict resolution analysts was hardly noticed in the conventional literature.

Edward Azar's Theory of Protracted Social Conflict (PSC)

Edward Azar was born in Lebanon in 1938, moved to the United States as a graduate international relations student, and subsequently specialized in what was at first a mainly quantitative analysis of inter-state conflict. His Conflict and Peace Research Data Bank, built up at the University of North Carolina, however, already included internal domestic as well as external international data, and he was progressively drawn to concentrate as much if not more on the former than on the latter, not least as a result of his increasing concern about the condition of his native Lebanon. This was further reinforced by his experience on a number of dialogue and discussion sessions, mainly on the Middle East, including participation in Herbert Kelman's and Stephen Cohen's Harvard University problem-solving workshops. This brought him into the mainstream of the new conflict resolution fraternity, whose attempted reconceptualization of the roots of large-scale contemporary violence he found congenial and confirmatory of his own thinking. In particular, he came to work closely in the 1980s with John Burton, and together they set up the Center for International Development and Conflict Management (CIDCM) at the University of Maryland. When Burton moved on to George Mason University, Azar stayed at Maryland, where he died in 1991 (see Fisher, 1997: ch. 4).

For Edward Azar, in a sustained sequence of studies published from the early 1970s (see References for Azar's main publications), the critical factor in protracted social conflict (PSC), such as persisted in Lebanon (his own particular field of study), Sri Lanka, the Philippines, Northern Ireland, Ethiopia, Israel, Sudan, Cyprus, Iran, Nigeria or South Africa, was that it represented 'the prolonged and often violent struggle by communal groups for such basic needs as security, recognition and acceptance, fair access to political institutions and economic participation' (1991: 93). Traditional preoccupation with relations between states was seen to have obscured a proper understanding of these dynamics. Indeed, in radical contrast to the concerns of international law, the distinction between domestic and international politics was rejected as 'artificial': 'there is really only one social environment and its domestic face is the more compelling' (Azar and Burton, 1986: 33). The role of the state (as also linkages with other states) was to satisfy or frustrate basic communal needs, thus preventing or promoting conflict (Azar, 1990: 10–12).

Drawing upon datasets of PSC compiled from the 1970s at the University of Maryland, Azar systematically developed and refined his understanding of the dynamics which generated violent and persistent conflict of this kind. At the time of his last writings in the early 1990s he identified more than sixty examples of this 'new type of conflict', which, 'distinct from traditional disputes over territory, economic resources, or East–West rivalry . . . revolves around questions of communal identity' (1991: 93). In the opening chapter of what is perhaps his most succinct summation of a decade and a half's work, *The Management of Protracted Social Conflict: Theory and Cases* (1990), Azar contrasts three aspects of what up until then had been a prevailing orthodoxy in war studies with his own approach. First, there had been a tendency 'to understand conflicts through a rather rigid dichotomy of internal and external dimensions' with sociologists, anthropologists and psychologists preoccupied with the former ('civil wars, insurgencies, revolts, coups, protests, riots, revolutions, etc.') and international relations scholars with the latter ('interstate wars, crises, invasions, border conflicts, blockades, etc.'). Second, prevailing frameworks of analysis had often been based on the functional differentiation of conflict aspects and types into sub-categories of psychological, social, political and economic conflicts, and into different 'levels of analysis'. Third, there had been a tendency to focus on overt and violent conflict while ignoring covert, latent or non-violent conflict, and on an approach to conflict dynamics in terms of conflict cycles in which the 'termination of violent acts is often equated with the state of peace'. In contrast, a study of PSC suggested that:

> many conflicts currently active in the underdeveloped parts of the world are characterized by a blurred demarcation between internal and external sources and actors. Moreover, there are multiple causal factors and dynamics, reflected in changing goals, actors and targets. Finally, these conflicts do not show clear starting and terminating points. (Azar, 1990: 6)

The term 'protracted social conflict' emphasized that the sources of such conflicts lay predominantly within (and across) rather than between states, with four clusters of variables identified as preconditions for their transformation to high levels of intensity.

First, there was the 'communal content', the fact that the 'most useful unit of analysis in protracted social conflict situations is the identity group – racial, religious, ethnic, cultural and others' (1986: 31). In contrast to the well-known 'levels of analysis' framework popularized by Kenneth Waltz (1959), which in its classic form distinguished system, state and individual levels, PSC analysis focuses in the first instance on identity groups, however defined, noting that it is the relationship between identity groups and states which is at the core of the problem (what Azar called the 'disarticulation between the state and society as a whole': 1990: 7), and how individual interests and needs are mediated through membership of social groups ('what is of concern are the *societal needs* of the individual – security, identity, recognition and others': 1986: 31). Azar links the disjunction between state and society in many parts of the world to a colonial legacy which artificially imposed European ideas of territorial statehood onto 'a multitude of communal groups' on the principle of 'divide and rule'. As a result, in many postcolonial multicommunal societies the state machinery comes to be 'dominated by a single communal group or a coalition of a few communal groups that are unresponsive to the needs of other groups in the society' which 'strains the social fabric and eventually breeds fragmentation and protracted social conflict'. As to the formation of identity groups themselves, as noted in chapter 2, Azar, like other conflict resolution theorists, drew on a rich tradition of research in social psychology and social anthropology to sketch the various ways in which individual needs come to be mediated and articulated through processes of socialization and group identity, themselves culturally conditioned (Lewin, 1948; Kelly, 1955; Sherif, 1966; Deutsch, 1973; Tajfel, ed., 1978).

Second, following other conflict resolution analysts, notably John Burton, Azar identified deprivation of human needs as the underlying source of PSC ('Grievances resulting from need deprivation are usually expressed collectively. Failure to redress these grievances by the authority cultivates a niche for a protracted social conflict': 1990: 9). Unlike interests, needs are 'ontological' and non-negotiable, so that, if conflict comes, it is likely to be intense, vicious and, from a traditional Clausewitzean perspective, 'irrational'. In particular, he cites security needs, development needs, political access needs and identity needs (cultural and religious expression), the first three corresponding to Henry Shue's three 'basic rights' of security, subsistence and freedom (1980). Arguing for a broader understanding of 'security' than was usual in academic circles at the time, Azar linked this to an equally broad understanding of 'development' and 'political access':

> Reducing overt conflict requires reduction in levels of underdevelopment. Groups which seek to satisfy their identity and security needs through conflict are in effect seeking change in the structure of their society. Conflict resolution can truly occur and last if satisfactory amelioration of underdevelopment occurs as well. Studying protracted conflict leads one to conclude that peace is development in the broadest sense of the term. (1990: 155)

Third, in a world in which the state has been 'endowed with authority to govern and use force where necessary to regulate society, to protect citizens, and to provide collective goods', Azar cited 'governance and the state's role' as the critical factor in the satisfaction or frustration of individual and identity group needs: 'Most states which experience protracted social conflict tend to be characterized by incompetent, parochial, fragile, and authoritarian governments that fail to satisfy basic human needs' (1990: 10). Here he made three main points. Whereas in western liberal theory the state 'is an aggregate of individuals entrusted to govern effectively and to act as an impartial arbiter of conflicts among the constituent parts', treating all members of the political community as legally equal citizens, this is not empirically what happens in most parts of the world, particularly in newer and less stable states where political authority 'tends to be monopolized by the dominant identity group or a coalition of hegemonic groups' which use the state to maximize their interests at the expense of others. Both through the mobilization of group interests and identities by ruling elites, and through the reactive counter-identification of excluded 'minorities', the 'communal content of the state' becomes basic to the study of PSC. Next, the monopolizing of power by dominant individuals and groups and the limiting of access to other groups precipitates a 'crisis of legitimacy', so that 'regime type and the level of legitimacy' come to be seen as 'important linkage variables between needs and protracted social conflict' (1990: 11). Finally, Azar notes how PSCs tend to be concentrated in developing countries which are typically characterized by 'rapid population growth and limited resource base' and also have restricted 'political capacity' often linked to a colonial legacy of weak participatory institutions, a hierarchical tradition of imposed bureaucratic rule from metropolitan centres, and inherited instruments of political repression: 'In most protracted social conflict-laden countries, political capacity is limited by a rigid or fragile authority structure which prevents the state from responding to, and meeting, the needs of various constituents.'

Finally, there is the role of what Azar called 'international linkages', in particular political-economic relations of economic dependency within the international economic system, and the network of political-military linkages constituting regional and global patterns of clientage and cross-border interest. Modern states, particularly weak states, are porous to the international forces operating within the wider global community: the '[f]ormation of domestic social and political institutions and their impact on the role of the state are greatly influenced by the patterns of linkage within the international system' (1990: 11).

Whether or not in any one case these four clusters of preconditions for PSC in the event activate overt conflict will depend upon the more contingent actions and events of 'process dynamics', which Azar analyses into three groups of determinants: 'communal actions and strategies', 'state actions and strategies' and 'built-in mechanisms of conflict' (1990: 12–15). The first of these involves the various processes of identity group formation, organization and mobilization, the emergence and nature of leadership, the choice of political goals (access, autonomy, secession, revolutionary political programme) and tactics (civil disobedience, guerrilla war), and the scope and nature of externalties. State actions and strategies form the second main element, with governing individuals and elites at any one time theoretically facing an array of policy choices running from different forms of political accommodation at one end of the spectrum to 'coercive repression' or 'instrumental co-option' at the other. In Azar's view, given the perceived political and economic costs involved in weak and fragmented polities and because of the 'winner-take-all' norm 'which still prevails in multicommunal societies', it is much more likely to be repression than accommodation. Finally, there are the various self-reinforcing 'built-in mechanisms of conflict' exhaustively studied by conflict resolution analysts once the malign spiral of conflict escalation is triggered.

Azar drew on the work of Sumner (1906), Gurr (1970), Mitchell (1981) and others to trace the process by which mutually exclusionary 'experiences, fears and belief systems' generate 'reciprocal negative images which perpetuate communal antagonisms and solidify protracted social conflict'. Antagonistic group histories, exclusionist myths, demonizing propaganda and dehumanizing ideologies serve to justify discriminatory policies and legitimize atrocities. In these circumstances, in a dynamic familiar to students of international relations as the 'security dilemma', actions are mutually interpreted in the most threatening light, 'the worst motivations tend to be attributed to the other side', the space for compromise and accommodation shrinks and 'proposals for political solutions become rare, and tend to be perceived on all sides as mechanisms for gaining relative power and control' (Azar, 1990: 15). All of this intensifies further as political crisis spirals into war, where new vested interests emerge dependent upon the political economy of the war itself, the most violent and unruly elements in society appear in leadership roles and criminality becomes a political norm. At the limit, disintegration follows. With sustained attrition, political structures buckle and collapse, a social implosion which subsequently sucks everything else in.

Azar saw PSC analysis as an attempt to 'synthesize the realist and structuralist paradigms into a pluralist framework' more suitable for explaining prevalent patterns of conflict than the more limited alternatives (1991: 95). We are not claiming here that Azar's analysis is the last word on the subject, nor that he was alone in pointing to the significance of mobilized identities, exclusionist ideologies, fragile and authoritarian governance, weak states and disputed sovereignty as chief sources of major armed conflict (we have only to think of the

Table 4.1 Azar's preconditions for protracted social conflict (PSC)

Relevant discipline	Preconditions for PSCs	Correlates
Anthropology, history, sociology	Communal content	Degree of ethnic heterogeneity
Psychology, biology, development studies	Needs	Levels of human development
Politics, political economy	Governance	State capacity and scales of political repression
International relations, strategic studies	International linkages	Volume of arms imports etc.; cross-border fomentation

work of David Horowitz (1985) and Anthony Smith (1986) in the mid-1980s); we claim only that his approach anticipated many aspects of what has since become orthodoxy, and that his ideas deserve more recognition than they have been given.

A further point is worth making. In terms of 'correlates of war', Azar's ideas were also seen to offer a framework for the analysis of prevailing patterns of war, which differed from what was usual when interstate war was the object of analysis (see the kinds of indicator suggested in Esty et al., 1998). Table 4.1 shows the way in which Azar's 'preconditions' widened the relevance of different disciplines to the study of protracted social conflict beyond what had hitherto been normal in mainstream international relations, and suggests indicatively the kinds of correlate that came into view as a result. Such statistical studies of non-interstate war are still in their infancy, and, as shown in the next section, remain controversial, but Azar's model offered a hopeful beginning.

Have More Recent Theories Confirmed or Discredited PSC?

In evaluating Azar's theory posthumously, we should of course remember that the writing on 'new wars' since his death assumes a knowledge of the post-Cold War world that he did not have. He could not have taken account in his published writings of the impact of the disintegration of the bipolar world or of Zartman's conclusion that: 'More than anything else, it is the uncertainty following the passing of the old order that allows conflict to break out with such abandon at the end of the millennium' (1997: 6). It is possible that Azar might have seen Mearsheimer's 1990 'Back to the Future' article, but, if so, for reasons already given, we can be pretty certain that he would have been unimpressed by its neo-realist interpretation.

Let us consider four more 'global level' interpretations that have become popular since the end of the Cold War and bear ambiguously on Azar's theory.

Huntington's 'clash of civilizations' hypothesis has recently been revived in the wake of the 11 September 2001 catastrophe (1996). Some have interpreted historic Muslim *ressentiment* against the West in these terms (Lewis, 2002), or pitted tribal fundamentalism (jihad) against secular consumerist capitalism (McWorld) (Barber, 2001). Others have been more circumspect (Armstrong, 2001; Shadid, 2002). Although identity groups play a key role in Azar's ontology, they are not 'the broadest level of cultural identity that people have short of that which distinguishes humans from other species', which is how Huntington defines a civilization (1996: 43). Azar would, we think, have regarded the latter not as a social *datum*, but as part of the ideological apparatus likely to be mobilized by political interests. He would also almost certainly have opposed Huntington's policy conclusions for western decision-makers.

Another issue area that Azar did not, so far as we know, forefront in his own analysis is that of 'environmental conflict'. This has become more prominent in the literature since his death, but in this case we do not see a contradiction with Azar's theory. In assessing the links between population growth, environmental scarcity and future violent conflict, for example, Thomas Homer-Dixon examines the likelihood of international 'simple scarcity' conflicts over water, forests, fishing and agricultural land, 'group-identity' conflicts triggered by population movements, and 'deprivation' conflicts caused by relative depletion of economic resources (1991, 1994). The latter two are evidently consonant with Azar's theory.

A third major strand of conflict analysis in the 1990s and early 2000s is more critical of conflict resolution. This is the international political economy critique that we mentioned in chapter 1. The central argument is, first, that the 'new wars' in the Third World are not symptomatic of local failures in governance, but are a product of the distortions of late capitalism, and, second, that the way they are now managed by donor governments, international financial institutions, aid and development agencies, and the United Nations perpetuates this. Development is seen to have been co-opted into a global security regime that uses conflict resolution and social reconstruction, as well as the more obvious instruments of international military control, to transform target societies in the image of the interveners in order to pacify the unruly periphery and maintain the status quo: 'the conflict resolution and post-war reconstruction concerns of liberal governance could be seen as the "riot control" end of a spectrum encompassing a broad range of "global poor relief" activities . . .' (Duffield, 2001: 9).

Is this a comprehensive rejection of Azar's analysis of PSC? We do not think so. Duffield's caricature of conflict resolution is just that – a caricature. Azar himself would have agreed – indeed, did agree – with much of the international political economy critique in the form he was familiar with in the 1980s, seeing the prevalence of PSC in the Third World as symptomatic of the distortions of postcolonial economic and political structures. He did not identify conflict resolution solely with 'micro' techniques, such as principled negotiation, facilitative mediation or problem-solving workshops. As Ronald Fisher notes, Azar saw these as important mechanisms for achieving short-term breakthroughs, but emphasized throughout his work that 'long-term development is essential to address fundamental causes' (1997: 97) – for Azar, 'peace is development in the broadest sense of the term'. In the final chapter of his book Duffield argues for a genuine 'cosmo-politan politics' that upholds international law and the search for participatory 'common values', as against the 'liberal governance' imposition of external norms and rules:

> Rather than searching for better policy or commissioning more detailed forms of analysis, the real task is reforming the institutions and networks of global governance to address complexity. . . . Reform would require turning rule-based bureaucracies into adaptive, learn-ing and networking organisations. (2001: 264–5)

Azar would simply say 'amen'. The idea of adaptive organization within a cosmopolitan world society is exactly John Burton's notion of 'second order learning', which, as we saw in chapter 2, he regards as essential for human survival.

Finally in terms of global-level interpretations, there is the whole discourse on 'new wars' in which state decay in some regions has been seen to coincide with the end of Cold War control, rapidly reduced costs and increased availability of weapons, and a change in tactics and the function of war, no longer aimed so much at decisive military victory as at perpetuating the economic and other gains associated with the continuance of violence (Keen, 1998; Kaldor, 1999; Reno, 1999). The emphasis is on the way new wars merge into forms of cross-border economic exploitation and criminal networks and are sustained often by the very measures taken to end them (although we have noted above how many or most of these features are far from new). As an analysis of what happens once large-scale violence has broken out, this is a further elaboration of Azar's understanding that PSCs 'do not show clear starting and terminating points' and often become self-perpetuating, capable of persisting at fluctuating levels for years, hardly noticed by the analysts of 'great power war' in his day. If the 'new war' analysis extends to a substantial reinterpretation of the deeper causes of such wars, however, then this would be much more significant for Azar's theory. So we will address this separately below when we look at theories about economic incentives for war (p. 95).

This short survey of post-Cold War global-level conflict analysis suggests that, having set aside the neo-realist and 'clash of civilizations' accounts, Azar would have found little difficulty in accommodating predictions of future conflict exacerbated by environmental constraints, the global distortions of late capitalism, or the privatization of violence and shifting technologies of warfare. We now turn to three other types of explanation for the prevalence of large-scale violence that have become more prominent since Azar's time, at regional, state and societal levels.

First, we may note those who have focused mainly on cross-border contagion and regional security complexes for explanations of the prevalence or absence of large-scale violence in 'zones of peace and war' (Lake and Rothchild, eds, 1997). Others attribute the contrast between 'zones of war' and 'zones of peace' to the stability of power structures in the various regions. Buzan and his associates, for example, studied 'regional security complexes' in the 1980s (that is, groups of states with interconnected security concerns). They found a spectrum ranging from regions in turmoil (marked by numerous conflict formations), through security regimes (where member states remain potential threats to each other but have reduced mutual insecurity by formal and informal arrangements), to pluralistic security communities (where member states no longer feel that they need to make serious provision for a mutual use of force against each other). They located the main determinants of regional stability in interstate factors: the numbers of state players within a given security complex, the patterns of amity and hostility and the distributions of power (Buzan, 1991: ch. 5). Change within a security complex could thus be measured in terms of four quite simple structural parameters: the maintenance of the status quo, internal change within the complex, external boundary change (states entering or leaving the complex), and 'overlay' – the dominant intrusion of an outside power. Since then, Buzan et al. have offered a more complex model in many ways closer to Azar's ideas.[8] Here, we suggest, we have an important supplement to Azar's model, and perhaps a qualification in those cases like Sierra Leone after 1991 where it may be external fomentation that is seen as a prime cause of war. This does not, however, contradict the main body of his work.

Another cluster of explanations for 'new wars' in the 1990s has come from those who place their main emphasis on the 'crisis of governance' precipitated by the impact of globalization on 'state decay' (Jackson, 1990; Ayoob, 1995). Brzoska explains how this has been characteristic of 'holistic' German explanations for new wars, for example, such as those of Munkler:

> The predominant cause of internal war, in this line of thinking, is the erosion of the capability of the state to govern. This can be the result of the weakening of the legitimacy of the state or of direct challenges to its monopoly of the use of force. (2005: 109)

We need not linger here, major topic though it is, because this is clearly compatible with, if not confirmatory of, Azar's strong emphasis on the key significance of 'governance and the state's role', including the importance of perceived legitimacy, in precipitating or inhibiting the escalation of PSC. It is also in line with Azar's observation that weak postcolonial states in the Third World are particularly vulnerable. It should be noted, though, that, since Azar thought that 'highly centralised political structures are sources of conflict', he himself advocated 'appropriate decentralised structures' (1986: 33–4). This is at odds with the recommendations of analysts such as Holsti, who advocate, on the contrary, 'the strengthening of states' (1996: xii). The discrepancy may not be as stark as at first appears, however, since Holsti agrees with Azar that 'vertical legitimacy' (political consensus between governers and governed about the institutional 'rules of the game') and 'horizontal legitimacy' (inclusive political community in which individuals and groups have equal access to decisions and allocations) are what ultimately underpin 'the strength of states' (1996: 82–98).

Turning to the societal level and what Azar called the 'disarticulation between the state and society as a whole', the increased prominence of nationalism and ethnicity in explanations for war in the 1990s would certainly have caused few problems for Azar (Esman, 2004). These were the kinds of conflict that he had been analysing since the 1970s. For example, neither van Evera's 'Hypotheses on nationalism and war' (1994) nor Lake and Rothchild's 'Containing fear: the origins and management of ethnic conflict' (1996) contradicts Azar's earlier conclusions. Lake and Rothchild argue that ethnic conflict is neither a result of 'ancient hatreds' nor caused by the sudden 'uncorking' of Soviet repression, but that:

> ethnic conflict is most often caused by collective fears of the future. As groups begin to fear for their safety, dangerous and difficult-to-resolve strategic dilemmas arise that contain within them the potential for tremendous violence. As information failures, problems of credible commitment, and the security dilemma take hold, groups become apprehensive, the state weakens, and conflict becomes more likely. Ethnic activists and political entrepreneurs, operating within groups, build upon these fears and polarise society. Political memories and emotions also magnify these anxieties, driving groups further

apart. Together these between-group and within-group strategic interactions produce a toxic brew that can explode into murderous violence. (1996: 41)

This is an almost word-for-word replication of Azar's description of the 'process dynamics' of PSC escalation. Azar would have added 'state actions and strategies' (merged by the authors under 'strategic interactions within groups' and 'confidence-building measures') and the interaction between these and 'communal actions and strategies'. He would also have added an analysis of what he saw as the underlying frustrations that formed the 'preconditions' for conflict in the first place.

Finally, we reach what has turned out to be the main frontal assault on Azar's style of PSC analysis in the 1990s – the so-called 'greed versus grievance' debate (Berdal and Malone, eds, 2000). As a somewhat ironic consequence of the neglect of his work, it is not Azar who is criticized by name here, but those who argue in the same way:

> Many, if not most, current conflicts stem from the failure of political, economic and social institutions to pay sufficient attention to the grievances and perceived needs of significant groups in the population. (Rasmussen et al., eds, 1997: 33)

In contrast to this, analysts such as Collier explicitly deny that 'grievance' causes major armed conflicts, and look instead to 'greed' – 'economic agendas as causes of conflict' (Collier 2000; Collier and Hoeffler, 2001). The argument is based on a claim of statistical refutation – that indicators of need-deprivation do not correlate closely with the incidence of armed conflict in comparison with indicators for economic incentives. The 'proxies' used to capture the economic agenda include: the share of primary commodity exports in GDP, since these are the most easily lootable assets (diamonds, drugs, timber); the proportion of young males between the ages of 15 and 24 in a society, since 'overwhelmingly the people who join rebellions are young men'; and the average number of years of education that the population has received as a proxy for employability and income-earning opportunities outside rebellion and war. These are then compared with 'grievance' proxies: ethnic or religious hatred, economic (horizontal) inequality, lack of political rights, and government economic competence. The conclusion is that 'The results overwhelmingly point to the importance of economic agendas as opposed to grievance':

> The combination of large exports of primary commodities, a high proportion of young men, and economic decline drastically increases risk. Greed seems more important than grievance. (Collier, 2000: 110)

We will not analyse the statistical evidence point by point here, but will focus instead on Collier's policy conclusions. The original stark contrast drawn between greed and grievance has been much softened by subsequent qualification, to the point where, surprisingly, policy recommendations from an 'economic agenda' basis do not differ significantly from those suggested by Azar's PSC analysis. For example, drawing from his joint study with Hoeffler of civil wars between 1965 and 1999 (2001: 147), Collier concludes that, in addition to measures for reducing the risk from an excessive dependence on natural resource exports, 'policies for conflict prevention' should include, first, policies to remedy 'low income and economic decline' and, second, policies to mitigate the dangers of 'ethnic dominance' such as to 'entrench minority rights in the constitution':

> This can be done by explicitly legislating either group rights or strong individual rights. . . . The scope for this approach depends upon the credibility of the checks and balances that the state can erect upon government power. Usually states are not strong enough for this degree of trust, and so they can usefully be reinforced by international and regional commitments. (Collier, 2001: 158)

We have seen how Azar's analysis led to precisely the same policy recommendations suggested by his first three PSC 'preconditions': the importance of managing ethnic dominance, countering lack of economic opportunity, and remedying government inability to protect minorities. Collier also stresses the significance of handling the influence of diasporas – Azar's fourth 'precondition' of cross-border linkages. In fact, when Collier turns to policy recommendations for 'postconflict peacebuilding', he explicitly reimports the language of 'grievance' itself, albeit with complex circumlocutions in an attempt to preserve a dubious distinction between 'objective' and 'subjective' grievance:

> The alternative to continuing the political contest but making the military option infeasible is to resolve the political contest itself. This requires at a minimum that the grievances be addressed, even if though on average they are not objectively any more serious than those in peaceful societies. If, indeed, group grievance has been manufactured by rebel indoctrination, it can potentially be deflated by political gestures. While grievances may need to be addressed objectively, the main purpose of addressing them is probably for their value in changing perceptions. (2001: 159)

In short, the analysis of economic incentives to violence from natural resource predation is, indeed, a substantial addition to Azar's PSC analysis, leading as it does to the classification of factional and criminalized wars in which political agendas play little part – these are already incorporated into our conflict typology in chapter 3 (see table 4.2). This may happen in any war as the self-perpetuating logic of violence takes hold. But it can hardly be seen to replace a PSC approach

Table 4.2 Primary commodity exports and the financing of conflict

Combatant	Resource	Period	Est. revenue
Angola rebels (UNITA)	Diamonds	1992–2001	$4–4.2 billion total
Sierra Leone rebels (RUF)	Diamonds	1990s	$25–125 million/year
Liberia government	Timber	Late 1990s	$100–187 million/year
Sudan government	Oil	Since 1999	$400 million/year
Rwanda government	Coltan (from Congo)	1999–2000	$250 million total
Afghanistan (Taliban, Northern Alliance)	Opium, lapis lazuli, emeralds	Mid-1990s–2001	$90–100 million/year
Cambodia government, Khmer Rouge	Timber	Mid-1990s	$230–390 million/year
Myanmar government	Timber	1990s	$112 million/year
Colombia (FARC rebels)	Cocaine	Late 1990s	$140 million/year

Source: Renner, 2002

as originally claimed – for example, in the kinds of cases that gave rise to Azar's conclusions such as the conflicts in Northern Ireland, the Spanish Basque country, Chechnya, Sri Lanka or the Israeli/Palestinian conflict.

More telling in this regard would seem to be those studies since the end of the Cold War that aim to analyse the complex, varied and lengthy processes by which incipient ethnopolitical conflicts do or do not escalate towards violence. Here results are exactly consonant with a PSC approach, as exemplified in the work of Azar's fellow scholar from Maryland, Ted Robert Gurr. In one way Gurr confirms Collier's finding that grievance rarely leads to overt rebellion, but he does so within an interpretative context of 'communal-based protest' that exactly mirrors Azar's approach:

> [T]he most common political strategy among the 275 ethnopolitical groups surveyed in the Minorities at Risk study was not rebellion: it was symbolic and organizational politics. . . . Equally important, the number of groups using armed violence has been declining after decades of increase. The eruption of ethnic warfare that seized observers' attention in the early 1990s was actually the culmination of a long-term general trend of increasing communal-based protest and rebellion that began in the 1950s and peaked immediately after the end of the Cold War. (2000: 275–6)

An Interpretative Framework for Conflict Analysis

Given the variety and complexity of the main post-Cold War conflict theories indicated above, we will end our survey of conflict analysis by offering a modified 'levels-of-analysis' model, which we think is the

Table 4.3 Sources of contemporary conflict: a framework

	Level	Example
1	Global	Geopolitical transition, North–South economic divide, environmental constraints, weapons proliferation, ideological contestation
2	Regional	Clientage patterns, spillover, intervention, cross-border social demography, diaspora
3	State	
	Social	Weak society: cultural divisions, ethnic imbalance
	Economic	Weak economy: poor resource base, relative deprivation
	Political	Weak polity: partisan government, regime illegitimacy
4	Conflict party	Group mobilization, intergroup dynamics
5	Elite/individual	Exclusionist policies, factional interest, rapacious leadership

most helpful framework for locating relevant interpretations and for specifying appropriate conflict resolution responses. Instead of Waltz's 1959 'system', 'state' and 'individual' levels (still used by most contemporary accounts, such as Crocker et al., eds, 2001: Part 1), we recommend a five-level model, comprising two 'international' levels (global and regional), one 'state' level divided into functional sectors, and two 'social' levels (conflict party and elite/individual). The relative emphasis accorded to these levels will shift according to the interpretation being considered or the conflict being analysed (see table 4.3). Azar's 'international linkages' can be recognized at global and regional levels, his 'communal content', 'deprivation of needs' and 'governance' at state level (social, economic, political sectors), and his 'process dynamics' at conflict party and elite/individual levels.

Global sources of contemporary conflict

Having looked at some of the main global-level theories in the previous section, we will confine ourselves here to noting the synergy between them – another reason why the sources of contemporary conflict are so difficult to handle. Geopolitical readjustment at the end of the Cold War ended some conflicts fuelled by superpower rivalry, but precipitated others, both along the perimeters of the former Soviet Union and in parts of the world where simplifying bipolar structures were suddenly removed. This phase may now be coming to an end in the Balkans (although not in Central Asia and particularly the Causasus). In its place the three interlocking factors of the North–South divide, environmental constraint and the proliferation of new technologies of

> **Box 4.2 Arms exports and conflict**
>
> Some $176 billion worth of weaponry was exported to the Third World between 1987 and 1991. Keith Krause (1996) notes three theoretical models of the relation between arms exports and conflict, each of which carries a different policy prescription. Weapon availability can be seen as: (a) an independent variable causing conflict, (b) a dependent variable following conflict, or (c) an intervening variable acting as a catalyst in conflicts caused by deeper factors. He favours the third alternative. In fact, many post-Cold War conflicts have been fought with small arms rather than heavy weapons (Boutwell et al., eds, 1995). Moreover, the recipients have increasingly been sub-state groups (Karp, 1994). On one estimate, the trade in small arms has been worth some $10 billion a year (*The Economist*, 12 February 1994: 19–21). Indeed, in many cases, as in Rwanda in 1994, the worst massacres have been perpetrated with machetes.

war are seen to have become more prominent: 'the combination of wealth-poverty disparities and limits to growth is likely to lead to a crisis of unsatisfied expectations within an increasingly informed global majority of the disempowered' (Rogers and Ramsbotham, 1999: 749). Some see, in addition, a global ideological struggle between religious fundamentalism and secular modernity which draws on these tensions and transmutes them into new forms of conflict. Lowering over this is the threat that rogue states, terrorist groups and criminal networks could gain access to weapons of mass destruction.

Regional sources of contemporary conflict

The end of the Cold War and the 'regionalization' of world politics have highlighted the importance of the regional level of explanation. As noted in chapter 3, conflict data show clear regional differences in contemporary conflicts. This confirms those studies that emphasize the importance of overspill from one area to another, or where a common precipitating factor has generated violent conflicts in a vulnerable region; for example: the Great Lakes area of Africa (identity/secession conflicts and refugee movements), West Africa (factional conflicts following the breakdown of postcolonial states), the Caucasus (identity/secession conflicts following the collapse of the Soviet Union), Central Asia (identity/secession and factional conflicts following the collapse of the Soviet Union).

The regional effects are both outwards ('spill-over', 'contagion', 'diffusion') and inwards ('influence', 'interference', 'intervention') (Lake and Rothchild, eds, 1997) (see box 4.3 and map 4.1). 'Internal' wars have external effects on the region through the spread of weaponry, economic dislocation, links with terrorism, disruptive floods of

Box 4.3 A regional pattern of conflict interventions

A number of Tutsi exiles from Rwanda helped President Museveni of Uganda in his successful bid for power, were integrated into the Ugandan army after 1986, and subsequently defected with their weapons to the mainly Tutsi-led Rwanda Patriotic Front forces which eventually seized control of Rwanda in 1994. This led to a consolidation of Tutsi control in Burundi and, in the autumn of 1996, to cross-border action in what was then Zaire against the Hutu militia responsible for the 1994 Rwanda massacres who were being sheltered by President Mobutu. With enthusiastic backing from the Zairean Tutsi Banyamulenge, who had been discriminated against by Mobutu's Western Zairean based regime, this swelled into concerted military support for Laurent Kabila in his march on Kinshasa and eventual deposition of Mobutu. This in turn had a knock-on effect in Angola by depriving UNITA's Jonas Savimbi of Mobutu's support, and encouraging the sending in of Angolan troops to Congo-Brazzaville to help reinstall Denis Sassou-Nguesso as President in October 1997. Meanwhile, similar incursions were beginning to tip the scale in the long-standing conflict in Sudan.

Map 4.1   Regional conflicts in Africa: spill-over effects

refugees, and spill-over into regional politics when neighbouring states are dragged in or the same people straddle several states. Conversely, regional instability affects the internal politics of states through patterns of clientage, the actions of outside governments, cross-border

movements of people and ideas, black market activities, criminal
networks and the spread of small arms. There are also evident sources
of regional conflict where river basins extend across state boundaries
(Gleick, 1995),[9] or where a regional mismatch between state borders and
the distribution of peoples (usually as a result of the perpetuation of
former colonial boundaries) lays states open to the destabilizing effects
of large-scale population movements (Gurr, 1993; Gurr and Harff, 1994).

The role of the state

At this point we move from a consideration of *contextual* factors at
international level to *structural* factors at state level. Wherever its other
sources may lie, it is at the level of the state that the critical struggle is
in the end played out. Despite predictions of the 'end of the state'
under the twin pressures of globalization and what Falk calls 'the local
realities of community and sentiment' (1985: 690), the state is nevertheless seen to remain 'the primary locus of identity for most people'
(Kennedy, 1993: 134). Clark agrees that the state is still the key
mediator in the continuously oscillating balance between forces of
globalization ('increasingly potent international pressures') and fragmentation ('the heightened levels of domestic discontent that will
inevitably be brought in their wake') (1997: 202). Given the juridical
monopoly on sovereignty still formally accorded to the state within
the current international system, all conflict parties are in the end in
any case driven to compete for state control if they want to institute
revolutionary programmes (Type 2 conflict), safeguard communal
needs (Type 3 conflict), or merely secure factional interests (Type 4
conflict). Even in 'failed' states this usually still remains the ultimate
prize for the warring elements. And the same applies to the various
forms of contemporary terrorism. Unlike classic interstate wars, or
lower levels of domestic unrest, therefore, the major deadly conflicts
with which this book deals are defined as such through their becoming integral crises of the state itself, problematically cast as it still is as
chief actor on the international stage and chief satisfier of domestic
needs. It is the interconnection between three sectors here that is
critical – social, economic and political – and, in addition, at a certain
level of escalation two other sectors come into play: a law and order,
and security. It is useful to bear these in mind when looking at prevention (chapter 5) and post-war reconstruction (chapter 8).

In the *social sector* we are concerned with the major types of social
division around which conflict fault lines may develop. In recent years
the debate between those who emphasize the 'vertical' (ethnic) roots
of conflict and those who emphasize the 'horizontal' (class) roots
(Munck, 1986) has been further complicated by the advent of other

revolutionary ideologies such as Islamist and Hindu nationalist movements (but also Jewish, Christian and even Buddhist). On the other hand, others again have noted the inadequacy of western preoccupations with class and ethnicity in determining the social roots of conflict in parts of the world, such as Africa, where social life 'revolves, in the first instance, around a medley of more compact organizations, networks, groupings, associations, and movements that have evolved over the centuries in response to changing circumstances' (Chazan et al., 1992: 73–103). According to the Commonwealth Secretary-General, forty-nine of the fifty-three Commonwealth states are ethnically heterogeneous, and, as John Darby notes, given complex settlement patterns and the mismatch between state borders and the distribution of peoples, 'ethnic homogeneity, on past evidence, is almost always unattainable' (Darby, 1998: 2).

In the *economic sector* once again there is some measure of agreement that protracted conflict tends to be associated with patterns of under-development or uneven development. This is a much discussed topic, with some evidence, first, that, *contra* certain traditional theories of social and political revolution, there is a correlation between absolute levels of economic underdevelopment and violent conflict (Jongman and Schmid, 1997; Stewart and Fitzgerald, 2001; Collier et al., 2003);[10] second, that conflict is associated with over-fast or uneven development where modernization disrupts traditional patterns, but does not as yet deliver adequate or expected rewards – especially where this is associated with rapid urbanization and population growth with a resulting increase in the relative numbers of untrained and unemployed young males (Newman, 1991); and, third, that, even where there are reasonable levels of development in absolute terms, conflict may still be generated where there is actual or perceived inequity in the distribution of benefits (Lichbach, 1989). In all three cases mounting discontent offers fertile recruiting ground for ideological extremism and racial exclusionism.

For many analysts it is the *government sector* that is the key arena, since social and economic grievances are in the end expressed in political form. Three main patterns may be discerned here. First, conflict can become endemic even in established liberal democratic states when party politics become ascriptively based and one community perceives that state power has been permanently 'captured' by another, and is therefore driven to challenge the legitimacy of the state in order to change the situation, as in Canada, Belgium, Spain (Basques) or Northern Ireland (Lijphart, 1977; Gurr and Harff, 1994: ch. 5). This has also been a feature in a number of non-western countries, such as Sri Lanka (Horowitz, 1991). Second, conflict is likely in countries where authoritarian regimes successfully manipulate the state apparatus in order to cling to power and block political access to all those not part of their own narrow patronage network, eventually becoming little more than exploitative 'kleptocracies' as in some post-Soviet Central Asian and postcolonial African states. Here politics has indeed become 'zero-sum' and change can only be effected through a direct challenge to the incumbent regime. Third, there is what seems to be the growing phenomenon of 'failed' or 'collapsed' states (Helman and Ratner, 1992–3; Zartman, ed., 1995; Rotberg, 2004), which, in the absence of adequate means for raising revenue or keeping order, succumb to endemic and chaotic violence. In a report on Africa presented to the UN Security Council in April 1998, Secretary-General Kofi Annan concluded:

> The nature of political power in many African states, together with the real and perceived consequences of capturing and maintaining power, is a key source of conflict across the continent. It is frequently the case that political victory assumes a winner-takes-all form with respect to wealth and resources, patronage, and the prestige and prerogatives of office. Where there is insufficient accountability of leaders, lack of transparency in regimes, inadequate checks and balances, non-adherence to the rule of law, absence of peaceful means to change or replace leadership, or lack of respect for human rights, political control becomes excessively important, and the stakes become dangerously high. (Annan, 1998)

Finally, we should note how, at a critical stage in conflict escalation, it is the *law and order* and *security sectors* that become increasingly prominent. This is the moment when domestic conflict crosses the Rubicon and becomes a violent struggle for control of the state itself. The two clear indicators are, first, in the law and order sector when the legal system and the civilian police come to be identified with particularist interests and are no longer seen to represent impartial authority, and, second, in the security sector when civil unrest can no longer be controlled by non-military means and armed militia emerge. At this stage, as Barry Posen has noted, the 'security dilemma', familiar to analysts of international relations, now impacts with devastating effect on the inchoate social-state-international scene (1993). Once this genie is out of the bottle and armed factions are organized and active, it is very difficult to put it back again. Gurr is one of those who has charted what is usually the ten-or-more-year period between the manifest onset of conflict and its escalation to military confrontation – the crucial window of opportunity for preventive measures.

Group mobilization and inter-party dynamics

Having outlined some of the *contextual* and *structural* sources of contemporary conflict, we move on to consider *relational* sources at conflict party level. Here Ted Gurr (1993, 1995, 2000) shows how national peoples, regional autonomists, communal contenders, indigenous peoples, militant sects, ethnoclasses and other groups tend to move from non-violent protest, through violent protest, to outright rebellion in an uneven escalation that takes many years in most cases. This is the time-lag that gives major incentives for the proactive prevention of violent conflict, as discussed in the next chapter. Goals variously include demands for political access, autonomy, secession or control, triggered by historical grievances and contemporary resentments against the socio-cultural, economic and political constraints outlined in the previous section. New threats to security, such as those felt by constituent groups in the break-up of former Yugoslavia, and new opportunities, often encouraged by similar demands elsewhere, will encourage mobilization, and the nature of the emergent leadership will often be decisive in determining degrees of militancy. When it comes to demands for secession, usually the most explosive issue, a history of past political autonomy, however long ago, is often critical.

Elites and individuals

Turning, finally, to the elite/individual level, we will not dwell on the complex arguments about the relative significance of 'agency' or 'structure' in explication of social and political change (itself a lineal descendant of earlier debate about the relative roles of 'great men' and 'vast impersonal forces' in history). The importance of leadership roles seems self-evident if comparison is made between, say, the effect of Slobodan Milosevic and Franjo Tudjman in Yugoslavia, and F. W. de Klerk and Nelson Mandela in South Africa. For Human Rights Watch, communal violence is rarely the product of 'deep-seated hatreds' or 'ancient animosities', as promoted by those with an interest in doing so, and those who like to suggest as a result that they are 'natural processes' about which little can be done:

> But the extensive Human Rights Watch field research summarized here shows that communal tensions per se are not the immediate cause of many violent and persistent communal conflicts. While communal tensions are obviously a necessary ingredient of an explosive mix, they alone are not sufficient to unleash widespread violence. Rather, time after time the proximate cause of communal violence is governmental exploitation of communal differences. (Human Rights Watch, 1995: 1–2)

Brown agrees that the academic literature 'places great emphasis on mass-level factors' but is 'weak in understanding the role played by elites and leaders in instigating violence'. Most major conflicts, in

Table 4.4 Proximate causes of internal conflict

	Internally driven	Externally driven
Elite-triggered	Bad leaders (23)	Bad neighbours (3)
Mass-triggered	Bad domestic problems (7)	Bad neighbourhoods (1)

Source: from Brown, ed., 1996: 582, 597.
Figures in brackets allocate numbers from Brown's list of 'major active conflicts'

his view, are triggered by 'internal, elite-level activities – to put it simply, bad leaders – contrary to what one would gather from reviewing the scholarly literature on the subject' (Brown, ed., 1996: 22–3) (see table 4.4).

Conclusion

This chapter has outlined a framework for the analysis of contemporary conflict that draws on Edward Azar's account of protracted social conflict, and then updates it via a 'levels of analysis' approach at international, state and sub-state levels. This framework is not a theory of conflict, but a model for locating the chief sources of contemporary conflict. The possibility of a revival of interstate war is by no means ruled out, but more unruly multilevel conflict seems likely to remain the predominant pattern for the immediate future.

Although the theories reviewed in this chapter may seem confusingly various, the main conclusion to be taken from it for the rest of the book is relatively simple. Given the complexity of much contemporary conflict, attempts at conflict resolution have to be equally comprehensive. Although peacemakers striving to maximize humanitarian space and the scope for peace initiatives in the middle of ongoing wars (chapter 6) or aiming to bring the violent phase of conflict to an end (chapter 7) usually have to work within quite narrow power constraints, long-term peacebuilders who aspire to prevent violent conflict (chapter 5) or to ensure that settlements are transformed into lasting peace (chapter 8) have to address the deeper sources of conflict. This is clarified in the hourglass model in chapter 1 (figure 1.3). Here is the framework within which conflict resolution would also seek to address threats generated by criminal greed (see chapter 5) and political terror (see chapter 11). This is likely to involve *contextual* change at international level (for example, via more equitable and accountable global and regional arrangements), *structural* change at state level (for example, via appropriate constitutional adaptations and the promotion of good governance – including state-building in critical cases), *relational* change at conflict party level (for example, via community relations and reconciliation work), and *cultural* change at all levels (for example, via the transformation of discourses and institutions which sustain and reproduce violence). It is to these themes that we now turn.

Recommended reading

Berdal and Malone (2000); Brown, ed., (1996); Collier et al. (2003); Duffield (2001); Kaldor (1999/2001); Martin (2003); Reno (1999).

Preventing Violent Conflict

> Conflict, including ethnic conflict, is not unavoidable but can indeed be prevented. This requires, however, that the necessary efforts are made. Potential sources of conflict need to be identified and analysed with a view to their early resolution, and concrete steps must be taken to forestall armed confrontation. If these preventive measures are superseded by a sharpening of the conflict, then an early warning must be given in time for more rigorous conflict containment to take place.
>
> *Max van der Stoel, OSCE High Commissioner on National Minorities, 2005*

Preventing violent conflict has been a central aim of the conflict resolution enterprise from the start, as illustrated in chapter 2 through Kenneth Boulding's early ambition to create early warning conflict 'data stations' with a view to timely preventive action, and Quincy Wright's proposed project for a 'world intelligence centre' in the first issue of the *Journal of Conflict Resolution*. A remarkable feature of the post-Cold War era forty years later has been the growing consensus on the importance of prevention in the UN and among many international organizations, governments and NGOs. This is partly a reaction to the catastrophes in Rwanda, Yugoslavia and elsewhere, and partly a realization that it may be easier to tackle conflicts early, before they reach the point of armed conflict or mass violence. Major-General Romeo Dallaire's assertion that a mechanized brigade group of five thousand soldiers could have saved hundreds of thousands of lives in Rwanda in the spring and summer of 1994 has reverberated throughout the international community. So has a realization of the cost-effectiveness of prevention when compared with the exorbitant bill for subsequent relief, protection and reconstruction if prevention fails. The new preoccupation with prevention is also a response to the globalization of contemporary conflicts. Not only do 'wars of the third kind' have causes related to the global system, as the previous chapter noted; they also have global effects, through worldwide media coverage, refugee flows, the impact of diasporas and the destabilization of surrounding regions. At the same time, the weakening of the norms of sovereignty and non-interference is beginning to open space for international interventions. In the late 1980s many were predicting catastrophe for South Africa, while few foresaw calamity in Yugoslavia. The dramatic contrast in their subsequent fates underlines the case for prevention. If violent conflict has so far been minimized in the former, could this not also have been achieved in the latter?

This chapter explores how conflicts can be prevented from becoming violent. It first examines the epistemological issues involved in prevention and how we can know that prevention has worked. It then examines the factors that contribute to the prevention of interstate and non-interstate wars. This leads to a review of possible policy measures and to discussion of the roles of the various agencies involved in conflict prevention. The chapter ends with some examples. The question that underlies the analysis is this: what forms of prevention are effective, and what are the circumstances under which they can work?

We noted earlier how 'conflict prevention' is a misnomer, since it is clearly impossible to prevent conflict from taking place. It would also be undesirable, for conflict is a creative and necessary means of bringing about social change. Here, we restrict our definition of conflict prevention to those factors or actions which prevent *armed* conflicts or mass violence from breaking out.[1]

A difficult underlying question here is whether it is a good thing to try to prevent violent conflict in the first place: may violence not be the only way to remedy injustice? We have addressed this question in general terms in earlier chapters, where we argued, first, that violent social conflict usually results in a lose–lose outcome for all main parties and for the population at large, and, second, that attempts to prevent violence must involve the satisfaction of human needs, the accommodation of legitimate aspirations and the remedy of manifest injustices.

Causes and Preventors of War

> Wars are much like road accidents. They have a general and a particular cause at the same time. Every road accident is caused in the last resort by the invention of the internal combustion engine . . . (But) the police and the courts do not weigh profound causes. They seek a specific cause for each accident – driver's error, excessive speed, drunkenness, faulty brakes, bad road service. So it is with wars. (A. J. P. Taylor, quoted in Davies, 1996: 896)

If Taylor is right, perhaps we can learn something about the prevention of wars from the prevention of traffic accidents. It is usually possible to point to particular factors that might have prevented an individual accident. If the driver had not been inebriated, if the weather had not been foggy, if the road had been better lit, the accident might not have happened. But it is hard to be sure of the influence of any particular cause in a single incident. Only when we have a large number of traffic accidents to study can we hope to establish a relationship between accidents and the factors associated with them. This may suggest generic measures that can make roads in general safer. For example, when driving tests were introduced in Britain, there was a measurable impact on the number of accidents per driver per year. Better lighting on roads has also reduced accident figures.

The prevention of fires is similar. Managers of buildings hope that the occupants will not start fires. But they do not place all their trust on the good sense of the occupants. Instead they invest in sprinklers, fire alarms, fire extinguishers and other measures designed to prevent the risk of fires getting out of control. They introduce 'preventors' of fire.

There is a case, similarly, for introducing preventors of war. This is not entirely new: there are already preventors at work, present alongside causes of war.

Light and deep prevention

Active measures to prevent conflict can be divided into two types. One is aimed at preventing situations with a clear capacity for violence from degenerating into armed conflict. This is called 'light prevention'. Its practitioners do not necessarily concern themselves with the root causes of the conflict, or with remedying the situation which led to the crisis which the measures address. Their aim is to prevent latent or threshold conflicts from becoming severe armed conflicts. Examples of such action are diplomatic interventions, long-term missions and private mediation efforts. 'Deep prevention', in contrast, aims to address the root causes, including underlying conflicts of interest and relationships. At the international level this may mean addressing recurrent issues and problems in the international system, or a particular international relationship which lies at the root of conflict. Within societies, it may mean engaging with issues of development, political culture and community relations. In the context of post-Cold War conflicts, light prevention generally means improving international capacity to intervene in conflicts before they become violent; deep prevention means economic and political measures to address the sources of conflict by encouraging economic development, meeting the needs for identity, security and access of diverse groups, strengthening shared norms and institutions, addressing the sources of conflict in poverty, marginalization and injustice, and building domestic, regional and international capacity to manage conflict. This distinction between 'light' and 'deep' prevention can be related in turn to the immediate and more profound causes of war discussed in the previous chapter. Readers will find different terminologies in the literature. For example, the influential 1997 report of the Carnegie Commission on Preventing Deadly Conflicts calls light prevention 'operational prevention' and deep prevention 'structural prevention'.

Causality and prevention

We have seen that Suganami (1996) distinguishes three levels on which the causes of war can be explained. First, 'What are the conditions which must be present for wars to occur?'; second, 'Under what sorts of circumstances have wars occurred most frequently?'; and, third, 'How did this particular war come about?' The first is a question about the necessary causes of wars, the second about the correlates of war, the third about the antecedents of particular wars. We can reformulate the further question, 'What prevents violent conflicts?' in a similar way: first, can war be prevented by removing its necessary conditions? Second, can the incidence of wars be reduced by controlling the circumstances under which they arise? And, third, how can this particular conflict be prevented from becoming violent?

Suganami (1996: 62) identifies three conditions that are logically necessary for war: the 'capacity of human beings to kill members of their own species'; 'sufficient prevalence of the belief among a number of societies, in particular the states, that there are circumstances under which it is their function to resort to arms against one another, and in doing so demand the cooperation of society members (without which no organized armed conflict could take place between societies)'; and 'the absence from the international system of a perfectly effective anti-war device'. Surprisingly, he ignores a further necessary condition which has been pointed to by many students of war: the existence of weapons.

It is clear that if any of these necessary conditions could be removed, war as an organized activity would be prevented. Following the order of Suganami's conditions, war could be prevented by changing human nature, by reducing the prevalence of the belief that resort to arms is a legitimate function of the state or by introducing a perfectly effective anti-war device, although all of these face serious practical difficulties, as does achieving general disarmament. The difficulty lies in the fact that war is an institution, and as such it is rooted in the social systems which give rise to it (Rapoport, 1992). So long as the belief that states can legitimately order people to participate in war is prevalent and preparations for war are made, wars remain a possibility. For practical reasons, then, most effort has concentrated on searching for ways to prevent some wars, or to prevent a specific war.

In the last chapter we noted attempts to identify correlates of war: factors related to the incidence of war, which might be suggestive about both the causes and the preventors of certain types of war. This has stimulated an immense literature. Pioneers such as Wright (1942) and Richardson (1960b) undertook systematic examinations of war incidence in history and attempted to discover causal factors, and many others have followed them. These efforts have produced significant increases in our understanding of the complex causes of both interstate and non-interstate wars (Geller and Singer, 1998). The same statistical approach can suggest relationships between structural factors and the non-occurrence of armed conflicts, or, more positively, peaceful change.

Suganami's third approach, of identifying the causes of a particular war, has its parallels in efforts to prevent a particular conflict from becoming violent. This is a matter of tackling the background, intermediate and trigger causes of a particular potential war. If one can transform the background causes, the war-prone situation may not arise. If one can modify the intermediate causes, the conflict may be prevented from coming to a head. If one can remove the triggers, violence may be avoided even if conflict remains. However, it is difficult to ascertain the causes of particular wars, and similarly it is difficult to plan or assess the effects of prevention. If historians cannot agree on the causes of a war, how can anyone agree on what policy might prevent a potential war? When a preventive policy has been carried out, how can anyone agree on whether it has been effective? There are no cast-iron answers to this question: we can only rely on the use of judgement and evidence. When peaceful relations are maintained, or a particular conflict is settled peacefully, there are historical questions to be asked about what factors made this possible, and these are in principle no different from the kinds of question we ask when we consider which factors caused a particular war.

For example, consider the intervention of the OSCE High Commissioner for National Minorities (HCNM), Max van der Stoel, in Estonia. In 1993 the citizens of Narva voted by an overwhelming majority to secede from Estonia. They were almost all Russians who had been dismayed to become what they saw as second-class citizens in their own country. The Estonian government declared that the referendum was illegal and threatened to use force if necessary to prevent the break-up of Estonia. Russian vigilante groups began to arm themselves and in Russia the President warned that he would intervene if necessary to protect the rights of Russian speakers. At a time when it appeared that this deadlock could lead to the outbreak of fighting, Max van der Stoel interceded. After meeting with representatives of the Narva city council and the government, he suggested that the Narva council should regard the referendum as a declaration of aspiration without immediate effect. At the same time he suggested to the Estonian government that they abandon their threat to use force against the city. His suggestions were adopted and no armed conflict took place.

But how can we be sure that it was the intervention of the HCNM that was responsible for preventing the armed conflict? To answer this question, we have to enter a difficult field much disputed by historians, philosophers and philosophers of science: namely, the issue of causation and counterfactuals.

In order to attribute the non-occurrence of armed conflict to the presence of the HCNM, we have to know, first, that the non-event could not be attributed to other preventive factors; second, that in the absence of the HCNM the causative factors would have resulted in a violent conflict; and, third, that the intervention of the HCNM not only preceded and was associated with the avoidance of conflict, but is also sufficient to explain it.

These are, of course, demanding requirements. Even in retrospect, historians have great difficulty in agreeing how particular wars have been caused or how much importance to place on a particular causal factor. We can rarely be sure that a particular cause would have had a particular effect, or that it was the agent for a particular effect. The clock cannot be turned back and the sequence of events rerun with the factor in question removed. In history, causes operate together and in combination. The effect of a cause is dependent upon other background conditions. Nor are events in history simply linked by predictable linear effects like physical laws, which can suggest, given a first event, a sequence of knock-on effects.[2] Rather, history is intrinsically made up of events that are connected by *meaning*, by the purposes and thoughts of those who act in history. This is what Pitrim Sorokin called the 'logico-meaningful' dynamics of history. Wars often arise from the juxtaposition and combination of previously unrelated chains of events. At the same time, what matters most is what these sometimes surprising combinations of events mean to those who are responsible for taking decisions. We cannot properly explain events unless we understand the mental world of the participants and the connections *they* make between them. It is this which makes wars particularly difficult to predict and sometimes gives them their surprising and dramatic quality.

In the Estonia case, we have to weigh the importance of various factors: the lack of mobilization of the Russian-speaking identity, the unwillingness of Russia to get involved at a stage when it was dependent on western support, and the capacity of the Estonian political system to manage its own disputes. Nevertheless, the situation was fevered and dangerous, and the intervention of the OSCE High Commissioner undoubtedly reduced the sense of crisis and opened the way to a protracted process of political negotiation over the issue, instead of a resort to force. It contributed to the easing of the immediate political risks associated with a declaration of secession, which had the potential to trigger a violent episode.

In sum, historians deploy different levels of explanation in explaining wars: there are immediate triggering factors, underlying sources of tension, and deeper structural conditions which shape events (Nye, 1993). The longer-term and the immediate causes work together to bring about war. Neither by themselves can satisfactorily explain war. The great catastrophes of history are 'a fatal combination of general and specific causes' (Davies, 1996: 896). In a similar way, structural prevention, such as the presence of adequate constitutional capacity for managing conflict, combines with operational and direct prevention, such as Max van der Stoel's diplomatic interventions, to head off a potential conflict. It is clear that both light and deep conflict prevention are required. If light prevention is relied upon alone in a situation that is prone to violent conflict, the underlying causes of conflict will remain and may still produce a violent conflict, in a slightly different configuration. To be satisfactory, conflict prevention must be about preventing not only particular possible wars, but a family of possible wars. In short, it must be about improving capacity, strengthening relationships and building justice as well as fighting particular fires.

Early Warning

With these general and epistemological considerations in mind, let us now turn to consider the contemporary effort to establish an early warning system for violent political conflict, along the lines of Boulding's proposed 'social data stations' which he saw as analogous to networks of weather stations in the identification of 'social temperature and pressure' and the prediction of 'cold or warm fronts' (see Kerman, 1974: 82). This is widely seen as essential for monitoring particular areas of potential conflict, and seeking ways to act early enough to nip a potential conflict in the bud where this is feasible and appropriate. There are two tasks involved here; first, identification of the type of conflicts and location of the conflicts that could become violent; second, monitoring and assessing their progress with a view to assessing how close to violence they are.

One line of approach, which addresses Suganami's second question, aims to establish the circumstances under which wars are likely to take place. We can take Ted Gurr's work as an example of this approach. Using data from his Minorities at Risk project, he identifies three factors that affect the proneness of a communal group to rebel: collective incentives, capacity for joint action, and external opportunities. Each concept is represented by indicators constructed from data coded for the project, and justified by correlations with the magnitude of ethnic rebellions in previous years. The resulting table makes it possible to rank the minorities according to their risk-proneness (Gurr 1998b). The assumption is that the more risk-prone are those with high scores on both incentives for rebellion and capacity/opportunity. Using this type of risk assessment Gurr was able to anticipate a relatively high probability that the Kosovo Albanians and East Timorese would rebel, and that other disadvantaged groups would not.

Econometric forecasting takes a similar approach. For example, Collier (2003: 53) finds that 'countries with low, stagnant and unequally distributed per capita incomes that have remained dependent on primary commodities for their exports face dangerously high risks of prolonged conflict'. The World Bank is developing economic 'at risk' indicators which classify countries' risk of conflict from a range of indicators of security (such as armed diasporas, arms imports), social cohesion (such as ethnic dominance), economic performance and governance (Cleves et al., 2002).

Other comparable approaches focus on indicators of genocide (Davies et al., 1997), human rights abuse (Schmid, 1997: 74), state failure (Esty, 1995), refugee flows, food crises, tracking arms flows, and indicators of environmental conflict (Davies and Gurr, eds, 1998); Austin (2004) reviews other early-warning models.

These statistical approaches blur the case-specific and context-specific information which area experts would use. They offer a guide as to where conflict prevention agencies might concentrate their efforts, but offer a probabilistic measure of conflict-proneness rather than a precise warning.

Turning from quantitative to qualitative conflict monitoring, a mass of information is available on particular societies and situations. It includes the reports of humanitarian agencies (now linked together on the ReliefWeb site on the Internet), qualitative analyses of particular conflicts and groups of conflicts at risk by the International Crisis Group, analyses by the media and by the academic community, and of course the diplomatic and intelligence activities of states and international organizations. Qualitative monitoring offers vastly more content-rich and contextual information than quantitative statistical analysis, but presents the problems of noise and information overload. Given the current state of the art, qualitative monitoring is likely to be most useful for gaining early warning of conflict in particular cases: the expertise of the area scholar and the local observer, steeped in situational knowledge, is difficult to beat. Networks of country experts, policy-makers and analysts, as brought together by the International Crisis Group, or networks of practioners and agencies monitoring particular situations, can both warn and encourage actions (Austin, 2004).

Even when observers have issued 'early warnings', it is by no means certain that they will be heard, or that there will be a response. Governments and international organizations may be distracted by other crises (as in the case of Yugoslavia), or unwilling to change existing policies (as in the case of Rwanda). The governments of countries seen to be vulnerable are also likely to resist external interference. Given the unpredictability of human decision-making, no system of forecasting is likely to give certain results. Nevertheless, there is already sufficient knowledge of situations where there is proneness to war to justify an appropriate response. For some time it has been realized that the key issue is not, in fact, providing early warning, but mustering the political resources to make an appropriate early response.

In many cases, it is possible to anticipate likely conflicts simply because existing conflicts are recurrent and protracted, and because conflicts tend to spill over in conflict regions. 'Enduring rivalries', that is, protracted disputes between pairs of states or peoples, have accounted for half the wars between 1816 and 1992. These may be expected to be sources of further disputes. It is not difficult to point to regions – such as West Africa, the Great Lakes region of Africa, the Caucasus, the India–Pakistan border and parts of Indonesia – where future violent conflicts can be expected. We also know from economic indicators that the risk of civil war in poor states, especially those with previous civil wars, is far higher than in more developed states (Collier, 2003). There are therefore plentiful indicators of areas where a preventive response is needed. What form should this response take?

Deep or Structural Prevention

We referred in chapter 1 to the hourglass model of conflict resolution (see figure 1.3). In this model, the freedom of action to deal with conflict is at its widest at the early stage of pre-violence prevention and at the late stage of post-violence peacebuilding. At these stages, the issues of conflict management, which narrow down to a few critical choices at the point of crisis, widen out to embrace the broader political context. Here the questions of how to prevent and manage conflict become very similar to the classical questions that we ask of any polity. How are resources and roles to be allocated in a way that is legitimate and accepted? What is the basis of political community? How are relationships to be conducted between individuals and groups within and between political communities? What are the accepted values, norms and rules of the community? How are public goods to be provided? How are the community's values, norms and rules to be upheld?

When there is an agreed and legitimate basis for a political community and the community provides public goods and secures the accepted values of its members, violent conflict is likely to be avoided. When coercion is used as the basis for the allocation of resources and roles, and when this allocation is uneven, illegitimate and unacceptable to people, violent conflict is more likely to occur.

This applies at any level of political community: at the level of global society as well as at national level and at the level of particular communities. Conflict formations run through our political communities at all levels, from the global to the national to the local. Moreover, these conflict formations are intertwined. The agenda for conflict prevention is thus to deal with conflict formations at the global, national and sub-national levels. If we see the context of conflict as forming a vital element of conflict transformation, there is no possibility of addressing local and regional conflicts without also taking the global and international setting into account.

Conflict prevention at the global level

Globalization is increasingly drawing the human population into a common community of fate, where the outcomes and life chances of individuals and groups are influenced more and more by factors outside their own political community's control. The development of conflict formations at the global level are increasingly clear, as the last chapter indicated. Despite overall gobal economic growth, the gulf between the richest and poorest societies has grown more stark and more widely resented in the last two decades. Global environmental change is putting the interests of developed and developing countries on an apparent collision course. The security of the well-off seems to come increasingly at the expense of the disadvantaged and the marginalized (Rogers, 2000).

However, there is only a limited extent to which a global political community exists. There is little sense of shared identity or shared responsibility. The procedures for allocating resources reflect the existing inequalities of power in global markets. Provisions for supplying public goods (such as a clean environment) are weak. Despite the urgency of global conflicts and the pressing need for some legitimate form of global governance, capacity to manage conflict at the global level is clearly insufficient.

Conflict prevention at the international level

What does exist is a certain amount of capacity at the international level, incorporated into international law and international institutions, and embedded in the practice of the major international and financial institutions, such as the UN, the G8, the World Bank, and so on. In so far as capacity to prevent conflict at the international level exists, it is directed primarily to conflicts between states and secondarily to conflicts within states in the developing world. There is an uneasy tension between actions at the international level to prevent armed conflicts and the global forces which also fuel armed conflicts.

First, it is important to note the sharp reduction from the past in the level of interstate conflict as noted in the previous chapter (Holsti, 1996). In Europe, for example, there was a historical trend towards the pacification of internal warfare, as states developed and slowly also began to control wars between themselves – although the motivations for regulation were weaker than the incentives for wars until warfare began to become truly destructive for whole nations. Over the last two centuries, there is a clear variation between periods of general war, and periods when an international order has kept the risk of large conflicts contained (Hinsley, 1963, 1987; Wallensteen, 1984: 217–46; see also table 2.1 in chapter 2).

From the end of the nineteenth century a new international basis for conflict prevention developed in the emerging commonality of interest between the liberal democratic powers. The democracies, with shared elites and shared economic interests, cooperated in war, and imposed democratic systems on the losers. In this way they gradually constructed and extended a liberal peace (Rasmussen, 2003). There were evolutionary, systemic effects too. As Mitchell et al. argue:

> War increases the share of democracies in the system because democracies win wars more often than non-democracies and defeat in war often leads to some form of regime change. . . . Thus, war more often than not leads to democratization through the effects of both winning and losing wars. (1999: 790)

This process led to a well-established security community among the European and North American states, which is now in the throes of being extended. At the same time, these states and their institutions are seeking to extend conflict prevention into the zones outside the liberal peace – while still retaining the use of coercion at will, and profiting from insecurity in the 'zones of war' through the sale of arms and the extraction of raw materials.

The remarkable achievement of this process has been the dramatic limitation of interstate war in recent decades. Claims have been made that mutual nuclear deterrence inhibited war between the super-powers during the Cold War. Others have looked deeper. Mueller (1989) has argued that war is becoming obsolescent between major states because it is too destructive to be a usable policy instrument, and irrelevant to the real conflicts of interest that divide major states. Keohane and Nye (1986) stress the role of interdependence in transforming relations between states: when states' interests are tied together in a web of interrelated issue areas, governments tend to move towards bargaining as the main instrument for resolving conflicts of interest. Others stress the importance of international institutions and regimes, which have become more universal with the end of the Cold War. For example, Axelrod and Keohane (1986) argue that institutions strengthen contacts between governments, make their actions more transparent, diminish security dilemmas and create a basis for reciprocation and mutual gains. Besides these changes in the structure of relations between states, the nature and importance of the state itself is changing, through globalization. Non-militarized economic power is seen to bring a greater enhancement of influence and ability to defend interests than investment in military power. As major states pool more of their powers and delegate others downwards, they are becoming different kinds of actors from what they used to be; and interstate wars of the old kind, between adjoining states disputing territory and power, may be becoming anomalies.[3]

Is democratic government, then, a preventor of interstate war? The answer is not clear-cut. The democratic peace proposition does not assert that democracies are peaceful. They are found to have fought just as many wars as other types of polity. Major powers that are democracies fight more wars than minor powers that are autocracies. The United States and the United Kingdom have both been involved in frequent wars in recent years and so democratic governance is not in itself a predictor of non-participation in war. The significant finding is that, with few exceptions, democracies have not fought other democracies. They tend to fight more wars against autocracies than do other autocracies. Raknerud and Hegre (1997) show that the tendency of democracies to join in wars waged against autocracies explains the apparent discrepancy between their abstinence from war with other democracies and their propensity to fight wars in general.

An important question is whether, as democratization progresses, new democracies will also be peaceful, or whether the inter-democratic peace will break down if states with serious conflicts between them become democracies. Doyle (1986) and Russett (1993) argue that democratization will extend the area of inter-democratic peace. Ward and Gleditsch (1998) argue that the transition period has unsettling effects. The recent experience with the eastern enlargement of the EU has had mixed consequences, but does not disconfirm the inter-democratic peace proposition. In some cases it has produced political conflicts which have not escalated into armed conflict (for example, Hungary–Slovakia, Hungary–Romania). In others, a clash between democratization and autocracy has led to war (former Yugoslavia). The NATO war against Yugoslavia became a classic example of a liberal interstate war, fought between a large coalition of democracies and a lone autocracy. Contested democratization appears likely to increase the risk of armed conflicts between democratic states and autocracies, without necessarily threatening the inter-democratic peace.

It is worth noting that there have been significant examples of zones of interstate peace where not all states are democracies. The European Union is perhaps the most dramatic example of a regional organization that has presided over the end of centuries of war among its member states. But ASEAN is another organization that has managed to regulate interstate disputes among its members, while avoiding mutual interference in the frequently troubled internal arrangements of its member states. The essence of the ASEAN system is *mushuwara*, the Malaysian village system for consensual decision-making, which has been applied to the international level (Askandar, 1997). In Latin America, an unusually low level of interstate wars has prevailed since 1945, without the existence of a security community of the kind Deutsch describes or strong bonds of interdependence. The explanation is unclear, although, as in the South-East Asian case, there is a common preoccupation with internal challenges (Holsti, 1996: 150–82).

Prevention of internal conflicts

The literature on the correlates and preventors of non-interstate wars is less extensive than that on interstate conflicts, but it is growing rapidly. We will explore first the evidence that appropriate forms of governance, economic development and respect for human rights are preventors of intrastate conflicts.

Governance is closely associated with conflict regulation. In the past, establishing common governance has been a crucial means of overcoming internal conflicts. It is also well recognized that the legitimacy of governance is the basis of consent. There may be different forms of legitimacy in different culture areas.

In the West, democratic governance has been basic to political legitimacy in recent decades, although what constitutes adequate democratic governance is of course a subject of lively debate. In non-western countries, imposed democracies have not always been successful. There is evidence that settled democracies are less prone to civil wars than other regime types. Stable autocracies also experience relatively few civil wars. It is semi-democracies and transitional regimes that have the highest incidence (Hegre et al., 2001). This is partly because such polities tend to be unstable, and political instability and regime change clearly increase the probability of civil war. But even allowing for this effect, a higher level of civil war is found in 'semi-democracies' (ibid.: 43).

In many cases, the issue of what kind of democracy is to be established is perhaps more crucial than whether a polity is democratic, especially if, as in some Central and Eastern European countries and many African countries, democratic institutions are a matter more of form than of substance (Schöpflin, 1994; Clapham, 1996). Societies that offer avenues for peaceful change and regulation of conflict, in which people can live fruitful and productive lives, will be peaceful whether or not they conform to contemporary stereotypes of liberal democratic forms. Moreover, there is a wide range of practices across different cultures for managing conflict. Western practices should not be regarded as superior. Indeed, practices transplanted into non-western societies may well be inferior to indigenous methods. Avoiding war depends most of all on whether local domestic institutions can provide adequate models for dealing with conflict and fostering development in locally acceptable ways. Locally adapted proportional voting systems, for example, appear to have been strikingly successful in preventing violent conflict (Reynal-Querol, 2002).

Other qualities of governance besides democratic forms are important. Where governance is legitimate and accountable to citizens, and when the rule of law prevails, armed conflict is less likely. Azar theorized that armed conflict degrades governance, deforms institutions and destroys development. The reverse can be shown to be true: good governance, sound institutions and effective development inhibit the incidence of armed conflict (Miall, 2003).

Development is an important preventor. Henderson and Singer (2000), in a study of the onset of civil wars in postcolonial states in Africa, Asia and the Middle East, identify development, demilitarization and full decolonization as factors that tend to inhibit the inception of civil wars. Collier and Hoeffler (1998) and Hegre et al. (2001)

confirm the widely accepted view that high levels of development reduce the risk of civil war. In contrast, mal-development creates a 'conflict trap' that the poorest countries find difficult to escape (Collier et al., 2003). The risk of violent civil conflict is highest in the poorest group of countries. In turn, violent conflict impoverishes people and puts development into reverse. So the poorest group of countries, with stagnant economies and a history of past conflicts, are most at risk. Middle-income countries have a lower risk of civil war and this risk is diminishing over time as development proceeds. OECD countries have an almost negligible risk of civil war. Collier (Collier et al., 2003: 187) argues that if a package of policy measures were introduced that obtained a sustained growth rate of 3 per cent per year in the poorest countries, shortened conflicts by a year and cut the rate of relapse into conflict of post-conflict societies, the global incidence of civil war could be halved.

Another significant factor is the level of inequality between different groups. Stewart (2002) argues that these horizontal inequalities add significantly to the risk of conflict among low-income and middle-income countries. It follows that equity between groups and inclusivity are preventive factors.

Similarly, abuse of human rights is widely recognized as an indicator of incipient conflict. Human rights violations are often an early warning sign of impending conflict, and of course human rights abuses are both a trigger for escalation (as, for example, in Kosovo) and a concomitant of protracted fighting. In contrast, high levels of observance of human rights tend to accompany other related factors including democratic governance, level of development and quality of governance.

We conclude by highlighting the links between these findings and Azar's theory of protracted social conflict. Light or operational preventors of non-interstate war roughly correspond to Azar's 'process dynamic' variables in protracted social conflict, including flexible and accommodating state actions and strategies, moderate communal actions and strategies on the part of the leaders of challenging groups, and mutually de-escalatory 'built-in mechanisms' of conflict management. Deep or structural preventors address Azar's 'preconditions' for protracted social conflict. They include adequate political institutions and good governance, cohesive social structures, opportunities for groups to develop economically and culturally, and the presence of accepted legal or social norms capable of accommodating and peacefully transforming these formations. A stable and peaceful wider regional setting is also often of vital importance. As table 5.1 shows, preventors of internal conflict can operate at a number of different levels.

Table 5.1 Preventors of intrastate conflict

Factors generating conflict	Possible preventors
Global level	
Inappropriate systemic structures	Changes in international order
Regional level	
Regional diasporas	Regional security arrangements
State level	
Ethnic stratification	Power-sharing/federalism/autonomy
Weak economies	Appropriate development
Authoritarian rule	Legitimacy, democratization
Human rights abuse	Rule of law, human rights monitoring/protection
Societal level	
Weak societies	Strengthening civic society, institutions
Weak communications	Round tables, workshops, community relations
Polarized attitudes	Cross-cultural work
Poverty, inequality	Poverty reduction and social reforms
Elite/individual level	
Exclusionist policies	Stronger moderates

[handwritten annotations: "what kind of changes?"; "how?"; "?"]

Light or Operational Prevention

When disputes are close to the point of violence, light or operational prevention comes into play. This is often called 'preventive diplomacy', but we prefer the more general term since it allows for a wider range of actors. Although much attention has been focused on external interveners in operational conflict prevention, the protagonists themselves can play the most decisive role by pursuing moderate and constructive strategies (Kriesberg, 1998). Moreover, direct negotiations between the contending parties may limit the risk of conflict escalation at an early stage (Zartman, 2001). In some of the most cited cases of conflict prevention, such as Macedonia and Estonia, a combination of actions by internal and external actors combined together to limit potential conflicts.

A wide range of policy options are in principle available for light prevention (Creative Associates, 1997: 3–6). They range from official diplomacy (mediation, conciliation, fact-finding, good offices, peace conferences, envoys, conflict prevention centres, hot lines) through non-official diplomacy (private mediation, message-carrying and creation of back-channels, peace commissions, problem-solving workshops, conflict resolution training, round tables) to peacemaking efforts by local actors (church-facilitated talks, debates between politicians, cross-party discussions). In some cases exploratory talks and trust-building by respected mediators are crucial. In others, positive and negative inducements by relevant states are significant. The literature (Carnegie Commission, 1997; Wallensteen, ed., 1998; Leatherman et al., 1999; Zartman, 2001; Hampson and Malone, eds, 2002) explores a range of political measures (mediation with muscle, mobilization through regional and global organizations, attempts to influence the media); economic measures (sanctions, emergency aid, conditional offers of financial support); and military measures (preventive peacekeeping, arms embargoes, demilitarization).

Operational prevention thus goes wider than conflict resolution, if that is conceived as bringing parties together to analyse and transform a dispute. However, the effort to resolve conflict at an early stage is at the heart of prevention. It involves identifying the key issues, clearing mistrust and misperceptions and exploring feasible outcomes that bridge the opposing positions of the parties. Finding ways to negotiate agreements, agree procedures and channels for dispute resolution and transforming contentious relationships are central to the enterprise. These were characteristic of the work of Max van der Stoel, the OSCE High Commissioner for National Minorities, whose intervention in Estonia has been cited above, and whose work in Central and Eastern Europe in the 1990s is one of the beacons of quiet preventive diplomacy in practice (Kemp, 2001). They are also the hallmarks of efforts by internal and external non-governmental peacemakers.

In some cases quite protracted conflicts continue at a political level, with successive negotiations, breakdowns, agreements and disagreements, but the conflict is eventually settled or suspended without violence breaking out. The long struggle over South Tyrol was negotiated between the Austrian and Italian governments and the local parties in Alto Adige. In other cases a negotiation process prevents a political conflict reaching any risk of violence. The peaceful divorce of the Czech and Slovak republics, and the negotiations between Moscow and the Tatar government over the status of Tatarstan within the Russian Federation are examples (Hopmann, 2001: 151–6).

Non-governmental organizations, development agencies and social actors also take significant steps to address conflict and attempt to prevent violence at an early stage. It is difficult to evaluate the impact of this kind of 'preventive peacebuilding', especially when the main intended impact may be to improve relations between specific groups or address needs at a community or regional level. It is only when there is an obvious relationship between programmes at the local and community level and impact on the elite level that conflict impact assessment is clear. The work can sometimes be very challenging. For example, the programme by Conciliation Resources in Fiji supported a Citizens' Constitutional Forum which contributed to the adoption in

1997 of a power-sharing system. This was intended to address the domination of the indigenous Fijians over the Indian-Fijian group. But following the coup which overthrew the constitution in 2000, the situation became more polarized than ever. Conciliation Resources continues to work with its partners to encourage multiculturalism, respect for human rights and the re-establishment of the constitution.

Development agencies have a range of impacts, some positive, some highly negative. Large government donors typically work with the local government and may have negative impacts on local communities when centrally financed development programmes impact on them. For example, EU support for irrigation schemes in the Awash valley in Ethiopia have led to the intensification of latent conflict between local Afar clans and the central government, although this has been partly offset by a small-scale local project with the regional government (of which the central government disapproved). Development agencies bring substantial resources into poor countries and it is difficult for them to avoid enmeshment in local conflicts.

The effectiveness of measures to prevent violent conflicts depends on circumstances. As Stedman (1995) argued, they can exacerbate some situations. As Lund (1995) countered, they can mitigate others. Efforts to prevent latent conflicts from becoming violent are always justified, but they must be informed, sensitive and well judged, and carried out with representatives of the affected population, if they are not to do more harm than good.

Mainstreaming Prevention: International Organizations and the Evolution of Norms and Policies

Fifty years after the idea was first examined by the pioneers of the conflict resolution field, it is remarkable how the idea of conflict prevention has been adopted as the leading edge of international and multilateral conflict management policy. Mechanisms for peaceful change and systems for anticipation of future issues, two of the key perquisites for international peace and security which were absent from all of the historic peace treaties noted by Holsti in chapter 2 of this book (see table 2.1), are now being designed into the security architectures of regional and international organizations through the commitment to programmes of conflict prevention.

The UN's concern with conflict prevention evolved from the Agenda for Peace (1992), through the Brahimi Report (2000), to the Secretary-General's Report on Conflict Prevention to the 55th Session of the General Assembly in June 2001, which made conflict prevention a priority of the organization. Kofi Annan urged his staff to develop a 'culture of prevention'. Similarly, UN Security Council Resolution 1366 of August 2001 identified a key role for the Security Council in the prevention of armed conflict. A Trust Fund for Preventive Action has been established and a system-wide training programme on early warning and preventive measures initiated. The so-called 'Annan Doctrine' which prioritized conflict prevention has influenced a wide range of actors to follow suit. Within the UN family, the UNDP defined its role in post-conflict peacebuilding through a conflict prevention strategy adopted in November 2000 and 20 per cent of UNDP track 3 funding is set aside for 'preventive and curative activities'.

The Organization for Security and Cooperation in Europe (OSCE) has fifty-five participating states spanning Vancouver to Vladivostok, and has evolved as a primary regional organization for early warning, conflict prevention, crisis management and post-conflict rehabilitation. Its conflict prevention structures and roles include a Conflict Prevention Centre, an Office for Democratic Institutions and Human Rights and, as we have seen, a High Commissioner for National Minorities (HCNM) whose task is to identify and seek early resolution of ethnic tensions that might endanger peace, stability or friendly relations between the participating states of the OSCE. The HCNM gathers information, mediates, promotes dialogue, makes recommendations and informs OSCE members of potential conflicts; significantly, the HCNM does not require approval by states of the OSCE before becoming involved.

The European Union made its commitment to conflict prevention at its Gothenburg Summit in June 2001, when it declared:

> Conflict prevention calls for a cooperative approach to facilitate peaceful solutions to disputes, and implies addressing the root causes of conflicts. The EU underlines its political commitment to pursue conflict prevention as one of the main objectives of the EU's external relations. It resolves to continue to improve its capacity to prevent violent conflicts and to contribute to a global culture of prevention.

This statement of commitment by the EU was an integral step in the process of developing a Common European Security and Defence Policy, growing out of the previous Helsinki Summit (December 1999) and the Lisbon Council (March 2000). The European Commission launched Conflict Prevention Assessment Missions to areas of conflict including Papua New Guinea, the Solomon Islands, Fiji, Indonesia and Nepal. The Organization for Economic Cooperation and Development (OECD), through its Development Assistance Committee, has also produced guidelines for conflict prevention which depend on long-term structural preventive measures built into developmental assistance programmes (Ackermann, 2003). Many of the agencies of the UN, and other international regional, and sub-regional organizations, were themselves also developing policies and programmes that emphasized the importance of robust values and structures for conflict prevention (Ackermann, 2003; Mack, 2003; Smith, 2003). It is also widely recognized that conflict prevention is a less costly policy than intervention after the onset of armed conflicts. Chalmers (2004) argued that for every £1 spent on preventive activity, an average of £4.1 will be generated on savings for the international community, compared to the costs of intervention after the onset of violent conflict.

It is nevertheless generally recognized that when it comes to conflict prevention in practice, there is a long way to go in translating rhetoric into reality. This is especially the case as far as the UN is concerned, where the resources available for preventive programmes are meagre. However, the significance of the UN's shift to a culture of prevention through the Annan Doctrine lies in its important role in innovation and norm-setting. Ackermann has pointed out that in general, norm-setting evolves through three stages: awareness-raising and advocacy, acceptance and institutionalization, and internationalization (Ackermann, 2003: 7). In the period of the first decade of the new century it is anticipated that conflict prevention will have made strong progress towards the second stage.

The 2001 Report to the General Assembly and Security Council Resolution 1366 both recognized that it was important for member states and organizations of civil society to commit to conflict prevention. Many have responded. The G8 countries produced their Rome Initiative on Conflict Prevention in July 2001, concentrating on small arms and light weapons, conflict diamonds, children in conflict, civilian policing, conflict and development, the role of women and the contribution of the private sector in conflict prevention. The government of the United Kingdom launched its Global Conflict Prevention Pool in 2001, combining the three key departments (Ministry of Defence, Department for International Development, and the Foreign Office) in an attempt to coordinate strategy around policy development and programme delivery (Kapila and Vernmester, 2002). The budget of £74 million in 2004 was limited, but the rhetorical commitment was clear. NGOs have continued to research, advocate and implement appropriate conflict prevention activities, including International Alert, the International Crisis Group, and the European Centre for Conflict Prevention, whose database of conflict prevention organizations listed about 850 organizations active in 2004 (<www.euconflict.org>).

The effects of this intensified commitment are hard to establish. We saw in chapter 3 how in most recent surveys the incidence of major armed conflict has been going down since the mid-1990s (see figure 3.1), although Hegre (2004) shows the number of new wars oscillating. Gurr et al. (2001) identify a decline in internal wars between 1993 and 2000 and associate the easing of discrimination amongst minority groups with a more benign policy environment. The statistical evidence also suggests a shortening in the duration of wars, which could be due to a diminishing of the factors previously fuelling violent conflicts, such as less support from superpowers and proxy states for armed factions, although it may also be due to greater involvement in peacekeeping, peacemaking and peacebuilding by the international community and local actors. Once again statistical correlations can indicate likely causal factors, but cannot prove them.

Recent Experience and Case Studies

Having examined structural and operational prevention at the interstate and the intrastate levels and the actors involved in prevention policy, we end the chapter by considering the application of conflict prevention policies to specific conflicts in the post-Cold War period and the early years of the twenty-first century.

First, let us note the existence of very different risks of violent conflict in different types of states, as indicated in chapter 3. In the OECD, no new internal or interstate wars within or between member states have started for many years. Clearly the combination of cross-cutting interests and identities, international institutions, dispute settlement mechanisms and membership of common security bodies in this area has largely eliminated the risk of intra-OECD warfare. In Eastern Europe and the former Soviet Union a long period without armed conflict was broken by the break-up of the Soviet Union and the former Yugoslavia, but after a burst of new conflicts, mainly over secession and self-determination, the number of new conflicts in this area is falling. Latin America has experienced no new internal wars since 1985. This leaves South and South-East Asia, the Middle East and North Africa, and Sub-Saharan Africa, all as regions with continuing inceptions of new wars as well as continuing old ones. Sub-Saharan Africa is the only region which has experienced an increase in the level of armed conflicts.

Capacity to prevent conflict varies regionally too. Capacity exists at an international level (in the form of international institutions, norms), at the national level (in the form of state institutions, parliaments, laws, etc.) and at sub-state levels (local communities, civic associations, etc.). It is very weak or non-existent in countries where states have failed or are failing and economies are stagnating. A combination of factors, including different configurations of structural causes and preventors of conflict, distinguish regions with little or no violent conflict from those with endemic violent conflicts.

We can illustrate how deep structural and light operational prevention have interacted by reference to one or two examples from Europe, and one or two from Africa.

The Baltic states present one of the most significant examples of conflicts that have been prevented, or averted. The secession of Lithuania, Estonia and Latvia from the Soviet Union might well have given rise to armed conflicts, both between the new states and Russia and between the Baltic and Russian citizens in the Baltic states. But this did not happen. In the case of Estonia, which we looked at above, the outcome can be attributed to a combination of light and deep prevention. On the light side, the effective diplomatic interventions of Max van der Stoel and others, combined with the moderate positions taken by the Estonian President, de-escalated the crisis. At a deeper level, the membership of all the concerned parties in the OSCE, and their acceptance of OSCE standards on citizenship and minority rights, created a legitimate framework for consultation and mediation. Both the Baltic states and the Russian Federation sought entry into European institutions; this gave European institutions some weight in the conflict. Crucially, the West, the Baltic states and the Russian government were all keen to avoid an armed conflict, but to be effective this wish had to be translated into practical measures and bridge-building institutions in the Baltic states, including voting systems in which politicians had to seek support from both the main ethnic communities in order to gain power. Moreover, the Russian-speakers were divided. The majority of them saw their best hopes for the future in participating in the Estonian economy, which had better prospects of development and trade with the West than that of Russia (Khrychikov and Miall, 2002).

Macedonia is perhaps the best-known case with a significant experience of conflict prevention measures. While the international community failed to prevent the spread of violent conflict from Croatia to Bosnia, it made great efforts in Macedonia to significant effect. When Yugoslavia broke up, Macedonia was a weak state with dubious viability. Four neighbouring states had potential claims on its territory (Pettifer, 1992). The government of Greece claimed prior ownership to the name. There was a potentially serious latent conflict between the majority Macedonian Slavs and the Albanians in Macedonia, who constituted about a quarter of the population (Mickey and Albion, 1993). It was very reasonable to fear that if conflict were ignited in Kosovo it could spill over into Macedonia and trigger an armed conflict there.

In response to these warning signs, the UN deployed its first ever preventive peacekeeping mission, in Macedonia in January 1993, initially as part of UNPROFOR, later renamed UNPREDEP in 1995. This effectively placed an international guarantee on Macedonia's territorial integrity. The peacekeepers prevented several incursions by Yugoslav troops from turning into violent incidents. The international community also supported the Macedonian economy and attempted to intervene in the conflict between Albanians and the Macedonians, with rather limited success. The OSCE High Commissioner also attempted to mediate between them, securing an agreement to establish a higher education institution in Tetovo. Despite several violent incidents, including the demonstrations in Tetovo in 1995, the conflict was contained. A crucial factor here was the moderate leadership of the Macedonian president and the internal political accommodation between the Albanian and Macedonian political parties. From the start, the government was a coalition between Albanian and Macedonian parties, and this gave powerful incentives for the elites to pursue moderate policies.

Macedonia's precarious stability was severely tested by the outbreak of war in Kosovo, and the temporary flight of 350,000 Kosovo Albanians into Macedonia. The UN was forced to withdraw UNPREDEP, when China refused to renew its mandate in response to the Macedonian government's decision to recognize Taiwan. NATO's KFOR replaced UNPREDEP, but it seemed that this might deepen the divide between the Macedonians, who were critical of the NATO war on Serbia, and the Albanians who supported it. A further crisis arose in 2001 with the appearance of the NLA (National Liberation Army). This group was made up of KLA (Kosovo Liberation Army) fighters from Kosovo and Albanians from Macedonia. It combined advocates of Albanian rights in Macedonia and probably criminals who wanted to protect their drug-running operations – a good example of the combination of greed and grievance in a rebel group. For a while, the Macedonian government seemed unable to contain the rebellion, and the risk that it could spread and ignite a major conflict was obvious. But it did not. Yet again, the elite accommodation held the situation in check. With the help of US and EU mediators, the Albanian and Macedonian parties signed the Ohrid agreement, which provided for new elections, arms to be collected by NATO troops, a revision of the constitution to give more rights to Albanians, and civilian monitors to assist the return of refugees. The agreement provided for devolution of power to local governments, the legalization of the university at Tetovo and the use of the Albanian language in state institutions. The Albanian rebel leader Ali Ahmeti came into politics. Disputes continued in 2004 over the boundaries of these local governments, and on the ground economic difficulties and polarization between the ethnic communities continue to maintain a risk of further conflict. An EU-led military force, Operation Concordia, took over from NATO in March 2003. As in the Estonia case, the underlying conflicts are not yet fully reconciled, but Macedonia has managed to remain a unified state and to avoid an internal war. In this case the combination of cooperation between the political elites and international support has avoided what might well have been a bloody extension of the Yugoslav wars.

In both these European cases, international involvement to avoid conflict was strong, and these were relatively advanced economies. But Sub-Saharan Africa too, despite its proneness to armed conflicts, has striking cases of countries which have avoided armed conflict. Botswana, for example, is a diamond-rich developing country which has avoided the conflicts that have beset other diamond-rich countries like Sierra Leone and other Southern African countries like Angola and Mozambique. The country has had a democratic system since independence, though one party has dominated the political system. Traditionally a cattle-rearing aristocracy, Tswana society was reduced to a proletarianized peasantry under colonialism, but an educated group emerged on independence and invested its gains from education in cattle and trade. Botswana has managed to avoid the intense conflicts over control of the state between ethnic groups and downplays ethnic differences. Indigenous systems of land tenure have been gradually integrated with modern systems, and Land Boards, which have acquired powers formerly held by chiefs, grant land rights and manage disputes. Botswana's political stability and strong economic development have enabled it to escape the conflicts in the region, though unfortunately not the ravages of AIDS which have had a devastating impact on society in recent years.

Kenya has suffered from inter-ethnic conflicts associated with the control of the state by dominant ethnic groups. Stagnant or declining economic growth in the 1990s combined with conflicts in peripheral areas (such as among the pastoralists in the north-east) seemed to threaten the country's stability. However, the elections of 2002 brought the opposition to power peacefully – an unusual event in Africa. The new government's policy of providing free education, encouraging agricultural cooperatives and tackling corruption gained dividends initially in economic progress and international support. Notwithstanding its ethnic and economic divisions, Kenya has avoided large-scale internal conflict.

Similar stories of relative peace can be found if we turn from the country to the group level of analysis. Although ethnicity has been a frequent source of ethnic conflict in the 1990s and 2000s, there are

Table 5.2 Success and failure in confict prevention		
	Success	**Failure**
Light measures	Armed conflict averted	Armed conflict
Deep measures	Peaceful change	Conflict-prone situation

many ethnic groups which have lived peaceably, though not without conflict, together with majority communities: for example, the Chinese community in Malaysia, the French-speaking population in Canada, the Macedonian community in Albania, and so on. Horowitz (1985) and Gurr (2000) give examples and analyses of the factors that have prevented potential conflicts in these cases.

Assessing conflict prevention evidently depends considerably on the frame of analysis chosen and the criteria used to assess proneness to conflict. Wallensteen (2002b) offers a list of thirty candidates for conflict prevention analysis since the end of the Cold War where operational conflict prevention of some kind took place. A much larger list could be compiled to examine the impact of structural prevention. The study of the impact of both operational and structural prevention on conflict incidence, and of their interaction with forces fuelling conflict, is still in its infancy.

Conclusion

In this chapter we have looked at the causes and preventors of contemporary armed conflicts. If, as A. J. P. Taylor suggests, wars have both general and specific causes, then systems of conflict prevention should address both the generic conditions which make societies prone to armed conflicts, and the potential triggers which translate war-pronenss into armed conflict. If structural conflict prevention is successful in providing capacity to manage emergent conflicts peacefully at an early stage, it should make societies less conflict-prone. If operational conflict prevention is successful, it should avert armed conflicts, without necessarily removing the underlying conditions of proneness to armed conflict (see table 5.2). Both light and deep approaches to conflict prevention are clearly necessary.

The cases we have quoted suggest that conflict prevention is not easy. It is difficult for the preventors to gain a purchase in situations of violence or chaotic change, and episodes of violence can readily overwhelm them. Nevertheless, where preventive measures have begun, and where circumstances are propitious, a cumulative process of peacebuilding can be seen. The challenge is gradually to introduce and strengthen the preventors, and to foster a culture of prevention, with early identification, discussion and transformation of emergent conflicts.

Recommended reading

Hampson and Malone, eds (2002); Leatherman (1999); Wallensteen (1998).

CHAPTER 6

сдерживание

Containing Violent Conflict: Peacekeeping

Certainly the idea of an international peace force effective against a big disturber of the peace seems today unrealizable to the point of absurdity. We did, however, take at least a step in the direction of putting international force behind an international decision a year ago in the Suez crisis. The birth of this force was sudden and it was surgical. The arrangements for the reception of the infant were rudimentary and the midwives had no precedents or experience to guide them. Nevertheless, UNEF, the first genuinely international police force of its kind, came into being and into action. . . . We made at least a beginning then. If, on that foundation, we do not build something more permanent and stronger, we will once again have ignored realities, rejected opportunities and betrayed our trust. Will we never learn?

> *Extract from Lester Pearson's Nobel Peace Prize acceptance speech referring to his comments on the origins of United Nations Peacekeeping, 1957*

UNEF – UN Emergency Force (Middle East)

Sadly, in the 50th year of UN peacekeeping operations, the perceived failures and costs of the UN mission in former Yugoslavia, and recent experiences in Somalia, have led to widespread disillusionment. Yet if the world loses faith in peacekeeping, and responses to the new world disorder are limited to the extremes of total war or total peace, the world will become a more dangerous place. Rather than lose faith in the whole peace process, we need to analyse the changed operational circumstances and try to determine new doctrines for the future

> *General Sir Michael Rose, Commander UN Protection Force in Bosnia, 1994–5*

For critical theory, structural transformation based on social struggles immanent in globalization processes will introduce new forms of democratic peacekeeping in the short term if not rendering it largely obsolete in the long run.

> *Michael Pugh, Peacekeeping and Critical Theory (2004: 54)*

132

I N this chapter we examine the role for conflict resolution in the most challenging of environments – in areas of heated conflict where violence has become routine and the prevention of violent conflict has failed. In terms of the hourglass model in chapter 1 (figure 1.3), we noted how higher levels of violence need more robust forms of intervention. We suggested that peacekeeping is appropriate at three points on the escalation scale: to contain violence and prevent it from escalating to war; to limit the intensity, geographical spread and duration of war once it has broken out; and to consolidate a ceasefire and create space for reconstruction after the end of a war. The first of these relates to topics covered in chapter 5, the third to topics covered in chapter 8, so in this chapter we focus on the second: intervention to limit and contain the terrible effects of ongoing war. Here we are examining options at the most narrow part of the hourglass, where political and humanitarian space is most severely constrained. We focus on the changing role of UN peacekeepers in these situations (creating security space), and recognize that this peacekeeping role is integrally linked to the role of NGOs, UN civil agencies and aid agencies in responding to humanitarian needs (creating humanitarian space). There is a growing recognition that these agencies need to work together to link mitigation and relief to the political tasks that are necessary to settle the conflict and resolve it within a sustainable peace process (creating political space). The central argument in this chapter is that peacekeepers and the various humanitarian and development agencies working in war zones need to be aware of the conflict resolution dimension of their work. In short, there is a vital conflict resolution role for peacekeeping to play even during the most intense period of destruction (see table 6.1).

We begin by looking at the emergence and development of peacekeeping as a conflict resolution mechanism, outlining the principles and practices which defined it as it evolved through two phases, generally termed first- and second-generation peacekeeping missions. We then look at the results of research into the dynamics of war zones (the targeting of civilians, the destruction of social and cultural

Table 6.1 Conflict containment and peacekeeping

Phase	Mode of peacekeeping	Negative role	Positive role
Violence	Prevention (see ch. 5)		
War	Limitation	Limit spread	Create security space
		Limit intensity	Create humanitarian space
		Limit duration	Create political space
Ceasefire	Stabilization (see ch. 8)		

institutions, the persistence of 'warlords') which challenged second-generation peacekeeping missions in the 1990s to the point where they were seen, by some critics at least, as inadequate to protect civilians and restore peace. In the light of this, we look at the associated intervention controversy and focus on the current debate about the ways in which UN peacekeeping can be reformed as a more robust conflict resolution intervention mechanism appropriate to the challenges of the twenty-first century. These third-generation operations are sometimes called 'peace support operations' (PSOs) or 'peace operations', to distinguish them from the more circumscribed nature of traditional peacekeeping. We conclude by noting how all of this is contested by critical theoretic transformationists, and look at some of the (admittedly still rather embryonic) policy implications suggested by them.

First- and Second-Generation UN Peacekeeping, 1956–1995

United Nations peacekeeping and academic conflict resolution have much in common conceptually, and both emerged as distinct areas of theory and practice at about the same time – in the mid-1950s. When the first conflict resolution centres and journals were being established (see chapter 2), UN Secretary-General Dag Hammarskjold and UN General Assembly President Lester Pearson were defining the basic principles of peacekeeping in order to guide the work of the United Nations Emergency Force (UNEF I), created in response to the Suez crisis in the Middle East in 1956. Peacekeeping is not mentioned in the UN Charter, prompting the suggestion that it operated somewhere between Chapter 6 (the peaceful settlement of disputes) and Chapter 7 (enforcement) – Chapter 6½. Although *The Agenda for Peace* in the early 1990s attempted to override the principle of consent and the minimum use of force in certain circumstances, the UNEF I principles served to define the essence of UN peacekeeping at least until the mid-1990s, and were based on the consent of the conflict parties, the non-use of force except in self defence, political neutrality (not taking sides), impartiality (commitment to the mandate) and legitimacy (sanctioned and accountable to the Security Council advised by the Secretary-General).

During the period of the Cold War thirteen peacekeeping operations were established, mostly deployed in interstate conflicts (although ONUC in the Congo 1960–4 was an exception). Their main function was to monitor borders and establish buffer zones after the agreement of ceasefires. The missions were typically composed of lightly armed national troop contingents from small and neutral UN member states.

These early missions are usually termed 'first-generation peacekeeping' (Fetherston, 1994). Like the categorization used in chapter 2, the use of the idea of 'generations' of peacekeeping development is not intended to be exact and watertight. Some missions elude neat classification, persisting across the generational categories adopted here or incorporating activities that went beyond the traditional monitoring function (UNFICIP in Cyprus and ONUC in the Congo, for example). Nevertheless, peacekeeping has evolved to meet the differing challenges of conflict in different periods and contexts; doctrines and practices of peacekeeping have changed as lessons learned from deployment in more complex conflict environments are reflected and acted upon. Thus the expansion of peacekeeping in the deployments into hot civil wars in the Balkans and in Africa especially in the 1990s can be reasonably described as second-generation peacekeeping (what the British military called 'wider peacekeeping'). The further development of doctrine from the late 1990s, reflected in the use of the terms 'peace support operations', or 'peace operations', marked a third generation of peacekeeping, where missions operated under a Chapter 7 mandate and where they were more robustly equipped to enforce that mandate. Here, we use this idea of three generations of activity to trace the development of peacekeeping and its function in war zones.

From the late 1980s, and most noticeably following the publication of UN Secretary-General Boutros-Ghali's *Agenda for Peace* in 1992, there was a dramatic increase in the number and size of peacekeeping operations. At the beginning of 1988, when the Cold War was coming to an end, there were only five operations in the field: three in the Middle East, a small observer mission in Kashmir, and UNFICYP in Cyprus. Six years later there were three times that number (see table 6.2).

The numerical growth of peacekeeping operations during the 1990s was accompanied by a fundamental change in their nature, their function and their composition. The single ceasefire maintenance

Table 6.2 The growth of UN peacekeeping					
	1988	**1992**	**1994**	**2000**	**2004**
Number of active missions	5	11	17	14	16
Number of troop-contributing countries	26	56	76	89	103
Military and police	9,605	11,650	75,523	37,338	62,271
International civilian personnel	1,516	2,606	2,260	3,243	3,949
Annual UN peacekeeping $b	2.30	1.69	3.61	2.22	2.82

Source: UNDPKO

function associated with traditional operations evolved into a multi-plicity of tasks involving security, humanitarian and political objectives. At the same time, the composition of post-Cold War peacekeeping operations became more diverse and complex: peacekeepers were drawn from a wider variety of sources (military, civilian police and diplomatic), nations and cultures. Second-generation peacekeeping was multilateral, multidimensional, and multinational/multicultural. By the mid-1990s the number of countries contributing to peacekeeping missions had almost tripled, from twenty-six in the late 1980s, and this trend has continued to the point that currently there are now more than a hundred different nations contributing forces to UN peacekeeping missions, amongst whom the dominant contributors are not the small neutral nations normally associated with peacekeeping (Canadians, Irish and Scandinavians, for example), nor the world powers or Security Council P5 countries, which became very involved in the mid-1990s in the Balkans (especially British and French troops); but, rather, it is nations in Asia (Bangladesh, Pakistan, India) and Africa (Nigeria, Ethiopia, Ghana) that make the major contribution to current missions.

Multilateralism implies the involvement of several levels of actors in an operation: these could be the two or more conflicting parties, the peacekeepers themselves, as well as the UN and other international actors. The new operations were multidimensional, incorporating military, civilian police and other civilian components, all of which fulfilled their distinct functions. The military component, i.e. the land, naval and air forces contributed by UN member states, included both armed and unarmed soldiers (the latter are often referred to as military observers). Essentially, the military component's function was to serve in a supporting role: to guarantee and maintain a secure environment in which the civilian components could conduct their work. Civilian police components (CIVPOL) also became increasingly important players in peacekeeping operations. Operating under the authority of the UN Security Council, international police monitors assisted in the restoration of the rule of law and in the maintenance of public order. Finally, there developed a sizeable civilian component consisting of two main groups. Firstly, there were inter-governmental organizations (IGOs), or organizations which are mandated by agreements drawn up between two or more states. This includes all UN agencies, regional organizations such as the OAU or the OSCE, as well as the International Committee of the Red Cross/Red Crescent (ICRC). Second, there was a wide variety of non-governmental organizations (NGOs), national and international organizations that are constituted separately from the government of the country in which they are founded. In contrast to the military component, which draws its strength from the effective coercive influence it can exercise over belligerents, the civilian component's power base may be diplomatic, economic, ideological, scientific and technical, humanitarian, and/or legal.

The development and deployment of these second-generation missions took place in the context of a new mood of optimism that conflicts could be managed and resolved peacefully through multilateral initiatives in which the UN, with the decline of superpower rivalry post-Cold War, could take a leading role. The optimism was expressed most clearly in the *Agenda for Peace*, which placed UN peacekeeping operations as key instruments within a new and broader context of collective human security. This UN vision for security, developed in the early years of the 1990s, was based around the value of positive peace and included a commitment to satisfy basic human needs, to protect human rights, and to promote economic equality and political participation. Significantly, according to Boutros-Ghali: 'in . . . situations of internal crisis, the United Nations will need to respect the sovereignty of states, [but the] time of absolute and exclusive sovereignty has passed . . . [and] it is the task of leaders of states today to understand this and to find a balance between good internal governance and the requirements of an ever more interdependent world' (Boutros-Ghali, 1992: 9).

However, as table 6.2 shows, the confidence in peacekeeping, at its height in the mid-1990s, began to wane in the closing years of the decade. The number of troops deployed, the number of deployments and the budget committed to peacekeeping all declined (although not the number of troop-providing countries). Peacekeepers faced seemingly insurmountable problems and were frequently exposed as powerless to protect civilians, humanitarian workers and even themselves, in the civil wars in former Yugoslavia, in the genocide in Rwanda and in Somalia.

The debacle in October 1993, when eighteen US soldiers were killed and publicly humiliated as part of the UNOSOM II mission in Somalia, effectively ended any possibility of US troops participating integrally and in significant numbers in UN-led missions in future. At the end of the decade the UN published the reports of inquiries into two other events which marked the nadir of its experience in trying to resolve conflicts. Approximately 800,000 people were killed during the 1994 genocide in Rwanda between April and July 1994. A UN peacekeeping mission (UNAMIR) already in Rwanda, but with its force numbers severely reduced, was largely powerless to prevent the killings, despite the pleas of its force commander, because the Security Council was reluctant to intervene so soon after the Somalia disaster. A year later, in one of the worst war crimes committed in Europe since the end of the Second World War, the Bosnian Muslim town of Srebrenica fell to a siege by Serb militias, during which 8,000 Muslims were killed under the eyes of the UN peacekeeping contingent deployed when Srebenica had become the world's first civilian safe area in 1993 (Security Council Resolution 819; 18 April). Two UN reports concluded that, faced with attempts to murder, expel or terrorize entire populations, the neutral, impartial and mediating role of the United Nations was inadequate. Both also called for a process of reflection to clarify and to improve the capacity of the United Nations to respond to various forms of conflict, and especially to 'address the mistakes of peacekeeping at the end of this century and to meet the challenges of the next one' (UN Report, 1999, 1999b).

When a new set of security challenges manifested themselves in the form of the attack on the USA on 11 September 2001, followed by the invasions of Afghanistan and Iraq, the world organization appeared even more marginalized. Nevertheless, as the world turned its attention to these new challenges to security, it should be noted that UN peacekeeping has not only continued, it was also revived and even modified. As table 6.2 above illustrates, by 2004 more countries than ever before were contributing to UN peacekeeping missions, and the sixteen missions active in that year deployed numbers of peacekeepers close to the historic highs of the mid-1990s.

War Zones, War Economies and Cultures of Violence

Amongst the most challenging situations which confront those wishing to engage in conflict resolution are those where warlords and militias have come to establish their power over civilian populations. In such situations, 'not only is there little recognition of the distinction between combatant and civilian, or of any obligation to spare women, children and the elderly, but the valued institutions and way of life of a whole population can be targeted' with the objective of creating 'states of terror which penetrate the entire fabric of grassroots social relations . . . as a means of social control' (Summerfield, 1996: 1). Civilians and humanitarian staff are the targets in these wars, not the accidental victims of it. In the First World War over 80 per cent of battlefield deaths were combatants; by the 1990s over 90 per cent of war-related deaths were civilians, killed in their own homes and communities, which have become the battlefields of many contemporary wars. As Nordstrom has remarked, the least dangerous place to be in most contemporary wars is in the military (1992: 271). 'Dirty war' strategies, originally identified with state-sponsored terrorism, are now a feature of a widening band of militias, paramilitaries, warlords and armies seeking control of resources through depredation, terror and force. The threat posed to civilians is perceived to be greater still following the events of 11 September 2001, when global mass casualty terrorism and the actions of suicide bombers became a new or at least a more persistent concern for the international community (with an estimate of more than 7,000 killed in some 190 terrorist attacks in 2002).

Are these behaviours in contemporary wars senseless and irrational convulsions of violence, expressions of ancient hatreds and regressions to tribal war and neo-medieval warlords, as some argue (Kaplan, 1994)? Or are there more systematic explanations, as those writing from an anthropological and radical political economy perspective suggest? An appropriate conflict resolution response will depend upon what answers are given to these questions.

In a pattern that has been well documented in recent years, for example in parts of Africa such as Tigray, Eritrea, Southern and Western Sudan, Northern Uganda, Angola and Somalia (Macrae and Zwi, eds, 1994: 13–20), scorched earth tactics are common, with livestock seized, grain stores attacked and looted, wells and watering places poisoned. Forced population movements are engineered to perpetuate dependency and control. Actors like the international drug cartels in Central and South America, the Taliban in Afghanistan and rebel groups in West Africa had effectively set up parallel economies, trading in precious resources such as hardwoods, diamonds, drugs and so on. In Cambodia the Khmer Rouge leadership profited so much from the smuggling of timber and gems across the Thai border that it saw little incentive to demobilize its forces as agreed under the Paris Peace Accords of 1991, while there is evidence of some collusion between the Khmer Rouge and the Cambodian Army in mutual profiteering from this trade (Keen, 1995). Although this does not apply to all internal conflicts, there are war-zone economies where civilians are seen as 'a resource base to be either corralled, plundered, or cleansed' (Duffield, 1997: 103). Humanitarian and development aid is captured, and humanitarian workers kidnapped, held hostage and killed. These wars can be seen to be both lucrative and rational for those who can take advantage and are prepared to act violently to gain power.

This is the point at which to re-engage with the economic analyses of what perpetuates endemic wars of this kind, as discussed in chapter 4. We saw how, through the project on 'The Economics of Civil War, Crime and Violence', Collier and his colleagues at the World Bank have offered important new insights into the difficulties faced by peacekeepers and other agencies active in areas of conflict (Collier et al., 2003).[1] They started from a concern that large-scale political and criminal violence was trapping large parts of the developing world in a cycle of poverty and low or negative economic growth. Their suggestion is that a significant element of the motivation for political violence does not come from a politics as grievance discourse (the assumption of much conflict research and of the *Agenda for Peace*), but from a dynamic where the economic motivation to pursue conflict becomes compelling. World Bank-sponsored research suggests that financial/economic factors explain the onset of civil war more powerfully than political grievance factors, although as rebel groups mobilize they gain recruits rapidly by the development of ideologies based on grievances and political claims. From this perspective most civil wars are driven not by ideology or grievance, but by greed and predation. In chapters 3 and 4, we argued that there are genuine identity-based and ideology-based conflicts that are fuelled by failures of existing government structures to accommodate legitimate political aspirations or to satisfy needs, and that economic motives do not explain the deeper dynamics of most major armed conflicts. Nevertheless, in fragile 'quasi-states', particularly where formal structures have hollowed out and war economies have become endemic, such analysis is compelling. Cooper (2001) argues that the trade in conflict goods, generating opportunities to acquire wealth and the means to continue financing arms acquisition, has significant implications for peacekeeping and peacebuilding activities in areas of conflict of this kind. He suggests that the development of strategies for restricting the trade in conflict goods (such as the controls placed on trade in Sierra Leone's conflict diamonds) may be as significant as programmes which prioritize arms control and disarmament in peace processes. The development of conflict goods control programmes is still at a rudimentary stage in war-zone conflict management, although it is becoming increasingly recognized that those who benefit from, and who are therefore motivated to perpetuate, war economies need to be addressed in the early stages of conflict stabilization in peacekeeping.

Strategies to achieve this are now beginning to be identified in the form of a range of policies that can be pursued by governments, regional organizations and the UN. In identifying some of these strategies and policies, researchers have pointed to important implications for the role of peacekeeping forces. Thus it has been suggested that UN peace operation mandates need to be formulated with an awareness of the economic reality of particular conflicts, especially so that peacekeeping forces can be deployed to establish control over resource-rich areas in order to prevent illicit exploitation and smuggling by factions which wish to use the proceeds to perpetuate conflict. The UN operation in Sierra Leone (UNAMSIL) is presently deployed in the Kono diamond district in what has proved to date to be a successful effort to curtail such activities (Wilton Park Conference, 2003).

For analysts like Outram, however, in his account of the civil war in Liberia, theories of economic predation of this kind do not go far enough, because they do not explain the extent and absurdity of the violence involved. The violence goes beyond rational expectations of what can be gained economically, for a rational warlord would not kill the goose that lays the golden egg. To explain it, we have to take into account socio-psychological considerations as well as economic motivations. In Liberia, accumulated fears drove people beyond killing the 'ethnic enemy' into factions which practised a general and undirected vengeance (Outram, 1997: 368). We can understand this phenomenon further by considering the work of Nordstrom. While Outram concentrated on the experience of the warring factions and the political economy which they constructed, Nordstrom has worked on the experiences of the victims of the violence. Following field research in Mozambique and Sri Lanka, she explained the many stories of absurd destruction and the use of terror in warfare as deliberate efforts to destroy the normal meanings that define and guide daily life (Nordstrom, 1992: 269). This is the process whereby dirty war becomes the means through which economies of violence merge with what Nordstrom calls 'cultures of violence'. As she puts it, 'violence parallels power', and people come to have no alternative but to accept 'fundamental knowledge constructs that are based on force' (ibid.). So this is yet another dimension of endemic war zones that peacekeepers and conflict resolvers have to try to understand if they venture to intervene in active war zones.

Working in war zones, then, clearly does create serious challenges for conflict resolution, and requires the analyst or intervener to be aware of their particular dynamics. We have commented elsewhere, with reference to humanitarian intervention, how principles of humanity, impartiality, neutrality and universality are necessary to guide action, but also how they are unavoidably compromised in the intensely politicized environment of active conflict (Ramsbotham and Woodhouse, 1996). Conflict resolvers have to be aware of this, while nevertheless continuing to search for an effective and internationally legitimate antidote to the untold misery inflicted on so many by ongoing war.

To Intervene or Not to Intervene? New Requirements for Third-Generation Peacekeeping

In response to such challenges, the search for a doctrine for third–generation peacekeeping begins from the prior question: can there be any role for conflict resolution activities, or indeed for UN peace-

keeping, in these circumstances? May it not even be counter-productive? Providing a negative response to these questions, a series of
highly critical accounts appeared in the academic literature from the
mid-1990s, questioning both the efficacy of UN peacekeeping and the
conflict resolution model with which it was associated.

From one direction came criticism of the ineffectiveness of impartial
and non-forcible intervention in war zones (Rieff, 1994). The alternatives
of either letting the conflicts 'burn themselves out' or of intervening
decisively on one side were seen as better options (Luttwak, 1999; Betts,
1994). From the other direction, as noted in chapter 1, came criticism of
the inappropriateness of what were seen to be attempts to impose western liberal democratic models, together with associated conflict resolution assumptions, behind which lurked the self-interest of powerful
intervening countries (Clapham, 1996b). The requirement for an effective and internationally legitimate third generation of peacekeeping
had to meet both these criticisms, somehow combining greater military robustness with commitment to genuine international norms.
We can illustrate the attempt to do this by way of two examples. The
key UN initiative has been the *Report of the Panel on United Nations Peace
Operations*, the Brahimi Report (2000). However, the shift in peacekeeping doctrine was initiated from both 'lessons learned' within the
Department of Peacekeeping Operations of the UN, and also by the
national defence academies of countries that had participated in
the larger-scale deployments in the 1990s, and that would no longer
agree to send their military forces into conflicts for which they are
inadequately prepared and supported. This new way of thinking can be
exemplified by looking first at the development of British peacekeeping doctrine.

The British military refers to this new form of peacekeeping as
'peace support operations' (PSO). A PSO is defined as:

> An operation that impartially makes use of diplomatic, civil and mili-
> tary means, normally in pursuit of United Nations Charter purposes
> and principles, to restore or maintain peace. Such operations may
> include conflict prevention, peacemaking, peace enforcement, peace-
> keeping, peacebuilding and/or humanitarian operations. (UK, Ministry
> of Defence, 2004: 103)

And here is the most recent UK PSO doctrine statement on *The Military
Contribution to Peace Support Operations* (May 2004):

> For the foreseeable future United Kingdom (UK) foreign policy is likely
> to underpin its conflict prevention activities with the regeneration or
> sustainment of fragile states. The UK government usually undertakes
> such operations as part of United Nations (UN) led operations or as
> part of multilateral endeavours, occasionally it undertakes unilateral

actions as in Sierra Leone in 2000. The generic title of Peace Support Operations (PSOs) is given by the military to these activities. Typically, the UK's Armed Forces are given responsibility for preventing or suppressing any conflict so that others can undertake activities that will alleviate the immediate symptoms of a conflict and/or a fragile state. Usually, there are associated activities to ensure stability in the long term. (Ibid.: 101)

Operational planning no longer separates combat operations from 'operations other than war' (OOTW), but envisages use of military capabilities across the full 'spectrum of tension' from traditional peacekeeping duties through to combat against spoilers and enemies of the peace. At the tactical level, 'where action actually takes place' and formation and unit commanders 'engage directly with adversaries, armed factions and the civil population', there is a similar – and very demanding – requirement to combine combat skills with those of negotiation, mediation and consent-generation. The aim of the new doctrine is to create peacekeeping operations that are sufficiently flexible, robust, combat-ready and sensitive to the overall peace-support purpose of the mission:

> In PSO, the desired strategic effect, or intent, is to uphold international peace and security by resolving conflicts by means of prevention, conciliation, deterrence, containment or stabilisation. (Ibid.: 3, sect. 3)

Peace support operations can thus be seen to be distinct from traditional UN peacekeeping on the one hand, and traditional war-fighting on the other (see table 6.3).

The PSO concept has, with variations, been embraced by an ever-increasing portion of the international military community, including NATO, and has consequently become the doctrinal basis for the launching of many modern peacekeeping operations. It is arguable that the deployment of KFOR in Kosovo was an early example of the

Table 6.3 Traditional peacekeeping, peace support operations and war

Traditional peacekeeping	Peace support operations	War
Universal consent	General consent of target populations, not of spoilers	No consent
Political neutrality between main conflict parties	No neutrality if a conflict party opposes the mandate	No neutrality
Impartiality in fulfilling mandate	Impartiality in fulfilling mandate	No impartiality
Non-use of force except in self-defence	Full spectrum of force needed to fulfil mandate	Full spectrum of force
International mandate	Normally uphold UN Charter purposes and principles	National interest

application of this strategy. Certainly, the use of Australian forces to lead the peace operation in East Timor in 1999 is a further example, as was the reinforcement of UN forces in Sierra Leone by British forces in the summer of 2000.

Turning now to the Brahimi Report concerning the future of UN peacekeeping, this lesson has been taken on board. The report was produced by a panel convened by Kofi Annan and chaired by Lakhdar Brahimi, the former Foreign Minister of Algeria. The panel published its findings in August 2000, laying out a wide-ranging set of recommendations for increasing the United Nations capacity for peace operations. The aim is to avoid the failures of the past by preparing forces in a more calculated way during the pre-deployment phase, and by more realistically appraising the level of forces and resources needed to achieve mandate objectives. The report recommends that forces must only be deployed if and when they have been given realistic and achievable mandates, and only when it is clear that they will be provided with the resources necessary to achieve those mandate objectives. In a clear intention to avoid the weaknesses of the second-generation model which did so much to undermine the credibility of the international organization, Brahimi insisted on the case for robust peacekeeping:

> No failure did more to damage the standing and credibility of UN peacekeeping in the 1990s than its reluctance to distinguish victim from aggressor. . . . Once deployed, United Nations peacekeepers must be able to carry out their mandate professionally and successfully. This means that United Nations military units must be capable of defending themselves, other mission components and the mission's mandate. Rules of engagement should be sufficiently robust and not force United Nations contingents to cede the initiative to their attackers. This means, in turn, that the Secretariat must not apply best-case planning assumptions to situations where the local actors have historically exhibited worst case behaviour. It means that mandates should specify an operation's authority to use force. It means bigger forces, better equipped and more costly but able to be a credible deterrent. In particular, United Nations forces for complex operations should be afforded the field intelligence and other capabilities needed to mount an effective defence against violent challengers. (Brahimi Report, 2000: x)

The purpose of this robust force structure is not as an end in itself, but to protect a continuum of activity from protecting people from harm to peacebuilding and conflict prevention. From the perspective of conflict resolution, there are several relevant structural changes that need to be made. The report recommends, for instance, that civilian police and human rights experts become better integrated into the peacekeeping mechanism. It also calls for more effective and integrated civilian roles in order to effectively augment and develop the military security function and, at the same time, to properly address the unique challenges of post-conflict peacebuilding.

To strengthen this process, the report supported efforts to create a pilot Peacebuilding Unit within the UN Department for Political Affairs, and recommended that this unit should be fully funded, subject to a positive evaluation of the pilot programmes. This proposal marks a new and welcome recognition that the civilian elements of peacekeeping operations, which are vital to the prospect of a long-term sustainability of the peace process, need to be adequately resourced, integrated and prepared. In terms of practice in the field, the UN has established peacebuilding support offices (PBSOs) in the Central African Republic, Guinea-Bissau, Liberia and Tajikistan on a pilot basis. These offices are designed to coordinate peacebuilding activities in the field by working with both governments and non-governmental parties and complementing ongoing UN development activities.

Responses to Brahimi have varied. For example, the International Peace Academy has conducted a series of regional dialogues on the Brahimi Report based on meetings in London (Europe), Johannesburg (Africa), Singapore (Asia) and Buenos Aires (Latin America). In summary, they reported that in both Africa and Europe the need for more robust peacekeeping mandates, enabling peacekeepers to deal with spoilers, was strongly supported. The idea of developing better-trained and better-equipped regional or even continental peacekeeping forces in Africa was also supported, with European contributors recognizing a role in supporting this capacity-building. However, in part to overcome suspicions of western interference in the affairs of the countries of the South, participants in the African, Asian and Latin-American dialogues expressed the need:

> to make peace-building a focus of peacekeeping activities and for greater local ownership of the processes of peace-building. The UN cannot deliver sustainable outcomes without utilizing the knowledge and experience of local and regional actors. Training and capacity building for local civil society actors, including a large proportion of women, should therefore be a priority. Emphasis should be on building the capacity for local governance, as in the later stages of the East Timor mission, rather than on deploying a vast number of international staff of highly uneven quality. (International Peace Academy, 2001)

This requirement is echoed in a UN Department of Peacekeeping Operations (DPKO) summary of lessons learned from a series of post-mission reports, which identified the support of the local population, sensitivity to cultural context and the need to build inclusive peace constituencies as essential prerequisites for any successful peacekeeping operation (see box 6.1). This is a theme that is looked at further in chapter 9.

Box 6.1 Conflict resolution, peacekeeping and the local community

- The local population should perceive the mission and its staff as being impartial. When the parties to a conflict attempt to use the mission or some of its staff to their own advantage, as they often do, the mission and its information component must be able to maintain and project its image of impartiality and neutrality. The effort to maintain impartiality, however, must not promote inaction. On the contrary, peacekeepers must discharge their tasks firmly and objectively.
- The United Nations must also demonstrate a commitment to the principles of transparency and accountability in its activities. It must not be perceived as being 'above the law'. Designating an ombudsman, or a focal point, to consider the grievances of the local population against the mission or its staff could be considered.
- Respect for the cultural traditions and social mores of the local population is an important part of maintaining good relations with the local population. Briefings on history, culture, and other aspects of life of the host country should be conducted for all staff.
- Efforts at peace-building – such as assistance in the restoration of basic civic services and support in rehabilitation and reconstruction of a devastated country – can be an effective way of winning over the local population and increasing grassroots support for the operation.
- In its peacekeeping and peacebuilding efforts, the operation is best advised to work through existing local authorities and community elders and its peace initiatives must be closely tailored to indigenous practices of conflict management, provided these do not contradict accepted international standards of human rights and humanitarian law. However, in areas of recent and ongoing conflict, the operation must exercise great caution in identifying local community leaders, since it is often unclear as to who actually represents the community. Due to strife, population displacements and other extenuating circumstances, traditional societal patterns and roles may have become blurred or have submerged under new, often militaristic, hierarchies.
- As peacekeeping missions become more multifaceted, peacebuilding is becoming an integral part of their activities. Emphasis should be placed on support of processes and institutions that reinforce reconciliation between warring parties and reconstruction of economic and social infrastructure, so that once the mission pulls out it does not leave behind a vacuum, but a foundation of peace and development that the country can build on.
- The United Nations must gear the composition of its peacekeeping forces to the new and changing role they are expected to play. The force could consist of mainly fighting troops when the imperative is maintenance of peace and security. This can be changed gradually, when the emphasis of the mission has changed to peace support and peacebuilding, to include more engineering or other units that could assist in the reconstruction of the country.
- Discretionary funds for peacebuilding should be made available to the SRSG [Special Representative of the Secretary-General] to enhance the SRSG's leverage with the local authorities and the humanitarian community. The mission could use these funds for quick-impact projects and infrastructure repairs, among other things.
- An integral part of United Nations peacekeeping should be the promotion of 'indirect peace-building', i.e. the resurrection of a web of non-governmental civic, professional, business and other associations.
- During the liquidation of an operation, consideration should be given to what resources could be left behind in the country to assist in post-conflict peacebuilding.

Source: Multidisciplinary Peacekeeping: Lessons From Recent Experience.
Lessons Learned Unit, DPKO website, <http://www.un.org./Depts/dpko/
dpko/index.asp.

Third-Generation Peacekeeping and Human Security

In this section we acknowledge the central criticism that third-generation peacekeeping from a conflict resolution perspective may be an attempt to combine what cannot be combined – greater military robustness with the service of genuinely cosmopolitan international norms. The key danger is that those with the military capacity will take on such intervention roles outside the ambit of the United Nations, and will thereby forfeit the international legitimacy upon which such operations in the end depend. Much of the debate about the evaluation of peacekeeping has been at the level of policy and operational aspects, with more than three hundred recommendations for reform being made in a series of major *fin de siècle* assessments and reports published in 2000. In the midst of this detail, commentators like Peou (2003) have suggested that this 'cult of policy relevance' has meant a failure to address the more fundamental critiques of peacekeeping pitched at the meta-theoretical level. Examined like this, third-generation peacekeeping can be understood as a component of a broader and emancipatory theoretical framework centred on the idea of collective human security, in turn situated within emergent institutions and processes of global cosmopolitan governance.

In relation to the UN, the theory was announced in the *Agenda for Peace*, and developed more recently in the Millennium Report, *We The Peoples: The Role of the United Nations in the Twenty First Century* under the leadership of Kofi Annan (United Nations, 2000). The 2000 Millennium Report was organized around the themes of the quest for freedom from fear (through conflict management and resolution), freedom from want (through economic development and growth) and sustaining the future (through careful husbanding of the earth's resources and ecosystem). According to Thakur, freedom from fear was central to the other two elements in Kofi Annan's trinity of objectives for the UN in the new century, putting peacekeeping and peacebuilding 'at the cutting edge of the UN's core function in the contemporary world' (Thakur, 2001: 117). So the normative basis for all this was the claim that a new security paradigm, collective human security, was emerging which gave sense, value and direction to the mission of the UN in the twenty-first century, and third-generation peacekeeping was integral to it. Similar conclusions were reached by the International Commission on Intervention and State Sovereignty (ICISS), initiated by the government of Canada at the UN General Assembly in September 2000 (see box 6.2)

Box 6.2 Human security

The meaning and scope of the concept of security have become much broader since the UN Charter was signed in 1945. Human security means the security of people – their physical safety, their economic and social well-being, respect for their dignity and worth as human beings, and the protection of their human rights and fundamental freedoms. The growing recognition worldwide that concepts of security must include people as well as states has marked an important shift in international thinking during the past decade. Secretary-General Kofi Annan himself put the issue of human security at the centre of the current debate, when in his statement to the 54th session of the General Assembly he announced his intention to 'address the prospects for human security and intervention in the new century'.

The traditional, narrow perception of security leaves out the most elementary and legitimate concerns of ordinary people regarding security in their daily lives. It also diverts enormous amounts of national wealth and human resources into armaments and armed forces, while countries fail to protect their citizens from chronic insecurities of hunger, disease, inadequate shelter, crime, unemployment, social conflict and environmental hazard. When rape is used as an instrument of war and ethnic cleansing, when thousands are killed by floods resulting from a ravaged countryside and when citizens are killed by their own security forces, then it is entirely insufficient to think of security in terms of national or territorial security alone. The concept of human security can and does embrace such diverse circumstances.

Source: ICISS, 2001: 15

Chaired by Gareth Evans and Mohamed Sahnoun, the ICISS was formed in an attempt to answer the crucial question posed by Kofi Annan at the UN General Assembly in 1999 and again in 2000:

> [I]f humanitarian intervention is, indeed, an unacceptable assault on sovereignty, how should we respond to a Rwanda, to a Srebrenica – to gross and systematic violations of human rights that affect every precept of our common humanity? (ICISS, 2001: vii)

The outcome of their investigation was to suggest a way of moving forward in the sovereignty/intervention debate by suggesting the use of the term 'responsibility to protect' (rather than the 'right to humanitarian intervention'). This was intended to provide a clearer way forward for the international community in pursuit of international human rights norms and the human security agenda. The principles that are seen to guide military intervention prioritize international legitimacy for the action, and the operational criteria are consonant with third-generation peacekeeping (or PSO) thinking.

The preoccupation with the reform of UN peacekeeping outlined above has been associated with a new phase of expansion in the new millennium, and at times sizeable and ambitious UN operations have been mounted. There has been a corresponding recovery in the number of UN peacekeepers. By 2001, the number of military and police personnel serving with UN peacekeeping missions, for example, had risen to 47,800 (see table 6.2 for comparison). By 2004 the number had risen again to more than 60,000 peacekeepers (the large majority of these from Bangladesh, Pakistan, Nigeria, Ethiopia, Ghana and India) deployed in sixteen missions. Of these sixteen, seven were new missions deployed between 1999 and 2004: in the DR Congo (MONUC, 1999), Eritrea-Ethiopia (UNMEE, 2000), East Timor (Timor Leste) (UNMISET, 2002), Liberia (UNMIL, 2003), Burundi (ONUB, 2004), Ivory Coast (UNOCI, 2004) and Haiti (MINUSTAH, 2004). All of these are sizeable missions with complex mandates and authorized with enforcement powers under Chapter VII of the UN Charter.

While this expansion suggests that peacekeeping remains a vital instrument in pursuing conflict resolution goals internationally, the problem is that in the context of the human security agenda outlined above, and in the light of Security Council Resolution 1296 (2000), which effectively confirmed that the deliberate targeting of civilians in armed conflict and the denial of humanitarian access to civilian populations in war zones constituted a threat to international peace and security, the potential demands on the duty to protect overwhelms the capacity of the UN to act. Robust peacekeeping missions are now being mounted, not under UN command, but by a small number of regional security organizations and coalitions of the willing and capable: such as NATO forces in Bosnia and Kosovo providing enforcement capacity (IFOR, SFOR and KFOR); Nigerian peacekeeping forces (ECOMOG); and a British-led IMAT (International Military Advisory Team) in Sierra Leone, working alongside but independently of the UNAMSIL force; and the Australian military providing the leadership of the force in East Timor (INTERFET/ UNTAET).

Chandler notes the danger of this subcontracting of peacekeeping:

> The transformation of the UN's peacekeeping role to that of the civilian rather than military tasks of peace operations will confirm the position of the UN as the handmaiden to NATO . . . the pre-eminent 'coalition of the willing', rather than the authorizing authority. While NATO powers will have an increasingly free hand to define the limits of sovereignty in the non-Western world, and intervene when they consider it necessary, the UN will have the task of cleaning up afterwards and will have to take responsibility for the unrealistic expectations raised by the growing internationalization of conflict situations. (2001: 17)

The way in which third-generation peacekeeping is in flux remains unclear. From early manifestations of third-generation peacekeeping we can identify two variants of the model. First, unilateral action by a nation, grouping of nations or a regional security organization, justifying intervention through the duty to protect principle (NATO in Bosnia and Kosovo), but subsequently and retrospectively gaining UN legitimacy. Second, the re-enforcement of an existing UN mission by more robust military forces under the command of a national centre, either working alongside the mission while independent of it, or providing its main command component (the British in Sierra Leone). We illustrate each of these below.

Case Studies

Third-generation peacekeeping in Kosovo

The intervention in Kosovo initially took the form of air strikes against Serbian forces in Kosovo and Serbia by NATO forces, while the post-conflict phase was entrusted to the UN with the peacekeeping force still under NATO command, but subsequently recognized by the UN. In June 1999, following an agreement between NATO and the Yugoslav army, and a second one with the Yugoslav government brokered by EU and Russian special envoys, NATO called off its air strikes. Concurrently, the UN Security Council announced its decision to deploy an international civil and security presence in Kosovo under UN auspices.

This resolution to the conflict was to be based on the following principles, adopted on 6 May by the Foreign Ministers of the G8:

- an immediate and verifiable end to violence and repression;
- the withdrawal of all military, police and paramilitary forces of the Federal Republic of Yugoslavia (FRY);
- the deployment of an effective international and security presence, with substantial NATO participation and under a unified command;
- the safe return of all refugees;
- initiation of a political process to provide for self-government and for the demilitarization of the KLA;
- a comprehensive effort towards economic development of the crisis region.

The security force, KFOR, authorized under Chapter VII of the UN Charter and commanded by NATO's North Atlantic Council, entered Kosovo on 12 June 1999. The Security Council authorized the Secretary-General to establish an interim civilian administration in the region. By mid-July 1999, the Secretary-General presented a comprehensive framework for the work of what was to become known as the

United Nations Mission in Kosovo (UNMIK). UNMIK was given authority in Kosovo over all legislative and executive powers, as well as for the administration of the judiciary. Its work was to be integrated into five phases, and encompassed support for returning refugees, the restoration of public services (including health, education and social services), the deployment of civilian police (CIVPOL), the development of an economic recovery plan and the development of stable institutions for the promotion of democratic and autonomous self-government.

UNMIK was divided into four sections, each of them involved in the civilian aspects of restoring peace. These sections are known as the 'four pillars'. Pillar One consists of the civilian administration under UN direction; Pillar Two carries out humanitarian assistance led by UNHCR; Pillar Three is concerned with democratization and institution-building led by the Organization for Security and Cooperation in Europe (OSCE); and Pillar Four, led by the European Union, is charged with economic reconstruction.

This structure serves as a good example of just how a coalition of organizations is working to implement the broader goals of conflict resolution and peacebuilding. While it is still too early to comment on how well this project in Kosovo will work, it does seem clear that military interventions alone do not in themselves restore peace. We must, therefore, come to understand, first, how to mobilize and utilize local and international resources effectively for peacekeeping and peacebuilding under the auspices of the UN and/or other regional organizations working in partnership with the UN. Second, we must find more effective ways to improve and coordinate links between the control and containment of violence in war-torn regions (the security and policing function) and the development of processes whereby trust and cooperation can be sustained or restored and peacebuilding activities realistically supported (the civilian conflict resolution function). These issues are taken up again in chapters 8 and 9.

Third-generation peacekeeping in Sierra Leone

British involvement following the near collapse of the UN Mission in Sierra Leone presented an early example of UK PSO doctrine in practice. The UN Mission in Sierra Leone (UNAMSIL) was deployed to help implement the 1999 Lomé Peace Agreement between Sierra Leonean warring parties. The UN force was mandated to assist in the demobilization of armed groups, to monitor adherence to an agreed ceasefire, and eventually to provide electoral support towards establishing a lasting peace. However, there was a strong likelihood of violent non-compliance by some of the parties, notably the Revolutionary United Front (RUF), not least due to acknowledged flaws in the Lomé agreement. Indeed, the

RUF duly violated the ceasefire, continued to abuse human rights and opposed demobilization. Ultimately, widespread fighting resumed, with which UNAMSIL proved unable to cope, resulting in the seizure of 500 of its peacekeepers by RUF militias.

According to Wilkinson (2000: 18), some of UNAMSIL's fundamental shortcomings included:

- a consensual peacekeeping and not peace enforcement mandate;
- poorly equipped and trained troops;
- the lack of a 'lead nation' to coordinate command and control structures;
- inadequate support from the Department of Peace-keeping Operations (DPKO) at UN Headquarters in New York.

Doctrinal confusion was a major contributing factor in UNAMSIL's problems. The operational environment clearly demanded an enforcement capability, but, despite UNAMSIL's Chapter VII mandate, agreement over such a robust approach within the UN system has proved much harder to achieve and many of the original troop-contributing countries (TCCs) to UNAMSIL did not, in fact, subscribe to PSO doctrine. An effective enforcement capacity requires a common 'doctrine, standard operating procedures, joint and combined operational planning and common training standards and experience' amongst TCCs, which was not the case in Sierra Leone. In May 2000 the RUF took 500 UN peacekeepers hostage. At the time of the kidnappings, UNAMSIL was a disparate collection of contingents from more than thirty countries, with no consistent operational infrastructure. Moreover, they arrived piecemeal and many had neither been trained nor equipped to cope with the rigours of enforcement. The British army had also learned that enforcement requires an accomplished military formation based on the lead-nation concept. Finally, UNAMSIL's operational support was supplied by planning capacity within the DPKO in New York, whose already insufficient capability had been further eroded by the withdrawal of 'gratis' officers for political reasons by the General Assembly in 1999.

UK PSO doctrine highlights three fundamental features of what was required to support peace in Sierra Leone effectively:

1 The threat to peace was multidimensional, demanding a multi-functional political approach, including national and regional diplomatic activities, military initiatives, humanitarian assistance and economic and development programmes.
2 The volatility of operational environment meant that it was injudicious to take parties' commitments at face value.

3 As these same parties only appeared to respect the use of force, so only an enforcement-capable force could establish the necessary stability to facilitate peacebuilding.

The UK's commitment of a balanced and capable combat force to assist UNAMSIL enabled the conduct of operations across the entire PSO spectrum (Wilkinson, 2000). UK intervention at such a critical juncture in Sierra Leone ultimately saved both the mission and the peace process. Bernath and Nyce (2002) describe how UNAMSIL was initially doomed until after the hostage crisis, which in fact spurred the UK and the international community not to allow another peacekeeping failure. In May 2000 UK forces were landed to evacuate UK citizens, to secure the airport for UN personnel, and subsequently to release eleven British soldiers taken hostage by rebel militias in August 2000. This decision to take robust action in defence of the peace process was linked to all of the subsequent success factors associated with the UN's peace-making efforts in Sierra Leone (Langholtz et al., eds, 2002). Indeed, British interest in Sierra Leone and its position as a permanent member of the Security Council was likely to have been a major catalyst in the Council's agreement to expand UNAMSIL's strength to 17,500. The depth of the UK's contribution to UNAMSIL was summed up by Defence Minister Hoon, who declared that the UK was 'to all intents and purposes running the day-to-day operation of UN forces'. Although the UN and the wider international community were grateful for the UK input, there was some discontent that the UK had not been prepared to place the majority of its troops within UNAMSIL's command and control structure. The British troops' rescue of UNAMSIL, and their combined success in getting the peace process back on track, ultimately enabling 'free and fair' elections to return President Kabbah to power the following year, suggests the effectiveness of UK PSO doctrine in practice.

Conclusion: The Transformationist Critique

In chapter 1 we announced as one of the *leitmotifs* of this book the current debates within the conflict resolution field across the containment, settlement, transformation spectrum. We conclude this chapter by illustrating this in relation to peacekeeping.[2] Excellent summaries of the transformationist critique can be found in Bellamy and Williams, eds (2004) and in Bellamy et al. (2004).

We noted in chapter 1 how the transformationist agenda usually begins by invoking Cox's distinction between conservative problem-solving theory and radical critical theory (1981). It then classes most existing practice under the former, criticizing it as objectivist, non-reflexive and instrumentalist. It is seen to lack awareness of its own epistemological and ontological assumptions, condemned to reproduce existing power imbalances and inequalities even if it thinks that it is acting impartially. In contrast, radical critical theory sees its own stance as constructivist, reflexive and normative, conscious of the epistemological and ontological institutions and discourses that underpin existing exclusions, and therefore able to serve genuinely emancipatory purposes (Fetherston, in Woodhouse and Ramsbotham, eds, 2000: 190–218).

The advantages of the transformationist approach are self-evident in this account. Awareness of the normative underpinnings of existing power structures makes it possible to challenge them in the name of those who are excluded and exploited, thus opening up the possibility of a genuinely emancipatory agenda whose aim is to eliminate human insecurity. This casts a critical light on the role of powerful stabilization forces operating on the margins of or outside the UN, questions the effect of traditional peacekeeping within the existing global order, and requires the new doctrine of peace support operations to become more aware of its own assumptions. It insists that a critical peacekeeping agenda must be set within wider policy approaches that question existing practice in security, development and governance.

Nevertheless, despite critiques of this kind, newer UN operations such as those in Sierra Leone and in East Timor also met the requirements called for by Brahimi in being robust, complex and multidimensional operations. Thus within both the transformationist peacekeeping critique, and amongst those developing doctrine relating to peace support operations, analysts have suggested that a constructive and emancipatory role for peacekeeping may be fashioned both from the continued application of reforms coming out of the Brahimi process, and from the opening of theory and policy to the reflexive insights of critical theory (Bellamy and Williams, eds, 2004: 183). Suggested changes range across the ideas that these should be international civilian peacekeepers (non-military peacekeeping); that peacekeepers should be released from an overly state-centric control system; that they should be made 'answerable to a more transparent, democratic and accountable institutional arrangement' based on 'a permanent military volunteer force recruited directly among individuals predisposed to cosmopolitan rather than patriotic values' (post-Westphalian or democratic peacekeeping); and that 'in so far as a goal of transformation is to remove the injustices that give rise to conflict, the need for military-civilian interventions might be expected to fade' (Pugh, in Bellamy and Williams, eds, 2004: 53).

The types of peacekeeping associated with the four main theoretical perspectives identified above are outlined in table 6.4, where modes of

Table 6.4 A spectrum of current peacekeeping models and levels of conflict resolution (CR) capacity

	1	2	3	4
Theory	Quasi-realist	Pluralist	Solidarist	Cosmopolitan
Practice	Stabilization forces	Traditional peacekeeping	Enhanced peace support operations	UN emergency peace service
CR capacity	Zero or low CR capacity	Limited passive CR capacity	High military/ low civilian CR capacity	High military/ high civilian CR capacity

peacekeeping are linked with both the theoretical perspectives and with the levels of intended conflict resolution (CR) capacity built into the model.

We suggest that the current debate is now between realists who reject the whole concept of enhanced UN peacekeeping, pluralists who are only prepared to countenance traditional first-generation peacekeeping, the pragmatic solidarists who favour the incremental development of existing arrangements and those transformationists who argue for enhanced mulitidimensonal UN rapid reaction capability, which combines military robustness with civilian peacebuilding expertise, including sophisticated conflict resolution capacity (Langille et al., 1995; Kinloch, 1996; Langille, 2000; Hansen et al., 2004). We apply the term 'cosmopolitan' to the transformationist end of the spectrum for reasons which are elaborated (Held, 2004; Woodhouse and Ramsbotham, 2005). Needless to say, critics of this idea see it as inappropriate if controlled by an as yet unreformed United Nations. In the final part of this chapter we explore the implications for the development of peacekeeping emerging from perspectives linked with columns 3 and 4 in table 6.4.

In the 1990s a series of initiatives were suggested by the pragmatists. For example, a 'Friends of Rapid Deployment' group worked with the DPKO to secure support for developing a rapidly deployable mission headquarters (RDMHQ). Since 1994 a DPKO team has organized the UN Stand-by Arrangement System (UNSAS) to expand the quality and quantity of resources that member states might provide. To complement this arrangement, the Danish government, in cooperation with thirteen regular troop contributors, organized a multinational Stand-by High Readiness Brigade (SHIRBRIG). Further studies were conducted by governments keen to move the concept on. The December 2004 Report of the UN High Level Panel included proposals along these lines:

> Deploying military capacities – for peacekeeping as well as peace enforcement – has proved to be a valuable tool in ending wars and helping to secure States in their aftermath. But the total global supply

of available peacekeepers is running dangerously low. Just to do an adequate job of keeping the peace in existing conflicts would require almost doubling the number of peacekeepers around the world. The developed States have particular responsibilities to do more to transform their armies into units suitable for deployment to peace operations. And if we are to meet the challenges ahead, more States will have to place contingents on stand-by for UN purposes. (Executive Summary: 5)

At the same time, towards the more radical end of the spectrum, a number of national studies focused on attempts to define the measures necessary to institutionalize a permanent UN standing peacekeeping capability. In 1995 the government of the Netherlands issued *A UN Rapid Deployment Brigade: A Preliminary Study*, which argued that developing crises could only be met by dedicated units that were instantly deployable: 'the sooner an international "fire brigade" can turn out, the better the chance that the situation can be contained' (cited in Langille, 2000). The report recommended that, rather than develop the existing Stand-by Arrangements System, a permanent, rapidly deployable brigade would guarantee the immediate availability of troops when they were urgently needed.

Another report was issued by the government of Canada, which, in September 1995, presented the UN with a study entitled, *Towards a Rapid Reaction Capability for the United Nations* (cited in Langille, 2000). Among the elements deemed necessary were an early warning mechanism, an effective decision-making process, reliable transportation and infrastructure, logistical support, sufficient finances, and welltrained and equipped personnel. The final section of the report outlined the case for 'A UN Standing Emergency Group' composed of volunteer military, police and civilian elements (Canada Report, 1995: 60–3). In making the case for dedicated volunteers, who would be selected and then employed by the UN, the Canada Report acknowledged that, 'UN volunteers offer the best prospect of a completely reliable, well-trained rapid-reaction capability. Without the need to consult national authorities, the UN could cut response times significantly, and volunteers could be deployed within hours of a Security Council decision. . . . No matter how difficult this goal now seems, it deserves continued study, with a clear process for assessing its feasibility over the long term' (Canada Report, 1995: 62). Further, it noted the establishment and costs of a UN Standing Emergency Group would warrant further consideration should the more pragmatic short-to-mid-term options (the existing arrangements) prove inadequate.

In many of these and similar proposals the assumption was that any rapid deployment capability should assume responsibility for the initial stages of a peacekeeping mission and that the deployment should be both proactive and preventive (Langille, 2000).[3]

These ideas for a permanent UN capability, located at the 'visionary' end of the spectrum of policy options, echo the call made by Lester Pearson in his Nobel Peace Prize acceptance speech quoted at the head of this chapter.[4] This may seem to be a tall order given the overt hostility of the currently most powerful military power to any such idea, the unwillingness to participate of a number of other countries, and the suspicions harboured by many non-western states. But it is not an impossible aspiration. And the conflict transformationists who espouse such a vision are both patient and persistent. Langille suggests that the development of a UN Emergency Peace Service is no longer 'mission impossible', but an initiative that links and expands upon the work provided by the report of the Panel on UN Peace Operations (the Brahimi Report), the ICISS report *The Responsibility to Protect*, earlier multinational efforts to enhance UN rapid deployment, the ongoing emphasis on the prevention of deadly conflict, and the recent establishment of an International Criminal Court. The development of a UN Emergency Peace Service, or of a mechanism similar to it, is then a logical progression of the idea of the collective human security agenda to which the UN is committed (see box 6.3). Linking up with the critical peacekeeping agenda discussed above, this does indeed require

---

Box 6.3 Proposal for a UN emergency peace service

The future roles and potential tasks of the new service should include the provision of: reliable early warning with on-site technical reconnaissance; rapid deployment for preventive action and protection of civilians at risk; prompt start-up of diverse peace operations, including policing, peacebuilding and humanitarian assistance.

A UN Emergency Peace Service must include a robust military composition; one capable of deterring belligerents, defending the mission, as well as civilians at risk. Notably, recent UN peace operations have included mandates with authorization under Chapter VII for the limited use of force. While the proposed UN service would not be another 'force' for war-fighting, deployable military elements must have a capacity for modest enforcement to maintain security and the safety of people within its area of operations.

Three further requirements in the majority of recent UN operations are the prompt provision of incentives to restore hope, useful services to address critical human needs and civilian police to maintain law and order. Even at the outset of a deployment, there will be a need for prompt disaster relief and humanitarian assistance, as well as conflict resolution teams, medical units, peacebuilding advisory teams and environmental crisis response teams.

Source: Langille, 2002

new ways of thinking about the nature and roles of peacekeeping and about the function of peace operations in the emerging global order. As the critical theorists argue, in the end the touchstone should be to develop forms of peacekeeping that serve, not primarily the interests of the powerful, but mainly the interests of what Edward Said called 'the poor, the disadvantaged, the unrepresented, the voiceless, the powerless' (quoted in Bellamy and Williams, eds, 2004: 7). We will carry these ideas forward in Part II of this book.

Recommended reading

Bellamy et al. (2004); Goodwin (2005); Woodhouse and Ramsbotham (2000, 2005).

Ending Violent Conflict: Peacemaking

Friends, comrades, and fellow South Africans. I greet you all, in the name of peace, democracy and freedom for all.

Nelson Mandela on his release from prison, 11 February 1990

I knew that the hand outstretched to me from the far side of the podium was the same hand that held the knife, that held the gun, the hand that gave the order to shoot, to kill. Of all the hands in the world, it was not the hand that I wanted or dreamed of touching. I would have liked to sign a peace agreement with Holland, or Luxembourg, or New Zealand. But there was no need to. That is why, on that podium, I stood as the representative of a nation that wants peace with the most bitter and odious of its foes.

Yitzhak Rabin, Memoirs, 1996, with reference to shaking hands with Yasser Arafat in Washington on 13 September 1993

IN this chapter we turn from the question of the role of conflict resolution in ongoing wars to the question of war endings. We will focus especially on efforts to bring armed conflicts to an end in the post-Cold War era, and the factors that have contributed to their success and failure. Having examined the nature and difficulties of ending violent conflict, we will move on to explore 'transformers' of conflict, and the place of de-escalation, pre-negotiations, mediation, negotiations and peace talks in ending violence and restoring peace. We illustrate these themes with examples of successful peace processes and of peace processes that have failed or coexisted uneasily with protracted conflict.

Conflict resolution is broader than conflict termination, and the relationship between conflict resolution and the ending of violent conflict is not necessarily direct. The root causes of conflict may persist without either war or a peace settlement doing anything to address them. Wars often generate additional conflicts, which add to and confuse the original issues. It is quite possible that efforts to resolve a conflict may not end a war, and efforts to end a war may not resolve the underlying conflict.

159

The Challenge of Ending Violent Conflict

How have major post-Cold War armed conflicts ended, and what are the obstacles to conflict resolution?

How major post-Cold War conflicts have ended

Although there have been significant cases of conflicts that have come to an end through peace agreements, this is not the normal pattern. More often, conflicts fizzle out, dropping below the thresholds that researchers used to classify them as armed conflicts. The underlying reasons for the conflict remain, and they are prone to break out again. This is consistent with the pattern of protracted social conflicts identified by Azar (see chapter 4). Between 1989 and the end of 1999, Wallensteen (2002b: 29) and his co-researchers counted a total of 110 armed conflicts; an additional 6 have been fought up to 2002 (Eriksson et al., 2003). Of these 110, 75 had fallen below the threshold of 25 battle-deaths a year by 2000, but only 21 ended in peace agreements, 22 ended in victories and in 32 the conflict became dormant. Nevertheless the post-Cold War era has seen some significant peace agreements, as well as some less well known ones (see box 7.1).

What constitutes a war 'ending' is itself a tricky question. Wallensteen and his colleagues use a miminal definition that no armed violence occurred in the following year; but peace settlements often break down, and repeated violence occurs. Cambodia, which produced a 'comprehensive political settlement' in 1990, was again

Box 7.1 Peace agreements in armed conflicts, 1988–2000	
Ethiopia-Somalia 1988	Niger, Air and Azawad 1995
Iran-Iraq 1988	Bosnia-Serb Republic 1995
Namibia 1988	Croatia-Eastern Slavonia 1995
Morocco-Western Sahara 1989	Guatemala 1996
Chad-Libya 1990	Liberia 1996
Nicaragua 1990	Philipines, Mindanao 1996
Lebanon 1990	Tajikistan 1997
Cambodia 1991	Central African Republic 1997
Chad 1992	Bangladesh, Chittagong Hill Tracts
Mozambique 1992	1997
El Salvador 1992	Northern Ireland, 1998
Djibouti 1994	Guinea-Bissau 1998
India, Jharkand 1994	Ecuador-Peru 1998
Bosnia-Croat Republic 1994	East Timor, 1999
Mali, Air and Azawad 1995	Eritrea-Ethiopia 2000

Source: Wallensteen, 2002b

a high-intensity conflict in late 1996 (Schmid, 1997: 79). The Lomé peace agreement of July 1999 in Sierra Leone broke down in renewed fighting which the intervention of UNAMSIL and the elections of May 2002 largely brought to an end. A war ending is not usually a precise moment in time, but a process. A violent conflict is over when a new political dispensation prevails, or the parties become reconciled, or a new conflict eclipses the first.[1] Perhaps for this reason, interstate peace agreements have been easier to conclude than intrastate agreements: only a quarter to a third of modern civil wars have been negotiated, whereas more than half of interstate wars have been (Pillar, 1983; Licklider, 1995).[2] However, armed conflicts *do* end eventually, if we take a long enough time period (Licklider, 1995).

Licklider finds that civil wars ended by negotiated settlements are more likely to lead to the recurrence of armed conflicts than those ended by military victories; on the other hand, those ended by military victories are more likely to lead to genocide. His findings point to the need for continuing peacebuilding efforts to resolve the underlying conflicts.[3]

Obstacles to conflict resolution

Chapter 4 has indicated some of the reasons why contemporary international-social conflicts are so hard to end. Sources of conflict, which usually persist in intensified form into the ensuing war, were identified at international, state and societal levels, and were also located in the factional interests of elites and individuals. To these are added the destructive processes and vested interests engendered by the war itself, as described in chapter 6. The economic destruction wrought by wars makes societies more likely to suffer war again (Collier et al., 2003). Violence spawns a host of groups who benefit directly from its continuation. Soldiers become dependent on warfare as a way of life, and warlords on the economic resources and revenue they can control (King, 1997: 37; Berdal and Keen, 1998). Even in low-intensity conflicts, protagonists may depend, economically or psychologically, on the continuation of the conflict, such as the people in Belfast who sustain paramilitary operations through protection rackets. Leaders who have become closely identified with pursuing the conflict may risk prosecution, overthrow or even death once the war is over, and have strong incentives for intransigence (for example, Karadzic in Bosnia, Savimbi in Angola, Vellupillai Probhakaran in Sri Lanka). Local and regional party officials or military officers who have made their careers in the conflict may develop a stake in its continuation (Sisk, 1997: 84). For such protagonists, peace may bring loss of role and status, and thus directly threaten their interests (King, 1997).

It would be easy to draw the conclusion that conflict resolution is not possible, and that political groups, like nations, will fight to the death to achieve their ends. However, we need to keep the obstacles in proportion. Most violent conflicts impose massive costs on the societies concerned, and so there is usually a large segment of the population which will benefit from the conflict ending. This is a shared interest across the conflicting communities, affecting security and economic welfare. Moderate politicians and constituencies, who may have been silenced or displaced by the climate of violence, will be keen to re-establish normal politics. Ordinary people will welcome a return to peace and wish to put the distress of war behind them. There is, therefore, a large reservoir of potential support that peacemakers should be able to foster.

We can point to a number of cases where conflicts have been settled by negotiation: examples include the ending of apartheid in South Africa, the ending of the internal conflicts in Nicaragua, El Salvador and Guatemala, the settlements in Mozambique and Namibia and the Ta'if Accord which brought the civil war in Lebanon to an end. Given political vision, engaged peacemakers, moderation and the right conditions, conflicts *can* be brought to a negotiated end. It is, therefore, worth trying to identify the ingredients of an effective conflict resolution approach, and the conditions under which attempts to end conflict are likely to succeed.

Conflict Resolution and War Ending

In looking at the scope for conflict resolution in ending violent conflict, we will follow Väyrynen in adopting a broad approach which recognizes the fluidity of the conflict process. Conflicts are inherently dynamic and conflict resolution has to engage with a complex of shifting relations:

> The bulk of conflict theory regards the issues, actors and interests as given and on that basis makes efforts to find a solution to mitigate or eliminate contradictions between them. Yet the issues, actors and interests change over time as a consequence of the social, economic and political dynamics of societies. Even if we deal with non-structural aspects of conflicts, such as actor preferences, the assumption of stability, usually made in the game theoretic approach to conflict studies, is unwarranted. New situational factors, learning experiences, interaction with the adversary and other influences caution against taking actor preferences as given. (Väyrynen, ed., 1991: 4)

The requirements are best seen as a series of necessary transformations in the elements which would otherwise sustain ongoing violence and war.

Väyrynen (ed., 1991) identifies a number of ways in which conflict transformation takes place. His ideas complement those of Galtung (1984, 1989, 1996, 2004), who has developed his views on the resolution of inter-party and intra-party conflicts, in their structural, attitudinal and behavioural aspects, into a full theory of non-violent conflict transformation. From these sources, and informed by Burton, Azar, Curle and the related theorists mentioned in chapter 2, we outline five generic transformers of protracted conflict which correspond to the outline framework for the analysis of contemporary conflict offered in chapter 4.

First, *context transformation*. Conflicts are embedded in a social, regional and international context, which is often critical to their continuation. Changes in the context may sometimes have more dramatic effects than changes within the parties or in their relationships. The end of the Cold War is the prime recent context transformation which has unlocked protracted conflicts in Southern Africa, Central America and elsewhere. Local conflicts which are fuelled by global forces may not be resolvable at the local level without changing the structures or policies which have produced them.[4]

Second, *structural transformation*. The conflict structure is the set of actors and incompatible goals or relationships which constitutes the conflict. If the root causes of the conflict lie in the structure of relationships within which the parties operate, then a transformation of this structure is necessary to resolve the conflict. In asymmetric conflicts, for example, structural transformation entails a change in the relationship between the dominant and weaker party. Empowerment of the weaker side (for example through international support or recognition or mediation) is one way this can be achieved. Another is dissociation – withdrawal from unbalanced relationships, as for example in the Kosovar Albanians' decision to boycott the elections in Serbia and set up a 'shadow state'.

Third, *actor transformation*. Parties may have to redefine directions, abandon or modify cherished goals, and adopt radically different perspectives. This may come about through a change of actor, a change of leadership, a change in the constituency of the leader, or adoption of new goals, values or beliefs. Transformation of intra-party conflicts may be crucial to the resolution of inter-party conflict. Changes of leadership may precipitate change in protracted conflicts. Changes in the circumstances and interests of the constituency a party represents also transform conflicts, even if such changes in the constituency take place gradually and out of view. Splitting of parties and formation of new parties are examples of actor transformations.

Fourth, *issue transformation*. Conflicts are defined by the conflicting positions parties take on issues. When they change their positions, or when issues lose salience or new ones arise, the conflict is transformed. Changes of position are closely related to changes of interest and changes of goals, and hence to actor transformation, and also to the context and structure of the conflict. Reframing the issues may open the way to settlements.

Fifth, *personal and group transformation*. For Adam Curle, this is at the heart of change.[5] The former guerrilla leader, committed to victory through any means, becomes the unifying national leader, offering reconciliation; the leader of an oppressive government decides to accept his opponents into the government. Excruciating suffering leads in time through mourning and healing to new life (Montville, 1993).

Transformations of this kind do not necessarily move in a benign direction. It is characteristic of conflicts that they intensify and widen, power passes from moderate to more extreme leaders, violence intensifies and restraint and moderation wither. These five types of transformation are useful, however, as a framework for analysing steps toward conflict resolution and for thinking about interventions in conflict.

The middle three transformers (structure, actor, issue), correspond to the conflict-level factors identified in our typology of conflict causes in chapter 4: context transformation corresponds to the global, regional and state levels, and individual and group transformation to the individual-elite level.

In many cultures conflicts are explained as 'tangles' of contradictory claims that must be unravelled. In Central America, the phrase 'we are all entangled', as in a fisherman's net, best describes the concept of conflict, and the experience of conflict is '*enredado*' (to be tangled or caught in a net) (Duffey, 1998). At the root of conflict is a knot of problematic relationships, conflicting interests and differing world-views. Undoing this knot is a painstaking process. Success depends on how the knot has been tied and the sequencing of the untying. The timing and coordination of the transformers is crucial (Fisher and Keashly, 1991). They need to develop sufficient energy and momentum to overcome the conflict's resistance.

This broad view of conflict transformation is necessary to correct the misperception that conflict resolution rests on an assumption of harmony of interests between actors, and that third-party mediators can settle conflicts by appealing to the reason or underlying humanity of the parties. On the contrary, conflict transformation requires real changes in parties' interests, goals or self-definitions. These may be forced by the conflict itself, or may come about because of intraparty changes, shifts in the constituencies of the parties, or changes in the context in which the conflict is situated. Conflict resolution must therefore be concerned not only with the issues that divide the main parties but also with the social, psychological and political changes that are necessary to address root causes, the intra-party conflicts that may inhibit acceptance of a settlement, the global and regional context which structures the issues in conflict and the thinking of the parties, and the social and institutional capacity that determines whether a settlement can be made acceptable and workable. The response must be 'conflict-sensitive' at a number of different levels.

Having outlined the main general requirements for ending violent conflicts in terms of conflict transformers, we now apply this in more detail, first to the issue of the conditions under which conflicts do end, second to the role of mediation and third-party intervention in war ending, and third to the nature of successful negotiations and peace settlements. We examine the significance of turning points and sticking points in peace processes, and the challenge of securing peace against the wishes of sceptics who may reject the terms of a particular peace agreement and spoilers who may want to wreck any settlement.

De-escalation, Ripeness and Conditions for Ending Violent Conflict

The end of the Cold War itself was a significant factor in transforming the context of many conflicts. It contributed to the ending of a significant number of post-Cold War conflicts. A notable factor was the reduction in the capacity or willingness of external powers to support fighting factions. In Central America, South Africa and South-East Asia, geopolitical changes, the end of ideological justifications for intervention and reductions in armed support for rebel groups contributed to conflict endings (for example, in El Salvador, Nicaragua, Mozambique and Cambodia). Even Northern Ireland's long conflict was positively influenced by the end of the Cold War, as the Republican belief that the UK had a strategic interest in Northern Ireland fell away.

As Hegre (2004: 244) shows, the global incidence of civil wars has fallen significantly since the end of the Cold War, reversing a forty-year increase to 1990. The rise before 1990 was mainly due to an increase in the duration of wars, rather than new starts; and the decline since 1990 has been due to changes in duration. A central factor has been the capacity of rebel groups to finance their struggles. Rebel groups have increasingly turned from external state support to contraband and plunder of natural resources. There remain a group of insurgencies in the peripheries of weak states, in the 'global badlands', which remain very resistant to the ending of violent conflict (Fearon, 2004).

Although external interventions are usually important and sometimes decisive in conflict endings, a crucial factor is the willingness of the conflicting parties themselves to consider a negotiated agreement.

A host of significant factors may bring about this willingness, and it is difficult to generalize across the heterogeneous group of post-Cold War conflicts (for discussions of de-escalation, conciliatory gestures and the factors influencing feasibility of settlement, see, for example, Mitchell, 1999, 2000; Downs and Stedman, 2002). In armed conflicts, parties become willing to consider negotiated outcomes when they lose hope of achieving their aims by force of arms. Even then, their ability to carry sceptical factions and constituencies is essential for a settlement. In Northern Ireland, for example, the decision of leading Republicans to pursue a political strategy as well as an armed strategy gradually led to involvement in political negotiations and a political outcome. But this alone did not bring about the ceasefire. Other preconditions included the change in the position of the UK and Irish governments, from opposing protagonists to cooperating mediators, and the realization on the part of the Unionists that their preferred outcome, devolved government, also depended on multiparty negotiations.

Zartman (ed., 1995: 18) argues that conflicts are ripe for negotiated settlements only under certain conditions. The main condition is a 'hurting stalemate'. Both sides must realize that they cannot achieve their aims by further violence and that it is costly to go on.

The concept of 'hurting stalemate' is widely accepted in policy-making circles, and some diplomats, such as Chester Crocker, have deliberately attempted to bring about a 'hurting stalemate' in order to foster a settlement. Others refer to the need for a 'ripening process' to foster 'ripe moments' (Druckman, 1986).

Zartman argues that for negotiations to succeed, there must also be valid spokespersons for the parties, a deadline, and a vision of an acceptable compromise. Recognition and dialogue are preconditions, and for these to take place both parties have to be accepted as legitimate. In conflicts between a government and an insurgency, for example, the government must reach the point where it recognizes the insurgency as a negotiating partner. Similarly, a more equal power balance between the parties is held to favour negotiation: when the asymmetry is reduced, negotiations may become possible. Druckman and Green suggest that changes in relative legitimacy as well as relative power between regimes and insurgents affect the propensity to negotiate (Druckman and Green, 1995).

The 'ripeness' idea has the attraction of simplicity, but a number of authors have suggested modifications or criticisms. Mitchell (1995) distinguishes four different models of the 'ripe moment': the original 'hurting stalemate' suggested by Zartman; the idea of 'imminent mutual catastrophe', also due to Zartman; the rival model suggested by games of entrapment such as the 'dollar auction' (Rapoport, 1989), where a hurting stalemate leads to even greater commitment by the parties; and the idea of an 'enticing opportunity', or conjunction of favourable circumstances (such as, for example, the conjunction of conditions which encouraged the first IRA ceasefire in Northern Ireland: a Fianna Fail Taoiseach, a Democratic President with strong American Irish support, and an understanding between the Northern Irish Nationalists and Republicans). Others argue that the concept is tautological, since we cannot know whether there is a hurting stalemate until the actions that it is supposed to trigger takes place (Licklider, ed., 1993: 309; Hampson, 1996: 210–14). If a stalemate that hurts the parties persists for a long time before negotiations, as it often does, the value of the concept as an explanation for negotiated settlements must be qualified.

It has been argued that the simple 'hurting stalemate' model gives too much weight to the power relationship between the parties, and fails sufficiently to take account of changes within the parties or changes in the context which may also foster a propensity to negotiate (Stedman, 1991). Moreover, although it is possible to point to cases of successful negotiations which have followed hurting stalemates, it is also possible to point to hurting stalemates which do not lead to successful negotiations, for example Cyprus. It may be argued in these cases that the stalemate is not hurting enough; but then there is no clear evidence from case studies as to how long a stalemate has to last or how much it has to hurt before it triggers successful negotiations. And stalemates are likely to hurt the general population more than the leaders who in the end make the decisions. We should distinguish, too, between ripeness for negotiations to start and ripeness for negotiations to succeed; in Angola and Cambodia, for example, the conditions for settlement 'unripened' after negotiated agreements had been made, because one or other of the parties was unwilling to accept the settlement terms, even though the condition of 'hurting stalemate' still obtained. A model that sees conflicts moving from 'unripeness' through a ripe moment to resolution is perhaps too coarse-grained to take account of the many changes that come together over time and result in a settlement: redefinitions of parties' goals, changes in the parties' constituencies, contextual changes, shifts in perceptions, attitudes and behaviour patterns. 'Ripeness' is not sudden, but rather a complex process of transformations in the situation, shifts in public attitudes, and new perceptions and visions among decision-makers.

Mediation and Third-Party Intervention

While the primary conflict parties have the most important role in determining outcomes, a feature of the globalization of conflict has been the increasing involvement of a range of external agencies in mediation efforts and third-party interventions of all kinds. These are not necessarily benign. Intervention in general (including by interested parties and outside powers) has tended to increase the duration of civil wars. Nevertheless, both domestic and external third parties are often important catalysts for peacemaking.

Conflict resolution attempts involve different kinds of agency (international organizations, states, non-governmental organizations, individuals), address different groups (party leaders, elites, grassroots), and vary in form, duration and purpose. Chapters 1 and 2 referred to this developing practice, including Track I, Track II, Track III and multitrack diplomacy, employing a spectrum of 'soft' and 'hard' intervention approaches, ranging from good offices, conciliation, quiet or 'pure' mediation at one end, through various modes of mediation and peacekeeping, to peace enforcement at the other. There have been fierce debates over whether third-party intervention should be impartial or partial, coercive or non-coercive, state-based or non-state-based, carried out by outsiders or insiders (Touval and Zartman, eds, 1985; Curle, 1986; Mitchell and Webb, eds, 1988; van der Merwe, 1989; Lederach, 1995; Bercovitch, ed., 1996). Attempts to integrate different approaches, such as Fisher and Keashly's (1991) 'contingency model'[6] and life-cycle models of conflict (Creative Associates, 1997: 3–4) suggest appropriate responses at different phases of conflict, though such models do not resolve the ethical issues involved, or the practical issues of coordination (Webb et al., 1996). They do, however, point to the conclusion that third-party interventions usually need to be coordinated (Jones, 2002) and continued over an extended period, and that 'third parties need other third parties' (Hampson, 1996: 233).

At the softer end of the spectrum third parties are often essential in contributing to issue transformations. They typically help the conflicting parties by putting them in contact with one another, gaining their trust and confidence, setting agendas, clarifying issues and formulating agreements. They can facilitate meetings by arranging venues, reducing tensions, exploring the interests of the parties and sometimes guiding the parties to unrealized possibilities. These are tasks that are usually contentious and even dangerous for the conflictants to perform themselves. By allowing the parties to present their cases, exploring them in depth, framing and ordering the discussion, and questioning the advantages and disadvantages of different options, before the parties have to make a commitment to them, mediation can sometimes perform a valuable role in opening up new political space.

Mediation is especially important at a stage when at least some of the conflicting parties have come to accept that pursuing the conflict is unlikely to achieve their goals, but before they have reached the stage of accepting formal negotiations. At this point, face-to-face meetings may be very difficult to arrange, and mediation and 'back-channels' become important. They played a large role in the peace processes in Northern Ireland, South Africa and the Israel/Palestine conflict. In the Northern Ireland case, for example, the SDLP, Sinn Fein and the Irish government established communications by sending secret messages through representatives of the Clonard monastery, a religious community which ministers to Republican families living on the 'front line' in Belfast; this prepared the ground for the Hume–Adams proposals (Coogan, 1995). In the South African case, the contacts arranged between the ANC and the government by third parties enabled preliminary communication between the two sides, before they were ready to negotiate openly.

International organizations, governments and non-governmental organizations (NGOs) all play a role at this stage. Although they usually have limited resources, NGOs are also able to enter conflicts. NGOs (such as the African Centre for the Constructive Resolution of Disputes (ACCORD), the Berghof Research Centre for Constructive Conflict Management, the Carter Center, the Community of Sant'Egidio, the Conflict Analysis Centre at Kent, the Harvard Centre of Negotiation, the Institute for Multi-track Diplomacy, International Alert and Search for Common Ground) have gained experience of working in conflict (van Tongeren, 1996; Serbe et al., 1997). They use a variety of approaches, including facilitation (Fisher and Ury, 1981), problem-solving workshops (de Reuck, 1984; Burton, 1987; Kelman, 1992; Mitchell and Banks, 1996) and sustained mediation.

It is possible to point to a number of cases where mediators from NGOs have contributed to transformation at key moments, usually in conjunction with governments and international organizations – the Community of Sant'Egidio in Mozambique (Hume, 1994; Msabaha, 1995: 221), Jimmy Carter in Ethiopia/Eritrea (Ottoway, 1995: 117), the Moravians and the Mennonites in Central America (Wehr and Lederach, 1996: 65, 69), the Norwegian organization FAFO in the Oslo talks between Israel and the PLO (Corbin, 1994) and the Conflict Analysis Centre in Moldova.

NGOs have sometimes been able to adapt their methods to the local culture, and can work usefully with one or several parties rather than with all. John-Paul Lederach, for example, found in his work in Central America that the parties look for *confianza* (trust) rather than neutrality in third parties, and that an 'insider-partial' would be more acceptable than impartial outsiders (Lederach, 1995; Wehr and Lederach, 1996).

The current trend in NGO interventions is away from entry into conflict situations by outsiders, towards training people inside the society in conflict in the skills of conflict resolution and combining these with indigenous traditions. We noted in chapter 2 how the constructions and reconstructions which took place in conflict resolution thinking placed great stress on the need to bring into the discourse of conflict resolution the ideal of a global civic culture which was receptive and responsive to the voices often left out of the politics of international order. Thus Elise Boulding envisaged the evolution of a problem-solving *modus operandi* for civil society, and Curle and Lederach defined the priorites and modalites of indigenous empowerment and peacebuilding from below. Indeed, it is in the encounter with local traditions that important lessons about conflict resolution are being learned, particularly about the limitations of the dominantly Euro-American model defined in chapter 2. In the study of the Arab Middle East, mentioned earlier, Paul Salem has noted a 'rich tradition of tribal conflict management [which] has thousands of years of experience and wisdom behind it' (ed., 1997: xi). Such perspectives are now beginning to emerge in contemporary understandings and practices of conflict resolution. Rupesinghe (1996) emphasizes the importance of building capacity to manage conflict within the affected society, a process which will necessarily involve the need for knowledge about the traditions of conflict management to which Salem referred. Kelman, Rothman and others have used an elicitive model in their workshops in the Middle East, drawing on the wisdom of local cultures to stimulate creative dialogue and new thinking at elite or grassroots levels. Participants in their workshops have gone on to play significant decision-making roles in the Israeli-Palestinian peace process (Rothman, 1992; Kelman, 1997). Similarly, community relations organizations in Northern Ireland have built networks of people across the communities who are a long-term resource for peacebuilding, and are changing both the society and the actors. Thus the encounter between conflict resolution ideas and social and political forces can subtly transform the context of conflict. NGOs also work towards structural transformation, for example by acting to empower the weaker side (van der Merwe, 1989; Lederach, 1995; Curle, 1996).

Of course, international organizations and governments still play much the largest role in managing conflicts in the post-Cold War world. The UN Secretary-General and his representatives exercise good offices in many parts of the world (Findlay, 1996), and made important contributions to the settlements in El Salvador, Cambodia, Mozambique and Namibia. The UN's legitimacy contributes to its special role, and its resolutions sometimes play a defining role in setting out principles for settlements (as in the case of Resolutions 242 and 338 in Palestine). It is true that the UN has also faced some dreadful failures in the post-Cold War world, including Bosnia, Rwanda and Somalia.[7] Nevertheless, as the instrument through which the international community arranges ceasefires, organizes peacekeeping, facilitates elections and monitors disengagement and demilitarization, the UN has an acknowledged corpus of knowledge and experience to bring to bear.[8]

Governments also play a prominent role as mediators. For example Portugal (with the UN) facilitated the Bicesse Accord in Angola (Hampson, 1996: 87–127), the ASEAN countries took a leading role in Cambodia, and the United States in Central America, Northern Ireland, India-Pakistan and elsewhere. The United States is especially significant in post-Cold War conflicts, given its unique international position, although its willingness to act as a mediator, rather than an interested party, diminished in the late 1990s. Governments are not always willing to shoulder a mediating role when their national interests are not at stake, and where they are, mediation readily blurs into traditional diplomacy and statecraft.

When governments bring coercion to bear to try to force parties to change position, they become actors in the conflict. Forceful interventions clearly can bring forward war endings in some circumstances, as in the case of Bosnia, where after many months of abstention the USA tacitly built up the Croatian armed forces and sanctioned NATO air strikes on Serb positions in order to force the Dayton settlement. The question is whether such interventions can lead to a stable ending of conflict, and whether imposed settlements stick.[9] We have discussed the dilemmas involved briefly in the previous chapter, and elsewhere (Ramsbotham and Woodhouse, 1996).

Peace Processes: Turning Points, Sticking Points and Spoilers

Conflict transformation may be gradual or abrupt; perhaps more typically, a series of rapid shifts are punctuated by longer periods of inertia and stalemate. If this process is to go forward, the parties and third parties must identify an acceptable formula for negotiation, commit themselves politically to a process of peaceful settlement, manage spoilers who seek to block the process, and return after each setback to fresh mediation or negotiation.

This suggests that there is a range of appropriate actions and interventions at different stages of the conflict, depending on the situation. If the parties are not ready for mediation or negotiations, it may still be possible to support constituencies which favour peacemaking, to work for changes in actors' policies and to influence the context that sustains the conflict. The international anti-apartheid campaign, for example, gradually increased the pressure on international businesses involved in South Africa, to the point where sanctions and disinvestment became a significant factor. External and internal parties can contribute to the structural transformations which enable parties to break out of asymmetrical relationships, by the process of conscientization, gathering external support and legitimacy, and dissocation as a prelude to negotiation and conflict resolution on a more symmetrical basis (see chapter 1, figure 1.11).

Once a peace process has begun, a dilemma arises as to whether to address first the core issues in the conflict, which tend to be the most difficult, or to concentrate on the peripheral issues in the hope of making early agreements and establishing momentum. A step-by-step approach offers the parties the opportunity to test each others' good faith and allows for reciprocation (see box 7.2), in line with the finding from experimental studies of conflict and cooperation that small tension-reducing steps are easier to sustain than one-off solutions in two-party conflicts (Osgood, 1962; Axelrod, 1984).[10] Since durable and comprehensive agreements are difficult to establish all at once, interim agreements are usually necessary in practice. They do need to address core issues, however, if the parties are to have confidence that the process can deliver an acceptable outcome. Interim agreements raise risks that parties may renege, or refuse to reciprocate after obtaining concessions. Agreements that give the parties some incentives to stay in the process (for example, transitional power-sharing arrangements), that are supported by external guarantors and that mobilize domestic support are therefore more likely to succeed (Hampson, 1996; Sisk, 1997).

The fate of the Oslo agreement in the Israel-Palestine conflict illustrates that both 'turning points' and 'sticking points' are characteristic of peace processes. 'Turning points' occur not only at single ripe moments, but at critical points when parties see a way forward through negotiations, either by redefining their goals, opening new political space, finding a new basis for agreement, or because the conjunction of political leaders and circumstances are favourable. 'Sticking points' develop when elites are unfavourable to the process (as in Israel), when parties to agreements defect (as in Angola, Cambodia, Sri Lanka), or when political space is closed or conditions are attached to negotiations which prevent forward movement. At turning points, the aim must be to find ways to capitalize on the momentum of agreement and the changed relationships that have led to it, building up the constituency of support, attempting to persuade the critics, and establishing process with a clear goal and signposts to guide the way towards further agreements and to anticipate disputes. At sticking points, the aim is to find ways around the obstacles, drawing on internal and external support, establishing procedures and learning from the flaws of previous agreements.

Box 7.2 Strategic dilemmas in peace processes

The obstacles to a peace process are almost always formidable. The parties to a violent conflict aim to win, and so they are locked in a process of strategic interaction which makes them acutely sensitive to prospects for gain and loss. Any concession that involves abandoning political ground, any withdrawal from a long-held position, is therefore resisted bitterly. This is reminiscent of aspects of Prisoner's Dilemma described in chapter 1.

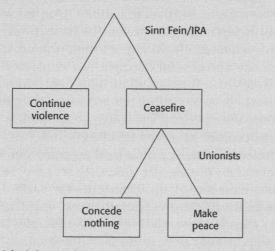

The strategic risks inherent in peacemaking can be illustrated in the tableau above, which is based on a simplified view of the Northern Ireland situation before the IRA ceasefire, but could apply to many other conflicts. Sinn Fein/IRA face a choice between declaring a ceasefire or continuing the violence. We assume they prefer a peace settlement to continuing the violence, but prefer to continue the violence than to stop if the Unionists hold out. The Unionists, too, we assume, prefer a settlement to a continuing conflict, but prefer holding out to settling. Sinn Fein/IRA have to choose first whether to cease fire, then the Northern Ireland Unionists choose between agreeing a settlement and holding out. Sinn Fein/IRA's dilemma is that if they declare a ceasefire the Unionists will continue to concede nothing; so the 'rational' strategy for the SF/IRA is to continue to fight.

The way out of this dilemma is for both parties to agree to move together to the option of peaceful settlement and so reach an option they each prefer to continued conflict. In order to do this, the parties have to create sufficient trust, or guarantees, that they will commit themselves to what they promise. For both sides, the risk that the other will renege is ever present. One way of making the commitment is for leaders on both sides to lock their personal political fortunes so strongly to one option that they could not go down the other path without resigning. (This is an equivalent of throwing away the steering wheel in the game of Chicken.) Another method is to divide the number of 'moves' available to the parties into many steps, so that both parties can have confidence that each is taking the agreed route. In real peace processes, confidence-building measures, agreement on procedures or a timetable for moving forward, and public commitments by leaders are among the methods of building and sustaining a peace process.

As a negotiated agreement comes into sight, or after it has been negotiated, intra-party conflicts over the proposed settlement become very important. Lynch (2002) argues that 'sceptics', as well as 'spoilers', are crucially important. Sceptics are factions who reject the terms of the proposed settlement but are not against a settlement in principle. Spoilers are fundamentally opposed to any agreement and attempt to wreck it. Stedman (1997) suggests the former may be managed by offering inducements and incentives to include them into the agreement, or by offering means to socialize them. The latter, he argues, have to be marginalized, rendered illegitimate or undermined. It may be necessary to accelerate a process for example by a 'departing train' strategy, that sets a timetable on negotiations and hence limits the time for spoilers to work. In successful peace processes, the moderate parties come to defend the emerging agreement, and spoilers can even serve to consolidate a consensus in the middle ground.

Peace processes involve learning (and second-order learning), with the parties gradually discovering what they are prepared to accept and accommodate. Elements of an agreement may surface in early talks, but they may be insufficiently comprehensive, or sufficiently inclusive to hold. They then fall apart; but the main principles and formulas of agreement remain, and can be refined or simplified, until a final agreement is devised. Negotiators and mediators learn from each other and from previous attempts and other peace processes.[11] Eventually they may reach fruition in a negotiated settlement; but even this is only a step, and not the last one, in the conflict resolution process.

Negotiations and Settlements

What types of negotiated outcome are likely to resolve protracted conflicts? It is difficult to generalize here, since different types of conflict are associated with different families of outcomes (Horowitz, 1985; Falkenmark, 1990; Montville, ed., 1991; Miall, 1992: 131–63; McGarry and O'Leary, eds, 1993; Sisk, 1997).

Negotiation processes are often slow and gradual. They start from pre-negotiations (Harris and Reilly, eds, 1998: 59–68). Successive rounds of negotiations are typically punctuated by continuing conflict. Framing and reframing issues and changing parties' perceptions and understandings of the conflict and the potential outcomes are a crucial part of the process (Aggestam, 1999).

As regards outcomes of negotiations, we saw in chapter 1 how theorists distinguish *integrative* (or positive-sum) from *bargaining* (or zero-sum) approaches. Integrative approaches attempt to find ways, if not to reconcile the conflicting positions, then to meet the underlying interests, values or needs (Fisher and Ury, 1981; Galtung, 1984; Pruitt and Rubin, 1986; Burton, 1987). Examples of integrative approaches are: setting the issue into a wider context or redefining the parties' interests in such a way that they can be made compatible, sharing sovereignty or access to the contested resource, increasing the size of the cake, offering compensation for concessions or trading concessions in other areas, and managing the contested resources on a functional rather than a territorial or sovereign basis. Bargaining divides a fixed cake, sometimes with compensations by linkage to other issues. In practice, negotiations combine both approaches.

Albin (1997) offers examples of several of these approaches in her study of options for settling the status of Jerusalem. Both Israelis and Palestinians agree that the city is indivisible, but the dispute over control remains at the core of their long-standing conflict. Both parties claim control over the holy places and claim the city as their capital. Proposals for settling the conflict have included suggestions for increasing the city boundaries of Jerusalem and dividing the enlarged area between the two states, each with a capital inside it (resource expansion); establishing decentralized boroughs within a Greater Jerusalem authority elected by proportional representation (no single authority: delegation of power to a lower level); Israeli sovereignty in return for Palestinian autonomy (compensation); dual capitals and shared access to the holy sites (joint sovereignty); or their internationalization, return to a federated one-state solution with Jerusalem as the joint capital (unification of actors) and transfer of control to a city authority representing both communities, but organized on functional rather than ethnic or national lines (functional).

In ethnic conflicts, integrative solutions are especially elusive (Zartman, ed., 1995b); nevertheless, consociationalism, federalism, autonomy, power-sharing, dispersal of power and electoral systems that give incentives to inter-ethnic coalitions all offer ways out of conflict in some circumstances (Lijphart, 1968; Horowitz, 1985: 597–600; Sisk, 1997).

Good settlements should not only bridge the opposing interests, but also represent norms and values that are public goods for the wider community in which the conflict is situated. Quite clearly, justice and fairness are crucial attributes for negotiations (Albin, 2001). In a more cosmopolitan world, outcomes are expected to meet wider criteria than those that might have been accepted in bargains between sovereign groups. At the same time, the criteria of justice have become more contested.

Some negotiated settlements are more robust than others. Although generalization is treacherous, successful settlements are thought to have the following characteristics (Hampson, 1996: 217–21). First, they should include the affected parties, and the parties are more likely to accept them if they have been involved in the process that reaches them – this argues for inclusiveness and against imposed settlements. Second, they need to be well-crafted and precise, especially as regards details over transitional arrangements, for example demobilization assembly points, ceasefire details, voting rules. Third, they should offer a balance between clear commitments and flexibility. Fourth, they should offer incentives for parties to sustain the process and to participate in politics, for example through power-sharing rather than winner-take-all elections. Fifth, they should provide for dispute settlement, mediation and, if necessary, renegotiation in case of disagreement. And, sixth, they should deal with the core issues in the conflict and bring about a real transformation, incorporating norms and principles to which the parties subscribe, such as equity and democracy, and at the same time creating political space for further negotiations and political accommodation. To this we might add, seventh, they should be consistent with cosmopolitan standards of human rights, justice and respect for individuals and groups.

Case Studies

We now turn to contrast two of the peace processes which have been central stories in post-Cold War conflict resolution. Their uneven progress and dramatic reversals offer insights into the difficulties encountered in ending protracted conflicts, and the various kinds of transformations that shape their course.

First, South Africa. The transition from apartheid to multiparty elections in South Africa was one of the most remarkable cases of conflict resolution in the post-Cold War period. How did the white minority, which had been so determined to hold on to power, come to agree to majority rule? How was this extraordinary reversal in government achieved without a bloodbath?

Second, Israel-Palestine. When Israel's Prime Minister Yitzak Rabin shook the hand of PLO leader Yassir Arafat on 13 September 1993 to seal the signing of the Oslo Accords, it seemed that they were celebrating a historic breakthrough in the protracted conflict. The Accords opened the way to a self-governing Palestinian authority, mutual recognition of Israel and the PLO, and final-status talks on other dividing issues. Yet the failure to implement the Accords and Israel's continuing subordination of the Palestinians living in the occupied territories raise troubling questions about whether it was ever appropriate to attempt conflict resolution in the first place between such unequal parties.

South Africa

The *structure* of the conflict lay in the incompatibility between the National Party (NP) government which was determined to uphold white power and privileges through the apartheid system, and the black majority which sought radical change and a non-racial, equal society based on one-person one-vote. Transforming this conflict involved first the empowerment of the majority through political mobilization and the campaign of resistance against the apartheid laws. The revolt in the townships, political mobilization and movements like Steve Biko's 'Black Consciousness' all expressed the refusal of the majority to acquiesce in a racially dominated society. Externally, the international pressure on the South African regime partly offset the internal imbalance of power, through the anti-apartheid campaign, international isolation, sporting bans, partial sanctions and disinvestment.

Changes in the *context* cleared significant obstacles. While South Africa had been involved in wars in Southern Africa with Cuban-supported and Soviet-supplied regimes, it had been possible for white South Africans to believe that their regime was a bastion against international communist penetration, and for the ANC to believe that a war of liberation based in the front-line states might eventually succeed. With the waning of the Cold War and changes in the region, these views became unsustainable. This separated the question of apartheid from ideological conflicts, and concentrated the struggle in South Africa itself.

Another crucial contextual factor was economic change. It had been possible to run an agricultural and mining economy profitably with poorly paid black labour. But as the economy diversified and modernized, a more educated and skilled labour force was necessary. The demands of the cities for labour created huge townships, such as Soweto, which became a focus for opposition to the regime. The more the government relied on repression to control the situation, the more exposed it became to international sanctions and disinvestment.

Significant changes of *actors* also made a crucial impact in the process of change. On the side of the National Party, the change in leadership from Vorster to P. W. Botha brought a shift from an unyielding defence of apartheid to a willingness to contemplate reform, so long as it preserved the power and privileges of the white minority. The change in leadership from Botha to F. W. de Klerk heralded a more radical reform policy and the willingness to abandon many aspects of apartheid. Changes at constituency level supported these shifts. For example, the businessmen in South Africa were among the first to see the need for a change in the policy of apartheid, and took a leading role in maintaining contacts with the ANC at a time when the peace process seemed to have reached a sticking point, for example in 1985–6. The bulk of the white population gradually came to accept the inevitability of a change, and this influenced the result of the 1988 elections and the referendum in favour of reform in March 1992. The split in the white majority in 1992 created an intra-party conflict between white extremists and the NP.

On the side of the black majority, the most important actor change was the split that developed between the ANC and Inkatha, starting in 1976 and growing gradually more serious, until it became a new source of internal armed conflict that threatened the peace process in 1992–4. It seemed that Inkatha and the white extremists might prevent a settlement, but in the end they helped to cement the alliance of the government and the ANC behind negotiated change. We return to this below.

With regard to the *issues*, both parties in the conflict made significant changes in their positions and goals.[12] On the NP side, a series of shifts can be identified in the mid- and late 1980s. First there was Botha's shift from the defence of apartheid to the pursuit of limited reforms. He proposed a tricameral parliament which would include whites, Indian and coloured people, but exclude blacks. Botha also sought negotiations with Mandela, but Mandela refused to negotiate until he was released. The reforms failed in their intention to broaden the base of the government's support, and instead led to intensified opposition in the townships. This led to the government's decision to declare the State of Emergency, which contributed in turn to further international pressure and disinvestment. By 1985 the process had reached a sticking point, with the government unwilling to make further reforms, and the black population unwilling to accept the status quo.

It was at this point, with confrontation and no talks between the two sides, that third-party mediators made an important contribution.[13] A group of businessmen met with ANC leaders in Zambia, and afterwards issued a call for political negotiations and the abandonment of apartheid. Botha made a new shift in September 1986, offering blacks resident outside the homelands a vote on township councils, but they were boycotted. Botha's reforms had stalled. By 1987–8 the situation had reached a second sticking point. The white electorate now showed that it was unhappy with the pace of change in the 1988 elections, and F. W. de Klerk's win in the election for the leadership of the NP brought a change of direction.

On the ANC side, too, there was change. Before 1985, the ANC saw itself as a national liberation movement and expected to establish a socialist government by seizing power after a successful armed struggle. By 1985 it had begun to accept that this goal was unrealistic, and that a compromise was necessary.

A turning-point came in 1989–90. De Klerk shifted decisively towards a policy of negotiations: he began to end segregation, lifted the ban on the ANC, and finally released Mandela on 11 February 1990. By the Groote Schuur Minute of May 1990, the government agreed to 'work toward lifting the state of emergency', while the ANC agreed to 'curb violence'. The ANC had now accepted that the NP would remain in power while negotiations were carried out, and the NP that it would have to give up its monopoly of power. The government's aim was now a power-sharing agreement, in which its future role in a multiracial government would be guaranteed. In February 1991 the parties took a further step towards each others' positions when the government agreed to tolerate the continued existence of an ANC militia force, and in return the ANC agreed not to activate it. The government released political prisoners in April 1991 and in September the parties signed the National Peace Accord, which set up a code of conduct for the security forces and mechanisms for dispute settlement during the course of negotiations. This was followed by the establishment of the Convention for a Democratic South Africa (CODESA), which agreed on a list of principles for a new constitution and set up working groups to work out the details.

There was still a wide gulf between the parties' positions. The National Party sought to sustain white power by arriving at a federal constitution based on power-sharing, a bicameral parliament, proportional representation, protection of group rights and strong regional governments. The ANC in contrast wanted to see a short-lived interim government of national unity followed by elections based on one-person one-vote, and a constitution based on individual rights and a centralized government. After further negotiations, the parties compromised on a Transitional Executive Council which would oversee the government, and an elected constituent assembly which would produce a new constitution. But they could not agree on the proportion of votes which would be required for a majority in the constituent assembly.

Meanwhile, the 'spoilers' were becoming active on both extremes. White extremists, who regarded the National Party's position as an unacceptable compromise, and the Inkatha Freedom Party, which feared that an ANC-dominated government would override the Zulu regional power base, found a shared interest in wrecking the negotiations. At first, their pressure caused a hardening of positions. After winning a referendum among the whites approving his conduct of the negotiations, de Klerk refused to make concessions on the voting issue. The ANC, facing escalating violence in the townships, which Inkatha was suspected of fomenting with the connivance of the police, decided to break off negotiations.

This was the third and most dangerous sticking point. Violence was rising and the threat of breakdown was clear. The ANC called a general strike and mass demonstrations. The police cracked down and twenty-eight marchers were killed in Bisho, Ciskei in September 1992. This disaster reminded both sides of the bloodbath that seemed likely if negotiations failed. Roelf Meyer, the Minister of Constitutional Development, and Cyril Ramaphosa, the ANC's lead negotiator, continued to meet unofficially in hotel rooms as violence rose. In September 1992 the parties returned decisively to negotiations when de Klerk and Mandela agreed a 'Record of Understanding'. This spelt out the basis on which power would eventually be transferred: an interim, elected parliament to agree a new constitution, and an interim power-sharing government of national unity, to be composed of parties winning more than 5 per cent of the vote, to last for five years. The ANC had shifted to accept power-sharing and a long transition; the National Party had shifted to accept that the continuation of white power would not be guaranteed. By now the NP was fearful of losing support to the right unless it acted quickly, and it stepped up progress, accepting a deadline for elections in April 1994. The Transitional Executive Council, set up in September 1993, gradually took on more and more of the key political functions of government, and the NP and the ANC found themselves jointly defending the settlement against Inkatha and the white extremists, who now supported a confederal alternative providing autonomy for the regions in which they lived.

The six months leading up to the elections were thus a struggle between the NP–ANC coalition and the spoilers, with the conduct of the elections as the prize. Inkatha left the Transitional Executive Council and violence against ANC supporters in Natal intensified. Negotiations between the ANC and Chief Buthelezi, leader of the Inkatha Freedom Party, came to nothing and Buthelezi prepared to exercise his threat of boycotting the elections. At the last moment the ANC offered King Goodwill of the Zulus a major concession over the trusteeship of land in Natal. Buthelezi's followers refused to follow him into the wilderness, and he was forced to accept a last-minute deal and participate in the elections. The elections thus proceeded legitimately, and returned a parliament in which the ANC fell just below the two-thirds majority required to pass laws. Power-sharing would be a fact. Mandela became president of the government of national unity, with de Klerk and Buthelezi as ministers.

In the end, a process of negotiations and elections had replaced apartheid and white power (Waldmeier, 1998; Harvey, 2003). The legitimation of the black opposition had transformed the structure of the conflict, turning an asymmetrical relationship between minority and majority into a symmetrical relationship between parties and their followers. Though many tensions remained, and real socio-economic transformation was slow to come, the elections conveyed 'participation, legitimation and allocation, the three elements necessary to the settlement of internal conflicts' (Zartman, ed., 1995b: 339). The parties in South Africa had achieved an agreed and legitimate constitutional settlement, in a situation so unfavourable that many observers had previously judged it to be impossible.

The Oslo Accords: the elusive search for peace in the Middle East

Of all the peace processes of the 1990s, the Israeli-Palestinian process has rightly gained the most attention. It is therefore important to review how the setbacks to the process reflect on the thinking and practice of conflict resolution. When the Oslo Accords were signed in 1993, it was widely believed that the Norwegian facilitation had brought about a breakthrough in the long conflict. Ten years later, most of the provisions of the Accords were suspended, the key 'final status' issues of the conflict remained unresolved, the violent occupation of Gaza and the West Bank continued and Palestinian suicide bombers were retaliating by blowing up Israeli civilians. What had gone so wrong?

We will take two separate narratives of the events to illustrate some of the contested views. First, the view that Oslo was indeed a breakthrough, but the prospects for conflict resolution were destroyed by 'spoilers' on both sides, and by the fundamental asymmetry of the parties. We shall rely here on accounts by Shlaim (2000) and Smith (2004), and a variety of conflict research perspectives from Aggestam (1999), Galtung (2004) and Kriesberg (2001).

The second perspective is that the attempt at conflict resolution was fundamentally flawed from the outset, in the context of Israeli-Palestinian asymmetry. As an example of this viewpoint we will quote Jones (1999: 130), who argues that the peace process became a means whereby 'a stronger party slowly and deliberately crushes the aspirations of the weaker party'. In Jones's view (1999: 160), the Oslo Accords, and the process that led to them, 'reproduce structures of inequality and domination', implying that conflict resolution in such contexts is fundamentally problematic.

In favour of the first perspective, the choice of a facilitative, back-channel approach made possible a breakthrough, where the official diplomacy at Madrid was stalled. The Norwegian intervention was made in good faith, with the intention of reducing the suffering caused by the conflict. It opened the way to mutual recognition and to a partition of Palestine as a possible solution to the long conflict. The Accords aimed to reconcile the needs of the two peoples to live side-by-side, to give autonomy in Gaza and Jericho as a first step towards what the Palestinians and many outsiders saw as a two-state solution. The two sides agreed to resolve the major 'final status' issues in the conflict within three years. It is only through negotiation and exploration that two sides can reframe their views of a conflict and create a new reality which opens the potential for a new relationship (Aggestam, 1999: 173).

In favour of the second perspective, the Oslo process was launched at a time when the PLO was weak and desperate, and the Israeli government overwhelmingly strong. The outcome has certainly been one in which the stronger party has crushed and humiliated the weaker, and the arrangements imposed by Israel have ended up in a dismembered and impoverished Palestinian entity, lacking not only statehood but even autonomy (Said, 2002). The denoument of this process was the construction of what the Arabs call 'the apartheid wall', symbolizing the Sharon government's intention to keep the Palestinians down and out. There is no road to peace in this direction.

However, responsibility for the fact that events took the course they did should not be laid at the door of the Norwegian facilitators. The 'spirit of Oslo' dissolved even before the Accords were signed, as lawyers from the Israeli government hedged the agreement with restrictions and caveats (Corbin, 1994). Neither Rabin nor Peres were prepared at that time to accept a Palestinian state, and both lost opportunities to expedite the negotiations (Shlaim, 2000; Smith, 2004). Significant constituencies on both sides opposed the agreement. Violence on both sides followed the Accords: the Hebron massacre, attacks by Hamas, the assassination of Rabin. With the election of Netanyahu, the Israeli government turned decisively away from the Oslo process, stalling on implementation of the Accords and accelerating the construction of settlements in the occupied territories.

It may be argued that an incremental process necessarily left the cards in the hands of the Israeli government, and therefore exposed the weaker to the risk that the process would never proceed further. This indeed turned out to have been so. Nevertheless, subsequent developments suggest that a two-state solution may still be a possibility. At the Camp David talks in 2000, Israeli Prime Minister Barak went further than any of his predecessors in appearing to accept Palestinian sovereignty over East Jerusalem, and being willing to return 91 per cent – but not all – of the West Bank to the Palestinians (for a lively debate on what went wrong at Camp David, see Agha and Mulley, 2001; Morris, 2002). In October 2003, the unofficial Geneva Accords, between Beilin and other members of the Labour opposition and former Palestinian ministers, brought the Oslo process to an unofficial conclusion by agreeing a comprehensive settlement to the conflict. Under this peace plan, Israel would withdraw to the internationally recognized 1967 borders (save for a few territorial exchanges); Palestine would become a state. Jewish settlements, except those included in exchanges, would revert to Palestinian sovereignty; Jerusalem would be divided, with Palestinian sovereignty over Arab parts of East Jerusalem and the Temple Mount. In return, the Palestinian negotiators were prepared to concede the right of Palestinian refugees to return to their homes. It was a painful concession, abandoning a pillar of faith of the Palestinian struggle. Most Palestinians rejected the Geneva Accords on this account, while the Israeli government rejected the territorial proposals out of hand.

Nevertheless these negotiations, and significant steps by Arab states, have revealed at least the contours of a possible two-state solution that – if a right of return were accepted – could, potentially, become the centrepiece of a more comprehensive settlement for the Arab-Israeli conflict as a whole (International Crisis Group, 2002).

But a number of preconditions are required before such a settlement is feasible. First, evidently, the Israeli government would have to agree it. External and internal changes are necessary for that to happen. A weakness of the conflict resolution attempts, arguably, has been their narrow basis. Only politicians from the Israeli Labour Party and the PLO have been able to come somewhere close to – but still some way from – a framework for an agreement. It will require changes of perspective and discourse for the Sephardic Jews and others who have supported Likud and the religious parties to accept a two-state solution, and also for Islamists on the Palestinian side to come to terms with a Jewish state. Indeed, the exclusively Jewish basis that Israelis claim for their state appears difficult to reconcile with the rights of Palestinian refugees and Arabs within Israel.

This analysis highlights that conflict resolution cannot be left to the conflict region alone, but must also address the wider context in which the conflict is situated. Following Etzioni's (1964) idea of encapsulated conflict, the conflict transformation process must reach out from the local level to the wider levels in which it is embedded. To put the same thing in another way, the task of mediation is only a part of conflict resolution, broadly conceived. Overcoming the asymmetry of the conflict is also essential and this may sometimes require advocacy and support for one side, as Curle and Francis suggest (see chapter 1, figures 1.8 and 1.11). People in the role of mediators should not be advocates, but mediation and advocacy are complementary. Peace and justice are indivisible and have to be pursued together (van der Merwe, 1989: 7).

Galtung (2004: 103–9) suggests that the conflict must be balanced, by placing Israel and Palestine within a Middle Eastern community. Another way of balancing is to modify the US economic, military and political support for Israel, which remains a lynchpin of the conflict. Perhaps a stage will come when American support becomes more even-handed in implementing the road map towards a peaceful settlement. This seems far off at present: but such a change in context would have a transforming impact on the conflict. The precedent of disinvestment from South Africa is strong. The task of conflict resolution here goes beyond what facilitators and mediators can achieve, and raises issues of how the world society is to implement cosmopolitan standards of justice and human rights, in an even-handed way.

Conclusion

We have identified the characteristics of a conflict resolution approach to ending conflicts, while acknowledging that in many contemporary conflicts, such an approach is not applied. We argued that conflict resolution is more than a simple matter of mediating between parties and reaching an integrative agreement on the issues that divide them. It must also touch on the context of the conflict, the conflict structure, the intra-party as well as the inter-party divisions, and the broader system of society and governance within which the conflict is embedded. This suggests that interventions should not be confined to the 'ripe moment'. Peace processes, we argued, are a complex succession of transformations, punctuated by several turning points and sticking points. At different stages in this process, transformations in the context, the actors, the issues, the people involved and the structure of the conflict may be vital to move the conflict resolution process forward.

Even when settlements are reached, the best-engineered political arrangements can collapse again later, if new life is not breathed in to them by the will of the parties, their constituencies and external supporters to make them work. For this reason, reconstruction and peacebuilding remains a constant priority, especially in the post-settlement phase. The next three chapters tackle the question of how settlements can be sustained without a return to fresh violence.

Recommended reading

Collier et. al. (2003); Harris and Reilly, eds (1998); Stedman et al. (2002); Wallensteen (2002b).
Online sources on peace accords:
ACCORD <http://www.c-r.org/accord/index.shtml>
USIP   <http://www.usip.org/library/pa.html>
INCORE <http://www.incore.ulst.ac.uk/cds/agreements/>

Post-War Reconstruction

Peace agreements provide a framework for ending hostilities and a
guide to the initial stages of postconflict reform. They do not create
conditions under which the deep cleavages that produced the war
are automatically surmounted. Successfully ending the divisions
that lead to war, healing the social wounds created by war, and
creating a society where the differences among social groups are
resolved through compromise rather than violent conflict requires
that conflict resolution and consensus building shape all
interactions among citizens and between citizens and the state.

Nicole Ball (1996: 619)

When wars have ended, post-conflict peacebuilding is vital. The UN
has often devoted too little attention and too few resources to this
critical challenge. Successful peacebuilding requires the
deployment of peacekeepers with the right mandates and sufficient
capacity to deter would-be spoilers; funds for demobilization and
disarmament, built into peacekeeping budgets; a new trust fund to
fill critical gaps in rehabilitation and reintegration of combatants,
as well as other early reconstruction tasks; and a focus on building
State institutions and capacity, especially in the rule of law sector.
Doing this job successfully should be a core function of the United
Nations.

Report of the UN High-Level Panel on Threats, Challenges and Change – A
More Secure World: Our Shared Responsibility (2004)

THIS chapter and the next consider the contribution that the conflict
resolution field can make to peacebuilding at the fragile stage when
war ends but peace is not yet secure. We have seen in chapter 7 that
there are many ways in which wars come to an end either temporarily
or permanently: through military victory, through formal peace agreements, or when the fighting reaches a stalemate or peters out into a
precarious stand-off punctuated by sporadic localized violence. Having
brought a war to an end, the next task is to prevent a relapse into
violence and secure a self-sustaining peace. This involves demobilization of the warring parties and decommissioning of their weapons, the

185

re-establishment of a functioning political system, restoration of essential services, return of refugees and other urgent priorities.

At the end of the Second World War, post-war reconstruction in the defeated Axis powers was carried out by the occupation forces following their outright victory in the war. Having disarmed the defeated, the occupying forces installed new governments with democratic constitutions, supported physical and economic reconstruction and gradually handed power to new indigenous governments. During the Cold War, outright victories became rare and many conflicts became protracted and difficult to end. Most conflicts did not end in agreed settlements and agreements frequently broke down at the implementation stage. The period from shortly before the end of the Cold War to the 1990s proved to be a high point for post-settlement peacebuilding. The UN organized sustained peacebuilding operations that went beyond peacekeeping. The UN saw its task as facilitating a process in which the parties to a violent conflict would secure the peace and then reach agreement on a new political system. Since the end of the 1990s this has given way to a new period in which 'coalitions of the willing' have attempted to restore stable conditions after wars which have not ended in peace agreements, not necessarily with the authority of the United Nations or the agreement of the formerly fighting factions. The term 'post-war reconstruction' is now widely used to include these interventions.

This term indicates a shift of meaning from the earlier term, 'post-settlement peacebuilding'. Johan Galtung invented the term 'peacebuilding' and meant it to characterize progression towards positive peace following the ending of war. The main priority of international efforts, however, has been to secure sufficient stability to avoid the recurrence of war – and sometimes also to introduce a democratic system. As a result the term 'reconstruction' is problematic for some. For example, in Northern Ireland, Mari Fitzduff says, 'reconstruction is a "no go" term – it implies that one reconstructs society to resemble what it was like before the conflict . . . [this] implies going back to a past which exemplifies the very factors that created the conflict' (in Austin, 2004: 375). For others, however, the term reconstruction implies righting a moral wrong done to the victims of violence. In Norbert Ropers's words, 'giving up the perspective of re-construction might also be interpreted as giving up the right to return, to resettle and to rebuild the homes and livelihoods for all those affected by the war' (in ibid.: 376).

In the first edition of this book we looked particularly at cases of post-Cold War settlements in which the United Nations played a major role in supporting the implementation of peace settlements, including Namibia, Angola, Mozambique, Cambodia and El Salvador. In this edition we widen our analysis to assess a cluster of other attempts at post-war reconstruction undertaken since then, not necessarily after a formal peace settlement and not necessarily under the aegis of the United Nations. What all these cases have in common is that external interveners have played a leading role in post-war reconstruction, that they have declared their sole aim to be to stabilize the host country and lay the foundations for sustainable peace, and that they have then said that they would withdraw. For this reason they might collectively be called 'intervention, reconstruction and withdrawal' (IRW) operations to distinguish them from other post-war peacebuilding efforts (see chapter 9) – though clearly there is a sharp difference between operations conducted by the UN following civil wars and those carried out by major powers which were parties to the preceding conflict and continue to deploy their own forces in the aftermath.

At this point we lay ourselves open to misunderstanding. Whereas in the first edition our sample of UN-led post-settlement peacebuilding operations might be more easily seen as attempts at conflict resolution, the broader sample of post-war reconstructions considered in this second edition are more controversial. We do not suggest that recent episodes such as the attempts to reconstruct Afghanistan post-2001 and Iraq post-2003 should be seen as conflict resolution, nor are we concerned with the question of whether these interventions were justified in the first place. Our aim is to review the development of thinking and practice about post-settlement peacebuilding and post-war reconstruction and to offer an assessment of it from a conflict resolution perspective.[1] In chapter 9 we balance this with a survey of the genuinely conflict resolution concept of peacebuilding from below, and in chapter 13 we discuss the principles that should guide legitimate intervention in conflicts from a conflict resolution perspective.

Our focus in this chapter is primarily on external interventions. We do not wish to suggest, however, that external intervenors are necessarily the prime actors involved in determining outcomes. The internal actors and domestic constituencies are almost always the more important. But it is a feature of modern armed conflict that the devastation is so great and the civil population's need for support is so pressing that external support for reconstruction is often badly needed (though this is not always the primary motive for outsiders to intervene). Whether interventions turn out to be in the interests of the civil population or not is a matter for investigation. In what follows we wish to assess what types of external intervention are helpful and what types are unhelpful from a conflict resolution perspective, recognizing that as conflict persists in the post-war phase, so too must efforts at conflict resolution. We will conclude that the effectiveness of peacebuilding in contributing to conflict resolution depends heavily on its legitimacy in the eyes of the domestic population.

Intervention, Reconstruction, Withdrawal (IRW) Operations, 1989–2004

The 1978 Settlement Proposal in Namibia, devised by the Contact Group of western states, mandated the United Nations Transition Assistance Group (UNTAG) under Security Council Resolution 435 to assist a Special Representative appointed by the UN Secretary-General 'to ensure the early independence of Namibia through free and fair elections under the supervision and control of the United Nations' (Ramsbotham and Woodhouse, 1999: 167–72). The transition phase was to last a year. This unexceptional decolonization arrangement unexpectedly turned out to be the template for international post-war intervention and reconstruction programmes when it was revived ten years later in 1988–9 in very different circumstances. The ending of the Cold War drew a line under what had been an almost automatic backing of rival sides and regimes by the superpowers, and opened up the possibility of concerted external action to end debilitating wars or overthrow repressive and dangerous regimes, and subsequently help to create or rebuild domestic political capacity to the point where power could be safely handed back to a viable and internationally acceptable indigenous authority in the host country.

This remarkable era in world politics has unfolded in two main phases so far. First came the period between the Namibia Accords and the Dayton agreement in Bosnia (1995), in which it seemed to suit the major powers to encourage the United Nations to assume a lead coordinating role (this was the theme of the first edition of this book). This was followed by a period in which, in different permutations, the norm has become one of multilateral coalitions under a lead nation or nations, supported by regional alliances or organizations, international financial institutions, G8, and a number of relief and development bodies, with the United Nations and its agencies playing a variety of more or less central or peripheral roles. What has been characteristic of both periods has been that the shape of intervention policy has been decided by the politically and militarily more powerful states. This is natural – strong states intervene in weak states, not vice versa, which is why some commentators are opposed to the entire enterprise, a point to be considered later.

As suggest in table 8.1, at least five distinct types of intervention can be distinguished: transitional assistance for postcolonial independence, backing for a previously democratically elected government or to restore a disrupted democracy, post-settlement peace support, humanitarian intervention in ongoing conflict and/or weak states,

Table 8.1 IRW operations 1989–2004: intervention categories

	(a) Independence	(b) Democracy	(c) Peace support	(d) Humanitarian	(e) Defence/regime change
1989	Namibia		Nicaragua[1]		
1990					
1991			Angola[1] El Salvador[1]		
1992			Cambodia Mozambique	(Bosnia (UNPROFOR))[2] (Somalia (UNITAF))[2]	
1993			Rwanda		
1994		Haiti	Guatemala[1]		
1995			Bosnia (IFOR/SFOR)		
1996					
1997					
1998					
1999	East Timor	Sierra Leone[3]		Kosovo	
2000					
2001					Afghanistan
2002					
2003			DRC (Zaire)[1] Liberia		Iraq
2004		Haiti[3]		Sudan (Darfur)?	

1   The mandate of the UN Observer Group in Central America (ONUCA) in Nicaragua and Honduras was initially to verify an interstate non-intervention agreement. It was subsequently expanded to take on something of an IRW role. The UN Observer Mission in El Salvador (ONUSAL) was established in 1991 to verify human rights agreements. It was expanded after the January 1992 peace agreement to take on a full IRW role. The UN Verification Mission in Guatemala (MINUGUA) was deployed for human rights verification and trust-building from 1994, then its mandate was expanded in 1997 to include verification of wider peace agreements. Initiated by the July 1999 Lusaka agreement, full-scale IRW operations did not effectively begin in the Democratic Republic of the Congo until 2003.

2   Neither Bosnia 1992–5 nor Somalia 1992–3 is an IRW operation, although they are included in brackets here because they are often cited as such. Attempts to broker peace during the UN Protection Force (UNPROFOR) period in Bosnia proved abortive, while the UN Operation in Somalia (UNOSOM II) from May 1993 can be seen as a proto-IRW mission, but continued fighting precluded post-war reconstruction. The same applies to the Military Observer Group of ECOWAS (ECOMOG)'s interventions in Liberia from 1990 to 1996, much discussed in the humanitarian intervention literature, despite a UN presence after the abortive 1993 Cotonou agreement. The implementation of the 1996 Abuja II agreement through to the election of Charles Taylor in July 1997 is similarly not included, because it is better seen as an extension of Taylor's bid for power. Liberia truly enters IRW territory from 2003 after the negotiated abdication of Taylor under category (c).

3   Despite successful democratic elections in Sierra Leone in 1996, it was not until February 2000 that international efforts to restore elected President Kabbah evolved into a full IRW mission with the expansion of the October 1999 UN Mission in Sierra Leone (UNAMSIL). The 1994 IRW restoration of elected President Aristide in Haiti was initially seen as successful, with further elections following in 1995. The subsequent unravelling of the IRW effort, particularly in the wake of disputed elections in 2000, seems at the time of writing to have triggered a new IRW attempt in 2004.

and the rooting out of perceived threats to national and international peace and security (including the war on terror).

Before we go further, one general conclusion can already be drawn from table 8.1. There are good discussions in the literature on factors conducive to success in post-war peacebuilding (for example, Licklider, ed., 1993: 14–17; Downs and Stedman, 2002: 54–61). What table 8.1 adds to this is the difference that intervention types (a) to (e) make to the difficulty of the task. With due allowance for all the other variables, we can suggest that the first phase of the post-war reconstruction process tends to be easier to complete successfully: (a) in decolonization wars where the former master has agreed to independence, and (b) in support of already democratically elected governments with near unanimous international recognition.[2] The record of (c) post-settlement peace support operations has been mixed, but not nearly as poor as has sometimes been made out. Angola was a failure given the inability of the interveners to handle Jonas Savimbi, while Rwanda was disastrous in view of the unwillingness of the international community to reinforce the UN Assistance Mission for Rwanda (UNAMIR) when it became plain that genocide was being planned. But Nicaragua, El Salvador and Mozambique are usually classed as successes, with Cambodia more controversial – but for many analysts a partial success despite the defection of the Khmer Rouge before the elections and the subsequent subversion of the election result by Hun Sen. It is (d), humanitarian intervention in ongoing civil wars and weak states as in Liberia 1990–6 (despite repeated ceasefires), and particularly post-1992 Bosnia and Somalia, that proved much more difficult to manage, with the latter two examples fatally (and unfairly) discrediting all types of comparable intervention under the aegis of the UN as a result. This should not have been surprising had decision-makers in the UN Security Council considered the very different circumstances between a postcolonial independence operation (Namibia), a post-settlement peace process support operation (Mozambique) and a humanitarian intervention in ongoing conflict (Somalia). In the case of UNPROFOR, the peacekeepers were already in Bosnia to support the Croatia agreement before the Bosnian war started – they were subsequently loaded with successive Security Council mandates out of proportion to their force configuration.

Among the peace support operations, a significant factor has been whether an agreement among the warring factions to settle the conflict has been made, and the extent to which external third parties have the consent of internal parties. In Nicaragua, El Salvador, Guatemala and Mozambique there was external support for negotiations but little external coercion; the parties were the main driving force in reaching a settlement and the settlements stuck. In other cases, as in Bosnia and Cambodia, settlements were imposed and needed continuing external coercion or they became unstuck. Rwanda was a case where a settlement was agreed among the major parties, but badly needed external support to sustain it did not arrive.

At the time of writing the final outcome is uncertain in (e), the fifth category of 'defensive' intervention and regime-change in order to pre-empt perceived threats to national and international peace and security, but it seems evident that this is a highly challenging environment. The international 'footprint' in Afghanistan is relatively light given US reluctance to become enmeshed in post-war nation-building there and the resistance of Northern Alliance commanders (given a decisive role from November 2001) to the arrival of more sizeable intervention forces. Even the large-scale troop deployment committed to Iraq is scarcely adequate for pacification in hostile areas given the size of the country and continued armed resistance to the occupying forces. In both cases, the fact that there was ongoing war after the formal cessation of large-scale hostilities has, for obvious reasons, played a major role in complicating the task for interveners. It is significant from a conflict resolution perspective that the perceived legitimacy of the intervention among the host population seems to decrease concomitantly in general terms as we move from case (a) through to case (e).

Finally, we can also now see that none of these cases approximates to the post-1945 context of total defeat and unconditional surrender after a classic interstate war as in Germany and Japan, which is how many in the US administration seem to have seen the task of rebuilding Iraq after the March 2003 intervention. In 1945 the political conflicts were decided on the battlefield and were emphatically over before reconstruction began. This is not the situation in most 1989–2004 cases. Despite common parlance, these are precisely not 'post-conflict' contexts, as will be elaborated below. Nor is this an accidental feature, but is part of the transformation in the nature of major armed conflict in the latter part of the twentieth century. It is also the difference between, say, the Northern Ireland peace process involving the accommodation of undefeated conflictants, and the peace process in South Africa where the outcome of the main conflict had already been decided by the irrevocable defeat of apartheid. This does much to explain why, despite the much greater long-term difficulties facing the reconstruction process in South Africa, it has been the Northern Ireland peace process that has seemed to encounter the greater initial problems.

Filling the Post-War Planning Gap

Another important point about the 1989–2004 post-war reconstruction experience from a conflict resolution perspective is the fact that no one operating model can fit the needs and complexities of each country's situation. The crucial negotiations are ultimately those between domestic parties, their constituencies and the affected populations, but these are not always well supported by conflict-sensitive external policies. The United Nations lacks adequate capacity in this area and nationally organized interventions tend to be strongly influenced by national priorities and short-term political interests of the intervening states. There are extensive institutional bases and planning structures for relief and disaster work at one end of the spectrum, and for longer-term international development at the other end of the spectrum, both within national administrations and within international organizations including the United Nations. But there is nothing much in between, which is exactly where the requirements for support for reconstruction and peacebuilding are located. This means that those who look for enhanced international planning, coordination and implementation capacities of this kind tend to call for the building up of a new international agency 'that specializes in conducting postconflict peacebuilding missions and administering war-shattered states' (even including perhaps an ability to assume a 'temporary directorship' over affected countries) (Paris, 2001: 774–81). Short of this there are the kinds of incremental changes recommended in the August 2000 report of the Panel on United Nations Peace Operations – the Brahimi Report (2000) – such as the setting up of a Peacebuilding Planning Unit in the Department for Political Affairs. Although the UN has probably made more concerted attempts to learn from past experience than other major interveners, this has tended to coincide with the relative loss of its leading role in post-war reconstruction since the mid-1990s (see successive United Nations Reports). The December 2004 Report of the UN Secretary-General's High-Level Panel on building consensus about the UN's role summarized its recommendations in this area as follows:

> The report recommends the creation of a Peacebuilding Commission – a new mechanism within the UN, drawing on the Security Council and the Economic and Social Council, donors, and national authorities. Working closely with regional organizations and the international financial institutions, such a commission could fill a crucial gap by giving the necessary attention to countries emerging from conflict. Outside the UN, a forum bringing together the heads of the 20 largest economies, developed and developing, would help the coherent

management of international monetary, financial, trade and development policy. (Executive Summary: 6)

At national level attempts to bridge this planning gap require either efforts to build greater 'inter-agency cooperation' between the relevant planning components within government, or the creation of new structures and procedures. As we saw in chapter 5, the United Kingdom, for example, has attempted to remedy this in the area of prevention through the setting up in 2001 of African and Global 'Conflict Prevention Pools' to coordinate the efforts of the Foreign and Commonwealth Office (UKFCO), Ministry of Defence (UKMOD) and Department for International Development (UKDFID) (GCPP, 2003). But it is only in the wake of the 2003 Iraq war that anything comparable has been created for post-war reconstruction – what is at the time of writing planned to be a forty-strong interdepartmental Post-Conflict Reconstruction Unit. The intention is that the Unit, resourced through an independent budget, will provide the institutional continuity required to support a pool of some two hundred key personnel with expertise across the sectors relevant to post-war reconstruction ready to operationalize the UK's contribution at short notice.

In the USA a Joint Interagency Cooperation Group (JIACG) attempted something similar in the aftermath of the 2003 Iraq war, although the vast discrepancy in planning capacity between the military planning resources of the Department of Defense (USDOD), with a total personnel of nearly 1.3 million, and those of the Agency for International Development (USAID,) with a personnel of 1,000, made this difficult. The incoming Bush administration tore up the Clinton Presidential Decision Directive (PDD) 56 on Interagency Planning for Complex Contingencies, and there was a reluctance to think that anything could be learnt from previous UN experience in post-war reconstruction – hence the inadequacy of the original Office for Reconstruction and Humanitarian Assistance (ORHA) in 2003 Iraq, run from the Pentagon and almost immediately abandoned. A new Office of the Coordinator for Reconstruction and Stabilization was set up in August 2004 with an apparent brief to draw up 'post-conflict' plans for up to twenty-five countries seen to be at risk and a capacity to coordinate three reconstruction operations 'at the same time', each lasting 'five to seven years'. Many commentators are alarmed at the prospect of such grandiose national plans to reshape 'the very social fabric' of target countries, linked as they are to huge potential contracts for western (and in particular US) businesses.[3] This is linked to control of the World Bank, whose investment in 'post-conflict' countries has risen from 16 per cent of its lending in 1998 to 20–25 per cent.

In short, there is a dearth of institutional memory or learning capacity among those with the resources to organize large-scale interventions and post-war reconstruction operations of this kind. There is no alternative to complex international cooperation, a major lesson to be learnt with important conflict resolution implications.

Wittgenstein's Locomotive Cabin: The International Post-War Reconstruction Blueprint

Another surprising aspect of the 1989–2004 post-war reconstruction experience has been the extent to which there have been commonalities in the reconstruction and withdrawal components across the dataset, despite huge discrepancies in conflict contexts, types of intervention and intervener, and whether these were forcible or non-forcible operations. This is reminiscent of Wittgenstein's locomotive cabin, in which, despite the different functions that they perform, the driver is faced with a uniform set of handles. In particular, a major claim in this chapter is that what we may loosely call the 'IRW blueprint' can broadly be seen to have been shared across the pre-1995 and the post-1995 periods, so that what we wrote in the first edition of this book can still be seen to apply, even where interventions may have been motivated by the 'war on terror'.

We can see this best by observing the continuing relevance for current IRW operations of definitions of the programme from the earlier period. In response to the request from Security Council Heads of Government meeting on 31 January 1992 to draft general principles that would 'guide decisions on when a domestic situation warrants international action', the UN Secretary-General (UNSG) defined 'post-conflict peacebuilding' as 'actions to identify and support structures which will tend to strengthen and solidify peace in order to avoid a relapse into conflict' (Boutros-Ghali, 1992: 11). This was at first largely identified with military demobilization and the political transition to participatory electoral democracy, but was progressively expanded in subsequent versions to include wider political, economic and social dimensions. In the 1995 *Supplement to An Agenda for Peace* it was envisaged that post-conflict peacebuilding would initially be undertaken by multifunctional UN operations, then handed over to civilian agencies under a resident coordinator, and finally transferred entirely to local agents (Boutros-Ghali, 1995). In 1997 the new UNSG, Kofi Annan, used similar language, defining post-conflict peacebuilding as 'the various concurrent and integrated actions undertaken at the end of a conflict to consolidate peace and prevent a recurrence of armed confrontation'. He distinguished this from ongoing *humanitarian* and *development* activities in 'countries emerging from crisis', insofar as it has the specific *political* aims of reducing 'the risk of resumption of conflict' and contributing to the creation of 'conditions most conducive to reconciliation, reconstruction and recovery' (Annan, 1997c). The same body of ideas has been drawn on to inform what is now more usually termed 'post-conflict reconstruction' in the innumerable reports, policy papers and studies that are produced almost weekly by national capitals, regional organizations, international financial institutions, think-tanks and non-governmental organizations engaged in IRW operations – although, as we have noted, the context of intervention changes significantly when there is no peace settlement and when the intervenors are one of the formerly warring parties.

Four features common to these reconstruction and withdrawal programmes will enable us to draw up a summative matrix that we can then carry forward to the rest of the chapter.

First, we can note that at the heart of the definitions just given is the fact that post-war reconstruction is made up of the 'negative' task of ending continuing violence and preventing a relapse into war, and the 'positive' task of constructing a self-sustaining peace. In the words of the 2000 Brahimi Report:

> History has taught that peacekeepers and peacebuilders are insepar-
> able partners in complex operations: while peacebuilders may not be
> able to function without the peacekeepers' support, the peacekeepers
> have no exit without the peacebuilders' work.

In other words, the negative and positive tasks are mutually inter-dependent. Yet they are at the same time mutually contradictory. The logic inherent in the negative goal is at odds with important elements in the positive goal, while key assumptions behind the positive goal are often at cross-purposes with the more pressing short-term priorities of the negative goal. The task of mopping up a continuing war or preventing an early relapse back into war is likely to demand uncomfortable trade-offs that might jeopardize the longer-term goal of sustainable peace – for example, deals with unscrupulous power-brokers, or the early incorporation of largely unreconstructed local militia to shore up a critical security gap. Conversely, measures adopted on the assumption that it is market democracy that best sustains peaceful reconstruction long-term may en route increase the risk of reversion to war. On the governance front, conflictual electoral processes may exacerbate political differences and favour the 'wrong' politicians. On the economic front, the competitive nature of free-market capitalism may engender instability. On the social front, there are the well-known tensions between stability and justice. Both democ-racy and the market economy are inherently conflictual processes which may offer a greater measure of political stability in the long run, but, as is often noted, are likely to increase political instability during the transition phase, particularly where there is little or no prior experience of them (Mansfield and Snyder, 1995, 2001; Snyder, 2000; Boyce, 2002). Unlike the situation in pre-war prevention, these tasks cannot be temporarily sequenced, but must all be undertaken at the same time – a major headache for IRW planners.

The second feature to be noted is the commonality of *sectoral tasks* across the IRW database. This can be illustrated in terms of both announced programmes and components of missions. In 1992 the UN Secretary-General outlined the sectoral tasks as:

> disarming the previously warring parties and the restoration of order, the custody and possible destruction of weapons, repatriating refugees, advisory and training support for security personnel, monitoring elections, advancing efforts to protect human rights, reforming or strengthening governmental institutions and promoting formal and informal processes of political participation. (Boutros-Ghali, 1992: 32)

In 1997 they were seen to involve: 'the creation or strengthening of national institutions, the monitoring of elections, the promotion of human rights, the provision of reintegration and rehabilitation programmes and the creation of conditions for resumed development' (Annan, 1997c). This was reflected in the make-up of UN missions (see box 8.1).

Third, we must include commonality in planned *temporal phases* of IRW operations. Here there is no obvious formal pattern since different missions define phases differently. For example, UNTAC in Cambodia operated in terms of four phases and the UN Mission in Kosovo (UNMIK) envisaged five phases, whereas the early phases of

---

Box 8.1   Components of the UN Transition Authority in Cambodia

1 *Military component*: verify withdrawal of foreign forces; monitor ceasefire violations; organize cantonment and disarming of factions; assist mine-clearance.
2 *Civilian police component*: supervise local civilian police; training.
3 *Human rights component*: secure signing of human rights conventions by Supreme National Council; oversee human rights record of administration; initiate education and training programmes.
4 *Civil administration component*: supervise administration to ensure neutral environment for election in five areas – foreign affairs, national defence, finance, public security, information.
5 *Electoral component*: conduct demographic survey; register and educate voters; draft electoral law; supervise and verify election process.
6 *Repatriation component*: repatriate 360,000 refugees.
7 *Rehabilitation component*: see to immediate food, health and housing needs; begin essential restoration work on infrastructure; development work in villages with returnees.

In addition, there was an information division.

Source: United Nations, 1996: 447–84

the 2003 Iraq operation included phases of the war. Nevertheless, in general terms it seems best to work in terms of three broad reconstruction phases: an immediate post-war intervention phase (*phase one*) when the tension between the negative and positive tasks is likely to be at its sharpest; a political stability phase (*phase two*) when a host government has attained sufficient legitimacy and control to allow the first stage of international withdrawal; and a normalization phase (*phase three*) when the country is seen to have attained 'normal' levels of autonomy and viability sufficient to enable the final stage of intervention withdrawal (UK Ministry of Defence, 2004). Beyond this, it is worth identifying a fourth stage that includes progress towards further declaratory goals articulated by IRW interveners, but shared by most or all other countries and therefore no longer strictly part of the post-war reconstruction process. It is important to note that the temporal phases in post-war reconstruction and de-escalation are also not sequential, but are nested within each other, so that the transition to phase two evidently has to be achieved in phase one and so on (see figure 8.1).

Fourth, and finally, there is the staged withdrawal of the international intervention presence itself, which, as just indicated, should be seen as a *function* of the prior phased sectoral changes in the domestic situation in the host country.

Taking these four features together, we can draw up a matrix of the international post-war reconstruction project since the end of the Cold War in order to evaluate it from a conflict resolution perspective. Box 8.2 offers a summative matrix of its main rhetorical provisions in order to clarify what we are trying to assess. It can be seen to be an awe-inspiring undertaking.

A Conflict Resolution Assessment of Intervention, Reconstruction and Withdrawal Operations, 1989–2004

In evaluating this gigantic international post-war reconstruction enterprise from a conflict resolution perspective, we will look first at the literature on sectors and phases, and then at the literature on specific interventions. Most studies concentrate on either one or other of these, although some cover both (see works listed in note 1).

A sectoral assessment from a conflict resolution perspective

The matrix in box 8.2 should be understood as a framework model. The sectors intersect and there are cross-cutting issues such as gender or the environment. Its main usefulness, perhaps, is that it allows us to

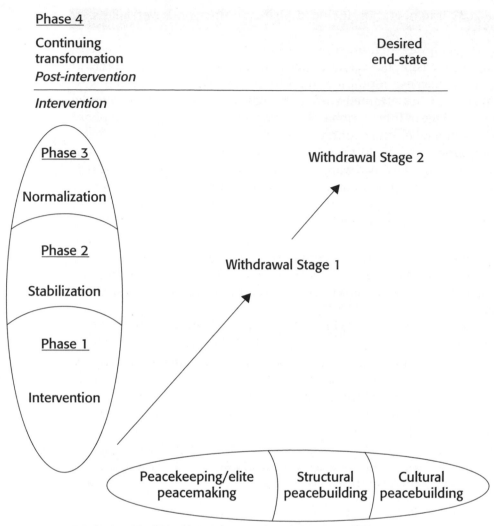

Note: Compare with the hourglass model (chapter 1, figure 1.3).

Source: Ramsbotham, 2004; for nested paradigms, see Dugan, 1996: 9–20 and Lederach, 1997: 73–85.

Figure 8.1   IRW operations: nested phases, nested tasks and withdrawal stages

discriminate within the sectors according to temporal phases. This is the most helpful format both for conflict resolution assessment and for IRW planners, because it brings out the phased cross-sectoral interdependencies more clearly in the ways and sequences in which they are experienced. Under *phase one* (intervention) we focus on the tradeoffs between the negative and positive priorities and note that this is where the security and law-and-order sectors are at their most significant. Under *phase two* (stabilization) we offer a brief analysis sector by sector of the interlocking requirements for political stability and note

Box 8.2 Post-war reconstruction/withdrawal matrix

Phases in host country post-war reconstruction

Sector A *Security*

Phase 1 International forces needed to control armed factions; supervise DDR; help reconstitute national army; begin demining.

Phase 2 National armed forces under home government control stronger than challengers.

Phase 3/4 Demilitarized politics; societal security; transformed cultures of violence.

Sector B *Law and Order*

Phase 1 International control of courts, etc.; break grip of organized crime on government; train civilian police; promote human rights/punish abuse.

Phase 2 Indigenous capacity to maintain basic order impartially under the law.

Phase 3/4 Non-politicized judiciary and police; respect for individual and minority rights; reduction in organized crime.

Sector C *Government*

Phase 1 International supervision of new constitution, elections, etc., prevent intimidation; limit corruption.

Phase 2 Reasonably representative government; move from winner-take-all to power-sharing system; stable relationship between centre and regions.

Phase 3/4 Manage peaceful transfer of power via democratic elections; development of civil society within genuine political community; integrate local into national politics.

Sector D *Economy*

Phase 1 International provision of humanitarian relief; restore essential services; limit exploitation of movable resources by spoilers.

Phase 2 Formal economy yields sufficient revenue for government to provide essential services; capacity to re-employ many former combatants; perceived prospects for future improvement (esp. employment).

Phase 3/4 Development in long-term interest of citizens from all backgrounds.

Sector E *Society*

Phase 1 Overcome initial distrust/monitor media; international protection of vulnerable populations; return of refugees under way.

Phase 2 Manage conflicting priorities of peace and justice; responsible media.

Phase 3/4 Depoliticize social divisions; heal psychological wounds; progress towards gender equality; education towards long-term reconciliation.

International intervention transitions

Phase 1 Direct, culturally sensitive support for the peace process.

Phase 2 Phased transference to local/civilian control avoiding undue interference/neglect.

Phase 3/4 Integration into cooperative and equitable regional/global structures.

the critical significance of the government sector at this point. Under *phase three* (normalization) we note the increased relative importance of the economic and socio-cultural sectors, and also discuss briefly the controversial relationship with phase four aspirations. The difficult trade-offs and dilemmas uncovered in this way show why many conflict resolvers have deep misgivings over the assumptions behind interventions of this kind – and why in some cases they disagree among themselves.

Phase one: intervention

Putting together the phase one tasks from across all five sectors of the matrix in box 8.2, we can observe at a glance what a daunting prospect the initial phase of the intervention is:

> *Control armed factions; supervise DDR (disarmament, demobilization, rehabilitation); help restructure and integrate new national armed forces; begin demining; reconstitute courts and prisons; break grip of organized crime; train police; promote human rights and punish abuse; oversee new constitution, elections and restructuring of civil administration; prevent intimidation; provide humanitarian relief; restore essential services; limit exploitation of movable primary resources by spoilers; overcome initial distrust between groups; monitor and use media to support peace process; protect vulnerable populations; supervise initial return of refugees.*

In this immediate post-intervention phase it can be seen that security (peacekeeping) and elite bargaining (peacemaking) predominate in ensuring the negative task of preventing a relapse into war. At the same time a transition has to be achieved from emergency relief towards the phase two political stability requirements. Three features determine the core challenges in phase one.

First, there is the fundamental *fact of continuing conflict*. Short of total prior military victory for one of the contending parties, the surviving undefeated conflictants are still intent upon achieving their pre-existing political goals. In the first edition of this book we called this 'Clausewitz in reverse', because in this sense the peace is best seen as a continuation of the war 'with the addition of other means'.[4] This is an insight that comes directly from the conflict resolution tradition. Where the war has been brought to an end by a peace process, its essence lies precisely in the effort to persuade undefeated conflict parties that their persisting and no doubt undiminished political aims can best be served by non-violent politics rather than by a perpetuation or a resumption of violence. Where the main power struggle has initially been decided by military means (as in Kosovo, Afghanistan and Iraq) the same still applies, inasmuch as surviving conflict parties continue to vie for post-war influence and additional actors and sub-actors emerge as the reconstruction process unfurls to complicate the situation further. What Grenier and Daudelin, drawing on experience in El Salvador, have called the peacemaking or post-war reconstruction 'market place' is focused around a series of trade-offs in which cessation of violence is traded for other commodities such as political opportunity and economic advantage (Grenier and Daudelin, 1995: 350). In phase one of the post-intervention process it is the interveners who usually play the key role in ensuring that there are incentives to discontinue violence by creating what the UN Secretary-General has termed negative and positive inducements (under the latter distinguishing the two conflict resolution approaches of 'civic action' and 'peace initiatives') (Annan, 1997c). This pattern can be seen across the range of IRW cases from international pressure to corral the South African administration and South-West Africa People's Organization (SWAPO) leaders into the Namibian elections in November 1989, through to the complex manoeuvring in Afghanistan from the time of the Bonn negotiations in November 2001, and on to the effort to keep all legitimate parties involved in the post-November 2003 preparations for a phased transfer of sovereignty in Iraq. In the words of the Brahimi Report (2000) with reference to the earlier period, 'United Nations operations did not *deploy into* post-conflict situations but tried to *create them*'. Even when armed conflict comes to an end, political conflict continues, which is why we should strictly refer to 'post-war' reconstruction rather than employ the usual 'post-conflict' misnomer. In Afghanistan and Iraq post-war reconstruction attempts began while the war was still continuing, albeit at a less intense level.

The second key feature is *the fact of the cost of war*, the fact that in the course of the preceding war (or under the preceding regime) the instruments of governance in all five thematic dimensions are likely to have been much debilitated if not destroyed. It is difficult to convey the scale of devastation: from huge loss of life (in the millions in countries like Cambodia and Afghanistan); hundreds of thousands of refugees and internally displaced people (a quarter of the population in Mozambique); ruined economies even in naturally rich countries (Angola's budget deficit 23 per cent of GDP; El Salvador per capita income 38 per cent of pre-war figures); the destruction of pre-existing political structures even in quite developed systems (in Kosovo with the collapse of Serb institutions; in Iraq with the instantaneous flight of public employees at all levels); and the substitution for all this of predatory warlords, criminalized economies and institutionalized 'kleptocracies' (Cranna, ed., 1994). In the Democratic Republic of Congo (DRC) in the four and a half years to autumn 2003, up to 3.5 million are estimated to have died as a result of the violence (International Peace Committee), with 3.4 million internally displaced and 17 million without food security out of a population of 53 million (UN Office for the Coordination of Humanitarian Assistance) (Swing, 2003: 25). In the first phase, intervening military forces are often the only large-scale organization with the capacity to respond, as in Basra (Iraq) from April 2003, when British troops found themselves having to run emergency services and begin rebuilding the whole of the local infrastructure. Bernard Kouchner, head of UNMIK in Kosovo, describes how the UN was initially dependent on NATO for much of its logistics and personnel (Kouchner, 2001). This raises critical questions about civil–military relations at many levels, including the staged handover to host-country civilian authorities that defines phase two (Williams, 1998). Faced with the task of disarming militias and beginning to reconstruct a national army, of training police and rebuilding courts and prisons, of producing electoral rolls and overseeing the creation of a new constitution followed by 'free and fair elections', of repatriating and resettling refugees and internally displaced persons (IDPs), of restoring emergency services and beginning to revive the economy, of introducing human rights training and safeguards for threatened minorities – all in the face of severe time constraints – it is little wonder that Gareth Evans, Australian foreign minister and one of the architects of the 1991 Paris Peace Accords in Cambodia, described the UNTAC mandate as 'overly ambitious and in some respects clearly not achievable' (Evans, 1994: 27). It remains to be seen what verdicts will be passed on the comparable efforts of the International Security Assistance Force (ISAF) and the United Nations Assistance Mission (UNAMA) in Afghanistan, and of the Coalition Provisional Authority (CPA) and its successors in Iraq.

The third key feature is *the fact that there are enemies of the reconstruction process – especially where wars are ongoing and parties see the interveners as combatants*. In peace processes, the spoilers range from ideologically implacable enemies, through disappointed political interests, to unscrupulous exploiters who profited from the previous dispensation and are reluctant to accept its demise (Stedman, 1997). Here there has been an evolution of experience since 1989, when the military component of IRW operations was still conceived as a variant on traditional peacekeeping, since the early cases were seen as the implementation of agreed settlements in which all the main players concurred. Bitter experience in Angola, Bosnia, Somalia and Rwanda taught that provision had to be made for the Savimbis, Karadzics, Aideeds and Interahamwe militias. As a result intervening forces have been asked to combine what had hitherto often been seen to be incompatible combat/enforcement and peacekeeping/consent-creating roles. As we have seen in chapter 6, combat troops are likely to find themselves in peacekeeping situations, while peacekeepers have been compelled to evolve also into peace-enforcers: 'neutrality' has been reinterpreted as robust 'impartial' support for the peace or reconstruction process. But one of the main conflict resolution insights applies here – in intense conflict zones no intervener will be seen as impartial. This has been a steep learning curve exacerbated by problems of coordinating best practice across what are often widely divergent national contingents, the lack of experience of such roles in some forces (including those of the United States), and the rapid turnover of troops just when such experience has been gained. Depending upon the type of spoilers involved, it is now generally recognized to be essential to make provision in advance for transforming spoilers into stakeholders in a peace process (as has happened for example in Northern Ireland) or failing that by accommodating those who are biddable without serious damage to the reconstruction process (a difficult question of judgement); for reducing the scale and significance of their support constituencies (a demanding exercise in 'winning hearts and minds'); and for defeating or marginalizing those who remain irreconcilable (a challenge for robust enforcement). This may be easier said than done. Spoilers have become increasingly sophisticated at deliberately exploiting the tensions and contradictions between the negative and positive tasks pinpointed above – for example, squaring the discrepant priorities of assuring the security of interveners and 'winning the hearts and minds' of the host population, or attempting to reduce initial expectations while at the same time being seen to be 'making a difference'. In Cambodia the Khmer Rouge succeeded in forcing the abandonment of the cantonment and demobilization plan in November 2002, but, surprisingly, not the 23 May 2003 national elections. In Afghanistan and Iraq, opponents of the post-war outcome have targeted UN and international aid workers with devastating effect, as well as those engaged in economic reconstruction and the nascent reconstituted police, armed forces and administration, using violence to frustrate the objectives of what they see as occupying forces.

In short, the main problem for conflict resolution in phase one is the fact that these are unavoidably militarized environments in which longer-term conflict resolution goals may be sacrificed to shorter-term security and emergency requirements. They also tend to be 'top-down' and 'external-actor-driven' processes in contradiction to the conflict resolution principles of 'bottom-up' and 'local-empowerment' peace-building.

Phase two: stability

Phase two is defined as the point at which enough progress has been made in stabilizing the domestic political situation to enable a safe handover of power to a host government and to undertake the first stage of international withdrawal. Reading across the sectoral phase two stipulations from the matrix in box 8.2 we can summarize the requirements as:

> National armed forces under home government control stronger than chal-lengers; sufficient indigenous capacity to maintain basic order impartially under the law; adequate democratic credentials of elected government with system seen to remain open to those dissatisfied with the initial result; a reason-ably stable relationship between centre and regions; a formal economy yielding sufficient revenue for government to provide essential services (with continuing international assistance); economic capacity to absorb many former combatants and progress in encouraging general belief in better future employment prospects; adequate success in managing conflicting priorities of peace and justice, protecting minority rights and fostering a reasonably independent yet responsible media.

Given the non-sequential and nested nature of post-war reconstruction phases, the attainment of these demanding phase two requirements is initially a task for phase one. Their consolidation, accompanied by further progress towards phase three goals, is the proper task for phase two. Here it is the 'structural peacebuilding' aspect of post-war recon-struction that predominates in general and the 'government' sector around which the other sectors can be seen to hinge in particular. This phase evidently poses particular problems for conflict resolution, because of the severe compromises that have to be made on conflict resolution principles in the name of stability. In order to clarify this, we will outline the phase two stability requirements here without criticism, and then summarize these difficult issues when we come on to consider phase three.

The literature on the *security sector* tasks is large, covering as it does the ponderously termed 'disarmament, demobilization, repatriation, resettlement and reintegration' (DDRRR) operations, and the (re)construction of national armed forces under the control of the government (Collier, 1994; Cillers, ed., 1995; Berdal, 1996; Ball, 1997; Kingma, 1997, 2002). This can be seen to include a wide range of more specific issues, from control of small arms and light weapons (UNIDR, 1996) to the reintegration of child soldiers (Goodwin-Gill and Cohn, 1994; McCalin, 1995), and demining (USDOD, 1998). In 1992–3 in Angola some 350 UNAVEM II military observers were expected to supervise the process for more than 150,000 combatants – and unsur-prisingly failed (Anstee, 1996). Since then, the international commu-nity has acquired a better understanding of what is required in these more challenging cases. For rebel forces or warlords to disarm is to give up their trump card, so there are huge incentives to cheat, and the interveners need clear vision, steady will and skill in applying the right combination of pressure, independent verification and positive political and economic inducements. The key point is reached when reconstituted national forces are, first, under secure host government control, and, second, decisively stronger than remaining undemobilized forces or private armies. Until this stage is reached, the situation is too volatile to contemplate withdrawal by intervening military forces (short of effective abandonment of the whole project), although current planning in Afghanistan appears to be prepared to risk this.

The *law and order sector* is equally well covered in the literature, with particular focus on the related topics of civilian policing (Call and Barnett, 1999), transitional justice (Kritz, 1995; Mani, 2002), and human rights (O'Flaherty and Gisvold, eds, 1998). Once courts and prisons have been rebuilt and the judiciary and police reconstituted and trained, the phase two requirement is that politically volatile elements should not be tempted to gain significant advantage through incitement to violence, and that criminal elements should not be able to operate with impunity. The 'impartiality' requirement is crucial, since otherwise the judicial and policing systems lose legitimacy, but this cannot be expected to go unchallenged, because disappointed interests will interpret the maintenance of order as suppression. As most of the 1989–2004 IRW cases suggest, law and order issues tend to get worse before they get better. The crime rate soars, as the peacetime economy is unable to absorb large numbers of unemployed ex-soldiers and their families as well as hundreds of thousands of returning refugees, while a continuing wartime black economy, a ready availability of weaponry, and the destabilizing effects of what has usually been an abrupt introduction of free market conditionalities further destabilize the situation. In El Salvador, for example, there were more killings per year in 1998 than there had been during the war. The lesson is that this must be expected and planned for. Negotiating acceptable conditions for justice and policing may involve issues that go to the heart of divided societies, as in post-conflict Rwanda, South Africa and Northern Ireland.

It is with the phase two *government sector* requirements that the heart of the post-war reconstruction challenge is reached. The literature on constitutional arrangements and elections is extensive and controversial (Kumar, ed., 1998; Sisk and Reynolds, eds, 1998). Unfortunately, this also tends to be the most testing and intransigent of the challenges, because it concerns the fundamental question over which all major political conflicts are in the end waged – who rules? Agreements have to be made on constitutional frameworks and electoral processes where domestic political interests want to secure advantages for themselves, and a process is needed to establish a structure that is in the interests of the population as a whole. The interveners have to tread warily, therefore, and this is where the international legitimacy provided in cases where the main domestic players have already agreed to the process in outline, and where it has been endorsed by regional organizations and the United Nations, is so beneficial. Evidently there are numerous possible constitutional arrangements that work in different circumstances, and there is no space to discuss the permutations here (Shain and Linz, 1995). But the phase two requirements are clear: first, sufficient perceived demo-cratic legitimacy for the government of the day, and, second, enough general confidence in the continuing openness of the system to encourage losers to continue their struggle non-violently within the constitution. This is absolutely critical to success in consolidating phase two and moving on to phase three, as we note in the next two paragraphs on the economy and the social sectors. In cases where there is little or no previous experience of such practices, or where there is a new state, or where central government has had little control over the provinces or has only imposed itself by authoritarian or tyrannical means, these requirements become very daunting indeed. For this reason some have questioned the wisdom of a 'rush to elec-tions' in intense and volatile political environments of this kind. Further discussion would include questions about the legitimacy of international democratic norms in relation to the power and interest of those promoting them and to the different cultures into which they are to be transplanted, about the role that external actors can or should be expected to play, and about the relative effectiveness of top-down government assistance programmes or those that work more from the bottom-up with civil society and non-government groups (see chapter 9).

In the *economy sector* the phase two benchmarks are determined by three main linked factors (Ball and Halevy, 1996; Kreimer et al., 1998; Pugh, 2000; Ball, 2001). The first is that the official economy should yield sufficient revenue for the government to be able to provide essen-tial services (with continuing support from international donors where needed). This is a major requirement that is closely dependent upon success in the 'government' sector because it presupposes progress in taming or pegging back the unofficial economy, and in many cases in overcoming the continuing reluctance of regional authorities to hand over revenues to the central government. The second requirement is to have understood and made strenuous provision to begin dismantling the entrenched war economy (or authoritarian kleptocracy) that allows exploiters to continue to resist reconstruction. We have seen that is likely to include an international regime to control exploitation of movable assets such as diamonds, drugs or oil. The third requirement is harder to measure because it involves the broad development of the economy as a whole. The phase two need is, first, to absorb enough of those previously employed in disbanded militia as will reduce disaffection to containable levels, and, second, more generally for there to be a sense that, however difficult and indeed miserable material conditions may be now, there is sufficient evidence of likely future improvement – particularly in employment prospects. Fortunately, the withdrawal of most or all of the intervening armed forces at this stage does not preclude longer-term engagement and commitment from external development agencies. Experience from 1989–2004 IRW teaches that it is the management of future expectation that is, if anything, even more important than the delivery of present gain. Several commentators advise that market conditionalities should not be imposed too precipitately, as was, by common agreement, the case to begin with in Mozambique. Paris is one who recommends a shift to 'peace-oriented adjustment policies' that recognize the priority of stimulating economic growth even at the risk of inflation, and that target resources at those hardest hit during the transition period (1997: 85–6). The central phase two aim in this sector is to persuade as many as possible that things will improve so long as they continue to participate in the reconstruction process.

Finally, in the *social sector*, the phase two benchmarks are not so clear-cut, beyond the aim of containing intergroup antagonism below levels that might threaten the reconstruction process and preventing its exploitation by unscrupulous political interests (UNRISD, 1995). This means adequate reassurances for threatened minorities (Gurr, 2000), the settlement of refugees (Stein et al., 1995; Black and Coser, eds, 1999) and the management of conflicting priorities of peace and justice (Boraine et al., 1997; Schuett, 1997; Skaar, 1999; Baker, 2001). Measurements of social divisions are very difficult to make, but most of the deeper recourses for overcoming them, including the healing of trauma and reconciliation, can only be expected to come to fruition over the longer term (see chapter 10). One key dimension now widely recognized as vital is what Luc Reychler calls 'the education, information and communication system':

> Here we look at the degree of schooling, the level of discrimination, the relevance of the subjects and the attitudes held, the control of the media, the professional level of the journalist, the extent to which the media play a positive role in the transformation of the conflicts, and the control of destructive rumours. (Reychler and Paffenholz, eds, 2001: 13)

Turning to the sixth part of the matrix in box 8.2, 'International intervention transitions', it should now be evident that the sectoral developments listed above, taken together, make up the demanding requirements for an ordered stage one *military withdrawal*. This should not be seen as an 'exit strategy' so much as a 'safe handover strategy' to indigenous civilian control. Interveners who are not prepared to see it in these terms should not intervene in the first place. As it is, the familiar tension between short-term 'negative' and long-term 'positive' goals now plays right through to the withdrawal process itself. On the one hand, the message to the wider population of the host country (as also no doubt to domestic constituencies in the intervening countries) is: 'We are not permanently occupying forces; we will be leaving very soon and handing over to you.' But at the same time the message to would-be spoilers has to be: 'It is no good waiting for us to go so that you can resume your old ways; we are here for the duration and will only pull out when the situation is secure. You had better realize this and join in the peace process on the best terms available to you while there is still time.' It is clearly easier to resolve the tension between these positions when the forces involved have international and domestic legitimacy.

As to the length of time that the stage one military–civilian transition takes, there are evidently no fixed rules. It depends upon the depth and complexity of the challenge in each case. In the heroic days of the early 1990s, for example, swift transitions were envisaged: for example, UNTAG in Namibia from April 1989 to March 1990; ONUSAL in El Salvador from July 1991 to April 1995; UNTAC in Cambodia from March 1992 to September 1993, etc. In some cases there was a handover to follow-on missions (UNAVEM II to UNAVEM III in Angola), in some there was a handover to a beefed-up intervention force (UNPROFOR to IFOR in Bosnia), and in some there was almost unconditional withdrawal (UNOSOM II in Somalia and UNAMIR in Rwanda). In the post-1995 period there has been a greater readiness to stay longer in Bosnia and Kosovo, since these were new political entities under effective international trusteeship (and in Kosovo with the added continuing uncertainty about future status). The operation in East Timor (now Timor Leste) lasted from 1999 to 2002. With Afghanistan and Iraq we seem to have returned to the breakneck pace of earlier transitions – at any rate in terms of announced timetables. The planning framework for the UK's Post-Conflict Reconstruction Unit being set up in 2004 is for eighteen months.

Phase three: normalization – and beyond

A cross-sectoral conspectus from the matrix in box 8.2 shows that many of the longer-term phase three requirements, commonly listed among the rhetorical aims of the intervention, constitute desiderata beyond the present capacity of many post-war countries (though they are very relevant to the current stage in Northern Ireland, for example):

> *Demilitarized politics; societal security; transformed cultures of violence; non-politicized judiciary and police; respect for individual and minority rights; reduction in organized crime; peaceful transition of power via democratic elections; development of civil society within genuine political community; equitable integration of local and national politics; development in the long-term interest of citizens from all backgrounds; depoliticization of social divisions; the healing of psychological wounds; progress towards gender equality; education towards long-term reconciliation; integration into cooperative and equitable regional/global structures.*

Here we reach a major difference of opinion among commentators between those who suggest that goals such as local empowerment, gender equality or reconciliation are better postponed in the interest either of stability or of conceptual and operational clarity, and those who insist that they are what justify the intervention in the first place and must therefore be forefronted from the start. This issue cuts across the conflict resolution community. For example, Michael Lund argues in the first direction: 'It is laudable to wish to improve society by eliminating as many of its deficiencies as possible . . . but such an approach risks making peacebuilding into a grab bag of unfulfilled human wants' (2003: 26). But others argue the opposite way (Lederach, 1997; Reychler and Paffenholz, eds, 2001).

We can now sum up conflict resolution criticisms of international post-war reconstruction efforts since the end of the Cold War, ranging from those who object to particular aspects of current practice or to particular interventions, through those who advocate a reformed international intervention capacity, to those who reject the whole idea of outsider intervention on the grounds that it inevitably serves the interests of the most powerful (see box 8.3). Paris describes the central tenet of peacebuilding as the assumption that the surest foundation for peace is 'market democracy, that is, a liberal democratic polity and a market-oriented economy':

> Peacebuilding is in effect an enormous experiment in social engineering – an experiment that involves transplanting western models of social, political, and economic organization into war-shattered states in order to control civil conflict: in other words, pacification through political and economic liberalization. (1997: 56)

This view merges with the radical critiques from international political economy and elsewhere as discussed in chapters 1, 4 and 6. We may note again here that from a conflict resolution perspective the primary aim is not to secure western norms but to reach agreements with parties aimed at reconciling differences in a way that is sensitive to local cultural and political conditions and in the interest of the

Box 8.3 A transformationist critique of IRW practice

At least eight components can be discerned in transformationist critiques over the 1989–2004 period:

1 An insistence on greater emphasis on 'bottom-up' rather than 'top-down' initiatives and the empowerment of indigenous grassroots participation.
2 Criticism of the relative neglect of the social-psychological dimension.
3 Unhappiness about sequenced and foreshortened time frames that fail to dovetail short-, medium- and long-term priorities properly.
4 A questioning of the motives of powerful interveners and an insistence that they be made accountable to host peoples and the international community.
5 A demand for more emphasis on gender equality.
6 An insistence on greater cultural sensitivity.
7 Unease about, if not opposition to, military involvement in and often control of what should be non-military tasks.
8 Disquiet at the way what were UN-led operations in the early 1990s have now come to be controlled by the militarily more powerful countries, with the UN increasingly sidelined and used as little more than a rubber stamp.

domestic population, and to mitigate the conflict-fuelling effects of external influences on the conflict.

In general from a conflict resolution perspective it can be seen that, whereas in phases one and two it is peacekeeping, elite peacemaking and structural peacebuilding that predominate, in order to secure the more far-reaching and deeply rooted declared sectoral goals of phase three normalization it is social and cultural peacebuilding that becomes more important. In other words, over time 'software' becomes relatively more significant than 'hardware'. Until this socio-cultural transformation happens, therefore, much of the formality of, say, an apparently independent judiciary or an electoral democracy or declaratory instruments on minority rights remains just that – a formality, behind which authoritarianism and partisan discrimination will continue to prevail.

As to the next stage of withdrawal of intervention personnel associated with phase three normalization, this is also less clear-cut than stage one withdrawal. It varies widely from case to case and merges into what might be termed 'normal' international presence and intrusion in developing countries, where it has been said, for example, that 'UNDP never leaves'. The sixth section of the matrix in box 8.2 describes the aim as 'integration into cooperative and equitable regional and global structures'. This emphasizes the importance of regional stability in IRW operations as noted in chapters 4 and 5. It also evidently begs the big questions about global equity and the global distribution of power that forms an important sub-theme of this book.

A Conflict Resolution Assessment: Evaluating Cases

Lack of space demands brevity in this section, even though it covers the other half of the extant literature, that on evaluating *individual cases*. The literature on individual post-war reconstruction cases is too large and diverse to select usefully here, although many of the general accounts already referenced also include specific cases (see works listed in note 1).

In general terms there is, unsurprisingly, a range of opinion here. The complexity of the intervention debate is shown in general terms through the fact that both proponents and opponents of intervention are found along the conservative, liberal, radical spectrum: Wolfowitz vs Luttwak, Wheeler vs Chandler, Kaldor vs Chomsky. A similar lack of agreement can be seen when it comes to evaluating individual interventions. For example, as Lund notes, Cambodia 1992–3 is variously classed as a 'success' (Doyle and Sambanis, 2000), a 'partial success' (Hampson, 1996) and a 'failure' (Durch et al., 2003).

One particularly useful feature of analysis of the kind undertaken in this chapter is that it clearly distinguishes phases when assessing the success of individual interventions. For example, in the literature the most common criterion used to evaluate success is the phase one negative security criterion (avoidance of a relapse into war), because this is the easiest to quantify:

> Surprisingly, once we have examined the many studies that take an interest in the restoration of minimum physical security, it is much harder to find rigorous, data-based analyses of the other desired outcomes of macro-level peacebuilding, especially using comparative data across several countries. (Lund, 2003: 31)

If a particular case drops out of readily available annual 'major armed conflict' assessments, as described in chapter 3, it can be classed as a success. From this perspective, 1992 Angola and 1993 Rwanda were spectacular failures because the loss of life in 1993 and 1994 respectively was far worse than before the intervention. Most of the others, however, are seen as successful – including Haiti right through to the end of 2003 (Lund, 2003: 30). The second most common criterion is the phase two stabilization government sector criterion of 'free and fair' immediate post-intervention elections. If this is taken as the yardstick, then another set of judgements is made, but once again this indicates success in most cases – despite continuing controversy about what constitutes a 'free and fair election' (Goodwin-Gill, 1994). And again this has tended to include Haiti after the 1995 elections.

That the two most popular criteria for measuring success are defective and could be misleading is shown, first, by noting the phase three normalization government sector criterion of a non-violent democratic transfer of power and, second, by taking into account all the other sectors. The phase three government criterion of a peaceful transfer of power delivers a dramatically altered – and sobering – result. Durch et al. (2003) suggest the survival of the political system through a second election as the criterion for 'effective transition', Doyle and Sambanis (2000) employ a standard of 'political openness' (see Lund, 2003: 31). A peaceful democratic transfer of power seems a more searching criterion. Very few IRW cases, even from the earlier period, pass this test. In Namibia, Cambodia and Mozambique, for example, all variously described as successes in the literature in the 1990s, the initial electoral winners are still clinging on to power 10–15 years later. In two of these cases (Mozambique and Cambodia) the incumbent was already *in situ* before the intervention took place. In one (Cambodia) the current leader even lost the initial election.

Similarly different results obtain if all the box 8.2 sectors are considered in evaluating success. In Haiti, for example, whereas phase one cessation of violence and phase two government first election criteria suggested success, it was evident from other criteria that this was precarious. Taking the five sectors in turn – the arming of President Aristide's own *Chimeres* militia instead of reliance on national armed forces and civilian police; the failure to prosecute political murders; the fiasco of an opposition boycott and 5 per cent turnout for the 2000 presidential election; the failure of the government to begin to provide essential services (exacerbated by the blocking of foreign aid); and the deepening social rift between Aristide's populism and business and professional interests – all clearly showed that, far from consolidation of phase two and progress towards phase three normalization, even the phase one achievements of the 1994–6 IRW effort were unravelling.

Finally, we must address the key question: 'Whose success?' Who decides on the overall criteria and the extent of their implementation? This will prove a decisive principle for conflict resolution intervention as discussed in chapter 13. It includes an evaluation of the motives of the interveners, but two other even more important criteria are international legitimacy, however difficult to evaluate, and, above all from a conflict resolution perspective, the opinion of the host populations themselves. Are those who are the targets of the intervention better off than they would have been without it? Have benefits outweighed costs? How can such responses be reliably elicited – particularly in highly contested political post-war environments? These are the questions that have to be satisfactorily answered if there is to be a reliable evaluation of post-war reconstruction efforts.

Conclusion

Setting aside intense disagreement about specific interventions, the argument in this chapter is that the success of post-settlement peace-building and post-war reconstruction efforts must be judged according to conflict resolution and conflict transformation principles. We have stressed the importance of domestic opinion within the host countries as the true arbiter, however hard it may be to ascertain, and have suggested that the perceived legitimacy of interventions appears to decrease as we move across the spectrum of intervention types in table 8.1. We have argued that the shift from UN-led post-settlement peacebuilding to mixed or non-UN interventions where there is no settlement or the settlement is imposed has compounded the problems of legitimacy. We have drawn attention to the reconstruction 'planning gap', which dictates that IRW enterprises have to be international. Whatever the initial war-fighting requirements may be in some cases, the overall post-war reconstruction effort requires coordinated efforts across national agencies, across civil–military operational divides, and across domestic–multinational/multilateral partnerships. Winning the peace makes even greater demands than winning the war. We have produced a matrix of the phased sectoral tasks that constitute the post-war reconstruction programme according to the principles of complementarity and contingency (box 8.2), and noted how, from a conflict resolution perspective, both phases and sectors are 'nested' (figure 8.1). The sectors interconnect, and the admittedly ambitious goals of phases three/four must imbue the entire undertaking from the start. This places a huge onus on effective cooperation between domestic parties and the interveners. In phase one (immediate post-intervention) when there is a situation of ongoing conflict, we have seen how the peacekeeping and elite peacemaking components tend to predominate. But, as elaborated in chapter 6, in a post-war reconstruction context military forces are there to support the peace process within an overall conflict resolution scenario. In phase two (stabilization) we noted how there is an unavoidable tension between the political stability requirements that enable a safe withdrawal of intervening armed forces, and the longer-term normalization and transformation norms that legitimized the intervention in the first place. It is the government sector and the political and economic tasks of structural peacebuilding that predominate in this phase. The key requirement of the intervening military at this point is that their withdrawal should be seen as a function of political stability in the host country orientated towards the construction of a sustainable peace. At all these stages it is important to draw parties into negotiations, hold open political space, and continuously develop and reframe the grounds for agreement. Finally, it is in phase three (normalization) and beyond that the full conflict resolution and conflict transformation goals can be attained. Cultural peacebuilding and the social-psychological sector come into their own here. We elaborate on this in the next chapter.

Recommended reading

Cousens and Kumar, eds (2000); Griffiths, ed. (1998); Hampson (1996); Kumar, ed. (1997); Lund (2003); Paris (2004); Reychler and Paffenholz, eds (2001); Stedman et al., eds (2002); Woodward (2003).

Peacebuilding

The struggle for humanization, for the emancipation of labour, for the overcoming of alienation, for the affirmation of men and women as persons . . . is possible only because dehumanization, although a concrete historical fact, is not a given destiny but the result of an unjust order that engenders violence in the oppressors, which in turn dehumanizes the oppressed. Because it is a distortion of becoming more fully human, sooner or later being less human leads the oppressed to struggle against those who made them so. In order for this struggle to have meaning the oppressed must not, in seeking to regain their humanity become in turn oppressors of the oppressors, but rather restorers of the humanity of both.

Paolo Freire, Pedagogy of the Oppressed

DURING the past ten years the literature on post-conflict peacebuilding has burgeoned, while within the conflict resolution field a number of scholar-practitioners have led a revision of thinking about the complex dynamics and processes of post-conflict peacebuilding, including the idea that effective and sustainable peacemaking processes must be based not merely on the manipulation of peace agreements made by elites, but more importantly on the empowerment of communities torn apart by war to build peace from below. This complements the account of international intervention and reconstruction offered in chapter 8. The revision of thinking has led to clearer understanding in three areas. First, in the recognition that embedded cultures and economies of violence provide more formidable barriers to constructive intervention than originally assumed. In these conflicts, 'simple' one-dimensional interventions, whether by traditional mediators aiming at formal peace agreements or peacekeepers placed to supervise ceasefires or oversee elections, are unlikely to produce comprehensive or lasting resolution. Second, in the specification of the significance of post-conflict peacebuilding and of the idea that formal agreements need to be underpinned by understandings, structures and long-term development frameworks that will erode

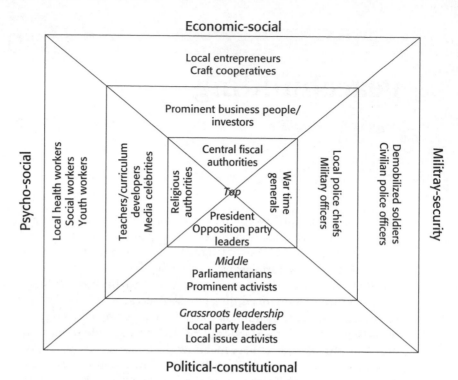

(*Source*: Reynolds Levy, 2004, developed from Lederach, 1995, 1997)

Figure 9.1   Framework for peacebuilding from below

cultures of violence and sustain peace processes on the ground. Third, in the related idea of the significance of local actors and of the non-governmental sector, and the links with local knowledge and wisdom. This alliance is to enhance sustainable citizen-based peacebuilding initiatives and to open up participatory public political spaces in order to allow institutions of civil society to flourish. The framework within which peacebuilding from below might operate, and examples of the peacebuilding constituencies involved, are shown in figure 9.1.

In this section we trace the emergence of this perspective, examine the development of peacebuilding theory and policy, and also examine the progress made in sustaining peace processes via authentic strategies based on the peacebuilding from below approach. We conclude the chapter with some reflections on the difficulties of implementing peacebuilding from below strategies, illustrated with reference to a case study of Kosovo. The conclusion is that peacebuilding from below cannot be seen in isolation from the broader process of cosmopolitan conflict resolution, acting to confront the global and higher level forces that impact on local communities.

The Idea of Peacebuilding From Below

Much of the development of thinking about peacebuilding came during the course of experience gained in supporting local groups trying to preserve or cultivate cultures of peace in areas of armed conflict in the 1990s. The wars in former Yugoslavia, for example, provided challenging situations for local peacemakers, and approaches to peacebuilding were developed, representing what Fetherston (1998) called anti-hegemonic, counter-hegemonic and post-hegemonic peace-building projects, and what Nordstrom referred to as 'counter-lifeworld constructs' that challenge the cultures of violence (1992: 270). The idea of peacebuilding from below also echoes Elise Boulding's insight, noted in chapter 12, that cultures of peace can survive in small pockets and spaces even in the most violent of conflicts.

These shifts in thinking moved the emphasis in conflict resolution work from an outsider neutral approach towards a partnership with local actors, and it is this relationship which is one of the key charac-teristics of peacebuilding from below. In this section the emergence of the approach is illustrated in the work of two scholar-practitioners, Adam Curle (see chapter 2) and John Paul Lederach. Throughout his academic career (which ended formally in 1978 when he retired from the Chair of Peace Studies at the University of Bradford), and also through the period of his 'retirement', Curle, a Quaker, has been deeply involved in the practice of peacemaking. In the 1990s much of this involvement took the form of supporting the activity of the Osijek Centre for Peace, Non-Violence and Human Rights, the site of the most violent fighting of the Serb Croat War from 1992. This involvement with the people of Osijek, who were trying to rebuild a tolerant society while surrounded by the enraged and embittered feelings engendered by the war, caused Curle to reflect about the problems of practical peacemaking. It was apparent, for example, that the model of medi-ation specified in his earlier book on mediation (*In the Middle*, 1986) and distilled from his experiences in the conflicts of the 1970s and 1980s was very difficult to apply on the ground in the confusion and chaos of the type of conflict epitomized by the wars in former Yugoslavia. It was still the case that the use of mediatory techniques would be much more likely to produce the shift in attitudes and understanding neces-sary for a stable peace, a resolution of conflict, than the use of conven-tional diplomacy alone: 'solutions reached through negotiation may be simply expedient and not imply any change of heart. And this is the crux of peace. There must be a change of heart. Without this no settle-ment can be considered secure' (Curle, 1992: 132). However, Curle real-ized through his involvement with the Osijek project that the range of conflict traumas and problems was so vast that the model of mediation based on the intervention of outsider-neutrals was simply not powerful or relevant enough to promote peace. As a result he made two important revisions to his peace praxis (Woodhouse, 1999).

First, Curle concluded that:

> Since conflict resolution by outside bodies and individuals has so far proved ineffective [in the chaotic conditions of contemporary ethnic conflict – particularly, but not exclusively, in Somalia, Eastern Europe and the former USSR], it is essential to consider the peacemaking potential within the conflicting communities themselves. (1994: 96)

He now saw the role of conflict resolution in post-Cold War conflicts as providing a variety of support to local peacemakers through an advisory, consultative-facilitative role via workshops and training in a wide variety of potential fields, which the local groups might identify as necessary. The task is to empower people of goodwill in conflict-affected communities to rebuild democratic institutions, and the starting point for this is to help in 'the development of the local peacemakers' inner resources of wisdom, courage and compassionate non-violence' (1994: 104). This in turn was linked in Curle's thinking to a deeper transformative quest to 'tame the hydra' of violence by understanding not only the politics of conflict but the deeper spiritual and philosophical sources of wisdom which would favour peace (Curle, 1999).

Second, Curle recognized an important role for the UN in this process of empowerment and in this sense sees the need to make connections between the official mandates of the UN agencies, including peacekeeping, and the unofficial roles of the NGOs in conflict zones. The approach of Curle has been to transform his original idea of active mediation as an outsider intervention process into an empowering approach, which is much more context-sensitive and which works to both empower civil society and to deepen its capacity for non-violent social change. In post-conflict peacebuilding, David Last has suggested that we face two challenges: first, to control violence (to stop violent behaviour) and, second, to link the control of violence to the rebuilding of relationships at the community level. At present we are faced with a model and practice where top-heavy military security mechanisms and political-administrative structures do not reach ordinary people, and where there are small, dispersed and under-resourced civilian NGOs frequently without the capacity to make a noticeable impact, beyond the symbolic, in conflict areas. The ideal is to seek for a complementary strategy in which peacekeeping missions and other IRW actions more broadly work to build local capacity, as indicated in figure 9.2.

John Paul Lederach, working as a scholar-practitioner within a Mennonite tradition which shares many of the values and ideas of the

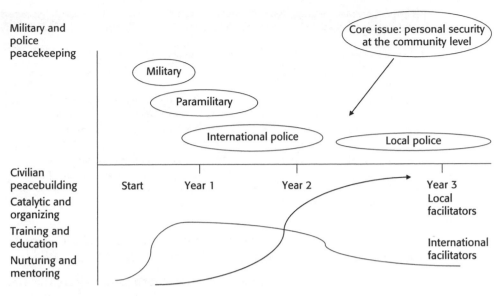

Military and police peacekeeping

Military

Paramilitary

International police

Local police

Core issue: personal security at the community level

Civilian peacebuilding

Catalytic and organizing

Training and education

Nurturing and mentoring

Start   Year 1   Year 2

Year 3
Local facilitators

International facilitators

Source: adapted from Last, 2000

Figure 9.2   Local–international and military–civilian sequences of a mission

Quakers, and with practical experience in Central America, has also stressed the importance of this approach, which he calls 'indigenous empowerment'. Both Curle and Lederach acknowledge the influence of the radical Brazilian educator, Paolo Freire, whose *Pedagogy of the Oppressed* was published in 1970, in the development of their ideas. Freire, working with the poor in Brazil and Chile from the 1960s, argued against the 'banking' or teacher-directed nature of education as a form of oppression, and in favour of 'education as liberation'. Freire was a visiting professor at Harvard in 1969, during the period when Adam Curle was director of the Harvard Center for Studies in Education and Development and beginning his own journey towards peace education. Curle's *Education for Liberation* was published in 1973, with strong influences from Freire, and his *Making Peace* (1971) represented his attempt to integrate his ideas on education and peacemaking in the broader project of liberating human potential and transcending violence. For Lederach, cognate ideas were explored and advanced in a series of highly influential publications from the mid-1990s (1995, 1997, 1999, 2003; Lederach and Jenner, 2002).

Within the conflict resolution field, then, peacebuilding from below became linked with the idea of liberating communities from the oppression and misery of violence in a project whose main goal was the cultivation of cultures and structures of peace (in Galtung's terms, positive peace). The pedagogy appropriate for this was defined

Table 9.1 Prescriptive and elicitive approaches to peacebuilding	
Prescriptive Training as transfer	**Elicitive** Training as discovery
Resource: model and knowledge of trainer	Resource: within-setting knowledge
Training as content-oriented: master approach and technique	Training as process-oriented: participate in model creation
Empowerment as learning new ways and strategies for facing conflict	Empowerment as validating and building from context
Trainer as expert, model and facilitator	Trainer as catalyst and facilitator
Culture as technique	Culture as foundation and seed bed

Source: Lederach, 1995: 65

as elicitive and transformative, rather than prescriptive and directive (see table 9.1). Thus for Lederach:

> The principle of indigenous empowerment suggests that conflict transformation must actively envision, include, respect, and promote the human and cultural resources from within a given setting. This involves a new set of lenses through which we do not primarily 'see' the setting and the people in it as the 'problem' and the outsider as the 'answer'. Rather, we understand the long-term goal of transformation as validating and building on people and resources within the setting. (1995: 212)

The approach also suggests that it is important to identify the 'cultural modalities and resources' within the setting of the conflict in order to evolve a comprehensive framework which embodies both short-term and long-term perspectives for conflict transformation. The importance of cultural relevance and sensitivity within conflict resolution theory has emerged, partly in response to learning from case experience and partly as an explicit critique of earlier forms of conflict resolution theory where local culture was given marginal significance (see chapter 15). In the former case both Lederach and Wehr, reflecting on their work in Central America, found that the 'western' model of outsider neutral mediators was not understood or trusted in many Central American settings, while the idea of insider partial peacemaking was. What has emerged then is the recognition of a need for what Lederach has called a comprehensive approach to conflict resolution that is attentive to how short-term intervention which aims to halt violence is integrated with long-term resolution processes.

This long-term strategy will be sustainable if outsiders/experts support and nurture rather than displace resources which can form part of a peace constituency; and if the strategy addresses all levels of the population. So here is another critical element in the programme. Lederach describes the affected population as a triangle (see chapter 1, figure 1.10). At the apex are key military and political leaders – those who usually monopolize media accounts of conflict. In the middle, at level two, are regional political leaders (in some cases more powerful than central government in their areas), religious and business leaders, and those who have extensive influence in sectors such as health, education and also within the military hierarchies. Finally at the grassroots level, level three, are the vast majority of the affected population: the common people, displaced and refugee populations, together with local leaders, elders, teachers, church groups and locally based NGOs. At this level also, the armed combatants are represented as guerrillas and soldiers in militias. Most peacemaking at the level of international diplomacy operates at level one of this triangle, but for conflict resolution to be successful and sustainable, the coordination of peacemaking strategies across all three levels must be undertaken. In this new thinking, peacebuilding from below is of decisive importance, for it is the means by which, according to Lederach, a peace constituency can be built within the setting of the conflict itself. Once again this is a departure from conventional practice where peacemaking resources from outside the conflict (diplomats, third-party intervenors, etc.) are valued more highly than peacemaking assets, which may exist within the community.

The Mainstreaming of Peacebuilding Models in International Policy

In much the same way that both conflict prevention policy and gender-sensitive approaches became 'mainstreamed' in the agendas of international organizations in the 1990s (as noted in chapters 5 and 12), post-conflict peacebuilding also emerged as an explicit policy objective of a wide variety of key actors concerned to define their role in the resolution of international conflict. As we saw in chapter 8, the process of post-conflict peacebuilding as far as the UN was concerned was defined in the *Agenda for Peace* in 1992. The *Supplement to An Agenda for Peace* in 1995 extended this definition as follows:

> comprehensive efforts to identify and support structures which will tend to consolidate peace and advance a sense of confidence and well-being among people. Through agreements ending civil strife, these may include disarming the previously warring parties and the restoration of order, the custody and possible destruction of weapons, repatriating refugees, advisory and training support for security personnel, monitoring elections, advancing efforts to protect human rights, reforming or strengthening governmental institutions and promoting formal and informal processes of political participation. (Boutros-Ghali, 1995)

During the 1990s most of the large international intergovernmental and non-governmental organizations published their own definitions and guidelines. In 1997 the Development Cooperation Committee (DAC) of the OECD produced its guide on *Conflict, Peace and Development Co-operation on the Threshold of the 21st Century* in which it argued that donor agencies working in the area of economic development should use peace and conflict impact assessments in order to link development policy with the task of building sustainable peace in conflict areas.

The World Bank has also emerged as a leading player in post-conflict peacebuilding. It has established a Conflict Prevention and Reconstruction Unit (CPRU), which in turn has administered a Post-Conflict Fund (PCF) since 1997. Established in 1944 as one of the Bretton Woods institutions to lead world recovery following the Second World War, it has evolved its role from rebuilding infrastructure to one dedicated to:

> a comprehensive approach which includes the promotion of economic recovery, evaluation of social sector needs, support for institutional capacity building, revitalization of local communities, and restoration of social capital, as well as specific efforts to support mine action, demobilize and reintegrate ex-combatants, and reintegrate displaced populations. (World Bank, 2003)

Recognizing that on average a country coming out of civil war has a 50 per cent chance of relapsing into conflict in the first five years of peace, and that it can take a generation to return to pre-war living standards, the World Bank devotes about 16 per cent of its total funding on projects that address the effects of war. During 2003, $13 million was disbursed to support countries in transition from conflict to peace, while a total of $61.5 million was approved for 120 grants for the period 1998–2005.

These initiatives have been paralleled by a host of other IGO, INGO and NGO peacebuilding initiatives since the 1990s. Within this wide and disparate constituency, attempts have been made to draw out common guidelines for ethical and effective practice, one example of which is given in box 9.1.

Implementing Peacebuilding From Below

In applying a peacebuilding from below approach the way in which a conflict is viewed is transformed: whereas normally people within the conflict are seen as the problem, with outsiders providing the solution to the conflict, in the perspective of peacebuilding from below, solutions are derived and built from local resources. This does not deny

Box 9.1　Preliminary peacebuilding checklist

Development and relief NGOs planning to incorporate peacebuilding into their programmes need a perspective and determination which:

- regards conflict and peace as multifactorial dynamic processes, often moving in and out of phases of peace and violence, and with actors who change over time; this means conflict is not linear and predictable;
- whilst seeing particular conflicts as unique and specific, looks at the experience of other violent situations and learns from peacebuilding and conflict resolution attempts in those places; a mix of appropriate, 'western' and 'non-western' methods should be utilized where possible, incorporating local and traditional conflict resolution and peacemaking processes;
- gives equal importance to relational influences as well as structural factors of conflict when designing programmes (especially psychological, social and cultural factors);
- incorporates in-depth surveying, analysis and understanding of the social fabric and relationships within a community where a peace-related programme is planned in order to ensure that more harm than good is not likely to result from such an intervention;
- engages and involves local people at the beginning of peacebuilding projects and programme design, and identifies indigenous sources of social energy and leadership;
- ensures that interventions are contingent and complementary with other official (Track I) and non-official (Track II) initiatives – cooperative and coordination mechanisms should be established, and peacebuilding networks supported;
- is clear about 'normative views' of society, about positions on human rights and justice, and encourages discussion of possible tensions between advocacy work and peace-related work like conflict resolution and peacebuilding programmes;
- trains and prepares their staff and those of their partners in non-violent conflict resolution methods and techniques appropriate to local conditions (an elicitive approach);
- sees peacebuilding as an integrated process; this has implications both for funding and longitudinal research and evaluation plans;
- is not afraid to take an eclectic approach, and to draw freely from different disciplines;
- is based on internationally accepted codes of conduct and operational behaviour.

Source: Lewer, 1999: 24–5

a role for outsider third parties, but it does suggest a need for a reorientation of their roles. Non-governmental organizations are decisive actors in the work of grassroots peacebuilding. There are more than 4,000 development NGOs in the OECD countries which work mainly overseas, and an estimated 20,000 other national NGOs outside the OECD countries which may become the field-based partners of the larger NGOs (that is, the international NGOs, or INGOs, which can operate in many countries and regions and which, like Oxfam and Save the Children, have a multinational organization). Finally there is a myriad of grassroots and community-based organizations (grassroots organizations or GROs, and community-based organizations or CBOs) which represent local interests, local opinion and local cultures. In the course of the most extreme conflict emergencies, the number of NGOs in the field can escalate dramatically; in Rwanda, for example, there were more than 200 NGOs active at the height of the crisis in 1994. Similarly, the number of NGOs active in former Yugoslavia went through a remarkable expansion as the crisis unfolded. Between February and September 1993 the number of NGOs virtually doubled, from 65 to 126, and while the majority of them were internationally based with more or less well-known reputations (90), a number were indigenous NGOs (the GROs and CBOs referred to above), often developed in response to the war (36).

Picking up a theme from the end of the previous chapter, how are we to assess the effectiveness of all these peacebuilding efforts? We saw in chapter 8 with reference to Lund's (2003) review of research literature on post-conflict peacebuilding that assessments of success and failure vary depending upon the criteria used. For example, Doyle and Sambanis (2000), using criteria of absence of major or lower-level violence and uncontested sovereignty two years after the war, found fifty-three successful and seventy-one unsuccessful peace processes since 1945, a success rate of 41 per cent. More demanding criteria, such as human security, increased gender equity, social healing and reconciliation, evidently lead to lower estimations of the success rate. Within this burgeoning literature on post-conflict peacebuilding there has developed a concern with developing methodologies for measuring the impact of international action in conflict-affected communities. Peace and conflict impact assessments (PCIAs) now form established methodological elements of policy-making (see box 9.2), and are used to minimize the likelihood of negative impacts of policy and to capitalize positive impacts (Bush, 1998; Menold, 2004).

What comes out of these studies is still being debated. There is criticism of the plethora of 'amateur' organizations that are drawn to conflict areas in competitive pursuit of funding and often refuse to be coordinated into the more formal post-war reconstruction efforts described in chapter 8 (often, they would argue, with good reason, as our case study below confirms). There is suspicion of the rubric of elicitive approaches where these simply mean reinforcing undemocratic, authoritarian, androcentric and at times corrupt local power structures. This is a highly complex and contested field in which, for example, advocates of gender sensitivity (see chapter 12) frequently find themselves at odds with advocates of cultural sensitivity (see chapter 15). There are the familiar criticisms that well-meaning peacebuilders often unwittingly prolong or worsen the conflict, serve the ends of those intent on 'pacification' in the interest of the powerful, distort local economies and encumber rather than empower local initiatives. Cases that confirm all these criticisms can be found, but those with experience are aware of all these pitfalls and insist that peacebuilding from below of the kind advocated by Curle and Lederach and as outlined in this chapter is essential as the only secure

Box 9.2 Peace and conflict impact assessment

An important element in assessing 'peacebuilding from below' is evaluating the effects of particular projects on the overall conflict dynamics. This raises methodological issues similar to those discussed in chapter 5 in relation to conflict prevention. How can we determine whether a particular intervention has positive or negative effects? There are two issues here: first, how to trace the chain of effects of a particular intervention in conflict; second, how to attribute any changes in the situation (such as a reduction in violent incidents) to a particular intervention.

Attempts to develop a methodology for peace and conflict impact assessment (PCIA) have developed rapidly in recent years. The main impetus for this tool has been the need of development agencies and donors to assess projects, and in particular to screen the positive or negative impacts on conflict of proposed projects. One approach, for example, is to develop indicators of the conflict, indicators of the project's effectiveness, and then to map the factors or variables that lie between the project and the conflict in an effort to trace connections. Impacts can be checked by interviews, questionnaires or focus groups with stakeholders. This micro-appraisal approach tends to relate a project to its immediate effects (for example, a workshop project might strengthen a particular constituency for peace; a cross-community training project might improve inter-ethnic relations in a particular locality). The next, demanding stage is then to assess how these low-level effects influence the overall conflict.

Another approach is pitched at analysing the overall impact of external interventions on a conflict's parties, dynamics and structure. Conflict analysis and conflict mapping are the main tools. DFID's Conflict Assessment approach, for example, combines conflict analysis, assessment of responses to the conflict by different departments of donor governments and analysis of strategic opportunities:

> The impacts of development policy and programmes at the macro- and micro-levels should be mapped. The approach is to make connections with the conflict analysis and consider whether development interventions have affected sources of tensions identified in the structural analysis; or affected incentives, capacities and relationships between warring groups identified in the actor analysis; or whether they have affected factors likely to accelerate or slow conflict identified in analysis of conflict dynamics. This draws on an analysis of the strategic context of the conflict and includes the preparation of conflict scenarios and identification of possible triggers for violence. (DFID, 2002)

As Hoffman (2004) warns, humility is important with regard to claims made for the impact of peacebuilding measures. The evidence to assess such claims may not always be available and the complexity of processes in conflicts will always make attribution difficult. Nevertheless, developing careful, well-evidenced evaluations of interventions by actors at different levels in conflict is a critical part of peacebuilding.

grounding for truly sustainable peace. Commenting on the many examples of local-level cross-community peacebuilding work in Eastern Croatia as a complement to the 1995 political-constitutional level settlement, for example, Judith Large concluded that, although it is easy for outside critics to be dismissive of these small-scale and usually unpublicized initiatives, this is not how things look from the inside. Here it was the practical transformative work of all those who opposed the violence that was cumulatively crucial: 'for activists inside, it mattered too much not to try' (1997: 4).

We are left with a final crucial issue. Putting together our analyses in chapter 8 and in this chapter, there is continuing discussion about which is more important in explaining success or failure – the emerging global model discussed in chapter 8 or the 'bottom-up' model outlined here. Tending in the first direction is the view of an increasing number of commentators in favour of the use of stronger and more long-lasting intervention mechanisms by the international community, including the revival of forms of trustee administration used by both the League of Nations and later by the Trusteeship Council of the UN, where the UN Charter allowed for mandated states 'to develop self-government [in each territory], to take due account of the political aspirations of the peoples, and to assist them in the progressive development of their free political institutions' (Article 73).

Events in Kosovo, Bosnia and Afghanistan have re-enforced arguments that:

> the most effective means of establishing new governmental institutions in war-shattered states is to rebuild these institutions from scratch, to staff them with international personnel, and then to gradually replace these officials with adequately trained and politically nonpartisan locals. . . . Because a trusteeship system would be geared toward the long-term administration of war-shattered states, rather than simply overseeing the reconstitution of governmental institutions in these states, trusteeship is believed to offer a more promising mechanism for the creation of durable and functioning governmental institutions. (Paris, 2003: 456; see also Paris, 2004)

Is the argument in this chapter incompatible with such an idea? In one sense there is no reason why it should be. The approach of conflict resolution, operating across the range of Lederach's model, but placing a high level of commitment at the base of the pyramid, provides the means to set the medium-term perspective of institution and national building within the longer-term goal of human security-oriented peacebuilding and reconciliation. There is no necessary conflict here with international responsibilities in weak or collapsed states where populations are at severe risk. But in another sense there are likely to be tensions given the current nature of international institutions. In the peacebuilding model described in this chapter, futures are negotiated, cultivated and legitimized through elicitive programmes of peace education and conflict resolution training, rather than prescribed and imposed by international bureaucracies. This introduces the idea of cosmopolitan conflict resolution as a corrective to unduly prescriptive international approaches, which will form the main theme of the second part of this book.

Case Study: Peacebuilding in Kosovo, 1999–2004

Some of the complexities of peacebuilding from below may be illustrated by reference to experience in Kosovo. Llamazares and Reynolds (2003) have analysed the dynamics of the post-conflict peacebuilding process there, and in particular the role of local NGOs. The assumption that NGOs – and particularly local NGOs – have a key role to play in building a positive peace in Kosovo is central to the peacebuilding policies and activities of the international community. However, despite the commitment to empowering and building from below, the role of local NGOs (LNGOs) and their relationship to international NGOs (INGOs) needs to be critically examined.

By the time the international peacebuilding mission began arriving in Kosovo in June 1999, the overall aims of the intervention had already been defined by UNSCR 1244 and by the coordinated agendas followed by major donor states. Moreover, while committing the UN administration of Kosovo to provide for the maximum self-government for the people of Kosovo, and to facilitate a process that would determine its final status, a vacuum remains about the nature of its final status which has continued the potential for instability and conflict. The arrival of an increasingly coordinated 'international peacebuilding community' to a fragile, war-torn society means that as LNGOs and CBOs begin to emerge from the rubble, there is often little room for 'alternative' forms of organization or local definitions of peace. The structures set up to implement post-war peacebuilding processes are often top-heavy, concentrating efforts and resources at the highest level of the intervention. In the case of Kosovo, the cumbersome UNMIK pillar structure (see case study in chapter 6) and hundreds of INGOs quickly overwhelmed a civil society already weakened by war. The trend towards greater coherence amongst international peacebuilding agencies severely challenges the ownership of the process by local actors.

The arrival of the international administration in Kosovo was a historic opportunity for the province, in which newly formulated international ideas about the reconstruction and stabilization of post-war societies were tested for the first time. The message coming from the top of the 'intervention pyramid' has been clear: the path to peace runs directly through the creation of a liberal, market-oriented democracy. The dominant international paradigm of a 'democratic peace' is undoubtedly colouring the emerging institutions and processes of post-war societies. In Kosovo, INGOs have been among the primary actors promulgating this particular vision of peacebuilding, creating or employing a host of local NGOs to assist in this process. However, the political culture that existed in Kosovo prior to the war has also shaped LNGOs, and these patterns of clientelism, fear of controversial advocacy, mistrust of government and state structures, lack of inter-ethnic cooperation, and so on, continue to hamper the ability of local agencies to contribute to a stable, multi-ethnic, democratic future for the province. International approaches to partnership have in effect reinforced these legacies and created a pattern of exclusive client–patron relationships that have, in some cases, reduced the vibrancy of Kosovar civil society.

In order for the tremendous 'social capital' found in Kosovo's civil society to become a true source of 'peace capital', a shift needs to take place in the peacebuilding endeavour. This could not only positively transform the nature of the relationships between international and local civil society actors in Kosovo, but it could also help the negotiation of a consensual definition and implementation of peacebuilding. As the international community winds down its level of activity in Kosovo, a number of recommendations are made by Llamazares and Reynolds.

One recommendation is that INGOs ought to encourage networking and coalition-building amongst LNGOs through, for example, the diversification of their local partners and an encouragement of horizontal cooperation amongst them. This way, each INGO would become the hub of a network of LNGOs based on geographical or programmatic proximity and developing working relationships that outlast the international partner's involvement. However, INGOs must avoid 'over-coordination' to the extent of promoting homogenization and centralization of programmes. The nature of these coalitions amongst LNGOs should be determined by the local partners to increase sustainability. Furthermore, to promote bridge-building between communities, this diversification of partners should ensure that it includes NGOs from both majority and minority communities.

Another recommendation strongly stresses the importance of establishing knowledge-sharing networks among civil society organizations in Kosovo. As the international community reduces its operational presence (funding and personnel) in Kosovo, cooperation with other local organizations will be increasingly important for effective programming. Existing networks such as the Kosovo Women's Network and the Kosovo Civil Society Foundation could serve as examples for this kind of cooperation.

A third recommendation is that the transfer of competencies and funding to municipal councils should be viewed not as a threat but as an opportunity. Kosovo's NGO sector has the opportunity to envision and create a new kind of complementary relationship with government at the local level. Effective relationship-building at this stage will pay off in the long term by helping to create responsive local governance, which can provide a bulwark against inappropriate centralization. However, there remains a confusion about the dynamic and trajectory of peacebuilding in Kosovo because of uncertainty about the its political status, which has yet to be resolved (unlike the situation in East Timor, and in other territories of the Balkans where there has been a clear transition to statehood).

Conclusion

It is now broadly accepted that a sustainable peace process must be rooted in the grassroots or communal levels of Lederach's conflict pyramid. However, what constitutes the authentic grassroots or the local community is frequently difficult to discern, and peacebuilding from below is subject to many of the same constraints, dilemmas and instabilities as elite-level peacebuilding. While respect for the cultural traditions and social mores of the local population is important, and while peacebuilding interventions should be conducted in partnership with community elders and leaders and in harmony with traditional conflict management practices, it should not be assumed that civil society operating at the local level is inevitably a quintessentially pure locus for peaceful activity and values. As a result of the impact of the conflict, of population displacement and of other factors, traditional communal relations may have become submerged under new militaristic hierarchies. Local groups may not be benignly autonomous actors and they are susceptible to the effects of structural global forces, structural pressures and national and regional power plays that characterize most violent conflicts. Indeed, local groups operating at the grassroots may well be highly disempowered and fragmented and lacking any capacity for peace activity; they may be local agents of stronger external groups, including militias or criminal groups or clan-based politics; or they may be peacebuilding organizations with authentic roots in the community, but compelled to speak the language of peacebuilding as defined by powerful donors.

For these reasons, peacebuilding from below is not a panacea that avoids the complex challenges of cosmopolitan conflict resolution and peacebuilding at all levels and dimensions of conflict. The fourth generation of conflict resolvers, whose ideas and work we have reviewed in this chapter, embedded the idea of peacebuilding from below as a core construct of contemporary conflict resolution. Having looked at the issue of long-term reconciliation in the next chapter, we will take up these challenges again in Part II, where we see them constituting the main task that faces the next generation of cosmopolitan conflict resolvers.

Recommended reading

Galama and van Tongeren (2002); Lewer (1999); Lund (2003); Reychler and Paffenholz, eds (2001); Woodhouse (1999).

CHAPTER 10

Reconciliation

I told those dedicated workers for peace and reconciliation that
they should not be tempted to give up on their crucial work
because of the frustrations of seemingly not making any
significant progress, that in our experience nothing was wasted,
for when the time was right it would all come together and,
looking back, people would realise what a critical contribution
they had made. They were part of the cosmic movement towards
unity, towards reconciliation, that has existed from the
beginning of time.

Archbishop Desmond Tutu, addressing an audience in
Northern Ireland in 1998

Reconciliation – restoring broken relationships and learning to live
non-violently with radical differences – can be seen as the ultimate goal
of conflict resolution. As suggested in chapter 8, the ending of direct
violence makes conflict resolution possible, negotiation between overlapping interests opens the door to settlement, and the overcoming of
structural injustice creates an enduring space within which further
transformations can occur. But it is the long-term process of reconciliation that constitutes the essence of the lasting transformation that
conflict resolution seeks – the hallmark of the integrative power that
alone binds disparate groups together into genuine societies. In the
terminology of chapter 1, figure 1.3, reconciliation constitutes the
heart of deep peacemaking and cultural peacebuilding.

Four Meanings of Reconciliation

But reconciliation in this broad sense is a complex process made up of
several components that all play their part. There is reconciliation in
the sense of acquiescence in what already exists ('I am reconciled to my
fate'). Although this seems negative, it captures the idea of voluntary
acceptance of what is as yet not an ideal outcome – a necessary

231

Table 10.1 Four dimensions of reconciliation		
	Aspects of reconciliation	**Stages of conflict de-escalation**
1	Accepting the status quo	Ending violence
2	Correlating accounts	Overcoming polarization
3	Bridging opposites	Managing contradiction
4	Reconstituting relations	Celebrating difference

element in peaceful politics. Then there is reconciliation in the sense of 'reconciling financial or other accounts'. This again may seem limited, but encapsulates the notion of comparison and correlation of stories to the point where they are at least not fatally incompatible or irreconcilable. Third, and more creative, is the idea of 'reconciling opposites' or bridging diversity. Here we begin to encounter the possibility of mutual change in the interest of opening up otherwise inaccessible opportunities. And finally we reach the culminating sense of 'reconciliation between former enemies' in which past enmity is set aside and emotional space is created for reforging new relationships (Pankhurst, 1998). This last stage more usually happens between individuals in small groups such as families or villages where personal contacts have been strong. But reconciliation between larger groups – even nations – is also possible, reaching from a reopening of diplomatic relations through to symbolic gestures such as the laying of wreaths or formal expressions of regret, and on to elaborate efforts to create common institutions or foster cultural exchanges as in Franco-German relations after the Second World War. Table 10.1 sets out these four senses of reconciliation and relates them to the stages of conflict escalation and de-escalation first introduced in chapter 1, figure 1.2. This shows how the first three meanings, although falling short of full reconciliation, are necessary constituent moments in the passage from violence and polarization to the peaceful management of contradiction and on to a final normalization of relations.

Between Separation and a Fusion of Identities

Needless to say, the road to reconciliation is long and tortuous. We ended chapter 8 by noting how in post-war reconstruction many insist that there is no point in attempting reconciliation in the early stages, and, indeed, that it might be counter-productive. Deeply traumatized individuals and groups are not ready for such an undertaking. This relates to controversy about the 'contact hypothesis' in conflict resolution, the argument that the more contact there is between conflict parties, the more scope there is for resolution (Hewstone and Brown, eds, 1986). A number of commentators deny this and advocate, on the contrary, a separation of conflictants wherever possible – good fences make good neighbours:

> [T]he data supports the argument that separation of groups is the key to ending ethnic civil wars. . . . There is not a single case where non-ethnic civil politics were created or restored by reconstruction of ethnic identities, power-sharing coalitions, or state-building. (Kaufmann, 1996: 161)

At the other end of the spectrum are those who argue that what is required is nothing less than an eventual redefinition of 'self/other' identity constructs themselves, so that a sense of 'we' replaces the 'us/them' split (Northrup, 1989: 80). Given the mismatch between state borders and the geographical distribution of peoples, we do not see physical separation as a feasible general strategy. And increasing interdependence in a globalized world dictates that, whatever conclusion is reached about the contact hypothesis, individuals and groups, including former enemies, will in most cases have to learn to accommodate difference and live together. On the other hand, we think that most of the problems of mutual accommodation lie on this side of a final transformation in basic identities.

Dealing with the Past: Trauma and Atrocity

Although there is a continuing general need for reconciliation within and between all societies in order to sustain social cohesion, the greatest difficulty from a conflict resolution perspective comes when conflict has escalated through the stages of difference, contradiction, polarization and violence to the point where atrocities have been perpetrated and deep injuries received. It is reconciliation after violent conflict that poses the most acute challenge. In these circumstances it is rarely a case of 'putting Humpty Dumpty together again' in any simple sense. Too much has happened, too many relations have been severed, too many norms violated, too many identities distorted, too many traumas endured. To reach the transformative levels of bridging differences and restoring trust requires a capacity for innovation and creative renewal likely to be beyond the capacity of many societies in the immediate aftermath of violence:

> People know if they are from a war-torn country how difficult it is to sit down across the table in the same room with an adversary. . . . It is likely that adversaries will say: 'we cannot negotiate because we despise

the other side too much. They have killed our children, they have raped our women, they have devastated our villages.' (Carter, 1992: 24)

Before reaching the point where it is possible to climb down the escalation ladder, it is necessary for individuals and groups to recover from trauma, and for the time-bomb of remembered injustice to be defused. In other words, we have to deal with the past in order to clear the ground in the present for the building of a shared future (Lederach, 1997: 27). We will, therefore, look at the challenge of overcoming psychological trauma and at the contentious debate about restoring justice before returning at the end of the chapter to a reconsideration of the wider role of reconciliation in conflict de-escalation and the reconstruction of a shared future.

Acknowledging trauma

There is only space to deal briefly with the complex and still controversial subject of psycho-social healing. The 'invisible effects' of war are often harder to treat than the physical effects:

> The first victims of war are often women and children. Even though they do not lose life or limbs, they are often deeply traumatised in ways not visible to the naked eye. Victims of violence and rape cannot just walk back into everyday life as if nothing happened. As we all know, in the former Yugoslavia, peace has yet to break out for many of the victims. That is why psycho-social work deserves to be a high priority in our emergency aid programmes. (Emma Bonino, European Commissioner with Responsibility for Humanitarian Aid, in Agger, 1995: foreword)

Whether western post-traumatic stress disorder (PTSD) approaches are appropriate in non-western cultural settings or not (Summerfield, 1996), the important point from the perspective of conflict resolution and reconciliation is, as Patrick Bracken explains, that psychological transformation has to accompany the relational tasks of reconciliation if the deeper processes of conflict resolution are to be achieved (Bracken and Petty, eds, 1998). These are evidently culturally sensitive and long-term undertakings, and many can never recover from such terrible injuries and losses.

Amnesia, justice or revenge?

A great deal has been written from a conflict resolution perspective on the relationship between justice and peace in attempting to rebuild social relations after large-scale violence and war (see the recommended reading at the end of this chapter). Here we will take Andrew Rigby's *Justice and Reconciliation After the Violence* (2001) and Rama Mani's *Beyond Retribution: Seeking Justice in the Shadows of War* (2002) as our initial guides.

Rigby frames his book by contrasting 'amnesia' or a forgive-and-forget approach as one way of 'moving on' for societies emerging out of 'division, bloodshed, and collective nightmare' with the alternative of 'trials, purges and the pursuit of justice' that he sees as at the opposite pole (2001: 2–3). He suggests that truth commissions and compensatory reparations lie somewhere between the two.

Mani distinguishes between three interdependent dimensions of public justice, all of which in our view have a role to play in opening the way to eventual reconciliation by providing an alternative to private vengeance. There is first what she calls legal justice or the rule of law, the 'entire apparatus of the justice system', that has usually been delegitimized if not effectively destroyed during the violence, and that needs to be rebuilt. Then there is 'rectificatory justice' to deal with past abuses in response to gross human rights violations, war crimes and crimes against humanity. Third comes 'distributive justice' to address 'the structural and systemic injustices such as political and economic discrimination and inequalities of distribution that are frequently underlying causes of conflict' (2002: 3–11).

Adapting these distinctions, we can usefully define the broad terrain of public justice that concerns us here by contrasting it with amnesia on one side (let us forget about the past) and private revenge on the other (let us avenge the past by taking the law into our own hands) (see table 10.2). Some societies seem able to 'forgive and forget' much more easily than others, and to achieve full reconstitution of relations between former enemies without having to go through the travails of justice, perhaps for cultural reasons – amnesia is the chosen path to reconciliation. Others appear to be unable to do so no matter what efforts are made by internal and external peacemakers – only private vengeance, it seems, can requite the burning sense of injustice. We return to these two alternatives below. But first we will try to clarify the resources that have been used by those societies that have chosen to deal with past atrocity through our broad definition of public justice.

Table 10.2 Justice: between amnesia and vengeance

Amnesia	Public justice	Vengeance
Forgive and forget	Dealing with the past publicly and collectively	I will repay

Peace or Justice? Not Exclusive Alternatives

It has often been said that there is a contradiction between peace and justice. Pauline Baker, for example, poses the question like this:

> Should peace be sought at any price to end the bloodshed, even if power-sharing arrangements fail to uphold basic human rights and democratic principles? Or should the objective be a democratic peace that respects human rights, a goal that might prolong the fighting and risk more atrocities in the time that it takes to reach a negotiated solution? (1996: 564)

She contrasts 'conflict managers' for whom the goal is peace (as in Angola, Cambodia and Mozambique) with 'democratizers' whose goal is justice (as in Namibia, El Salvador and Bosnia).[1]

Although we acknowledged a tension along these lines between the negative and positive tasks of post-war peacebuilding in chapter 8, we do not see the alternatives in such stark terms. Neither the concept of peace nor that of justice is as monolithic as is often made out. Although the negative peace of order and the cessation of direct violence may in some situations appear to be incompatible with the requirements of justice, the positive peace of reconciliation and psycho-social healing largely presupposes it. In other words, the passage from negative to positive peace runs through justice (see table 10.3). And, following Mani, we see justice itself as multidimensional, opening space for reconciliation via a range of combinations of truth commissions, trials, or reparation and rehabilitation measures, depending upon the legal capacity and the nature of the social divisions in the country in question. In other words, for reconciliation to be possible there usually needs to be sufficient *acceptance* by former enemies of the legitimacy of post-war rule of law, sufficient *correlation of accounts* to allow truth commissions and trials to defuse issues of rectificatory justice, and sufficient *bridging of differences* through compensation, reparation or structural adjustments to deliver adequate prospects of improved distributive justice in future. We will look at each of these in turn before exploring the possibilities for

Table 10.3 From negative to positive peace via justice

Negative peace	Justice	Positive peace
Absence of violence	Rule of law	Long-term reconciliation
	Truth commissions/trials	
	Reparation/distributive justice	

reconciliation in the full sense of a *reconstitution of relationships* in the final section.

Alternative Paths to Reconciliation

Having established our conceptual framework, let us briefly review the range of experiments undertaken by different societies in navigating the difficult journey from war to social reintegration in recent years. Good case studies can be found in Rothstein, ed. (1999), Whittaker (1999) and Rotberg and Thompson, eds (2000), as well as in Rigby (2001) and Mani (2002). We look first at amnesia as a deliberate policy choice, then at three linked approaches within the broad ambit of justice (truth commissions, trials, and compensations), and conclude with what seem to be the culturally conditioned opposites of ritual healing and a retaliatory settling of accounts.

Official amnesia – letting go of the past

As Rigby reminds us (2001: 2–3), despite the previous vindictiveness of Franco's regime in Spain, in the transition to democracy after his death in 1975 'there was no purge, but rather an exercise in collective amnesia'. Here the suggested explanation is that this was a 'pact of oblivion' made by two elites for fear of counter-coups by the Spanish military. Similarly in Cambodia, the initial renunciation of the 'spirit of revenge' was a consequence of agreements between 'the Cambodian political elite' and the surviving Khmer Rouge leadership. Some Cambodian school textbooks still devote fewer than ten lines to the Pol Pot years. In both cases Rigby notes that apparent general acquiescence in this approach may have been a result of the widespread complicity of grassroots membership on either side of the previous divide, often splitting families. Even so there are signs in both countries that a younger generation, born after the violent period and therefore not implicated, may well begin to demand more information and a public reckoning on the previous traumas, if for no other reason than to ensure that there can never be a repetition: 'lest we forget'. So perhaps there are some things best forgotten such as 'ancient hatreds' (here we need the waters of Lethe), but others we want to remember such as the memory of the victims and reasons why violence is best prevented (here we need the waters of Acheron). Ultimately, when all significant links with current politics are broken, we are no doubt left with pure historical enquiry – who can now really understand why Guelphs and Ghibellines were so passionately opposed to each other in medieval Europe?

Truth commissions – honouring the past

In contrast to this is the risky path of 'truth commissions' – what Desmond Tutu, Chair of the South African Truth and Reconcilation Commission, calls the 'third way' between 'Nuremberg and national amnesia' (Tutu, 1999: 10–36). Truth commissions have been set up in more than twenty countries, including abortive or half-hearted efforts in Sri Lanka and Haiti, and rather more substantial attempts in El Salvador, Chile and Guatemala. Each reflects the nature of the situation in that country (see box 10.1). A searching discussion of dilemmas and controversies can be found in Rotberg and Thompson (2000).

More elaborate still has been the most famous example: the Truth and Reconciliation Commission (TRC) in South Africa. The 1995

Box 10.1 Truth commissions

In El Salvador, the 'Commission on the Truth' set up on 5 May 1992 reported back to the UN Secretary-General and President Cristiani on 22 September with a 200-page assessment of 22,000 complaints received of violations perpetrated since 1980. Direct evidence was confirmed in 7,312 cases, and indirect evidence in a further 13,562, with 97 per cent of the human rights violations attributed to the 'rightist military, paramilitary, security forces, and death squads' and 3 per cent to the opposition rebels (UN Doc. S/25500). Perpetrators were named, despite protests from the ruling ARENA party, and 103 army officers were dismissed, but a blanket amnesty was granted by the ARENA-controlled National Assembly and recommendations for a purge of the Supreme Court of Justice were obstructed (Hampson, 1996: 156–7).

In Chile, the National Commission on Truth and Reconciliation set up in 1990, as a result of a deal with General Pinochet, had to complete its work in only 18 months, met behind closed doors and could name none of the perpetrators – although the report was handed to President Aylwin on television and a public apology was made. It was greatly aided by the thousands of transcripts on disappearances that had been collected during the seventeen-year Pinochet dictatorship by the Roman Catholic Church's Vicaria de la Solidaridad.

In Guatemala, the official Commission on Historical Clarification, despite a limited mandate and scant resources that frustrated some, used provisions in the National Reconciliation Law to recommend trials in a number of cases (Guatemala Memory of Silence Report, February 1999). This was supplemented by civil society initiatives, notably the Roman Catholic Church's unofficial Project for the Recovery of Historical Memory that recorded 6,000 testimonies in local Indian languages and disseminated its report via theatre, radio, workshops and ceremonies. The army and civilian self-defence patrols were blamed for most of the 150,000 deaths and 50,000 disappearances. Two days after the presentation of the report, its coordinator was beaten to death in Guatemala City (Crocker, 2000: 111).

Promotion of National Unity and Reconciliation Act required the TRC
to contribute to the building of:

> a historic bridge between the past of a deeply divided society charac-
> terised by strife, conflict, untold suffering and injustice, and a future
> founded on the recognition of human rights, democracy and peaceful
> coexistence and development opportunities for all South Africans, irre-
> spective of colour, race, belief or sex. (Quoted in Villa-Vincencio and
> Verwoerd, 2000, 280)

The plan was for societal reconciliation to be effected through as wide
a sample as possible of individual testimonies and responses. Avoiding
vindictiveness on the one hand, and a disregard for wrongs and suffering on the other, the hope was that full public disclosure of human
rights violations since 1960 and an attempt to harmonize competing
versions of the past within what Lyn Graybill calls 'a single universe of
comprehensibility' (1998: 49), together with some acknowledgement
of responsibility, if not expression of regret (Committee on Human
Rights Violations), as well as some measure of reparation for the
victims (Committee on Reparations and Rehabilitation), would open
up an emotional space sufficient for accommodation if not forgiveness, with the question of punishment or amnesty abstracted or postponed (Committee on Amnesty) (Asmal et al., 1996; Boraine et al., eds,
1997; Boraine, 2000). Needless to say, as a middle way, the TRC has been
severely criticized from opposite directions, by those arguing that the
country should not look back and risk causing new wounds, and by
others (for example, Steve Biko's family) arguing that human rights
violations should be tried and punished in courts of law (Gutmann
and Thompson, 2000).

Defenders of the TRC maintain that justice is broader than
retributists make out – including procedural justice as well as the wider
healing and therapeutic qualities of restorative justice, which are what
is needed in a raw politicized atmosphere where legitimacy is still in
question (Kiss, 2000). A punitive approach would be interpreted as partisan 'victor's justice'. These compromises are unavoidable aspects of
'transitional justice' in societies coming out of violence and attempting
to rebuild the foundations of social consensus (Kritz, ed., 1995). Rotberg
describes the TRC experiment as an 'enriched form of justice' in which
'truth for amnesty is said to achieve justice through reconciliation'
(2000: 14). We comment briefly on each of these components.

Many agree that in an environment where 'truth' is still bitterly
contested, a TRC can uncover 'truths' inaccessible to courts of law.[2]
Unlike most other truth commissions, proceedings in the TRC were
held in public and communicated as widely as possible. The outcome
was not a single 'official' version of the truth, but painfully and

emotionally elicited insights and understandings as the heart-rending stories of victims were listened to with the deepest respect in the Committee on Human Rights Abuses, and sometimes explicitly acknowledged by perpetrators. The commissioners *Final Report*, containing the evidence given by 20,000 victims, is an extraordinary and very moving record. Although falling far short of a full measure of atonement and forgiveness, many attest to the healing power of the process as past sufferings were acknowledged and honoured (Minow, 2000), and to the narrowing of the opportunities to continue to circulate unchallenged lies about apartheid.

As to the question of punishment or immunity, unlike what was done in many other countries, no blanket amnesty was given. Amnesty was awarded or withheld on an individual basis for more than 7,000 applicants, according to whether the Committee on Amnesty was satisfied that full disclosure had been made and that the motives had been 'political' rather than merely criminal – an admittedly difficult and loosely defined distinction. The judgments were often highly controversial and on occasion overturned by South Africa's High Court (Slye, 2000).

Such in outline was the compromise attempted in South Africa in conditions where the defeat of apartheid had been decisive, where there were sufficient resources to mount the TRC, where Christian and indigenous African *ubuntu* traditions could be drawn upon and, above all, where outstanding leadership was providentially displayed. Even then, a public opinion survey published in July 1998 suggested that two-thirds of South Africans at that time thought that the TRC had led to a deterioration in race relations rather than societal reconciliation (Rotberg, 2000: 19). Nevertheless, in our view this experiment, no doubt in its details unique to conditions in South Africa at that time, offers a magnificent and hopeful example of a creative attempt to handle the past in a way that furthers societal reconciliation in the present and promotes conflict resolution into the future.

Trials – bringing the past before the tribunal of the present

This is a large subject, but we will confine ourselves to one main point (for the wider debate about war crimes tribunals compare Mak (1995) and Meron (1993)). Although often presented as an alternative to truth commissions, we suggest that national or international criminal tribunals are better seen as complementary in most cases. We can see this through the example of Richard Goldstone, head of the 1992 commission to investigate criminal conduct in South Africa, and subsequently appointed as the first chief prosecutor of the United Nations International Criminal Tribunals for the former Yugoslavia and Rwanda. Goldstone acknowledges that the relationship between peace and justice is a complicated one, inasmuch as without a cessation of violence there is usually no hope of bringing perpetrators of atrocities to justice. Nevertheless, he insists that 'Without establishing a culture of law and order, and without satisfying the very deep need of victims for acknowledgement and retribution, there is little hope of escaping future cyclical outbreaks of violence' (1997: 107). The mention of retribution makes it appear that the non-retributory mechanism of truth commissions would not be deemed adequate. But in a chapter entitled 'The South African Solution: Is Truth Sufficient?' (2000: 59–73), he concludes that the TRC achieved results that 'made South Africa a better country' and could not have been achieved 'through normal criminal processes' which would have been long and costly and rejected as politically motivated by the majority of white South Africans: 'Suffice it for me to state here my great admiration for the awesome task it performed during its thirty-month existence. I have no doubt that South Africans will live to appreciate its work and legacy' (ibid.: 71–2). There are many critics of international tribunals, not least supporters of those indicted, who are usually convinced that the tribunal is a political tool of their enemies. But for the authors of this book they are an essential ingredient in the struggle to assert internationally endorsed humane standards, even in the crucible of intense conflict.

Reparation – future compensation for the past

We will say little about compensation and reparation except to remind ourselves that this is widely recognized to be a key element in the wider ambit of justice enabling greater scope for reconciliation. In Chile efforts were made to compensate survivors and the families of victims, while the Reparation and Rehabilitation Committee of the South African TRC recommended who should be compensated and by how much to Parliament (Rotberg, 2000: 11). In the event, victims rarely receive much and the spread of compensation is inevitably seen as arbitrary and controversial. Martha Minow (2000) includes not just money payments, but monuments, parks and renamed buildings as part of the compensation and sees this as essential to the long-term vision of social transformation. This merges into issues of reconstruction and improvements in distributive justice that become part of the wider peacebuilding effort.

Ritual healing – exorcizing the past

We end this section by noting two contrasting cultural responses to past violence in order to underline the particularity of different countries. Here we draw attention to resources found within many indigenous societies that have impressed conflict resolvers, such as the role of traditional healers in Mozambique (Nordstrom, 1995), or the work of lineage leaders in Somaliland to effect reconciliation through 'grassroots peace conferences' and 'peace-making endeavours' (Farah, 1993). In some cultures, where misfortune and violence is often attributed to possession by bad spirits, there is scope for remarkably swift reconciliation through public cleansing ceremonies. In these cases the war is seen as a calamity imposed from outside which was no individual's or group's fault. One of the criticisms of the Regional and Local Dispute Resolution Committees set up in South Africa after the 14 September 1991 National Peace Convention was that this was elitist and dominated by predominantly white business, and legal, political and church leaders out of touch with grassroots cultures which is where the deepest sufferings have been felt (Gastrow, 1995: 70–1). On the other hand, there are pertinent warnings against indiscriminately resourcing 'indigenous processes' which may turn out to represent transparent mechanisms for perpetuating local systems of oppression, exclusion and exploitation (Pankhurst, 1998).

Retaliation – cleaning the slate by avenging the past

A very different response comes in societies where traditions of clan-based reprisal and vendetta are endemic, as exemplified in the Balkans. Although usually – and rightly – condemned from a conflict resolution perspective as the antithesis of reconciliation, we must acknowledge that in the eyes of many in these traditions it is only after reprisal and redress that the balance of justice is restored and relations can be reformed. Needless to say the trouble with this is that what to one party is restoration of balance to another is usually a sharp disequilibrium. This can even be seen in the aftermath of the 11 September 2001 attack, where an initial wave of sympathy for the United States was enhanced by a widespread sense that the suffering there had somehow restored a measure of equivalence that opened space for reconciliation if used creatively. That was not how it was viewed in the United States, however, where the clamour for reprisal was loud.

Reconciliation and Conflict Resolution: Going Down the Escalation Ladder

In conclusion, having noted the political and cultural differences from case to case, we return to our main theme of the essential ingredients in the general process of what Mervyn Love calls 'peacebuilding through reconciliation' (1995). Conflict resolvers have made important contributions here over the years, notably Joseph Montville, whose work on reconciliation and healing in political conflict resolution comprises a three-stage 'conflict resolution strategy' for reconciliation through a process of 'transactional contrition and forgiveness' based on the problem-solving approach (1993: 122–8). Kelman offers a comparable method for 'transforming the relationship between former enemies' (1999). Lederach (1997, 1999, 2001) looks to Psalm 85, verse 10 for his inspiration that reconciliation is the place where 'truth and mercy have met together, justice and peace have kissed', while Kriesberg (1998) also sees the components as truth (revelation, transparency, acknowledgement), justice (restitution) and mercy (acceptance, forgiveness, compassion, healing) leading to peace (security, respect, harmony, well-being). Using a psychodynamic approach, Volkan et al. (1991) argue that the fundamental need is for public acknowledgement of past hurts, which lets the protagonists and victims begin to move on from rage and hatred to acceptance of loss and ultimately acceptance of each other. We end the chapter by retracing the four stages of reconciliation in relation to the de-escalation stages introduced in chapter 1: ending violence, overcoming polarization, managing contradiction and celebrating difference.

Political closure and acceptance: preconditions for reconciliation

The first requirement is for some measure of political closure, at least to the point where a return to violence has become unlikely. It is much harder to move forward with the deeper processes of reconciliation if the divisive political issues are still active and threatening. That is why reconciliation is often easier after decisive defeat and victory as in Germany and Japan after 1945, or Biafra after the Nigerian civil war. The losers may feel that they must 'reconcile' themselves to the outcome because it is unavoidable, while the winners may find it possible to be magnanimous. This goes far towards explaining the greater space for reconciliation in post-apartheid South Africa than in post-Dayton Bosnia, or Kosovo while the issue of final status is still undecided. If it is hard to forgive a defeated enemy, and harder to forgive a finally victorious enemy, it is harder still to forgive an enemy who is still seen to be an immediate and potent threat. The link here is between reconciliation in its first sense and peacekeeping after violent conflict.

Overcoming polarization and reconciling accounts

At the second stage of overcoming polarization, it is a question of combating what have often been irreconcilable accounts of the conflict entertained by rival parties. The deeper processes of reconciliation cannot be reached while dehumanized images of the enemy are still current and mutual convictions of victimization are widely believed. We enter the territory of reconciling stories, at any rate to the point where those with a political interest in demonizing the other lose influence, and it may become possible for each party to comprehend that all feel that they are victims and have suffered tragic losses. The key point is reached when the other is 'rehumanized'. Here the link is between reconciliation in its second sense and peacemaking – particularly among political elites and opinion-formers.

Managing contradiction and reconciling conflicting demands

With the third stage, the reconciliation process definitively enters the realm of transformation, as efforts are made to bridge continuing deep differences by structural political and economic rearrangements. These are often highly complex, but the chief requirement is that, even though there may not be a possibility of reparation in most individual cases, a general belief is strengthened that basic needs will be increasingly met through measures of more inclusive political representation and more equitable economic opportunity. The space for deeper reconciliation is much widened if parents feel that things are likely to get better for their children. The link is between the third sense of reconciliation and structural peacebuilding.

Celebrating difference and reconciling former enemies

Only when the fourth and final stage is reached has true reconciliation been achieved. Here we enter the realm of atonement and forgiveness. Former enemies are reconciled to the point where differences are not only tolerated, but even appreciated. Many never reach this stage, which often includes formal acts of acknowledgement and apology on behalf of previous generations, and general acceptance that a shared future is now more important than a divided past. This involves deeper levels of peacemaking and cultural peacebuilding that stretch from revisions of formerly polarized official accounts and media representations, through pluralization of education and stories told in school textbooks, and eventually on to leavening everyday experiences that affect localized transmissions of memory within communities and families (Kelly, 2002). Identities themselves become softened and transformed, as a broadening of self-understanding combines with a re-perception of others as fellow human beings. Transformation of this kind may be the exception. Perhaps only remarkable individuals can achieve it at a single leap. The argument here has been that earlier stages on the path to reconciliation are more likely to offer the space required for overcoming violent conflict. Nevertheless, it is this full measure of transformative reconciliation that inspires the sentiments expressed by Archbishop Tutu at the head of this chapter, and that in the end underpins the cosmopolitan vision to which we turn in Part II.

Recommended reading

Bracken and Petty, eds (1998); Kriesberg (1998b); Lederach (1997, 2001); Mani (2002); Minow (1998); Rigby (2001); Rotberg and Thompson, eds (2000); Rothberg, ed. (1999); Tutu (1999); Whittaker (1999).

COSMOPOLITAN CONFLICT
RESOLUTION

Terror and Global Justice

The terror that the world faces cannot be understood in theological terms. That its perpetrators claim to represent Islam is neither here nor there. Proving a thousand times that Islam is not what they say it is will change nothing. Nor is it about the presence of US troops in Saudi Arabia, nor about Palestine, nor about poverty, nor about the clash of civilisations, nor about 'Arab humiliation' whatever that means. The only way to deal with such terror groups is to treat them as the criminals they are.

Amir Taheri, The Times, 26 May 2003

Globalisation is forging greater interdependence yet the world seems more fragmented, between rich and poor, between the powerful and the powerless, and between those who welcome the new global economy and those who demand a different course. The September 11, 2001, terrorist attacks on the United States cast new light on these divisions, returning strategic military alliances to the centre of national policy making and inspiring heated debates on the danger of compromising human rights for national security. For politics and political institutions to promote human development and safeguard the freedom and dignity of all people, democracy must widen and deepen.

Human Development Report 2002: Deepening Democracy in a Fragmented World, Overview

Introduction

Many commentators now claim that the events and aftermath of 11 September 2001 have redefined the paradigm of global order and security. The consensus is that after the last epoch-marking event (the end of the Cold War) yet another profound historical shift has occurred. We do not yet know the full implications of what this shift will be, but we know at least, as Ken Booth and Tim Dunne have suggested, that when 'the victim of terror attacks of spectacular horror happens to be the greatest power on earth, the agenda is set' (2002: ix).

The attacks of 11 September 2001 dramatically illustrated the rapid and deep changes in international relations brought about by global-ization. As Part I of this book has shown, local conflicts are manifest-ing themselves globally and global conflicts locally, and the effects of conflicts can be felt far from their sites. As states and societies become more than ever open to events outside their borders, and images, belief systems, communications and ideas flow rapidly across societies divided by different ways of life and cultures, it is not surprising that conflicts of interest and perceived conflicts are experienced not only at the intrastate and interstate levels, but also globally. A hybrid mixture of local, regional and global conflicts has emerged, which we might call transnational conflict. Accompanying this change are uncertainties over how and where this form of conflict should be addressed. New doctrines of intervention and new understandings of 'peace and security' imply a redefinition of jurisdiction. If interests cut across states and communities, where does appropriate jurisdiction lie? How is democratic accountability to be effective in a world of inter-dependent decisions? How are conflicts to be resolved when they cross borders and levels of analysis? In this new 'neo-medieval' order, conflict resolution is challenged to redefine its scope and its praxis. We have used the term 'cosmopolitan conflict resolution' to indicate the need for an approach that is not situated within any particular state, society or established site of power, but rather one which promotes constructive means of handling conflict at local through to global levels in the interests of humanity.

The underlying argument in this chapter, which sets the framework for the second part of this book, is that addressing conflict formations both at the global and the local level is a necessary part of the response not only to new forms of global or mass casualty terrorism, but also to the threat of violence and frustrated needs in general. Terrorism, of course, is neither a legitimate nor a necessary outcome of these under-lying conflicts. But tackling conflicts which create the conditions in which terrorism flourishes is necessary in its own right, and is also an integral part of the response.

Inevitably this agenda is related to wider debates about transitions in international order and the emergence of cosmopolitan democratic governance (Held, 1995; Shaw, 2000). David Held developed his analy-sis of democratic theory and cosmopolitan governance from founda-tions in the democratic peace ideals of Immanuel Kant. For Kant: 'The greatest evils which affect civilised nations are brought about by war, and not so much by actual wars in the past or the present, as by never ending and indeed continually increasing preparations for war' (cited in Held, 1995: 226). Kant's remedy was his idea of an association of citizens who would form a moral community, a pacific federation in which war would be renounced as a means of politics. Similarly, cosmopolitan conflict resolution seeks to open new political spaces in which citizens from different parts of the world can tackle the transnational sources of violent conflict.

The idea of cosmopolitan conflict resolution rests on political, legal and moral foundations. Kant and his successors posited the possibility of a new level of political community, based on moral and political concerns beyond the borders of a particular state. The international law of human rights has given a legal basis for such concerns, setting out standards that states have committed themselves to uphold. Moral cosmopolitanism rests on the idea that the flourishing and well-being of human beings is a matter of concern to all. This applies to people equally, whoever they are, and it applies globally. In national politics it is a commonplace that the well-being of fellow citizens is a matter of common concern within a state, and that citizens of a state have rights and duties stemming from their citizenship. Cosmopolitanism widens these attributions to all human beings. It asserts that all have rights and needs that have to be protected, and duties to protect others. For example, cosmopolitanism implies that citizens have a responsibility for institutions which damage well-being elsewhere in the world, as Pogge (2002) argues in the case of world poverty. Similarly, there is a cosmopolitan responsibility for the lives and life-hopes of others being damaged through conflict. Cosmopolitan conflict resolution is justified, and should be held accountable, in terms of the contribution it makes to the long-term interests of the affected populations. Cosmopolitanism is therefore founded on ethical universalism, befitting the global age, as we argue in chapter 13, and on the view that the state-based international society of the late twentieth century has the potential to evolve into a world community, as we discuss in chapter 16. All of this is consonant with ideas about the evolution of a 'global civil society' as advocated by Mary Kaldor and others (Kaldor, 2003). In these respects, cosmopolitanism is a narrative that competes with terrorism and war, challenging particularist ethics and asserting the value and universal moral concern of each individual life.

Conflict Resolution and Terrorism

In the conflict resolution field, the United Nations Development Programme approach to combating international terrorism cited at the beginning of this chapter would receive more support than that of Amir Taheri. This is not to underrate the importance of traditional police responses to terrorism, nor to compromise moral clarity by condoning what are criminal acts – as universally agreed by the citizens of Madrid in March 2003, for example. But it is to insist that an effective response has to address the underlying sources of conflict as well as their symptoms.

Terrorism is not a new phenomenon and has been studied by writers on conflict resolution for many years – as indicated by the title of Burton's 1979 book *Deviance, Terrorism and War*. That is why, drawing on decades of analysis of the relationship between frustrated human needs and terrorism, Burton (2001) was one of the few who can be said to have predicted a dramatic increase in terrorism before the events of 9/11. We also applaud the refreshing frankness and courage of a theorist-practitioner like Lederach, who, within days of 9/11, offered his fellow Americans an imaginative conflict transformationist alternative at a time when calls for revenge were understandably loud (2001).

What follows should be seen to follow from the analysis of terrorism offered in chapter 3, where two conceptual clarifications are of particular relevance.

First, in chapter 3 we defined terrorism as a certain kind of political action, a means towards an end rather than an end in itself (see box 3.3). In most cases it is a strategy that is taken up and dropped by political groups according to how they assess the best way to gain their purposes in particular situations – as in the case of the Tamil Tigers in Sri Lanka, who pioneered the recent upsurge in suicide bombing campaigns, and have now, at any rate for the moment, abandoned them. Here is the clue for a conflict resolution response. The aim is not to eliminate terrorists, but terrorism. This neutralizes the familiar fact that in intense political conflict each side sees the other as the terrorists, and focuses instead on the core business of eliminating acts and tactics of terror no matter who is responsible for them. Does this mean being prepared to 'do deals with terrorists'? It means doing whatever is necessary within a wider strategy of the kind outlined below to persuade those who have adopted terrorist tactics no longer to do so. This is the way in which many, if not most, terrorist campaigns do in fact come to an end. There is no compromise in condemning terrorist acts. But political accommodation is made with legitimate political goals – although it is true that this will often involve difficult compromises in the area of amnesty and punishment, as discussed in chapter 10.

For example, in Northern Ireland terrorism has been the response of those who felt themselves oppressed, but not strong enough to meet their oppressor in battle. It is a characteristic tactic of the weaker side in what they perceive to be asymmetric conflicts. Characteristically, too, it is often undertaken by people who perceive themselves to be idealists righting previous wrongs. Yet in taking the struggle to the stronger enemy, its practitioners abandon the traditional restraints on war and directly attack civilians. Despite robust efforts on the part of the British government, policing alone did not prevent the growth of terrorism in Northern Ireland. The introduction of the army followed by the internment of Republicans greatly intensified an already serious political conflict. Terrorism continued throughout the Troubles, both in Northern Ireland itself and on the British mainland. Only when the conflict resolution process was launched that eventually led to the Downing Street Declaration and the IRA and Loyalist ceasefires did terror attacks begin to dissipate (even then, the worst atrocity, the Omagh bombing, came after the Good Friday agreement). Getting the guns out of politics has been a slow, frustrating and incomplete process. But the curtailment of terrorism could never have been achieved by policing and military methods alone.

The second conceptual clarification to note from chapter 3 is the way in which typologies of terrorism relate closely to conflict typologies, confirming the idea that most forms of terrorism should be understood within the more general context of the forms of conflict of which they are part (see table 3.4). The exceptions were seen to be state terrorism and international terrorism, which did not coincide with usual conflict categories. We include them here because our definition of terrorism does not discriminate between those who practise it – and in the case of the former, both historically and quantitatively, it has been governments that have been responsible for most such atrocities. In view of this, it is important to differentiate appropriate responses accordingly.

State terrorism, whether the sponsoring of terrorist acts abroad (as formerly in Libya) or as domestic oppression (as in Zimbabwe or Sudan), requires coordinated action against the offending government and support for civilian victims. Similarly with the three main kinds of *insurgent terrorism*, whether 'ideological' (aimed at changing the nature of government), 'national-separatist' (aimed at changing the identity of the state) or 'economic/factional' (aiming to control some or all of the assets of the state). The first two are often amenable to a combination of firmness and incentives, albeit usually only after sustained attrition, since resort to terrorism tends to come once the underlying conflict has more widely reached the level of ingrained violence in any case. The third kind of insurgent terrorism is closest to Taheri's description and is less open to political solutions. Finally, and now eclipsing all other forms, there is *international terrorism*, not in the sense in which most groups that practise terrorism have international links of supply and support, but in the sense that these are international networks that are not based in particular countries and whose primary political or ideological purposes are not confined to particular countries. Radical Islamist jihadis are now the most prominent examples, but earlier it was Anarchist, Bolshevik and Maoist networks. Much of this is controversial, with some questioning the existence of Al-Qaida, while others suggest that it has some 18,000 operatives in sixty countries (IISS, 2004) (see box 11.1). The situation is complex and volatile as it is often difficult to distinguish actors and motives, and multiple agendas complicate the simplified typology offered here. Is international terrorism so different to other forms of terrorism that it requires an entirely different response? Although we do recognize differences, we do not think so. But, before moving on to outline a policy framework for overcoming terrorism that we believe is consonant with a conflict resolution approach, we will take a further step here.

Box 11.1 Groups thought to have links with Al-Qaida

This list is impressionistic, since there may be few direct operational links in many cases. Al-Qaida acts as an ideological, logistical and financial hub – often through the offering of relatively small sums of money.

AFGHANISTAN
Hizb-I-Islami

ALGERIA
Armed Islamic Group (GIA)
Salafist Group for the Call and
   Combat (GSPC)

CHECHNYA
Islamic International
   Peacekeeping Brigade
Riyadus Silikhin
Battalion of Chechen Martyrs
Special Purpose Islamic
   Regiment

CHINA
Eastern Turkestan Islamic
   Movement (ETIM)

EGYPT
Al-Gamaa al-Islamiya (IG)
Al-Jihad (Egyptian Islamic Jihad)

INDONESIA
Jemaah Islamiya (JI)

LIBYA
Libyan Islamic Fighting Group

LEBANON
Asbat al-Ansar

MOROCCO
Jemaa serat al-Mustaqin (Salafist
   movement)
Moroccan Islamic Combat Group (GICM)

PAKISTAN/KASHMIR
Harakat ul-Mujahidin (HUM)
Jaish-e-Mohammed (JM)
Lashkar-e-Yayyiba (LT)
Al-Badhr Mujahedin
Harakat ul-Jihad-Islami (HUJI)

PHILIPPINES
Abu Sayaff Group (ASG)

SOMALIA
Al-Ittihaad al-Islamiya (AIAI)

SOUTH-EAST ASIA
Jemaah Islamiya (JI)
Kumpulan Mujahidin Malaysia (KMM)

TUNISIA
Tunisian Combat Group (TCG)

UZBEKISTAN
Islamic Movement of Uzbekistan (IMU)

YEMEN
Islamic Army of Aden (IAA)

An appreciation of the political culture of the groups involved and of the conscious and sometimes unconscious motives of the individuals who participate in terrorism can begin to foster a more reflective understanding of the phenomenon. According to some accounts, Islamist politics stem from a profound sense of humiliation and subordination at the hands of the western colonial powers, combined with a rejection of secular western commercial culture, which is seen to threaten Islamic values. Halliday (2002) brilliantly dissects the general and particular causes of this crisis. The original aim of the Islamists was to create a society and a state based on Islamic principles. This drew them into resistance to the secular, modernizing trends in Islamic states as well as to the sources of those trends. The movement bound together political movements in disparate conflicts, from Palestine to Afghanistan to Kashmir and beyond. Combined with the crisis of the state in the region, this led to what Halliday calls a general 'west Asian crisis'. The Islamists' seizure of power in Afghanistan, helped by Pakistani intelligence, Saudi finance and US support for the *mujahadin*, created conditions for a new, militaristic and large-scale training ground for terrorism to be established.

It is also important to try to understand the mind-set of those who carry out attacks on ordinary citizens, however difficult this may seem. Here we run into difficulties highlighted in chapter 14, where competing belief systems (including those of third parties) generate conflicting explanations. The self-understanding of those responsible for terror is, insofar as it seeks to justify it, evidently at odds with those (including the authors of this book) who reject all acts of terror as ethically and legally unacceptable. At times it may seem simply crass, as when Basayev, asked why his group had massacred more than 300 children at Beslan in North Ossetia in September 2004, replied that Russians had killed more than 40,000 Chechen children over the past ten years (Gregory, 2004). Nevertheless, there are those like Rowan Williams, future Anglican Archbishop of Canterbury, who was in New York on 11 September 2001, who are prepared to recognize in their own feelings of anger against those responsible a window of understanding into the hearts and minds of the perpetrators (Williams, 2002). From a psychoanalytic perspective, Britton (2002: 31) makes some suggestive observations on 'the suicidal act as a means of gaining approval and self-glorification'. The destructive drive, he suggests, is 'characteristic of a particular pathological organisation. . . . In this system death is believed to produce eternal union rather than loss, whereas continued life is felt to cause separation.' 'The fixation is to the infantile imago of an idealised parent who is more likely to be represented as God than as a human being.' Once again, we stress that all acts of terrorism are to be condemned as criminal, no matter how great the provocation. But at the same time an adequate response needs to include some attempt to understand what drives those who are attracted to terrorism, and why Osama bin Laden 'is a source of inspiration to Moslem youth all over the world' (Covington et al., eds, 2002: 113).

Conflict Resolution as a Response

It will now be evident why, from a cosmopolitan conflict resolution perspective, an adequate response to terrorism must do two things. It must operate where appropriate at all levels from the local to the global. And it must embed an intelligence/security-led *denial* response within a wider policy framework that also contains: a *prevention* strategy to address the breeding grounds for violent conflict and terrorism, a *persuasion* strategy to convince political groups and their constituencies that non-terror tactics are better and a *coordination* strategy to combine all these efforts under principles of contingency and complementarity (see box 11.2). It will also insist that this coordinated response must not in its execution itself contradict the anti-terrorism values in whose name the whole enterprise is undertaken.

A coordinated framework of this kind reflects the recommendations of the UN's Policy Working Group on the UN and Terrorism (UNPWG), set up by the UN Secretary-General to complement the work of the Counter-Terrorism Committee of the Security Council (UNCTC) (established under Security Council Resolution 1373 in September 2001):

> Terrorism is, and is intended to be, an assault on the principles of law, order, human rights and peaceful settlement of disputes on which the world body is founded. . . . So it is through a determined effort to bolster and reassert these guiding principles and purposes that the world body can best contribute to the struggle against terrorism. (A57/273 S/2002/875)

The UNPWG bases its recommendations on strategies of dissuasion, denial and the promotion of international cooperation.

The First Dimension: Prevention – Reducing Proneness to Terrorism

This dimension of the strategy links with the aim of structural conflict prevention in general, in the conviction that development-led strategies 'can facilitate the creation of opportunities and the political, economic and social spaces within which indigenous actors can identify, develop and use the resources necessary to build a peaceful,

Box 11.2	A policy framework for addressing terrorism	
1 Prevention	**Reducing proneness to terrorism**	
	Address perceived global inequalities and injustice	
	Address urban poverty among young men	
	Address lack of democratic opportunity (repressive states)	
	Address underlying conflicts – Iraq, Palestine, Kashmir, etc.	
In general:	*Treat legitimate grievance with proper seriousness and respect*	
2 Persuasion	**Reducing motivation and recruitment**	
	Uphold cosmopolitan values and human rights	
	Persuade insurgent groups and governments to choose political accommodation rather than violence and repression	
	Persuade domestic and diaspora support constituencies that non-terrorist options work best	
	Acknowledge and address feelings of hurt and motivations of supporters	
In general:	*Discredit terrorism/repression and alter calculations of its likely effectiveness among potential perpetrators and supporters*	
3 Denial	**Reducing vulnerability and defeating hardliners**	
	Limit target vulnerability to terrorism	
	Cut off supply for acts of terror (finance, weaponry, WMD)	
	Strengthen international policing capabilities	
	Break up terrorist networks and arrest activists	
In general:	*Strike correct balance between effectiveness and upholding the values being defended*	
4 Coordination	**Maximizing international efforts**	
	Apply principles of contingency and complementarity	
	Apply principle of comparative advantage	
	Respect the primacy of international law	
In general:	*Ensure that this is a genuinely international enterprise*	

equitable and just society' (UN Secretary-General's 2001 *Report on the Prevention of Armed Conflict*, Paragraph 29). This is seen to underpin the UNPWG approach:

> If such efforts assist societies to resolve conflict peacefully within the rule of law, grievances that might have been expressed through terrorist acts are more likely to be addressed through political, legal and social means. (UNPWG, 2003)

In addition, 'effective structural prevention measures would strengthen the capacities of States to avoid the type of protracted armed conflict that weakened Afghanistan and enabled the rise within its territory of transnational terrorist networks'.

Correcting undoubted gross global resource imbalances and discrepancies in the distribution of political power – often seen to fuel frustration and historic resentments in the Islamic world – is too large an agenda to link specifically to the prevention of terrorism. But the resentments in the Muslim world against the colonial powers and the continuing elements of foreign political and economic domination are very real. The most powerful states, above all the USA, need at least to acknowledge the legitimacy of these grievances, be seen to be addressing them purposively, and to conduct themselves 'with more humility and respect for the basic human aspirations of all people' (Austin, 2004). Other suggested 'breeding grounds' for terrorism include 'strong, authoritarian Arab and Muslim states' where the failure of socialist and nationalist alternatives in the 1950s, 1960s and 1970s left a vacuum filled by religious fundamentalism in the 1980s and 1990s. Western governments are seen as hypocritical because they 'espouse democracy and human rights worldwide, yet support elitist and non-democratic governments in these states' (Laqueur, 1999: 145; von Hippel, 2002: 36). Behind this lies the sense of alienation and lack of hope among young unemployed males in sprawling new conurbations (in 1975 one-third of the world's population lived in cities; by 2025 it is likely to be two-thirds, while in many of the poorest countries more than half the population is under 16: even in oil-rich Saudi Arabia two-thirds are under 30, of whom a third are unemployed). And all of this is kept at fever pitch by unresolved conflicts, as in Kashmir, Palestine, Chechnya and Iraq, which fuel perceptions of injustice in radicalized Muslim opinion.

Democracy as an Antidote to Terrorism?

One common prescription in all this has been the idea that the spread of democracy is the best long-term preventative antidote to terrorism. This is a common theme within the UN system, as seen in the UNDP extract at the head of this chapter. It has been built into the international response to the challenge of post-war reconstruction described in chapter 8. And it underpins the self-understanding of US policy-makers, where there is widespread cross-party agreement that the global extension of 'wider liberty' is the ultimate goal of US foreign policy (US National Security Strategy Report (NSSR), 20 September 2002).[1]

Can democracy fulfil these expectations? Does the 'democratic peace' extend from interstate relations, where it has been mainly discussed, to being the best domestic antidote to terror? We believe that it is as well at the outset to recognize that there are different understandings of democracy, which we cannot go into here, and that there are many difficulties to be resolved and overcome (see box 11.3). Developing a form of cosmopolitan democracy that offers a wider

---

Box 11.3   Ten challenges to democratic peace posed by terrorism

1   How to find 'cosmopolitan democratic' resources to meet the challenges of international political protests, insofar as they are fuelled by legitimate concerns about global inequalities and injustice.

2   How to manage the challenge posed by state sponsors of terrorism and non-democratic authoritarian regimes that 'breed' terrorism, without inconsistency and 'double standards'.

3   How to build democratic peace in weak, usually poor, states where central government is discredited or non-existent, and where loyalties and authority structures lie rather in indigenous tribal and family units.

4   How to satisfy social-revolutionary challenges that deny the efficacy or even legitimacy of democracy in meeting the needs of the poor.

5   How to respond to radical religious challenges when democracy is seen as *parti pris* to secular interests, in the name of revealed truth.

6   How to accommodate nationalist-separatist challenges to the identity of the state in the absence of agreed independent democratic mechanisms to determine it.

7   How to combat, in ways compatible with democracy, the challenge from warlords, 'economic terrorists' and international criminals impervious to democratic principles, and from spoilers implacably opposed to democratic peace processes.

8   How to respond to critics who argue that liberal democracy is a western concept inappropriate in other cultures.

9   How to respond to critics who argue that western democracies are still in many ways undemocratic.

10   How to answer the question whether liberal democracy and market capitalism are interdependent, separable or contradictory. Perhaps future developments in China, India and Russia hold the key here.

---

sense of political inclusion is part of the challenge. What we argue here is that if political actions are conducted in the name of democracy, then certain clear implications logically follow. The best response from a conflict resolution perspective is to spell these out.

The Second Dimension: Persuasion – Reducing Motivation and Support

This is the dimension of strategy that links the more general approach of prevention to the specifics of dealing with particular individuals, groups or governments that have either already taken up the terrorist option, or are contemplating it. There are three layers here: confronting ideologies of terror, persuading actual or potential terrorists to adopt non-terrorist options (and to persuade governments to act in ways that will maximize this), and reducing the appeal of terrorism within actual or potential support constituencies.

The confrontation with ideologies of terror is a large topic that can only be touched upon here. To understand the conflict means taking the relevant belief systems seriously (including those of past ideologues such as Maududi, Qutb and Khomeini in the case of Islamic groups influenced by them (Armstrong, 2001)), giving a hearing to those culturally best placed to counter them (for example, moderate Muslim interpreters of jihad and the newer generation of Islamic scholars), and demonstrating the greater humanity and efficacy of non-terrorist alternatives. Of particular significance here is the recent spread of the Wahhabi-Salafi movement that originated in Saudi Arabia, especially in the form known as the Salafi-Takfiris.[2] This is seen by many traditionalists as an unwarranted assault on the entire Islamic corpus by those who wrongly claim to be returning to the original Quranic inspiration: 'Salafism is a recent innovation that is completely different in form, content and above all ethical behaviour than traditional orthodox Islam' (Olivetti, 2001: 75). In particular, Takfiri belief and practice is identified as 'the source of – and license for – indiscriminate terrorism and slaughter' with the aim of igniting a global conflict between Islam and the West, thereby gaining control of the former and recreating their version of early Islam (ibid.: 77). Needless to say, this is highly contentious. We are in the realm of the 'ambivalence of the sacred' (Appleby, 2000), where the so-called 'desecularization of the world' since the time of the Iranian revolution in 1979 (Berger, 1999) has placed a premium on recognizing the way in which all the great religions can be co-opted to serve violent ends, but also contain resources for the promotion of conflict resolution and peace (Gopin, 2000). Here we may note the salutary and refreshing correctives offered by analysts such as Shadid (2002) and Feldman (2003), who argue that the earlier 'adolescent' stage of Islamic militancy is now giving way to a more widespread and mature activism in which younger generations, losing none of their ideological ardour, are nonetheless learning that they can best pursue their goal of reform by renouncing violence, engaging in grassroots work in civil society and transforming their authoritarian societies by democratic means.

At the core of the strategy of persuasion is the aim of affecting the calculations of those who have the power to determine policy options within governments and insurgent groups. It means understanding what motivates different kinds of groups, such as the commander-cadre model and the networked groups model analysed by Stern (2003). This applies to all those who are politically biddable and for whom terrorist means are only one possible alternative among others. It also includes prevailing upon governments to offer appropriate inducements to encourage and strengthen the voice of the moderates. We are familiar with this in general terms from earlier chapters, only now it is applied specifically to the issue of terrorism. In other words, 'moderate' here does not mean politically moderate, but those who are prepared to use non-terrorist means. For example, Ibrahim Rugova in Kosovo was politically intransigent (he insisted on full independence for Kosovo), but he was moderate in the sense that he espoused non-violent methods. It is right not to negotiate with those using terror to hold us to ransom, but the door must be open to induce those who have used terrorist tactics to move towards political means. In innumerable postcolonial transitions, designated terrorists have transformed themselves into government officials, if not heads of state: Kenyatta in Kenya, Makarios in Cyprus, Begin in Israel or, more recently, Adams in Northern Ireland and Mandela in South Africa. Even UK premier Margaret Thatcher, whatever her public stance, was pragmatic enough to countenance covert exchanges of messages via third parties with Sinn Fein/IRA. Without such contacts there could have been no progress towards an eventual ceasefire. In Sri Lanka a cessation of LTTE (Tamil Tiger) terrorism has come about in part as a result of Tamil resistance to its counter-productive effects, and in part through externally mediated negotiations on the substance of the political conflict.

Finally comes the challenge of reducing the scope for recruitment and support from potentially sympathetic constituencies. These are always much larger than the core intransigent group, and defined by the general appeal of the political programme at issue. This is well understood by those who espouse terrorism and often aim to provoke repressive government response in order to activate this wider support. The same applies to the diaspora, which plays a key role in sustaining terrorist capabilities in many cases. Here another factor comes into play – how governments in the diaspora countries react. All of this requires careful, well-judged and sustained management – as recognized by the UNPWG through its Subgroup on Media and Communications and in particular its Department for Public Information (UNDPI). The UNDPI was deputed to initiate a review of how the United Nations can reach local populations that support terrorist aims, using in-country teams as much as possible in order to determine the best means of conveying messages to target audiences. Among the UNPWG recommendations was that an international effort should be made 'to mount a direct concerted international challenge drawing from the main cultural and religious traditions against all forms of religious extremism which encourages terrorism' (this includes links with 'the growing number of institutes and think-tanks in Arabic-speaking countries'). A coordinated worldwide education programme under the aegis of UNESCO should also be launched 'to inculcate curricular reform which encourages the learning of tolerance and respect for human dignity while reducing mutual mistrust between communities, and to counter the efforts of some extremist groups who use education as a weapon of hatred and exclusion'.

The Third Dimension: Denial – Reducing Vulnerability and Defeating Hardliners

We will deal briefly with this dimension of the anti-terrorist policy framework, not because it is not of central importance, but because there is less that conflict resolution can contribute when faced with those implacably set on murderous policies.

Under UNSCR 1373 (2001) the purpose of the UNCTC of the Security Council was to 'improve the flow of information with and among international, regional and sub-regional organizations on counter-terrorism' with a view to helping member states to coordinate their duty to deny financial support, suppress safe havens, and share information about 'any groups practising or planning terrorist acts'. In monitoring implementation of UNSCR 1373, a good idea of the range of activity involved was offered in the February 2003 report where relevant bodies provided summaries of their 'activities, experiences and plans, including best practices, codes or standards they have developed' (S/AC.40/2003/SM.1/2; 26/2/03). This covered legislation and implementation machinery including police and intelligence structures, customs, immigration and border controls, weapons access controls, cooperation and information exchange, judicial cooperation between states on extradition and early-warning, as well as links to other threats such as arms trafficking, drugs, organized crime, money laundering, and the illegal movement of chemical, biological and nuclear weapons. Relevant associated bodies included the International Atomic Energy Authority, the UN Global Programme on Money Laundering established in 1997, and the Office for Drug Control and Crime Prevention, which launched a Global Programme Against Terrorism in October 2002, identifying countries needing assistance and coordinating the combating of transnational organized crime. The greatest single concern, dwarfing all the others, has been to prevent the nightmare scenario in which terrorist groups gain access to weapons of mass destruction.

But denial and suppression strategies need to be integrated with prevention and persuasion strategies. As an example of the former, we may note the failure to demobilize and integrate the Arab ex-*mujahideen* from the anti-Soviet war in Afghanistan in the late 1980s, earlier armed by the CIA even though they were known to be practising terrorist tactics against Soviet forces and civilians (Austin, 2004: 2). This sabotaged the UN's 1988 Geneva Accord and vastly increased the subsequent denial and suppression task when many of them refocused their efforts against the United States. As an example of the latter, we may point to the way denial cannot be separated from inducement in persuading key suppliers to suspend their support for terrorism. In addition, we may once again note the recommendations of the UN Policy Working Group, namely that 'States should be encouraged to view the implementation of UNSCR 1373 as an instrument of democratic governance and statecraft' and that 'all counter-terrorism measures must be consonant with international human rights law'. One suggestion was for the UNDPI, with the Office of the UN High Commissioner for Human Rights, to publish a digest of core jurisprudence of international and regional human rights bodies on the protection of human rights in the struggle against terrorism, and to convene a consultation with international, regional and sub-regional organizations and NGOs.

The Fourth Dimension: Coordination – Maximizing International Efforts

We end by stressing that tackling the conflicts likely to fuel conflict must be a genuinely international enterprise. For the UN's Policy Working Group the key role for the United Nations in the development of preventative strategy and policy is to provide a framework for cooperation in which regional organizations would be encouraged to develop strategies appropriate to their own regions and which worked on the benefits of the comparative advantages each of them possesses. The UNPWG proposed that meetings between the Secretary-General and representatives of regional organizations should develop an international action plan in which the United Nations would cooperate with regional organizations in identifying best practice in the field of counter-terrorism and promote its adoption: 'The potential role of the United Nations in working with regional multilateral efforts fits within the Organization's roles of norm-setting, coordination, cooperation and capacity-building.' But counter-terrorism is only one part of an effective response; the other is to address long-standing injustices and unequal life-chances. These have long been central concerns for the UN system.

Seen in this way, the response to terrorism is one part of a response to a much larger set of global issues, which have to do not only with violence but also with human rights, opportunities for livelihood and free expression, and the life-chances of ordinary people. It is in attending to these sources of conflict, rather than launching military interventions, that preventive action is needed. An opportunity is available to be seized, since there is a genuine international consensus that terrorist methods are entirely abhorrent and unacceptable, but also that where associated political aspirations are legitimate they must be seen to be addressed with the utmost seriousness. Global injustices and the failure of existing institutions to recognize and respect political aspirations need remedying for their own sake. But in the process, there is hope of addressing the sources of humiliation, rage and despair that are the fuel of terrorism. It faces many obstacles, but the cosmopolitan conflict resolution approach has a vital role to play.

Recommended reading

Booth and Dunne, eds (2002); Keeley 2003; Lacqueur (2003); Martin (2003: ch. 3); Stern (2003).

chapter 12

Gender in Conflict Resolution

It took the human race thousands of years to rid itself of human sacrifices; during many centuries it relapsed again and again. . . . So have we fallen back into warfare, and perhaps will fall back again and again, until in self-pity, in self-defence, in self-assertion of the right of life, not as hitherto a few, but the whole people of the world will brook this thing no longer. . . .We (the Womens' International League for Peace and Freedom) wish to loosen within our own members and in all people those natural and ethical human impulses which, once having their way in the world, will make war impossible.

*Jane Addams, American pacifist and founder member of Womens'
International League for Peace and Freedom*

This process of feminist reflection on the social order and its workings is more urgent than ever. Also, more of us are doing it. That development should be celebrated by exploring how women think about the future and the action models they generate to bring these futures into being.

Elise Boulding

Iᴛ has been pointed out by a number of observers that conflict reso-lution has, in its development, conceptualization and methods, been 'gender-blind' (Reimann, 1999; 2002). Gender, which is taken to mean the historical and social construction of role differences between men and women, implies a relationship of power, which has a pervasive effect on all areas of behaviour and in all social institutions and practices. Since the conflict-war continuum is also a constructed social practice embedded in a set of linked institutions, the field of conflict resolution, which attempts to engage non-violently with that continuum, if it is to be effective, cannot afford to be as gender-blind as its critics have implied.

Although much of it emanates from fields of enquiry outside the peace and conflict research field, there is an extensive literature on war, women and gender relationships (Perrigo, 1991). In the international

Box 12.1 Four stages in engendering conflict resolution	
Stage 1	Making women visible as agents of change in conflict resolution.
Stage 2	Removing male bias in conflict resolution data-collection and empirical research.
Stage 3	Rethinking conflict resolution theory to take gender into account.
Stage 4	Incorporating gender into conflict resolution policy-making and practice.

relations literature, for example, the work of Cynthia Enloe (1988, 1993, 2000) has been a major influence in subverting the gender-blind assumptions of realist and neo-realist theory, and has insisted on the importance of gendered analysis in the international system. Enloe has provided a potent analysis of what she sees as pervasive militarization, defined as 'the step-by-step process by which something becomes *controlled by*, *dependent on*, or *derives its value from* the military as an institution or militaristic criteria' (2000; 281), and argues that women globally are being incorporated and co-opted 'to the threshold of all those social institutions that promote militarization' (ibid.: 33). Other analysts stress the commonalities in the discourses implicated in the exercise of hegemonic power in the international system and in those of patriarchy in the family.

In this section we examine the progress made in developing a gender-sensitive approach in conflict resolution and in correcting the gender-blindness that has concerned critics. Pankhurst and Pearce (1998) suggest that, although different disciplines follow different paths, there seem generally to be four steps involved in the process of engendering a disciple or area study. First, making women visible as change agents; second, the removal of male bias in the collection of data and the conduct of empirical studies; third through the rethinking of theoretical constructs to take gender into account; and finally the stage where gender becomes part of the mainstream in terms of institutional policy-making and practice (see box 12.1).[1]

Stage 1: Making Women Visible as Agents of Change

Significant progress in the first of these steps, making women visible as change agents in peacemaking and conflict resolution, was made through the lifelong contribution of Elise Boulding, whose work in establishing the foundations of conflict research and conflict resolution was noted in chapter 2. As a young sociologist concerned, as were all of the pioneers of the new field of conflict research in the 1950s, to avoid the mistakes which led to World War II and which might lead again to a catastrophic nuclear third world war, she was influenced by *The Image of the Future* (1951), a study of 1,500 years of European history by Dutch historian-sociologist Fred Polak. In the efforts to rebuild a peaceful European and global society after 1945, Polak offered the idea of 'imaging' a better future as a way of empowering people to bring it about. The idea attracted Boulding, and her major contribution both to the foundation of conflict research and its gender sensitization was to open up a discourse and practice in contemporary conflict resolution, where women and children were included as radical change agents and empowered peacemakers. Taking Polak as her guide, as we saw in chapter 2, Boulding placed the idea of imaging the future within the context of what she called the '200-year present', that is the idea that we must understand that we live in a social space which reaches into the past and into the future: 'it is our space, one that we can move around directly in our own lives and indirectly by touching the lives of the young and old around us' (1990: 4). Boulding was a member of the Womens' International League for Peace and Freedom (WILPF, formed in 1915, the oldest womens' peace organization in the world), and was its International President from 1968 to 1971. This important organization provided a vehicle within which the voices of women in Boulding's '200-year present' could be activated and heard.

Her study of women in history, *The Underside of History* (1976), presented the case for a feminist project to abolish structural and behavioural aggression against women and to establish gender equity. However, she also insisted that 'equity feminism', while representing an important phase of feminist aspirations, was a limited mode of action. It needed to be augmented by a social and transformational feminism which focuses on the broader malformations that produce violence and oppression for both sexes, while also identifying women's culture historically as a resource for development and peace-building.

During the 1980s Boulding organized a series of 'Imaging a World Without Weapons' workshops, an extension of the idea of problem-solving workshops and influenced by Polak's thinking on future imaging. Initially western-oriented, the workshops were subsequently reformulated in an effort to incorporate perceptions and values globally. In *Cultures of Peace: The Hidden Side of History* (2000), she has surveyed more than fifty years of research on human culture and society, and on the activity of peace movements working within a culture of war, arguing that the resources and energies for peace cultures are deep and persistent and are nourished by collective and communal visions of how things might be. In a manner not often displayed by the value-neutral exponents of problem-solving-based conflict resolution, Boulding was explicit about the norms and objectives that characterized her transformative agenda. In 2001, at the age of 81, she imagined herself looking back at the way the world had changed in the 100-year future, that is looking back from 2101:

> By 2050 the population had, through both disaster and design, fallen below five billion: human life on earth became viable again. School-based peace education joined with health and social education, leading to mutual solving of problems in and across communities and faiths. Industrialization slowed down, older technologies and skills were revitalized, steady-state economies were achieved. Dismantling the military and its institutions began. People's organizations (NGOs) now provided vital communication networks round the world, linking the growing thousands of locally-run communities, sharing information, skills, problems, solutions.
>
> By 2100, the biosphere was beginning to recover from the destruction of the twentieth century, though used-up resources were gone for ever. National boundaries still existed for administrative convenience, but regional intergovernmental bodies skilled in conflict management handled disputes peacefully. . . . Humans had learned to listen to one another and the planet. (2001: 1)

Stage 2: Data-Collection and Case Studies

In view of this consideration of the feminist and gendered analysis of Elise Boulding, it is perhaps fair to comment that conflict resolution has not been quite as gender-blind as has been alleged. Nevertheless, following Boulding, a generation of women writers and activists have been highly effective in the field at the theoretical, policy and applied levels, and often committed to the radical and transformative agenda associated with her. It is women such as these who have engendered conflict resolution by making women visible and active, and also by effecting the second and third steps in the process of raising gender awareness mentioned at the beginning of this section, that is the removal of male bias in the collection of data and the formation of case studies, and the re-examination of theoretical constructs. We start with an example of the former.

The process of making women visible as change agents has produced a wider array of case studies where women have taken leading roles in peacebuilding, and recent studies which correct male bias in data gathering and analysis, especially in relation to the participation of women and girls in armed militias and fighting forces (McKay and

Mazurana, 2004). During the wars in former Yugoslavia, women and women's organizations sustained and developed local cultures of peace against considerable opposition in highly militarized and sharply polarized communities. One of the most influential of these initiatives was the Centre for Peace, Non-Violence and Human Rights (Centar za Mir for short) in the Croatian town of Osijek, as noted in chapter 9. The proximity of Osijek to the border with Serbia rendered it vulnerable to attack and the city was heavily shelled for almost a year, from August 1991 until June 1992. Most of the population fled, leaving some ten thousand people in the city. Around eight hundred people were killed, and many more were wounded (Jegen, 1996: 14). The city, surrounded on three sides by Serb forces, continued to experience sporadic shooting and other war-related incidents until 1995, but was never overrun.

In 1992, the Centar za Mir (CZM) came into being, addressing both the psychological and the social and human rights issues of the war, and has generated new projects to meet local needs. While not a feminist organization in any explicit sense, women held leading positions in the organization and the needs of women and children were firmly addressed in its projects and agenda. Its Director was Katerina Kruhonja, a doctor at the University Hospital of Osijek. A member of the Catholic Church from the beginning of the war, she sought to create an influence for peace in public prayer meetings outside the army headquarters in Osijek and by broadcasting prayers on the local radio network. She was supported by a teacher, Krunoslav Sukić. Kruhonja and Sukić affiliated the CZM with the anti-war organization, Anti-Ratna Kampanja (ARK) in Zagreb. The CZM has now grown into an organization well known throughout Europe, attracting visitors from across the world and providing a strong example to many small groups of peaceworkers who are attempting to sustain cultures of peace in zones of conflict and violence (Mitchels, 2003; ch. 4).

By the end of the 1990s it was recognized that many of the activities to sustain peace in countries beset by violence were conducted by a wide range of community-based organizations. Many of these were formed and run by women, who were involved across the spectrum of peacemaking, from activity in conflict areas through to supporting peace agreements in post-conflict peacebuilding. The way in which women's voices have emerged in peacemaking in recent years has still to be fully and properly chronicled, but, because of their relative exclusion from the formal political structures of war-torn societies, grassroots organizations provide an outlet for women in peacemaking roles, who are trying to respond to the various needs of their beleaguered communities (see box 12.2).

Box 12.2 Engendering conflict resolution: case studies of women responding to conflict

Case study research into the role of women and conflict resolution has increased dramatically in recent years. Among a number of examples, we can cite work done by International Alert, and by Peace Direct, whose *Unarmed Heroes* (2004) offers excellent case studies. From research sponsored by the United States Institute of Peace (USIP) (2000) come examples from war-torn countries such as:

- **Somalia**, where women have met in a variety of venues since 1993 to develop a long-term vision for Somali society, and there has been a proliferation of women's non-governmental organizations addressing issues of migration and displacement, and creating avenues for peace. Women have taken the initiative to restore destroyed schools, to establish clean water sources, and open an inter-clan dialogue on peace. An alliance of seventeen NGOs, formed and led by Somali women, emerged to coordinate peacebuilding activity, to exchange information between their different clan groupings, and to establish opportunities for dialogue.
- **Colombia**, where grassroots organizations led by women have been active in protesting about the prolonged civil war. Indigenous women have begun to speak out against the damage to their communities, caught in the cross-fire between Marxist guerrilla organizations, drug traffickers, right-wing death squads and the forces of the Colombia government.
- **The Middle East,** especially in relation to the Israeli-Palestinian conflict, where there are a number of cross-community efforts led by women to create opportunities for grassroots conflict resolution activities. One such project is the Jerusalem Link, which connects the Palestinian Jerusalem Centre for Women with the Israeli Bat Shalom. The Jerusalem Link has worked to develop an International Women's Commission, a tripartite and independent body of women of Palestine, Israel and the international community to provide a gender perspective on peacemaking and human security issues and to have a more specific mandate to have an advisory role in any formal negotiation processes related to Middle East peacemaking.
- **Northern Ireland**, where the Northern Ireland Women's Coalition (NIWC) provided an example of a political movement to enhance women's power and influence in an official peace agreement and the ensuing peace process. NIWC had representatives in the talks process and the outcome was that provisions of the Good Friday Agreement included clauses that related to human rights and equality issues, care for victims of the conflict, and provisions for a Civic Forum.

Source: Marshall, 2000

Stage 3: Rethinking Conflict Resolution Theory

In parallel with an accumulating body of empirical evidence about the experiences, roles and transformative influence of women in challenging cultures of violence and constituencies of war has come an increasingly powerful conceptual assault on ungendered assumptions in conflict resolution. Considering these two steps together, that is the research methods used in peace and conflict research on the one hand and the dominant theoretical constructs on the other, a younger generation of women in conflict research has now opened up areas of enquiry around categories of power and participation in their concentration on transformation as the deepest level of conflict resolution (Francis, 2002). For example, in terms of methodology, some women in the field of conflict research have argued strongly in favour of qualitative methods where the experiences of people are heard and recorded, rather than relying on the aggregation of conflict-related statistics – as we noted with regard to 'war zone ethnography' in chapter 6 (Nordstrom; Fetherston). This point is not only technical and methodological, but also has fundamental implications for theory. In particular, Vivian Jabri has identified the importance of embedding these perspectives in a more searching critical theoretic approach:

> Violent conflict generates a hegemonic discourse, which seeks to subsume subjectivity and its multiple forms of representation into a singular entity involved in a confrontational interaction with another assumed/constructed monolithic entity. (1996: 180–1)

These monolithic entities are also reproduced 'through the representation of observers, conflict researchers and third parties attempting mediation', especially if such third parties interpret the conflict through the definitions of its leading actors, in which case conflict resolution may merely 'reproduce the exclusionist, violent discourses and practices which perpetuate it' (ibid.). In order to subvert these ways of thinking, Jabri introduces the idea of an emancipatory politics as the most relevant discourse for conflict resolution and peace, in which the main stress is on the interrelated elements of public space, participation and individuality, thereby at the same time transforming institutional and discursive gender distortions. The production of new meanings in the encounter between the 'self' and the 'other' is seen to be at the core of these hoped-for transformations, and, as we will note further in chapter 14, the work of Habermas on discursive ethics and the theory of communicative action is looked at to provide the required critical theoretic framework.

If theoretical reformulations of this kind are sustained and developed, this might go some way towards meeting Reimann's complaint that conflict resolution has always been a 'gendered discourse' based on unexamined ontological and epistemological assumptions and methods which obscure its own gender-blindness. The way the causes, courses and endings of violent conflicts are examined has strong implications for the lived experience of men and women in society, so that 'to ignore gender as both constituting and being constituted by conflict in general, and conflict management in particular, is to valorize and leave unexamined the existing power structures' (1999: 18).

It is no longer possible for the conflict resolution field to ignore this theoretical challenge. Recent analyses, again from feminist-oriented versions of critical theory, have pointed to the limitations inherent in an unchallenged acceptance of binary categories (including femininity and masculinity), which excludes 'the variety of ambivalent and unsecured femininities and masculinities'. Gender-aware analysis of this kind has impacted on the field of conflict research by insisting on diversity: 'Allowing dissident, and not always affirming, voices to be heard can offer an element that celebrates uncertainty and multiplicity' (Väyrynen, 2004: 140).

Stage 4: Mainstreaming Gender in Policy-Making and the Empowerment of Women

The fourth stage in the engendering of an area of study is the mainstreaming of gender perspectives in the policy implications of research. An historically significant move in this mainstreaming was the passing of UN Security Council Resolution 1325 on 31 October 2000, described by Kofi Annan as 'a landmark step in raising awareness of the impact of armed conflict on women and girls, and of the vital role of women in conflict resolution and peacebuilding' (UN, 2002). Resolution 1325 called for fuller representation of women in peace negotiations and in the highest offices of the UN, and for the incorporation of gender perspectives in peacebuilding, peacekeeping and conflict prevention activities. We regard this as a landmark in the engendering of peace and conflict resolution policy as originally envisioned in the conflict resolution field by Elise Boulding. It was wonderful that, having suggested developments along these lines from the 1950s, she witnessed this moment of fruition half a century later when in her 80s.

We noted in chapter 2 that the UN, despite all its recognized limitations, has become a forum for and generator of seminal ideas of central importance in conflict resolution, and UNSCR 1325 was built upon on a series of treaties and conventions relating to women's rights and human rights since the inception of the UN in 1945 (see box 12.3).

It was because of disappointment with the lack of recognition of women's roles in peacekeeping and peacemaking in the Brahimi Report that women's organizations intensified their lobbying of the Security Council. Their goal was to press for a resolution that would mainstream the role of women in peace and security issues and confer the status of recognition in international law on that role. The immediate factor which influenced the passing of UNSCR 1325 was, therefore, linked to the lobbying conducted by the Coalition on Women and International Peace and Security, which consisted of Amnesty International, the Hague Appeal for Peace, International Alert, the International Peace Research Association, the Women's Commission

Box 12.3 Engendering peacebuilding and conflict resolution: the evolution of UN policy

1948 (Dec)   *Universal Declaration of Human Rights* (General Assembly Resolution 217A) recognized the equal rights of men and women.

1966 (Dec)   Resolution 2200A on the Protection of Women and Children in Emergency and Armed Conflict recognized that women suffered as civilians in armed conflict. Member states should make all efforts to spare women from the ravages of war and ensure they are not deprived from shelter, food and medical aid (Articles 4 and 6).

1975 (June)   First UN World Conference on Women, leading to the *Declaration of Mexico on the Equality of Women and their Contribution to Development and World Peace*. Recognized the multiple roles as peacemakers played by women at the level of the family and community, and at national and international levels. Called for fuller representation of women in international forums concerned with peace and security. The declaration had the status of a recommendation, and was not binding on states.

1979 (Dec)   General Assembly Resolution 34/180 on the *Convention on the Elimination of All Forms of Discrimination Against Women* (CEDAW), recognizing that global peace and welfare was linked to the equal participation of women in all areas.

1985 (July)   Nairobi Conference to Review and Appraise the Achievements of the United Nations Decade for Women. Produced the *Nairobi Forward-Looking Strategies for the Advancement of Women*, a collective plan of action for women and their advocates.

1989 (Nov)   UN Secretary-General reported to the Commission on the Status of Women to review the implementation of the Nairobi Strategies. Concluded that women remained victims of violence disproportionately, and that they had not progressed significantly in decision-making roles since 1985.

1993 (July)   The World Conference on Human Rights issued a *Programme of Action* to integrate women's needs into human rights activities. The Programme identified a variety of forms of discrimination against women, including the rape of women in situations of armed conflict.

1995 (Sept)   Fourth World Conference on Women, Beijing, held during the 50th anniversary of the formation of the UN, issued the *Beijing Declaration*, which identified six strategic objectives related to promoting the role of women in peacemaking, including commitments to increase women's participation in decision-making, to reduce military expenditures, to promote non-violent conflict resolution, and the contribution of women to fostering a culture of peace.

2000   Women in the Balkans and Rwanda claimed that systematic rape is a form of genocide. Influenced by the Women's Caucus for Gender Justice, the Rome Statute of the International Criminal Court recognized these issues for the first time as crimes against humanity and war crimes. The Rome Statute also demanded the equal participation of female judges in trials and on gender-sensitive processes in the conduct of trials.

2000 (Aug)   The UN conducted a comprehensive review of peacekeeping operations under the direction of Lakdhar Brahimi. The Brahimi Report produced a wide range of recommendations for the reform of peacekeeping, which, although it did make some proposals to increase the role of women in leadership positions in peacekeeping operations, did not fully recognize the significance of gender perspectives.

Source: adapted from Poehlman-Doumbouy and Hill, 2001

for Refugee Women and Children and the Women's International League for Peace and Freedom. The original project to review peace-keeping operations was declared in May 2000 in the form of the Windhoek Declaration from Namibia, a country which had itself experienced years of conflict and which had also provided a successful model for UN-led post-conflict peacebuilding. The Coalition on Women and International Peace and Security persuaded Namibia to hold an open session on women, peace and security during their month of Security Council presidency in October 2000, which ended with the passing of UNSCR 1325. One of the key campaigning groups in the coalitan, which secured the resolution, was the WILPF; another was the International Peace Research Association (IPRA). Elise Boulding served as Secretary-General of both these organizations.

Let us leave the last words of this chapter, therefore, to Elise Boulding, who expresses more eloquently than we can the underlying centrality of gender to all aspects of conflict resolution. This is, as she often noted, something that is still not properly recognized within the formal field of conflict resolution itself:

> We are a long way from our pre-industrial village sisters who under-stood very well the structures and resource systems within which they operated. One of the greatest dangers of our time is despair, and feelings of helplessness in the face of macro-level social forces. The possibility is there that the human race will self-destruct. It is precisely at this historical moment that it can be useful to reflect on the accumulated experience of women's cultures over the centuries in the work of feeding, rearing and healing humans, building their social and physical environments, and then rebuilding them after destruction. It was the need for that kind of reflection that led me to take a year of solitude in 1974 and begin the mental journey that led to the writing of *The Underside of History*.
>
> Today, 20 years later, this process of feminist reflection on the social order and its workings is more urgent that ever. Also, more of us are doing it. That development should be celebrated by exploring how women think about the future and the action models they generate to bring these futures into being. (Boulding, 1994)

Recommended reading

Nordstrom (1997); Pankhurst and Pearce (1998); Steans (1998); Vickers (1993).

The Ethics of Intervention

Who do we think we are? Is it justified for outsiders to choose among people or institutions, to make judgments about who or what is 'truly' a local capacity for peace? To what extent might our attempts to do so constitute dangerous and inappropriate social engineering? . . . The fact that aid inevitably does have an impact on warfare means aid workers cannot avoid the responsibility of trying to shape that impact. The fact that choices about how to shape that impact represent outsider interference means that aid workers can always be accused of inappropriate action. There is no way out of this dilemma.

Mary Anderson, 1999, Do No Harm: How Aid Can Support Peace – Or War

All that is required for evil to triumph is that good men do nothing.

Edmund Burke

THERE has always been a sense of unease about third-party intervention in the conflict resolution field. As Mary Anderson's comment at the head of this chapter shows, it is an unease shared by aid workers and others. Third parties have an effect on conflict dynamics, and their good intentions do not guarantee good outcomes. Even if they are invited in, there are legitimate questions to be asked about who invited them and why, what constituencies they represent, how well they understand their own motives and roles, and whether their actions are likely to have beneficial or deleterious consequences. These questions become more acute as the interventions become more coercive or even forcible. Not intervening also makes a difference and must be assessed as one of the policy options. We may recall British Prime Minister Neville Chamberlain's refusal to intervene in Czechoslovakia in September 1938, because it was a conflict 'in a faraway country between people of whom we know nothing' – or the refusal of the UN Security Council (UNSC) to intervene in Rwanda in April 1994.

In the conflict resolution field questions about the ethics of intervention have, therefore, been seen to be important from the start – as exemplified in contributions to classic texts such as the 1978 *Ethics of*

> **Box 13.1 A hierarchy of intervention relations, principles and criteria**
>
> **A**   General intervention relations
> **B**   Framework principles for international   *See figure 13.1*
>   intervention
> **C**   Criteria for forcible international intervention   *See box 13.2*

Social Intervention (Bermant et al., eds). Continuing in this tradition, we begin by looking at the nature of social intervention in general in order to define the main intervention relations, and from this elucidate framework principles for conflict resolution and comparable kinds of international intervention (including intervention by aid and development workers, and peacekeepers). Within this conceptual framework we can then consider guidelines for coercive and forcible intervention, insofar as this is seen to be needed to protect the international values being promoted and defended (see box 13.1).

Conflict Resolution Roles

We can begin with James Laue's thoughtful analysis of the ethics of conflict intervention, first offered in the 1970s (Laue and Cormick, 1978; Laue, 1981, 1990). Drawing on experience in 'labor-management relations, international and intercultural conflict, racial and community disputes, court diversion and other arenas', Laue based his analysis on the nature of conflict intervention roles:

> The major point of the typology presented here is that there are definable, analytically distinct intervention roles that cut across all the other variables of personality, skills, type of issue, system level of the dispute, etc. These roles are based . . . predominantly on an intervenor's base and credibility – for whom does the intervenor work, who pays for the intervenor to be there, and consequently what are the structured expectations for behaviour of the intervenor in that role? (1990: 268)

Laue identifies five main conflict intervention roles: the *activist*, 'who is in, and almost of, one of the parties', such as one of the tenants in a tenant–landlord dispute; the *advocate*, who works on behalf of one of the parties but is likely to play a less 'hard game' than the activist, perhaps in a formal consultative capacity or like a diplomat 'working on behalf of the interests of one party in international relations'; then comes the *mediator*, whose ultimate advocacy 'is for the process rather than for any of the parties *per se*'; followed by the *researcher*, such as a journalist or crisis observer, who might see the intervention as 'objective' or 'neutral, but 'once he or she engages in a conflict situation, the configuration of power in that situation is altered' and the intervener 'is likely to be used by the parties for their ends'; and, finally, the *enforcer*, including arbitrators, judges and police, who have 'formal powers to sanction either or all the parties' – funding agencies may have such leverage, and 'superior physical force' will often characterize enforcers in international conflicts (Laue and Cormick, 1978). Important questions are raised, for example about shifting intervention roles (see the discussion about figure 1.12 in chapter 1), and about the different expectations of powerful in-parties and powerless out-parties, with the former wanting classic 'neutral' conflict resolution from the third parties in order to preserve the status quo, while the latter seek assistance in their quest for 'power, justice and change'. These are issues with which we are now very familiar.

Conflict Resolution Intervention Principles

Figure 13.1 sets out the main intervention relations that in our view characterize all social conflict interventions of the kinds described by Laue, and the associated framework principles for ethical international intervention (Ramsbotham, 2005). If we consider large-scale international interventions, such as those described in chapter 8, the first three principles can be seen to concern relations with target populations, the fourth and fifth concern relations among the interveners, and the last three concern relations with the wider international community.

These principles are confirmed by a survey of two overlapping literatures: the rapidly expanding sets of principles and guidelines for ethical intervention produced by aid, development and conflict resolution organizations on the one hand, and the criteria recommended for principled and effective international peacekeeping on the other. As an example of this we may note the way in which the May 2004 UK Joint Warfare Publication on the British military contribution to peace operations, mentioned in chapter 6, stresses the importance of the liaison with non-military peacebuilders, and reproduces in an appendix extracts from the *Principles of Conduct for the International Red Cross and Red Crescent Movements and NGOs in Disaster Relief* as an overall guide. In addition to the overriding universal humanitarian imperative, these principles include: impartiality and non-partisanship in response to crises (including proper support for the role of women); respect for local cultures, and mutuality in the involvement of beneficiaries and the empowering of indigenous capacity; the importance of

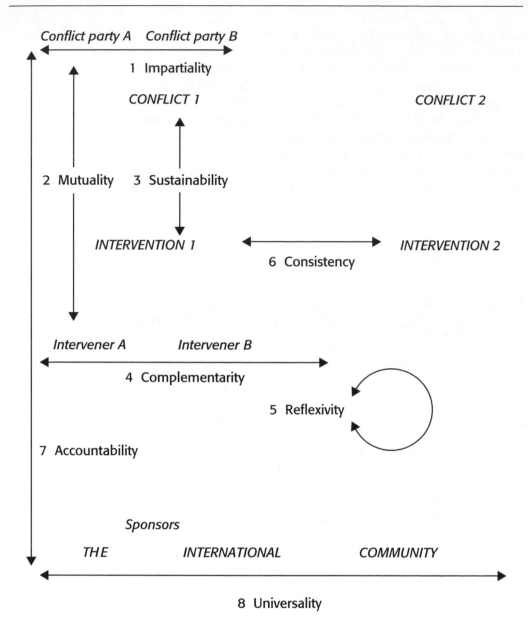

Figure 13.1   General intervention relations and framework principles

sustainability and reduction of future vulnerability; cooperation with other disaster relief agencies so that there is no damaging mutual competition; the integrity of the interveners in genuine commitment to their stated aims; and their accountability both to those assisted and to sponsors so that effectiveness can be transparently assessed.

The principle of impartiality

From a conflict resolution perspective, the principle of impartiality implies that, whatever role an intervener plays, conflict resolution is incomplete unless the interests of all those affected are properly taken into account. Behind this lies the whole idea of win–win outcomes and the importance of responding to human needs that we have seen to have played a central role in the evolution of the field.

This parallels the International Committee of the Red Cross (ICRC) idea of impartiality as non-discrimination in responding to need:

> The Red Cross makes no discrimination as to nationality, race, religious belief, class or political opinions. It endeavours to relieve the suffering of individuals, being guided solely by their needs, and to give priority to the most urgent cases of distress.

This is a core value, enshrined in Article 3, common to the four 1949 Geneva Conventions, and in Article 75 of the 1977 Additional Protocol I.

We should distinguish this from the related ICRC principle of neutrality, which means non-political engagement:

> In order to continue to enjoy the confidence of all, the Red Cross may not take sides in hostilities or engage at any time in controversies of a political, racial, religious or ideological nature.

Increasing involvement in intense internal conflicts (in contrast to the interstate wars that formed the usual original ICRC environment), since at least the time of the 1967–70 Biafran war, has put the principle of neutrality under growing strain. What Forsythe has called 'humanitarian politics' forces interveners to choose between the ICRC tradition based on consent from public authorities with little or no overt criticism of their behaviour, and more uncompromising approaches, such as that of Médecins sans Frontières, which are not afraid to disregard the wishes and legal claims of public authorities, both in condemning atrocities and intervening without permission (Forsythe, 1977: 227). This remains highly controversial.

In the evolution of peacekeeping doctrine, we saw in chapter 6 how the original idea of neutrality, in the sense of only operating with the consent of all parties, gave way in the 1990s to that of impartiality in fulfilling an international mandate as the key criterion that distinguishes principled peacekeeping from traditional interstate war (see table 6.3). Peacekeepers could not be neutral if one party was responsible for atrocities.

The conflict resolution field tends to confirm this logic, but is particularly aware of the fact that in intense conflict fields everything is politicized, so that the impartiality of interveners will be contested, no matter how elaborate their international mandates. In these circumstances the UNSC and International Criminal Tribunals are regarded as political tools by those whose interests they are seen to be damaging. This does not render the principle of impartiality otiose, but suggests that it is a value that has to be struggled for.

The principle of mutuality

The principle of mutuality is the fundamental intervention relation between interveners and those they purport to be assisting. It determines that interveners take care to ascertain that the intervention is seen to be likely to do more good than harm from the conflict parties' perspective. If there is little or no mutuality – if the arrow is not double-headed – then the outsiders are likely to be imposing their own concepts and values without due regard for the needs and wishes of the protagonists. Experience suggests that they will more often than not be oblivious to this. We noted in chapter 8 that there are problems in determining the views of target populations, and the situation will be complicated to the extent that the primary conflict parties have conflicting interests and perceptions and are internally divided. The principle of mutuality demands that indigenous initiatives and capabilities be forefronted and empowered, and that interventions are carried out without damage to local economies and with respect for local cultures. As we note in chapters 12 and 15, there may be tensions here, for example, between the priorities of recognizing and supporting the role of women as understood in international instruments, and the possibly conflicting patriarchal and authoritarian nature of local tradition.

The principle of sustainability

The principle of sustainability is central to humanitarian, development and conflict resolution interventions. Interveners who are not prepared to 'stay the course' or commit the resources required should not undertake the intervention in the first place. We saw in chapter 8 that this is also a key principle for military forces in intervention, reconstruction and withdrawal (IRW) operations. The principle requires careful estimates of the appropriateness and viability of entry strategies, given contingent conditions in the target states, and says that exit strategies should be determined by the needs of those on whose behalf the intervention has been undertaken, not by domestic opinion in the intervening countries or the interests of intervening governments. Once again there may be tensions in target countries between those wanting interveners to leave as soon as possible and those wanting them to stay.

The principle of complementarity

With the principle of complementarity we reach the important issue of relations between different interveners. Here the overarching requirement must be that the efforts of interveners should, where appropriate, complement each other for the greater good of those for whom the intervention is undertaken. The word 'appropriate' is a reminder that complementarity does not mean limiting diversity, which can often be beneficial. But the aim of the principle is to overcome the all-too familiar dangers of 'competitive altruism' by prohibiting damaging rivalries, unnecessary duplications and avoidable failures of communication. We saw in chapter 8 how in IRW operations the early preponderance of military tasks in assuring 'negative peace' progressively gives way, it is hoped, to the essentially non-military tasks of building 'positive peace', however difficult military–civilian relations may be from time to time.

The principle of reflexivity

The principle of reflexivity asks interveners to look at themselves. What are their motives, aims and interests? What constituencies do they represent? What kinds of advocacy do they pursue and why? On what authority do they act? What resources of power and influence do they bring? As in the equivalent just war principle of intentionality, motives and subjective purposes are notoriously difficult to self-determine or externally impute, but the underlying principle is clear – that interveners' purposes must at any rate not be incompatible with the declared aim of the intervention. For example, the unedifying spectacle of outsiders battening onto other peoples' disasters in order to raise their own profiles or to pull in extra funding is clearly ruled out by the principle of reflexivity.

The principle of consistency

With the principle of consistency we move from relations that concern interventions within a particular conflict arena to relations between interventions in different conflict arenas – although it may at times not be clear where one arena ends and another begins. The requirement is that in similar circumstances equal provocation or challenge should elicit equal response. The aim here is to meet often-voiced accusations of hypocrisy and double standards. In the context of IRW operations, this is subject to unavoidable dispute about what counts as 'similarity'. Apart from anything else, different states have different geographic and historic ties, which often determine who takes a lead, who is prepared to provide resources and who is acceptable in the target country.

The principle of accountability

The principle of accountability governs relations between interveners and those in whose name they claim to act. In individual cases these may in the first instance be sponsors such as governments, or international organizations. But sponsors are themselves part of the intervention they are sponsoring, so they too should be prepared to answer for their own motives and actions. Behind this may lie wider claims to be acting in the name of the conflict parties (which links this principle to the principle of mutuality) or of the international community as a whole (which links with the principle of universality below). The double-headed arrow represents the conferral of legitimacy in one direction (answering the question *quo warranto*? – by what authority do you intervene?) and transparency and accountability in the other (answering the question *quis custodiet ipsos custodes*? – who judges the judges?). Unlike equivalent traditional just war criteria, which concern prior estimations of likely future benefit and harm, the principle of accountability forefronts the importance of ongoing comparative assessments of the effectiveness of present and past operations. Here we enter the important and burgeoning field of 'impact assessments', essential for learning lessons and improving performance, albeit beset by difficulties such as those discussed at the beginning of chapter 5.

The principle of universality

Finally we reach the principle of universality. When it comes to cross-border intervention conducted in the name of the international collectivity, either because it is authorized by a regional or global international organization, or because it purports to be undertaken according to internationally endorsed values, the principle of universality rules that such enterprises must be cross-culturally endorsed. This, too, is an ICRC principle, and the renaming of the League of Red Cross Societies as the League of Red Cross and Red Crescent Societies in 1983 was a significant move in this direction:

> The Red Cross is a world-wide institution in which all Societies have equal status and share equal responsibilities and duties in helping each other. Our movement's universality stems from the attachment of each of its members to common values.

We have seen how claims to be acting in accordance with international law and in defence of international norms have been made by almost all interveners in IRW operations since the end of the Cold War. Similarly, one of the main themes of this book has been that the conflict resolution field has to reflect universal values if it is to qualify as a truly cosmopolitan enterprise.

From Just War to Just Intervention

Some of those in the conflict resolution field are either pacifists who do not condone the use of military force under any circumstances or those who would restrict conflict resolution to the attempt to make peace by peaceful means. For them there is no place for just war principles in conflict resolution. They would argue instead for the principles of non-violence: conflict is to be seen as a search for truth in which no party has final or valid answers; the intervener must take actions that are self-limiting and consistent in all respects with the ends sought; the intervener must seek to persuade and never to destroy other parties; the intervener must trust to the potential for transformation which is always present, however difficult to find (Wehr, 1979: 55–68). But others think that, when faced with murderous opponents of peace processes, there is a legitimate role for armed forces as neutralizers. For them the further question cannot be avoided: what are the circumstances in which such uses of force would be justified? They find it unavoidable to enter the territory of just war.

Galvanized by UN Secretary-General Annan's call for international consensus on 'developing international norms' against violent repression and the 'wholesale slaughter' of civilians (1999: 39), attempts have been made to suggest criteria for just international intervention in these cases (see Stromseth, 2003: 261–7, for a good account). Annan himself listed a number of factors to be considered by the UNSC when deciding whether to intervene: the nature of the breaches of international law and numbers affected; the inability or unwillingness of the governments responsible to remedy the situation; the exhaustion of peaceful or consent-based efforts; the UNSC's ability to monitor the intervention; the limited and proportionate use of force, mindful of effects on civilian populations and the environment. Further to Prime Minister Blair's Chicago speech of 22 April 1999, the UK government formulated six 'principles' to 'guide intervention by the international community', arguing that a set of agreed understandings or guidelines of this kind would aid the UNSC 'to reach consensus, thus ensuring effective and timely action by the international community' (Cook, 2000b, quoted in Stromseth, 2003). The guidelines were: that greater efforts at prevention should be made to preclude the need for intervention; that non-military intervention should be preferred, with military intervention as a last resort; that immediate responsibility for halting violence lies with the state in which it occurs; that the international community should intervene only where there is convincing evidence of impending catastrophe on a large scale which a government cannot prevent or is promoting; that use of force should be proportionate and effective and carried out in accordance with international law; and that 'any use of force should be collective' and 'wherever possible, the authority of the Security Council should be secured' (Cook, 2002, quoted in Stromseth, 2003). These suggested guidelines are intended to apply, for example, across all five types of international intervention considered in chapter 8.

We might also note the many attempts made during the Cold War to formulate similar criteria for legitimate 'unilateral' intervention ('self-help by states') in response to excessive humanitarian threats in other countries (Lillich, 1967). These have been well summarized by Chesterman: that the threats of abuse must be egregious; that there must be no realistic non-military alternatives; that collective action through the UNSC must have failed; that military action must be limited to what is necessary, must be proportionate, and must have a reasonable chance of success; and that the intervening state must act 'disinterestedly' so that the humanitarian objective is paramount (2001: 228–9). Finally, we may note the approach of the International Commission on Intervention and State Sovereignty's Report, *The Responsibility to Protect* (2001), which accepts one of the central traditional pro-interventionist arguments, that, since the duty to protect their own citizens is integral to the sovereign rights of states, a failure to do so limits those rights, and triggers both a right and a duty for the international community to intervene. Guiding principles for a use of military force are seen to include: a high threshold of large-scale threatened loss of life as just cause; right intention; last resort; proportional means; and reasonable prospects of success (ICISS, 2001: 32–7). Identical stipulations are made in the UN High-Level Panel Report on 'five basic criteria of legitimacy' for use of force: seriousness of the threat, proper purpose, last resort, proportional means, reasonable chance of success (2004: 57–8).

It can be seen that these suggested criteria for just forcible intervention nearly all come under one or other of the traditional just war criteria (see box 13.2). The difference lies in their content: just war criteria are internally transformed when converted into criteria for forcible international intervention. This transformation in content is what fits them for subsumption under the general framework principles for international intervention listed above (in box 13.1), thereby determining what the requirements are if just war is to serve the wider purposes of just peace.

Box 13.2 Western just war criteria transmuted into criteria for just intervention

For Thomas Aquinas, writing in the fourteenth century, 'three things are required for any war to be just': 'the first is the authority of the sovereign on whose command war is waged', 'secondly a just cause is required' and 'thirdly the right intention of those waging war is required, that is they must intend to promote the good and avoid evil'. Just war criteria today are usually divided into those that determine when it is right to wage war (*jus ad bellum*) and those that determine how the war should rightly be fought (*jus in bello*). There is no generally agreed list, weighting between criteria, or ruling on whether a war has to satisfy all criteria to count as just.

War decision criteria

Just cause: The difference from traditional just war is that military force is to be used to defend a range of international norms, including decolonization norms (East Timor), democratic norms (Sierra Leone), conflict settlement norms (DRC), humanitarian norms (Kosovo) and anti-terrorism norms (Afghanistan).

Legitimate authority: The difference is the idea that such interventions should be multilateral, and that UNSC authorization or at any rate subsequent cooperation should be sought.

Right intention: Here the loftiness and disinterestedness of the professed motive makes it harder to convince sceptics that the intervention is not conducted with a view to domestic politics, oil, or a quest for hegemony.

Prospect of success at acceptable cost: This, too, becomes more problematic – likely success and anticipated balance of benefit and loss are harder to assess when the aim is not just military victory, but reconstruction and nation-building.

Last resort: The difference here is, first, that every effort is made to induce target governments to act responsibly, and, second, that interveners climb the ladder of UN response: Chapter VI peaceful settlement, Article 41 sanctions (UNSC sanctions have been imposed on half the IRW target states in table 8.1 in chapter 8), and only when these are seen not to be viable, Article 42 all necessary means.

War conduct criteria

The aim of *in bello* criteria is to limit the use of force to the *minimum necessary*, and to ensure in each case that such use is *proportionate* and *discriminate* (non-combatants must not be deliberately targeted). In international interventions these criteria become even harder to determine, particularly in terms of targeting when conflict zones are chaotic and civilians are caught up in the fighting. Training for such interventions requires additional skills to those of normal combat, and the importance of transparent mechanisms for determining and punishing breaches of international law by the interveners becomes even more evident (see, for example, UK Ministry of Defence, 2004).

Conclusion: International Ethics, International Law and International Politics

Ethical principles of the kind considered in this chapter supplement international law, but not without controversy. For example, when it comes to the question of forcible intervention to uphold international values in the absence of explicit authorization by the UNSC to maintain or restore international peace and security, opinion is divided. At one end of the spectrum are restrictionists who rule out the legality of all such interventions and argue that to allow them would be 'inimical to the emergence of an international rule of law' (Chesterman, 2001: 217). From this perspective international ethics offers spurious justification for what is legally inadmissible, thus opening the door to 'vigilantes and opportunists to resort to hegemonial intervention' (Brownlie, 1973). At the other end of the spectrum are those who hold that such nominally illegal actions – for example in Kosovo in 1999 – may produce results 'more in keeping with the intent of the law [i.e. more 'legitimate'] – and more moral – than would have ensued had no action been taken', thus saving international law from being strangled by its own formalism (Franck, 2003: 226).

Linked to this is the harsh actuality of international politics – that, when it comes to full-scale international interventions, it is only the powerful who intervene in the affairs of the weak, not the other way round. International politics is the domain of the powerful. Interventions do not take place against the will of those governments that command the resources to carry them out. Beyond what is available through the UNSC, there is no international institutional capacity to decide where, when and how to intervene. And the UNSC only acts in accordance with the interests and historico-cultural instincts of the states that make it up. At the time of writing the possibility of intervention in the Darfur provinces of Sudan is being canvassed by the US and the UK, but is being blocked in the UNSC by Russia, China, Pakistan and Algeria.

So what is the point of attempts to formulate ethical guidelines if in the end all that counts are the interests of a handful of powerful elites in the most powerful countries, and the dominant foreign policy preoccupations of the most powerful states?

Let us end this chapter by remembering that the framework intervention principles in figure 13.1 are derived from the conjunction of basic intervention relations and the guidelines suggested in the growing IGO, NGO and peacekeeping literatures on good practice. We think that they are clear and well-grounded principles to guide conflict resolution in both domestic and international conflicts. The more difficult questions, on which the authors disagree, concern criteria for just forcible intervention. Box 13.2 summarizes the current transformation in just war criteria suggested by those – including the UN, some governments and international commissions – who want to find clear guidelines for UNSC decisions on when and how to intervene in cases for which international law is uncertain and ambiguous (Stromseth, 2003: 233). Two of us regard these, too, as fitting reasonably well under the more general framework principles. One of us believes that these principles are as likely to be distorted to justify the wars of the powerful and doubts that they are consistent with the framework principles. In other words, what both the framework principles indicate (for all of us) and what the more restricted just intervention criteria spell out (for two of us) are widely endorsed international requirements that must be fulfilled *if* those operations are to count in the way that political leaders claim. What we all agree on is that firm and carefully applied ethical criteria are an essential consideration for those who intervene in conflict, at any level. As the quotations at the top of this chapter indicate, one cannot avoid difficult ethical choices in this area. Both acts of omission and acts of commission carry moral dilemmas and risks. The search for a set of principles that can command adherence and respect is a central task for cosmopolitan conflict resolution. We hope the discussion in this chapter contributes to this task.

Recommended reading

Chandler (2004); Elshtain, ed. (1992); Holzgrefe and Keohane, eds (2003); ICISS (2001); Ramsbotham and Woodhouse (1996).

CHAPTER 14

Dialogue, Discourse and Disagreement

One does not make peace with one's friends. One makes peace with one's enemy.

Yitzhak Rabin, Memoirs, 1994

Tʜɪs chapter concentrates on the theme of communication and asks how successful conflict resolution has been in responding to the challenge of serious political disagreement, the chief linguistic manifestation of intractable conflict (it is taken from Ramsbotham *Radical Disagreement*, forthcoming). The communicative dimension of conflict resolution can usefully be considered under three headings. The purpose of *interactive conflict resolution* (originally called 'controlled communication') is to search for mutually acceptable outcomes to apparently intractable conflicts. The purpose of *dialogical conflict resolution* is to open channels of communication in order to overcome prejudice and misunderstanding and to build trust. The emergent field of *discursive conflict transformation* aims to deconstruct discourses that reproduce violence and to foster discourses of non-violence situated in 'the unhindered process of intersubjective communication'.

We will take Jay Rothman's adversarial, reflexive, integrative (ARI) conflict management framework as characteristic of interactive conflict resolution, because he makes a more concerted attempt than any other conflict resolver known to us to take full account of the phenomenon of serious political disagreement. As he says in relation to the Palestinian/Israeli conflict:

> One of the problems with previous human relations, activist and problem-solving dialogue efforts between Jews and Arabs is that they have largely been held among the already 'converted'. Thus, although participants may gain valuable insights and generate creative suggestions for solutions, these dialogues are not fully representative of the main-stream perspectives in one or both sides. (1992: 31)

He also elegantly links interactive conflict resolution both to dialogical conflict resolution and to discursive conflict transformation. ARI attempts to defuse the virulence of the initial 'adversarial' conflict frame, where disagreement predominates, by transmuting it through a linking dialogical or 'reflexive' frame into a final discursive or 'integrative' frame where substantive transformative resolution can be achieved. Rothman identifies these three ARI stages with three underlying methodologies: 'Empiricism, hermeneutics, and critical theory may be viewed as the deep conceptual structures . . . beneath, respectively, the adversarial, reflexive, and integrative conflict frames' (ibid.: 72).

Having examined the way in which disagreement is handled in ARI and interactive conflict resolution, we will look first at the hermeneutic or dialogical tradition in conflict resolution, and then at the critical theoretic or discursive tradition, and in particular at what their two generally acknowledged intellectual sources, Hans-Georg Gadamer and Jürgen Habermas respectively, say about disagreement. This will enable us to conclude by highlighting what still needs to be done by those conflict resolvers who want to take the phenomenon of radical disagreement seriously.

Interactive Conflict Resolution

The ARI approach incorporates features that are common across the related conflict resolution fields of principled negotiation (Fisher and Ury, 1981) and pure mediation (Curle, 1986); of alternative dispute resolution (Floyer Acland, 1995) and public conflict resolution (Dukes, 1996); and of interactive conflict resolution (Fisher, 1997) and analytical problem-solving (Mitchell and Banks, 1996).

In the adversarial or 'positional' disagreement phase the facilitators aim to help the conflict parties to bring into the open the incompatible beliefs that would otherwise block progress: 'Israelis and Palestinians, through the media, through proxies, or through shouting matches in public settings, blame each other for the conflict and articulate mutually exclusive political platforms' (Rothman, 1992: 23). In the ARI training chart it is assumed that participants will 'continue until the point at which discussions appear that they might break down altogether', at which moment the last rites can then be read on adversarial disagreement:

> You have now experienced a very familiar, and I am sure you will agree, a rather unconstructive approach to dialogue. Each of you stated your position, each of you suggested why the other side is wrong or to blame for the conflict. Few of you listened to anyone else, and, frankly, very little, if anything, new was learned. This is the normal approach that all of you have experienced perhaps every time you have discussed the situation with someone who holds a very different

> perspective than your own. I invite you now to experiment with a new way. (Ibid.: 170)

This negative characterization of radical political disagreement is common across the conflict resolution field. The aim of alternative dispute resolution, for example, is to transcend the fact that 'our culture and our legal system . . . are *adversarial*: they work on the basis of right or wrong, win or lose, either/or' (Floyer Acland, 1995: 9). Similarly, the purpose of transformative public conflict resolution is to revive participatory democracy by promoting 'productive dialogue' at all levels, rather than the undesirable oppositional disagreement and 'debate' seen to be characteristic of the 'Anglo-American adversary system' (Dukes, 1996: 130, 164–9).

Having exposed the negativity of disagreement, the aim of the second, reflexive, phase of the conflict resolution process is to translate adversarial judgements about objective issues (disagreement) into non-adversarial comments about the speaker's subjective pre-occupations (self-description):

> This reflexive dialogue allows sides to explain their own deep motivations and perceptions in the conflict, and begin to understand the salience of the memories, history and fears of the other side, in influencing the way they act in the conflict. (Rothman, 1992: 62)

The highlight comes when members of each side are asked to 'articulate the other side's core values, hopes and fears as if they were members of the other side'. This is often 'very poignant and powerful' and 'clears the way for an integrative approach to conflict management'. If participants slip back into adversarial language, they are reminded by facilitators that what we want is not 'positional debate' but 'questions for clarification, for understanding, for analytic empathy' (ibid.: 175). This process of objective-to-subjective translation is once again common across the conflict resolution field. Roger Fisher of the Harvard Negotiation Project advises that 'it is more useful to draft statements that describe feelings and the impact of what others do than to draft statements that judge or describe others' (Fisher et al., 1994: 27–8), while clients of alternative dispute resolution are reminded that people 'are not motivated by *facts*: they are motivated by their *perceptions* of the facts, their *interpretations* of the facts, their *feelings* about the facts' (Floyer Acland, 1995: 57; italics in the original). In this way the brutal asymmetries of radical disagreement are flattened out into the symmetrical juxtapositions of self-description.

With the third, integrative, phase we reach the heart of the conflict resolution process. The ground has been cleared for participants to learn how to reinterpret the conflict as a shared problem, to generate creative alternatives, to employ objective criteria in finding optimum agreements, and to seek cooperative implementation in overcoming remaining barriers. This is the essence of principled negotiation and problem-solving. Disagreement can now be discounted as superficial, and resolution can move deeper to look for the underlying interests, needs or sub-conscious origins where integrative transformation is achieved. The Harvard Negotiation Project advises 'principled negotiators' to disregard surface adversarial 'positions' characteristic of disagreement and to focus on reconciling submerged 'interests' (Fisher and Ury, 1981).[1] John Burton (1997) looks beneath the shallow squabbles characteristic of 'disputes' to the frustration and denial of basic human needs where deep-rooted conflict originates and can be resolved. In his Center for the Study of Mind and Human Interaction, Vamik Volkan seeks out the 'unconscious psychological factors which may render political processes unworkable and even malignant' (Volkan and Harris, 1993: 170–1, quoted in Fisher, 1997: 109–10).

What happens if, despite the strategy of neutralizing and bypassing radical disagreement via this three-stage process, workshop participants nevertheless reject the conflict resolution assumptions? What if both Israelis and Palestinians insist, for example, that, given the nature of the modern state system, exclusive sovereignty is the only essential safeguard for precisely the needs for safety, identity and autonomy that facilitators emphasize? Rothman admits that 'participants from each side of the divide' do indeed respond like this, but he then dismisses this as a relic of the original adversarial 'monologue of disbelief, mistrust and animosity', and reiterates that conflict parties must realize that 'at the deepest levels' they are, after all, 'alike in needs and motivations' so that 'a new opening for peace is promoted' and integrative conflict resolution can proceed (1992: 185–6).

Dialogical Conflict Resolution and Gadamerian Hermeneutics

Dialogical approaches in conflict resolution also often start by noting the fact of initial disagreement. In his advocacy of 'intercultural dialogue' in the wake of the 11 September 2001 atrocities, for example, Bikhu Parekh (2002) begins with two composite adversarial 'opening statements' which he describes as 'partisan, extreme, polemical, hurtful and sometimes deeply offensive'. He does not linger over them, however, but immediately looks in the opposite direction for the 'badly needed dialogue', 'better intercultural understanding' and 'broadly agreed view of the past' that he hopes will eventually produce 'mutually agreed compromise' on substantive issues. These aims are broadly shared by specialists in interpersonal and intergroup dialogue.

Interpersonal and intergroup dialogue

Dialogic approaches in interpersonal conflict resolution draw mainly from the communication, psychology and active listening literatures. Recent developments point beyond the original psychotherapeutic idea of 'projective' sympathy and empathy whose aim was to 'enter the private perceptual world of the other and become thoroughly at home in it' (Rogers, 1980: 142). Instead, the focus has shifted to the concept of 'relational' empathy in which a more dynamic and productive process is envisaged, whereby, in intense interpersonal exchange that is as much affective as cognitive, interlocutors together generate shared new meaning sometimes referred to as a 'third culture' (Broome, 1993). The aim is to reach an understanding through a dialogical exchange of views via mutual translation into a common language. Heavy demands are thereby made on participants, who are expected to be able to recognize that they can never escape the universal reach of prejudice and that the attempted 'fusion of horizons' will always be an ongoing project, never a completed programme. They are asked to decentre their own identities to the point where, instead of seeking 'certainty, closure and control', they welcome the tension between 'irreconcilable horizons' and adopt a 'playfulness' and open-mindedness appropriate to encounter new experience or the ultimately unabsorbable 'other' (Stewart and Thomas, 1986: 198). It can be seen that the fact of disagreement is treated purely privatively here – a symptom of what conflict resolvers are trying to avoid, not something from which they can learn.

A similar set of ideas can be found in the field of intergroup or intercommunal dialogue. This is a large set of enterprises illustrated, for example, in the work of the Community Relations Council in Northern Ireland.[2] Saunders (1999) offers a fine analysis of the role of 'sustained dialogue' in attempts to transform intractable 'ethnic and racial conflicts' – including the Palestinian-Israeli conflict. Here, in the wake of recent events, we will take as characteristic the related enterprises of comparative religious ethics and inter-religious dialogue. The coincidence of the UN 2001 *Year Of Dialogue Between Civilizations* with the catastrophe of 11 September projected these agendas rapidly up the scale of international urgency. Several different approaches can be found within the field of comparative religious ethics, but the most pertinent from a conflict resolution perspective is what Sumner Twiss terms the 'hermeneutical-dialogical' paradigm.[3] The aim of intergroup dialogue of this kind is to study 'others and ourselves as equals'. At its core is the goal of constructing a 'common moral world' between divergent traditions, which involves a dialectic of mutual translation and receptivity through continual dialogue in a constructive effort to answer the shared question: how should we live together? (Twiss, 1993). This involves 'normative appropriation' (fusion of horizons) between insider-participants of the kind mentioned above, and with similar implications.

Before moving on we should note in passing the cognate but distinct enterprise of inter-religious dialogue, such as the 1993 Parliament of the World's Religions that attempted to frame a shared 'global ethic'. The central purpose of the kind of dialogue envisaged in the 1993 Parliament was not to create new shared meaning, but to confirm that 'there is already a consensus among the religions which can be the basis for a global ethic – a minimum fundamental consensus concerning binding values, irrevocable standards, and fundamental moral attitudes' (Kung and Kuschel, eds, 1993: 18). The success of the enterprise depends once again upon 'bracketing out' serious disagreement, but this time on the assumption that whatever is left can be said to constitute the desired global religious consensus.

Gadamerian hermeneutics

It can be seen that both interpersonal and intergroup dialogical conflict resolution are steeped in the ideas of Gadamer, and in particular his concept of a 'fusion of horizons'. What did he mean by this term? Why is Gadamer's hermeneutics so influential in conflict resolution? And what does he make of the phenomenon of serious political disagreement in his central work, *Truth and Method* (1960/1975)?

Hermeneutics has traditionally concerned the interpretation of historical texts. What Gadamer calls 'romantic hermeneutics' equated the understanding of a text with 'getting inside' the initially alien world that produced it – rather like the tradition of 'projective empathy' in psychology. In contrast to this, Gadamerian hermeneutics begins with the perspective of the interpreter at the point where 'the natural life in which each means and understands the same thing is disturbed' (1960/1975: 158–9). We are pulled up short by a text, or encounter a 'Thou' that stands over against us and asserts its own rights against our proto-assumptions, prejudices and interests. This is the 'primary hermeneutical condition' where the concept of a 'horizon' first reveals itself: 'a hermeneutical situation is determined by the prejudices that we bring with us. They constitute, then, the horizon of a particular present, for they represent that beyond which it is impossible to see' (ibid.: 272). The 'true home of hermeneutics' is in this intermediate area 'between strangeness and familiarity', where we encounter the unfamiliar, and, through awareness of our conceptual limits, thereby transcend them: 'in the process of understanding there takes place a real fusing of horizons, which means that as the historical horizon is projected, it is simultaneously removed' (ibid.: 273). In other words, there is only a single (albeit repeated) movement of understanding, which, in positing difference (becoming aware of its horizon), thereby overcomes it. This is an endless process for a finite consciousness that is already part of the tradition it is trying to explore: a person 'who does not accept that he is dominated by prejudices will fail to see what is shown by their light' (ibid.: 324).

The key move that has made Gadamer so influential in conflict resolution is the central parallel that he then draws between the interpreter/text relationship in hermeneutics and the ego/alter relationship in interpersonal conversation or dialogue. Much of his insight is generated by examining 'the hermeneutical phenomenon according to the model of the conversation between two persons' (ibid.: 340). He admits that 'the hermeneutic situation in regard to texts' is not 'exactly the same as that between two people in conversation', because, unlike live interlocutors, texts are 'permanently fixed expressions of life' so that 'one partner in the hermeneutical conversation, the text, is expressed only through the other partner, the interpreter' (ibid.: 359). Nevertheless, he then carries over his hermeneutic insights into his definition of 'true dialogue'. Productive dialogue is a conversation in which both partners seek to create or recreate a shared world of understanding – as if each was interpreting the other's text. To do this each partner must be prepared to assimilate fore-meanings or prejudices by converting judgements or assertions into questions: 'all suspension of judgements and hence, a fortiori, of prejudices, has logically the structure of a question'. Only in this way can the space be opened for the 'imperceptible but not arbitrary' shifts in mutual understanding (exchange of views) through which the creation of a common language becomes possible. This repeated process of 'reciprocal translation' eventually forges common meaning (ibid.: 348). From a conflict resolution perspective, a shared reality is restored and the basis for a new community is established, neither my world nor your world, but 'a transformation into a communion in which we do not remain what we were' (ibid.: 341).

These are profound insights that have inspired conflict resolvers. But we can also discern here the origin of the comprehensive disregard for the phenomenon of radical political disagreement that is characteristic of dialogical conflict resolution. If 'to understand what a person says is to agree about the object' (ibid.: 345), then to disagree is to court misunderstanding. Since texts do not answer back in the way that conflictual conversational partners do, there is no analogue for disagreement in conversations modelled on the relationship between interpreter and text. To transmute judgements into questions is to remove the basis for disagreement. And if true conversation is a dialogue between Gadamerian partners, there is no room for contradiction. Mutual exploration of a question and a common search for shared meaning are attitudes that conflict resolvers want to encourage. But they are not attitudes that characterize serious disagreements or intense political disputes.

Discursive Conflict Transformation and Habermasian Critical Theory

For these and other reasons, a number of conflict resolvers and conflict transformers have been critical of interactive conflict resolution and dialogical conflict resolution and have turned instead to discourse analysis and critical theory. Discourse analysis tends to mean different things to different people – ranging from essentially Marxist insights in the tradition of Althusser (1970) which aim to unmask discourses that claim universality but are materially shaped by dominant economic interests, through the more diffracted lens of Foucault for whom discourses are concretions of power relations and 'practices which form the objects of which they speak'(1972: 49), and on to the disparate understandings of social constructionism clustered around the idea that there is no one truth, only competing socially and discursively produced realities and knowledges (Burr, 1995). Here we will take Vivienne Jabri's *Discourses on Violence* (1996) as our main sample of an application of discourse analysis to conflict resolution, in her case aligned most closely with Habermasian critical theory.

Discursive conflict transformation

Edward Said was among those on the Palestinian side who disputed the capacity of 'cooperative' conflict resolution to address severe asymmetric conflict:

> There is still a military occupation, people are still being killed, imprisoned and denied their rights on a daily basis [so only when there has been an] end to occupation [and] we are on a reasonably equal footing with the Israelis [can we] begin to talk seriously about cooperation. In the meantime cooperation can all too easily shade into collaboration with Israeli policy. (1995: 37)

Some commentators agree that 'uncritical conflict resolution', operating in situations of quantitative or qualitative power asymmetry, simply reinforces the status quo (Kuttab, 1988; Rouhana and Korper, 1996). This has inspired others to invoke critical social theory as a remedy (Hoffman, 1987; Jabri, 1996; Fetherston, 1998). Rothman himself equates the integrative stage of ARI with critical theory, whose epistemology seeks not to take existing institutions and social relations for granted, but to problematize and challenge them. The aim is to 'transform the status quo . . . by approaching it with a normative view as to what it ought to become' (Rothman, 1992: 73).

How does this work? How can discourse analysis and critical theory bring about the fundamental transformation that neither the 'objectivist' (rational actor/bargaining) approach, nor the 'subjectivist' (communications/problem-solving) approach, can achieve – and that even the 'structuralist' (institution-building) approach misses? The starting point for Jabri (1996) is to address the embedded symbolic or representative orders, linked to differential access to resources, of which specific conflicts are taken to be a manifestation. Positivist or cognitivist assumptions about language as a transparent medium are seen to ignore the central role that language plays in the reproduction of the structures of domination and exclusion that generate and perpetuate violence. Jabri employs a threefold strategy to counter this. First, analysis of the 'discourses on violence', the discursive and institutional continuities that perpetuate war; second, identification of an independent locus for a transformative 'discourse on peace'; third, the invocation of Habermasian discourse ethics to provide a secure critical standard from which to expose the workings of the former and to ground the latter.

Jabri (1996) identifies two specific discursive mechanisms for the production and reproduction of war. The first mechanism (dealt with by her in chapter 4) is legitimation through repertoires of meaning linked to the state system and drawn upon by strategically situated agents. Here, militarism and just war are singled out as 'dominant modes of discourse which are implicated in the reproduction of war as a continuity within social systems' (ibid.: 97). The second mechanism (dealt with in chapter 5) is the construction of exclusionist identities via discourses that reify particular 'ways of knowing' (ibid.: 140).

The key point for those interested in the phenomenon of radical disagreement is that the critical struggle against these hegemonic discourses does not take the form of disagreement at all, and cannot do so. Hegemonic discourse must be undermined and exposed as ideology, not taken on its own terms in counter-argument. To do the latter would be to play according to the rules of the hegemon by buying into the illusion of symmetry. That is why, for example, Jabri does not engage with any of the arguments about just war. She does not mention the voluminous literature on just war criteria (disagreement about its 'regulative rules'), nor the equally large literature that includes pacifist and realist critiques of the whole just war approach (disagreement about its 'constitutive rules'). Since the conscious legitimations offered by situated agents do not include acknowledgement – or even consciousness – of the institutionalized power relations, social roles and diurnal routines that shape them, 'first-order' disagreements must be decisively set aside in favour of the 'second-order' discourse analysis that is alone capable of uncovering them. Only in this way can the hegemon's 'shared world of meaning' be delineated as just that, thereby opening the way for the possibility of an entirely independent counter-discourse. This is the strategy suggested by discursive conflict transformation for dealing with all asymmetric power struggles.

Having cleared the ground in this way, Jabri invokes the framework of Habermas's communicative ethics to reconstruct a transformative 'discourse on peace'. It is the rules that determine when communicative action is genuinely free from domination, rather than any specific arguments or outcomes resulting from the application of those rules, that are decisive. There is no other court of appeal. Actions and institutional arrangements can only be said to be legitimate when they result from a *process* of unconstrained discourse in which all affected parties participate freely.

What happens when the assumptions on which discourse ethics rest are themselves challenged, for example by religious beliefs which reject the very idea of 'an intersubjective space of equal interpretation and contestation'? It is a situation which seems to leave no room for discourse ethics, because it 'does not allow the occurrence of discourse and precludes any possibility of an emergent dialogic relationship' (ibid.: 166–7). As Jabri says, this is characteristic of 'some of the most pervasive conflicts of late modernity'. It is also central to the issue of radical disagreement. Jabri's response demonstrates again why such disagreement is not taken seriously in discursive conflict transformation. Put simply, she acknowledges 'value differentiation and heterogeneity' of this kind, but then incorporates it as 'lived experience' and 'moral substance' within what remain 'universal constitutive rules framing communicative action' (ibid.: 167). The objectors are located beside other voices under the general designation 'difference as a formative component of subjectivity', and are redefined in terms of 'contextualized social relations'. Their objection is thereby neutralized.

To enter the realm of communicative ethics, therefore, is, for Jabri, to enter 'a zone of peace based upon dialogic principles':

> The Habermasian model of discursive ethics . . . does not provide a substantive definition of the contents of peace, but provides for a

process of which peace is necessarily constitutive. It also provides a framework through which war as an institution may be put to question. (Ibid.: 166)

In other words, the discourse on peace is raised above the turbulence of political disagreement by the discursive framework itself. This explains much of its power and appeal to conflict resolvers and trans- formers. In our view it deserves this attention and is one of the most exciting recent developments in the field. Nevertheless, we may for the same reason note how and why serious disagreement is once again disregarded in the process.

Habermasian critical theory

We have seen why a number of advocates of discursive conflict reso- lution and transformation now appeal to Habermasian discourse ethics to ground their methodology. Others make a similar appeal in order to connect the field with cognate enterprises, also built along Habermasian lines, such as the promotion of cosmopolitan democracy and citizenship (Linklater, 1998; Jones, 1999: 80–104: reference to Held, 1995), or with parallel discussion in the field of international rela- tions. We would do well, therefore, to ask how the phenomenon of disagreement is handled in Habermas's foundational text, *The Theory of Communicative Action*. For the sake of brevity we will confine our read- ing to volume 1 (1984).

It turns out to be a somewhat complicated story. Habermas himself offers no systematic analysis of the phenomenon of disagreement, despite the fact that it plays such a crucial role at every stage in his argument. His account can nevertheless, we believe, be reconstructed as follows:

1	Disagreement-as-threat		Disagreement as threat *to* the unity of reason
2	Disagreement-as-remedy	(A)	Disagreement as equal partner *in* the unity of reason
		(B)	Disagreement as subordinate component *of* the unity of reason
		(C)	Disagreement as guarantor of difference *within* the unity of reason

At the heart of Habermas's treatment is the double role of disagree- ment as both threat and remedy. As *threat*, disagreement is seen to be symptomatic of the breakdown of pre-modern forms of solidarity, reproduced in the disruptions of the everyday and encountered in the perennial risks that menace 'the intersubjectivity of ethical life'; as *remedy*, it is integral to the theory and practice of argumentation, upon which the explication and repair of communicative rationality depends. As Seyla Benhabib notes:

> Discourses arise when the intersubjectivity of ethical life is endangered; but the very project of discursive argumentation presupposes the ongoing validity of reconciled subjectivity. (1986: 321)

Both roles are constitutive, but they coexist uneasily. It is essential for Habermas's theory that, at one and the same time: (A) serious disagreement should be seen to be what distinguishes 'real discourse' from strategic steering and monological imagining; (B) disagreement should nevertheless be contained entirely within the wider economy of action oriented to reaching understanding as a subordinate and reflective moment; and (C) that, despite all this, disagreement should after all make a final reappearance when the curtain comes down, unconstrained and with renewed vigour, to represent the free play of difference in the emancipated social world that discourse ethics aspires above all to promote.

The defining feature of moment (A) is the formal symmetry between agreement and disagreement in Habermas's theory of argumentation. This can be seen in the only substantial passage devoted exclusively to the phenomenon of disagreement:

> Someone who rejects a comprehensible speech act is taking issue with at least one of these validity claims. In rejecting a speech act as (normatively) wrong or untrue or insincere, he is expressing with his 'no' the fact that the utterance has not fulfilled its function of securing an interpersonal relationship, of representing states of affairs, or of manifesting experiences. It is not in agreement with *our* world of legitimately ordered interpersonal relations, or with *the* world of existing states of affairs, or with *the speaker's own* world of subjective experiences. (1984, 1: 308)

Habermas's account of the 'world-relations' of disagreement, therefore, maps exactly one-to-one onto his general model of communicative rationality, where 'communicatively achieved agreement is measured against exactly three criticisable validity-claims' and actors who come to an understanding about something 'cannot help embedding their speech acts in precisely three world-relations'. In this way the sharp asymmetries in terms of world-relations that are exactly what characterize serious political disagreement are ironed out into the formal symmetries of *pro* and *contra*.

At the same time, under moment (B), Habermas by no means treats disagreement and agreement symmetrically. On the contrary, it is essential for his theory that it is agreement ('reaching understanding') that is 'the telos of human speech' and that 'the use of language with an orientation to reaching understanding is the *original mode* of language use, upon which indirect understanding . . . and the instrumental use of language . . . are parasitic' (ibid.: 1: 288; original italics) – as also the phenomenon of disagreement. For example, in his procedural rules for argumentative speech Habermas insists that proponents:

> thematize a problematic validity claim and, relieved of the pressure of action and experience, in a hypothetical attitude, test with reasons, and only with reasons, whether the claim defended by the proponents rightfully stands or not. (Ibid.: 1: 25; original bullets removed)

Argumentation is detached from political urgency, stripped of conviction and translated into hypothetical mode. No traces of serious political disagreement remain.

And yet, despite all this, under moment (C) Habermas has to reintroduce the idea of substantial disagreement after all in order to guard against the accusation that his theory implies a hegemony of social coordination that stifles dissent and smothers what it purports to emancipate: 'Nothing makes me more nervous' than the imputation that the theory of communicative action 'proposes, or at least suggests, a rationalist utopian society' (Habermas, 1982: 235). He wants to claim that only the idealizations presupposed in 'the intersubjectivity of linguistically achieved understanding' can open up the space for divergent voices to be heard:

> linguistically attained consensus does not eradicate from the accord the differences in speaker perspectives but rather presupposes them as ineliminable . . . More discourse means more contradiction and difference. The more abstract the agreements become, the more diverse the disagreements with which we can non-violently live. (1992: 140)

In this passage from disagreement-as-threat (radical dispute) to disagreement-as-tolerated-difference (the celebration of diversity) we recognize the transmogrification aimed at in discursive conflict transformation. Habermas himself does not have to look at specific examples of serious political disagreement, because he already knows in advance what the formal requirements for communicative action are. And, if these are not fulfilled, we do not have disagreement in his eyes at all, but perhaps something more akin to Max Weber's 'polytheism of gods and demons' struggling inarticulately with one another – reminiscent of Matthew Arnold's dark chaotic plain 'where ignorant armies clash by night' (Habermas, 1984, 1: 249).

Conclusion: Taking Radical Disagreement Seriously in Conflict Resolution

How seriously have scholars and practitioners in the conflict resolution and conflict transformation field taken the challenge of deep value incompatibilities and 'thick' cultural differences? In particular, what do they tell us about the phenomenon of radical disagreement, the chief linguistic manifestation of the conflicts in question? For the reasons given above neither interactive conflict resolution nor the dialogical and discursive traditions associated with it can be said hitherto to have paid adequate attention to the phenomenon of deep political disagreement. It is treated as a purely privative and limiting concept, not as an important feature of intense conflict fields that is worthy of empirical study in its own right. This may be understandable, since the main purpose of classic conflict resolution has been to move the conflict parties away from the locked positions in which they find themselves. But our contention is that it is an omission more likely to limit the field than to enhance it – as shown by the insights to be derived from studies such as Julie Mertus's *Kosovo: How Myths and Truths Started A War* (1999) that begin to forefront it. In the area of communication and language, significant tracts of empirical data lie unexamined, an unnecessary impoverishment that forecloses further insights into the nature of radical conflict. This is pursued further in *Radical Disagreement* (Ramsbotham, forthcoming) through: a parallel investigation into the conceptualization of serious political disagreement in conflict analysis; a central comparative study of the anatomy of deep disagreement in order to test existing models; an evaluation of practical implications of taking radical disagreement seriously; and an evaluation of theoretical implications. The significance of the results fully justifies the effort. We suggest that this will be an important new undertaking for conflict resolution in the future, as attempts are made to get to grips with the conceptual gulfs that underlie deep value conflicts – such as those between Palestinians and Israelis or the challenge to western secular liberalism and American hegemony laid down so brutally on 11 September 2001.

Recommended reading

Abi-Ezzi (forthcoming); Aggestam (1999); Burr (1995); Dukes (1996); Fisher (1997); Floyer Acland (1995); Jabri (1996); Ramsbotham (2004b, 2005b, forthcoming); Rothman (1992); Saunders (1999).

Culture, Religion and Conflict Resolution

Much of the field of conflict resolution . . . is based . . . on the fundamental belief that resort to physical violence in the processing of social conflict . . . is a prime example of wrongheaded problem solving. And the fact that most cultures at some point . . . sanction this solution is proof to these conflict resolutionists that culture needs to be not only analysed and understood for purposes of activist conflict resolution, but rethought and re-imagined – *re-engineered* – as well.

Avruch, 1998: 20–1

Verité en deçà des Pyrenées, erreur au-delà (what is truth on this side of the Pyrenees, is error on the other)

Pascal: Pensees, 1660

W ITH the topic of culture and conflict resolution we reach an underlying motif that has resonated throughout this book. Indeed, for us it is in the end the most important issue of all. Most of the definitions and models offered in chapter 1 were seen by the founders of the field as generic – they applied across cultures and societies. Cultural variations were emphasized – less by those who defined conflict 'objectively' in terms of structure, behaviour and power struggle over scarce resources, more by those who defined it 'subjectively' in terms of perceived incompatibility of interest, interpretation and belief – but even the latter did not usually regard cultural variation as particularly problematic, since they tended to come from a background in individual and social psychology rather than in cultural studies. It was above all the influx of anthropological ideas into the field that first sharpened awareness of the culture question, then leavened most aspects of conflict resolution thinking, and then challenged the validity of many of its basic assumptions.

The fundamental question is this: *how far down does cultural variation reach?* We will suggest in this chapter that conflict resolvers have given three different answers to this question – not at all, a little way down, and a long way down – but that they agree in rejecting a fourth possibility – the whole way down – or there would not be a coherent field of conflict resolution at all.

Let us remind ourselves of the recurrence of the culture theme in this book. In chapter 2 we saw how, although the inspiration from precursors came from many religious traditions, the founders of the formal field in the 1950s were mainly from Northern Europe and North America. Latterly there has been a proliferation of conflict resolution centres throughout the world raising questions about many of these assumptions. Chapters 3 and 4 raised similar questions about conflict analysis, and chapters 5 to 8 about conflict resolution responses – for example, about the appropriateness of intrusive prevention strategies across cultural boundaries, about the problems of multinational peacekeeping in third countries, about how radically negotiation and mediation are affected by cultural difference, about the suitability of universal democratic market economy models in post-war reconstruction in non-western settings, or about cultural variations in approaches to reconciliation. Part II of the book has also been drawn to this theme, whether the topic was the refusal to see ideologies that condone or encourage terrorism as legitimate cultural alternatives, the tension between the principle of gender equality and patriarchal cultures, the universality of conflict resolution intervention principles, or the relative neglect of the challenge from radical disagreement in dialogic and discursive conflict resolution.

How Far Down Does Cultural Variation Reach?

There is limited space to indicate the wider debates about cultural variation that have informed conflict resolution. But paramount here was the influence of the anthropologist Franz Boas, and particularly of his students, such as Ruth Benedict and Margaret Mead, with their emphasis on the uniqueness of different cultures and critique of earlier value judgements about evolution from primitive to civilized cultures (Benedict, 1934). This came to be associated with refutation of the idea of biologically determined human instincts for rapacity, violence and war, and with promotion of the idea of what Sponsel (1996) called 'the anthropology of peace' that saw cooperation and coexistence as natural, war as an 'invention',[1] and the causes of violence lying in the organizational structures and psycho-cultural dispositions of particular societies. Ross's *The Culture of Conflict* (1993) adopts this approach, comparing ethnographic data from ninety pre-industrial societies in an attempt to answer the question 'Why are some societies more conflictual than others?' His answer as to why among the Yanomamo of southern Venezuela a 'militant ideology and the warfare associated with it are the central reality of daily existence' (Chagnon, 1983), whereas the Mbuti pygmies of the Zaire rain forest are 'at peace with themselves and with their environment' (Turnbull, 1978), is that:

> In the most general terms, the psychocultural dispositions rooted in a society's early socialization experiences shape the overall level of conflict, while its specific pattern of social organization determines whether the targets of conflict and aggression are located within a society, outside it, or both. (1993: 9)

He then generalizes this 'culture of conflict theory' to post-industrial societies and – surprisingly – finds it precisely confirmed in explaining the protracted conflict in Ireland and the 'relatively low levels of conflict in Norway' (ibid.: ch. 9). Animal ethologists have taken the predisposition to peace and war even further back: for example, de Waal (1989, 1998) shows that primate societies practise reconciliation – a different emphasis from that of Jane Goodall in her observation of the murderous propensities of our genetically nearest cousins, the chimpanzees (1986).

Similar conclusions have been drawn in attempts to explain human aggression, where the 'determinism' of Freud (the innate self-destructiveness of his death drive *thanatos*) and Lorenz (his 'hydraulic' model in which the drive to aggression builds and seeks outlet) are partially challenged in the 'frustration/aggression' theory of Dollard and his associates (1939), and refuted in the 'social learning theory' of Bandura (1973) with the idea that aggression is not an innate drive nor an automatic reaction to frustration, but a learned response. Via this route psychologists could join anthropologists and ethologists in denying the evolutionary functionality of competition and war, and emphasizing the cultural malleability of individuals and societies with a view to fostering conditions for the non-violent resolution of conflict. So it is that, having looked at 'cultural influences on conflict resolution' and offered examples of varying practice from culture to culture, the editorial 'final words' of Fry and Bjorkqvist's *Cultural Variation in Conflict Resolution* are:

> We conclude that the source of conflict lies in the minds of people. External, social conflict is a reflection of intrapsychic conflict. External control does not solve the roots of the problem. If we wish a conflict really to disappear, then a change in attitude is needed. Only when people learn to understand and respect each other can peaceful coexistence begin. (eds 1997: 252)

It is interesting at this point to consider the implications for conflict resolution of the wider current battle between anti-evolutionism of this kind and a new generation of evolutionists. On the surface it might seem portentous, since each accuses the other of professional unreliability, political bias and dire consequences for understanding and responding to conflict. We will argue that it turns out to be less serious than might at first appear.

The new evolutionists attack what Tooby and Cosmides (1992) call 'the standard social science model' currently dominant in sociology, anthropology and social-psychology, and attempt to reassert the primacy of biology (Dawkins, 1998; Wilson, 1998; Pinker, 2002). This is said to represent a confluence of ideas from 'four frontiers of knowledge' – mind, the brain, genes and evolution – that, it is claimed, are at last bridging the gap between biology and culture and finally providing a secure basis for the understanding of human nature (Pinker, 2002: ch. 3). The 'politically correct' assumption that human nature is a benign 'blank slate' on which different cultures can 'construct' variation uninhibited by innate characteristics is rejected, including the idea that:

> violence has nothing to do with human nature but is a pathology inflicted by malign elements outside us. Violence is a behavior taught by the culture, or an infectious disease endemic to certain environments. (Ibid.: 307)

Pinker rejects this as 'the central dogma of a secular faith', and points to human bodies and minds for 'direct signs of design for aggression' (male body size, the effects of testosterone, anger and teeth-baring, fight-or-flight response of the autonomic nervous system, aggressive acts initiated by circuits in the limbic system), to the transculturally rough-and-tumble behaviour of boys, 'which is obviously practise for fighting', to evidence that the 'most violent age is not adolescence but toddlerhood', to the 'shockingly high homicide rates of pre-state societies, with 10 to 60 per cent of the men dying at the hands of other men', and so on. Pinker espouses Hobbes's analysis that morality has been a late invention only 'discovered by our ancestors after billions of years of the morally indifferent process known as natural selection' in which violence paid off in certain circumstances for rational and self-interested agents – in response to competition for the scarce resources required for survival and self-reproduction; in response to fear of others similarly motivated; and in response to the male cultures of 'honour' that resulted (ibid.: ch. 17).

Anti-evolutionists have in turn fought back, identifying the political agenda of evolutionary psychology as 'transparently part of a right-wing libertarian attack on collectivity, above all the welfare state' and rejecting its claims as 'not merely mistaken, but culturally pernicious' legitimizing male 'philandering', the favouring of our genetic kin and human aggression, as if a propensity to violence was biologically imprinted in human nature between 100,000 and 600,000 years ago on the Pleistocene savannahs where homo sapiens originated (Rose and Rose, eds, 2001: 8, 3, 2).

We do not think that debate at this level of abstraction does have portentous implications for conflict resolution. The arguments of psycho-cultural theorists such as Ross, or Fry and Bjorkqvist, point to the significance of manipulating structural and psychological aspects of culture in order to produce non-violent societies. But the implications suggested by the evolutionary theorists for conflict resolution turn out to be not too different. We saw in chapter 1 how, in the light of iterated game theory, Dawkins's 'selfish gene' hypothesis suggests that over a sufficient time span and under non-apocalyptic conditions 'nice guys come first'. Similarly, the two main conflict resolution conclusions from Pinker's chapter on violence are, first, that democratic state structures are the best political antidote to the three Hobbesian 'reasons for quarrel', because 'by inflicting penalties on aggressors the governing body eliminates the profitability of invading for gain', which in turn 'defuses the Hobbesian trap in which mutually distrustive people are each tempted to inflict a premptive strike', while a system of laws disinterestedly applied 'can obviate the need for a hair trigger for retaliation and the accompanying culture of honour' (2002: 330). The fact that the state is democratic is seen to be the best way to neutralize the danger that the state authorities themselves may turn violent. The second main conflict resolution conclusion that Pinker derives from his evolutionary theory is that the central psychological aim should be to bring potential enemies 'into each other's moral circles by facilitating trade, cultural exchanges, and people-to-people activities' (ibid.: 335). Since for Pinker mind is a 'combinatorial, recursive system' we not only have thoughts, but thoughts about thoughts, etc., so, in a passage reminiscent of Burton's second-order learning argument, he sees the 'advances in human conflict resolution' as 'dependent on this ability'. For Pinker, the mindsets predisposed to violence 'evolved to deal with hostilities in the ancestral past, and we must bring them into the open if we are to work around them in the present'. Anti-evolutionists avert their gaze from 'the evolutionary logic of violence', because they fear that 'acknowledging it is tantamount to accepting it or even to approving it':

> Instead they have pursued the comforting delusion of the Noble Savage, in which violence is an arbitrary product of learning or a pathogen that bores into us from outside. But denying the logic of violence makes it easy to forget how readily violence can flare up, and ignoring the parts of the mind that ignite violence makes it easy to overlook the parts that can extinguish it. With violence, as with so

many other concerns, human nature is the problem, but human nature is also the solution. (Ibid.: 336)

In short, both evolutionists and anti-evolutionist culturalists in the conflict resolution field turn out in the end to be deriving remarkably similar policy recommendations from their apparently incompatible theories.

Culture and Conflict Resolution: Three Responses

In reply to the question 'How far down does cultural variation reach?' conflict resolvers give three different levels of response (see table 15.1). We will comment briefly on each in turn.

We have already noted how the central conflict resolution approach of Burton is based on the claim that deep-rooted conflict is caused by the failure of social and political institutions to satisfy non-negotiable ontological human needs for recognition, security, development and so on (chapter 2). In the Burtonian model culture operates at the shallower level of values, and therefore does not affect the conflict resolution imperative of mining down to the underlying level of universal or generic human needs. As Avruch puts it, Burton's theory of conflict 'marginalizes the role of culture to the extreme, silencing it as effectively as does the power-based realist paradigm, which Burton so clearly opposes in most other ways' (1998: 89–90).

In the second category, we find conflict resolution specialists who recognize the significance of cultural variation, but regard it as one variable among others, important to take account of but not serious enough to transform generic approaches. Perhaps the best examples come from the negotiation literature. Prominent here have been studies such as Gulliver's pioneering 1979 analysis of cross-cultural negotiations in quasi-Gadamerian terms as interlocutions in which

Table 15.1 Three conflict resolution answers to the culture question

	Response	Responder
1	Cultural variation is not relevant to conflict resolution	Burton, Zartman
2	Cultural variation should be taken into account in conflict resolution, but only as a variable	Bercovitch, Cohen, Gulliver
3	Cultural variation is fundamentally significant in conflict resolution	Avruch, Black, Lederach, Galtung
4	Cultural variation reaches right to the bottom, precluding cross-cultural generalization	

both parties have to try to educate each other (1979), and Cohen's analysis of Israeli-Egyptian culturally based misunderstandings and miscommunication leading to damaging ˙ 'dialogues of the deaf' (Cohen, 1990, 1991). This work relates to that of Jervis on 'perception and misperception' in international politics (1976) and Janis on 'groupthink' (1973). In sharp contrast to this has been the scorn poured by Zartman on the significance of culture for international negotiation: 'Culture is indeed relevant to the understanding of the negotiation process . . . every bit as relevant as [the] breakfast [the negotiators ate], and to much the same extent' (1993: 17; quoted from Avruch, 1998: 42). Zartman gives three reasons for this, each challenged by Avruch (that negotiation is a universal process and 'cultural differences are simply differences in style and language', that in any case there is now a universal culture of diplomacy, and that cultural difference is trumped by considerations of power) (Avruch, 1998: 42–55). In general, conflict resolvers vary in the weight they accord cultural variation in this area. In the view of Avruch neither those who approach the study of negotiations from an analytical social-psychological perspective (such as Pruitt and Carnevale, 1993), nor those who adopt the more popular and prescriptive 'how-to' approach (Fisher and Ury, 1981) take much note of cultural factors. Others do pay more attention, such as Bercovitch (1996), as also many of those whose main focus is on cross-cultural mediation (Augsburger, 1992).

In the third category come those conflict resolvers for whom cultural variation is of fundamental significance. We may point here to three contributions in particular: to the comprehensive and highly effective critique of culture-blind 'generic' conflict resolution mounted by Avruch and Black (1987, 1991; Avruch et al., 1991); to Lederach's definition of conflict transformation in terms of a culture-sensitive 'elicitive' approach rather than an externally imported 'prescriptive' approach drawn originally from his experience of the different assumptions about mediation in Latin America (Lederach and Wehr, 1991; Lederach, 1994, 1995); and to Galtung's comparison of Occidental ways of thinking with Oriental and Hindu cosmologies and traditions, usually to the disadvantage of the former (1990; 1996: 196–264).[2] In this category also come numerous individual and comparative ethnographic studies of differing ways of handling conflict across diverse cultures. Fry and Bjorkqvist, for example, include a section that compares conflict resolution practices among the Semai of Malaysia (community resolution through the *becharaa'* process), the Toraja of Indonesia (avoidance strategies), the Margariteno of Venezuela (formal and informal resolution, 'non-violent but often cruel') and the kingdom of Tonga (the *kava* drinking circle), and then set this in turn beside conflict resolution initiatives in contemporary major armed conflicts as in Sri Lanka, Mozambique or Latin America, and beside smaller-scale conflict in inner cities and schools (eds, 1997: 51–231). In our view, the wealth and diversity of this kind of material at the moment swamps most attempts at detailed cross-cultural analysis on this scale. So there is still much work to be done here.

We will leave the last word with Avruch, whose careful overall assessment we are happy to endorse. In defining conflict, Avruch warns us to guard against six 'inadequate ideas' which oversimplify and 'fail to reflect the "thickness" or complexity of the phenomenological world [they seek] to represent' (1998: 12). The six conceptual inadequacies are: to assume that culture is homogenous; to reify culture as if it were a 'thing' that could act independently of human agents; to ignore intercultural variation by assuming that it is uniformly distributed among members of a group; to assume that an individual possesses only one culture; to identify culture superficially with custom or etiquette; and to assume that culture is timeless (ibid.: 12–16). Avoiding these pitfalls leads to an understanding of culture as inherited experience in responding to life's problems (possibly genetically rooted), that is at the same time continually being locally transformed: 'This means (contrary to the reified or stable or homogenous view of culture) that culture is to some extent always situational, flexible, and responsive to the exigencies of the worlds that individuals confront' (ibid.: 20). In terms of the scope for cross-cultural understanding, Avruch frames the debate in terms of two approaches drawn from anthropology:

> One strategy is based on an actor-centred, thickly described, and context-rich – an emic – way of looking at culture. The other strategy is based on an analyst-centred, 'objective,' and transcultural – an etic – way of looking at culture. (Ibid.: 57)

The emic approach 'brings with it all the strengths of ethnography: the attention to context and detail and nuanced translation' (ibid.: 62). On the other hand, there are criticisms that this can end up being 'merely descriptive', may prevent comparisons and cross-cultural insights, and might suggest unhelpful ideas that reify cultures and see them as timeless and uniform: 'this is how the such-and-such people think'. In contrast, etic schemes identify 'underlying, structurally deep, and transcultural forms' that 'enable efficient, retrievable handling of large amounts of cultural data' and allow comparison across cases (ibid.: 70).[3] The weakness of etic approaches is that they tend to oversimplify: 'When the continuums are turned into dichotomies (as they usually are, despite the cautions of their authors), these schemes become very crude instruments for measuring rather fine aspects of culture' (ibid.: 68). In short, Avruch rejects theories that see cultural variation going all the way down to the bottom as in some forms of cultural relativism, because in that case no cross-cultural conclusions could be drawn at all and this would preclude the prescriptive principles on which conflict resolution is based (for a classic discussion on 'rationality and relativism' see Hollis and Lukes, eds (1982); on 'universalism vs. communitarianism' see Rasmussen, ed. (1990)). But, within these constraints, he lays his greatest stress on the importance of an understanding of and sensitivity towards what he and Black have called ethnoconflict theory and ethnoconflict praxis in conflict resolution – the indigenous conflict understandings and resolution practices among the principle parties in the conflict in question (Avruch and Black, 1991; Avruch et al., 1991). This is precisely Lederach's 'elicitive' approach described in chapter 9.

Religion and Conflict Resolution: Islamic and Buddhist Approaches

We now look briefly at Islamic and Buddhist approaches to conflict resolution in order to emphasize the richness of transcultural capacities. What has been called the 'ambivalence of the sacred' (Appleby, 2000) emphasizes the widely recognized point that within all the great world religions are traditions that can be co-opted to legitimize violence and war, but also deep resources for promoting non-violent conflict resolution and peace (Gopin, 2000). This is a function of the way in which these religions emerged from certain social and political backgrounds, and subsequently, as a result of their success, came to permeate every aspect of culture, society and politics in those parts of the world where they prevailed. This enmeshed the deep spiritual teachings in the changing political institutions, social arrangements and cultural practices within which they were reflected, variously understood and transmitted. So it was, for example, that the theme of warfare, endemic in the Jewish scriptures and often enjoined by God at a time when the Jewish people first achieved political self-consciousness as a distinct people in a hostile environment, is not developed further during the long period after 70 CE when there was no longer a Jewish state, but then became prominent again from 1948. Early Christians were predominantly pacifist (to become a soldier meant swearing allegiance to non-Christian gods), but ever since the conversion of Constantine in the fourth century CE just war doctrines have prevailed. The Meccan suras of the Koran are notably eirenic compared with the post-Medina suras when Mohammad was administering the first Islamic *umma* and fighting wars – followed by one of the most remarkable phases of military expansion after his death. The Hindu *Mahabharat* is full of battles, including the setting for Gandhi's favourite text, the *Bhagavad Gita*, which he interpreted as a spiritual allegory. Even Buddhism, usually seen as a peace-loving religion, can become a rallying point for militant chauvinism, as witnessed in Sri Lanka. Religion can be used to sharpen exclusive identities and lend conviction and passion (including a promise of future reward) to destructive political programmes. But, of course, it also offers a deep source for understanding, reconciliation and human fellowship that transcends secular divisions.

Islam and conflict resolution

We noted in chapter 1 Salem's argument that the 'western' assumptions on which conflict resolution rests are not applicable universally (1993; Salem, ed., 1997). In particular, he suggested that concepts and values related to peace and conflict were not necessarily understood in the same way in the Arab-Muslim Middle East as they might be in Europe and North America.

Mohammad Abu Nimer has pointed out that attempts to develop peacebuilding strategies in the Middle East and in other Muslim countries have been constrained because of a dominant stereotype of a bellicose and intolerant Islamic world-view, which brands Islamic and Arab culture and religion as inherently violent (2003). There are also internal characteristics which have inhibited the development of democratic pluralist and peacebuilding activities. This has been linked to a crisis within Islamic thought, where the traditional practice of *ijtihad*, which means the continuous and evolving interpretation of the Qur'an, has declined and been replaced by dogmatic and narrow interpretations. Muslim scholars are now engaged in a process of critical re-examination of Islamic belief systems and are identifying a rich tradition of non-violent conflict management ideas and practices which are vital in the quest for appropriate responses to the political and developmental challenges of the region.

In a partial challenge to Salem, Abu Nimer insists that Islamic tradition encompasses a whole galaxy of ideas, principles and practices which are entirely consonant with a conflict resolution approach – and of course long predate it. In the light of this he identifies guidelines for non-Muslim activists to take into consideration when engaging in predominantly Muslim societies. Initiatives properly set within well-informed cultural and religious frameworks might entirely transform the possibilities for cross-cultural cooperation.

There is an abundance of cultural and religious indigenous practices and values in Muslim communities that can be drawn upon in designing models of intervention to promote social and political change and development; there is no need to mechanically import western-based models which may at best produce a short-term impact, but in the long term typically do not take root in the life of the community. They also eventually run up against certain problematic core values in the socio-cultural structures of many Muslim communities (especially in the Muslim Arab context), such as hierarchy, authoritarianism, patriarchy, and so on. These structures are threatened by the democratic partici-patory elements of community peacebuilding. This is an inevitable confrontation that ought to be anticipated by both interveners and community members. Utilizing the community's local forces for change in such projects is an important step in overcoming some of those structural challenges.

There are therefore significant differences between western modes of conflict resolution and the assumptions, rituals and practices of the Arab-Islamic world. Cosmopolitan conflict resolution in the context of Middle East peacemaking means that peacemakers have to be aware of specific indigenous methods of conflict resolution and reconciliation.

George Irani (1999) has identified *wasta*, which is patronage-based mediation, and the rituals of *sulh* (settlement) and *musalaha* (reconcili-ation) as key elements of traditional practices widely used at the village level throughout the Middle East. This offers a good example of cultural variation in reconciliation mentioned in chapter 10. Through *sulh* and *musalaha*, conflict management takes place within a communal, not an individualized, framework. Kinship and patriarchy are important aspects of the process and elements of the conventional western model are reversed. Mediators are respected not for their neutrality, but for their authority and their ability to both determine and apply a solu-tion. Reactions to being wronged in a conflict range across a spectrum from revenge to reconciliation, and there are strong customs and ritu-als, justified in the Qur'an, which work in favour of reconciliation. Thus while the Qur'an provides for equity in cases of revenge, it also favours forgiveness in cases of apology and 'remission'. Irani (1999) has pointed out that in the Qur'an, the Prophet Muhammad describes the extent and limits of punishment (*qisas*) and retribution:

> O you who believe!
> The law of equality
> Is prescribed to you
> In cases of murder:
> The free for the free,
> The slave for the slave,
> The woman for the woman.
> But if any remission
> Is made by the brother
> Of the slain, then grant
> Any reasonable demand,
> And compensate him
> With handsome gratitude.

This is a concession
And a Mercy
From your Lord

The process of *musalaha* which follows from this injunction is one based on transformation and empowerment. Therefore in order to increase the efficacy of conflict resolution and peacebuilding initiatives in Muslim communities, there is a necessity to emphasize justice, empowerment of the weak, social solidarity and public support.

Both Abu Nimer and Irani conclude that such a use of non-violent peacebuilding strategies and activities in Muslim communities has potentially far-reaching consequences in terms of political and religious leadership, non-governmental organizations and third-party interveners.

A practical example of an attempt to bridge differences and build consensus in problem-solving and conflict resolution on issues of common concern can be seen in the post-11 September 2001 dialogue between the League of Arab States (LAS) and the Organization of the Islamic Conference (OIC) and the European Union. In March 2003 the EU Council President (Greek Foreign Minister George Papandreou), in a speech to the Arab League Summit at Sharm-el-Sheik, set out a common agenda for such an interchange (see box 15.1).

Box 15.1 Proposal for an EU–Middle East dialogue

The European Union believes in a strong, united Arab voice. The European Union desires that the Arab world and civilization take an active part in world developments. We believe you can and should help shape events in a positive way. The European Union actively fights any notion of stereotypes and discrimination, and rejects the notion of a 'culture clash'.

But if we are to avoid culture clash, if we are to create a different vision for the world, we must be able to open up a serious and sincere dialogue – at all levels and on many difficult questions – respecting each others' views as equals. Just some of the questions we need to respond to are:

- How do we address the issue of weapons of mass destruction effectively? Whether in North Korea, Iraq, or elsewhere, Europe does not want to see the proliferation of weapons of mass destruction.
- How can we strengthen multilateral solutions to global crises?
- How do we deal with new security threats such as terrorism in an effective way? How do we understand and define terrorism? What are its causes and how do we address them together?
- How do we enhance our citizens' participation? How do our cultures communicate? Our peoples? Our citizens?
- Can we take practical initiatives together on critical global issues, such as working together to eliminate poverty?

Source: EU Council President (Greek Foreign Minister George Papandreou) in a speech to the Arab League Summit at Sharm-el-Sheik, March 2003

Buddhism and conflict resolution

The idea that conflict resolution is not a western inheritance, but a universal human skill that different cultures practise and understand in different ways, gained further strength with the realization that conflict resolution practices can be found embedded at the heart of Buddhism. Guatama Siddhartha, the Buddha, himself personally practised mediation, as well as meditation, in Northern India in the fifth century BC. He intervened in a dispute over water between neighbouring Indian states and brought them back from the brink of war (McConnell, 1995: 315–29). He also mediated between his own monks when they split into factions, meeting no success until he withdrew from the monks and induced them to reconsider (ibid.: 284–314).

John McConnell has shown how closely a contemporary view of conflict fits with a Buddhist view. He reads conflict into the four noble truths as follows:

1 Conflict (suffering) is part of the human condition.
2 Understanding the deep roots of conflict is the first step to transforming it.
3 By engaging with and transforming the roots of conflict, peace can emerge from conflict.
4 Peace is a way of life, a process, not something that lies in the future, but something to be engaged in now.

A basic idea in a Buddhist understanding of conflict is that 'the causes of the situation are not in the past, where they would be inaccessible, but in the present, where they can be tackled if we have the tools' (ibid.: 185). The causes lie in the minds of the conflictants, and especially in how they 'concoct' wants, desires and illusory projections of the self, to which the self clings.

Conflict arises from *loba* (greed, craving for fixed goals, striving for mastery), *dosa* (hatred, or generalized suspicion) and *moha* (self-distorted perceptions). The self attaches itself to the goals one adopts, misperceives the self as the self-and-the-objects-desired, and suspects others of thwarting its desires. 'Greed, hate and delusion interact within and between the minds of conflictants, manifesting themselves in perceptions and behaviour.' Using these categories, and the precise understanding of successions of mental changes incorporated in the *paticca-samupadda*, the practitioner can 'trace the origins and history of a conflict and observe the psychological interactions that perpetuate it in the present' (ibid.: 7). The mediator, like the meditator, uses awareness as the key tool to transform the seeds of anger, craving, and so on into seeds of compassion and understanding.

One of the best-known exponents of a Buddhist approach to conflict resolution and peacemaking is the Vietnamese Buddhist master Thich Nhat Hanh (1988). As a champion of the Buddhist 'third way' in the Vietnam war, Nhat Hanh developed a non-violent approach to the conflict that rejected both communist and capitalist doctrines, and took an active part in the anti-war movement. Since those days he has practised and taught in the West, expounding 'engaged Buddhism' as a response to conflict and injustice. Speaking to audiences in both the East and the West, his approach achieves a remarkable synthesis of different cultures.

Conclusion

Let us end by reminding ourselves of Avruch's point in the quotation at the head of this chapter. He noted how, contrary to conflict resolution beliefs, most cultures 'at some point' sanction resort to violence in processing social conflict. We have seen how both the Islamic and the Buddhist traditions contain deep resources for non-violent conflict resolution. But we are aware that, like other religions, they can also be used to justify violence and repression. For this reason Avruch concludes that culture needs not only to be understood, but also to be 're-engineered'. He sees this as possible, because he rejects the 'reified or stable or homogenous view of culture' and favours the idea that 'culture is to some extent always situational, flexible, and responsive to the exigencies of the worlds that individuals confront' (1998: 20). We agree with him, but are painfully aware that conflict parties as often as not have a very reified and homogenous view of culture, and that this represents their accepted discourse on culture and identity and the pragmatic interest of those who seek to use it to further political goals.[4] Indeed, a naturalized view of culture can be seen as more universal than the fashionable western social science view that claims to be able to recognize its contingency and fluidity. Irony tends to be in short supply in intense conflict – including that between western constructivists and non-western fundamentalists. This, in our view, is the most testing challenge to conflict resolution in the culture debate today. It carries forward our discussion about radical disagreement in chapter 14.

Recommended reading

Abu Nimer (2003); Avruch (1998); Avruch et al. (1991); Cohen (1991); Coward and Smith (2004); Fry and Bjorkqvist, eds (1997); Galtung (1996: Part IV); Gulliver (1979); Irani (1999); Lederach (1995); McConnell (1995); Ross (1993, 2 vols).

Future Directions: Towards Cosmopolitan Conflict Resolution

History says, Don't hope
On this side of the grave
But then, once in a lifetime
The longed for tidal wave
Of justice can rise up
And hope and history rhyme

So hope for a great sea-change
On the far side of revenge
Believe that a further shore
Is reachable from here
Believe in miracles
And cures and healing wells

Seamus Heaney, extract from The Cure at Troy

IT is notoriously difficult to make predictions about the future in the social sciences. How many Sovietologists predicted the collapse of the Soviet system, even five years before its demise? How many Iranian scholars or academic experts on Islam predicted the replacement of the Shah by an Islamic theocracy, even on the eve of the 1979 revolution? How many analysts or academics warned about the impending attacks on the United States before 11 September 2001, and how many are able to foretell with any confidence the likely outcomes of the war on terror launched by the US administration in response to those attacks? Perhaps the only thing that can be safely predicted is that commentators will later read back into their accounts of the past the *post hoc* knowledge that was so conspicuously absent before. Nevertheless, in this final chapter we will attempt to take stock of the conflict resolution enterprise, first by framing it within a broad assessment of the current state of evolution of world politics, second by summing up the main conclusions of the book within this context, and third by suggesting what some of the key tasks are therefore likely to be for the next generation of those who will be working in the conflict resolution and conflict transformation field.

The Nature of the International Collectivity

Has progress been made from a conflict resolution perspective in the evolution of something approximating to a true international community over the past fifty years, as the first generation of founders? It has long been fashionable in critical circles to scorn the eighteenth-century enlightenment idea of social and political progress, particularly on a world scale (Bury, 1932). But we do not take this view. In critical theoretic terms, as we saw in chapter 14, those in the conflict resolution field tend to follow Habermas (or Held or Linklater) in challenging the ineluctability of Weber's iron cage, or the self-torment of Adorno's negative dialectic, or the infinitely refracting mirror of Foucault, or the all-dissolving solvent of various postmodernisms. Conflict resolution rejects determinism, whether in realist or in Marxist guise. Instead, conflict resolution and conflict transformation insist that, although human conflict is inevitable, the path to violence is not. It offers robust criteria for guiding policy choices in the positive handling of potentially damaging conflict, set within equally clear-cut principles for addressing underlying structural or cultural asymmetries. The field makes no apology for its straightforward value commitment and practical orientation. Of any policy or specific initiative, it is always a good conflict resolution question to ask: but how can we determine if it is likely to work in practice to the advantage of those it purports to help? As chapter 13 made clear, the final conflict resolution criterion for testing whether or not this is the case is the verdict of those affected by it, however difficult it may be to find out what that verdict is, either practically or in a politically or theoretically uncontroversial manner.

In orientating the conflict resolution enterprise within the current phase of world politics, our starting point is the observation that the international collectivity is not a homogeneous entity. It is made up of successive layers of economic, political and cultural deposits, in which later accretions rarely replace earlier strata entirely, but come to predominate or are themselves absorbed in unpredictable patterns. The continuing debate about the nature, significance, novelty and impact of globalization tells us that we should not expect unambiguous answers here (Held et al., 1999). The same is true of disputed understandings about the causes and best policy response to international terrorism. In table 16.1 we offer a schematized model of five coexisting aspects of the international collectivity, none of which can be finally reduced to the others.

The first aspect is the continuing survival of pre-state structures (albeit continuously transformed by rapid changes in communications and technology) in various parts of the world, interspersed with

	Aspect	Organizing principle	Theory
1	Pre-state alternatives	(Charisma)	(Traditionalist)
2	International system of states	Power	Realist
3	International society of states	Order	Pluralist
4	International community	Legitimacy	Solidarist
5	World community	Justice	Cosmopolitan

Table 16.1 The international collectivity: five aspects

newer urban sprawls. Here a genuine Hobbesian anarchy may prevail as older traditional forms of authority succumb to the worst features of marginalization and an often criminalized modernity (which is why the terms 'charisma' and 'traditionalist' are bracketed in table 16.1) (Jackson, 1990; Kaplan, 1994; van Crefeld, 2000).

The second aspect is the unregenerate state system in which state interest remains the political currency and militarized power the main organizing principle. This can be recognized as still dominant in regions like the Middle East and South Asia, and in some eyes continues to prevail at geopolitical level in neo-conservative US circles (Mearsheimer, 1990; Gray, 2002; Waltz, 2002).

Third, there is the international society of states, distinguished by a sufficient reciprocity and mutuality of interest to underpin a reasonably ordered and predictable intercourse of nations. Here, relative power is acknowledged, but even the most powerful share an interest in mutual restraint: non-intervention and cultural pluralism are the presiding values, and international order the organizing principle (Bull, 1977; Wight, 1977; Bull and Watson, 1984; Jackson, 2000).

Fourth comes the international community – an informal term not defined by specialists, but widely used by non-specialists (in more formal terms we define international community as at the Grotian end of the broad spectrum of international society). Here, for the first time non-state actors move into prominence, as well as states, the presiding values are solidarist and the chief organizing principle is international legitimacy as determined through relevant international institutions, international organizations and international law (Doyle, 1999; Wheeler, 2000).

Finally, we can discern the still faint outline of a possible world community in which particularities have been overcome to the extent that genuine cosmopolitan values prevail, suitable instruments of global governance have evolved and international justice is widely accepted as the overarching organizing principle (Falk, 1995; Held, 1995; Linklater, 1998; Kaldor, 2003).

These five aspects coexist, and none is yet finally reducible to the others. Our question about progress within the world collectivity from a conflict resolution perspective can now be made a little more precise. Can we discern a relative overall shift of emphasis over, say, the past 500 years – and particularly over the past 50 years – in a general direction from aspect 1 towards aspect 5? To the extent that this is the case, is it to be welcomed? Is it likely to continue? If so, what are the tasks for conflict resolution? If not, what are the implications?

The Arrow of the Future: Conflict Resolution and World Politics

The response from the field of conflict resolution would be in the form of a 'yes' to the first two questions. Despite manifold setbacks and disappointments, there appears to be an overall direction to world politics so far, in which the development of a global international society of states, and the partial development of an international community, have finally brought conflict resolution principles and practices to prominence within world politics. This is seen as a benign development. Looking to the future, despite all the dangers and challenges, conflict resolution sees every prospect of further evolution in the same direction – so long as strenuous international efforts continue to be made to ensure that this takes place. It is not 'vast impersonal forces' that are seen to determine what will happen. For conflict resolution the future is what we make of it. To recall Elise Boulding, conflict resolution refers to 'those activities in which conflict is dealt with in an integrative mode – as choices that lie at the heart of all human interaction' (Boulding, 1990: 140). We are all agents of this process because we operate intersubjectively, where our perceptions, interests and needs are constantly encountering the perceptions, interests and needs of others. The way in which, and the structures in which, these conflicting encounters are negotiated 'determines whether we are "peacemakers" or "warmakers"'.

As can be seen in table 16.2, in line with conflict resolution principles, we now replace the one-dimensional realist understanding of power, as represented in table 16.1, with Kenneth Boulding's more sophisticated 1989 tripartite analysis, as outlined in table 1.3 (chapter 1). Here 'threat power' is seen to predominate under the realist definition of international system, 'exchange power' under the pluralist conception of international society, and 'integrative power' under the solidarist and cosmopolitan understandings of community. We noted earlier how Boulding saw these as 'fuzzy sets', in as much as each aspect also contains elements of the other two. In chapter 1 we identified three complementary conflict resolution responses to escalation and de-escalation conflict phases (figure 1.3). Here we suggest

Table 16.2 Three forms of power and three associated conflict resolution responses		
Aspect	Predominant form of power	Conflict resolution response
System	Threat power	Conflict containment (also applies to pre-state anarchy)
Society	Exchange power	Conflict settlement
Community	Integrative power	Conflict transformation

the appropriateness of extending this analysis more widely by aligning the three main conflict resolution responses – conflict containment, conflict settlement, conflict transformation – to the three aspects of the international scene where they most aptly apply. The interpenetration of aspects, together with the principle of complementarity, determines that in practice all three conflict resolution responses will need to be applied at the same time in most cases (for example, in regions of 'pre-state anarchy' the violence has to be contained, but at the same time settlements must be reached where possible between biddable and legitimate parties, while attempts are also made to transform the broader structural and cultural contexts within which a sustainable peace may eventually be attained).

It is at this point that a conflict resolution approach can be seen to part company from most realist, many Marxist and some radical interpretations of global politics.

In a Hobbesian world in which every individual is engaged in a power struggle with every other, or states 'have no permanent friends, only permanent interests', conflict resolution has little to build on. This would be a future dominated by a revival of violent great power rivalry, or by an epochal clash of civilizations, or by a collapse of authority into lawless anarchy, or by a 'world-rending cataclysm' in which inchoate market states contend for control in a world bereft of coherent leadership and awash with lethal weaponry – all predicted in quasi-realist writings since the end of the Cold War. Similarly, in a totally hierarchical world, in which classes or castes are immutably divided by relations of dominance, there is nothing to mitigate the permanent and violent conflict between the dominant and the dominated. This would be a future in which the final convulsions of late capitalism eventually implode under the accumulated pressures of internal contradiction, as the global majority of the dispossessed at last learn how to turn the vulnerabilities of capitalism against itself and use this knowledge to vent their rage – as predicted in quasi-Marxist vein. Finally, from a different angle, comes a bewildering kaleidoscope of predicted post-structural futures in which inherited categories and certainties are deconstructed to the point where wheels begin to spin and there is no longer enough purchase to propel a recognizable conflict resolution programme forwards.

In these three visions of the future there is little or no room for conflict resolution. To find examples of the kinds of future that conflict resolution presupposes, we turn instead to those politicians and authors whose predictions and advocacy are variously couched in terms of a continuing evolution of the current international society of states, or a progressive strengthening of genuine international community, or the eventual possible emergence of a universal world community. This is a wide spectrum of possibilities across which different dimensions of the conflict resolution response come into prominence in turn. We will illustrate this through Robert Jackson's analysis of the future of international society in his book *The Global Covenant: Human Conduct in a World of States* (2000), and Richard Falk's vision of a future world community in *On Humane Governance: Toward a New Global Politics* (1995).

Jackson defends the virtues of the present international society of states and predicts that it will continue to predominate in future. He sees it as the best practical response to irreducible human diversity, reflecting the realities of human nature and protecting pluralist values under international law:

> If I had to place a bet on the shape of world politics at the start of the twenty-first century, my money would still be on the prognosis that our great-great-grandchildren will live in a political world that would still be familiar to us, that would still be shaped politically by state sovereignty. Peoples around the world will still be organized and recognized as independent states. They will still coexist and communicate and transact their political business to a significant extent via the *societas* of states. . . . Notwithstanding its very real limitations and imperfections, to date the *societas* of sovereign states has proved to be the only generally acceptable and practical normative basis of world politics. (2000: 424–5)

This is a world in which the *conflict settlement* dimension of conflict resolution is forefronted. The concepts, methodologies and practices of conflict settlement, ranging from diplomacy through negotiation and mediation to various forms of institutional accommodation, can be seen to be integral to the whole enterprise of preserving order and allowing space for communities to develop in their own way within the overarching framework of the international society of states. Within this framework the conflict settlement approach provides the essential capacity for managing unavoidable deep conflicts non-violently.

Falk is more visionary, as befits a leading contributor to the World Order Models Project (WOMP), which for many years has conducted its research in terms of individuals, vulnerable groups and the wider environment within a global analytic framework, rather than in terms of the state system. His idea of humane governance is a normative project that 'posits an imagined community for the whole of humanity, which overcomes the most problematic aspects of the present world scene' (1995: 243). The normative project is summed up under ten dimensions, which range from the abolition of war, through the protection of human rights including the economic and social concerns of the poor, and on to a proper stewardship of nature and cosmopolitan democracy. Falk describes this ambitious programme as 'attainable', while acknowledging that it will be 'incredibly difficult' to achieve given the strength of the top-down forces of militarist, market-driven, materialist globalization. In the end it is driven by the imperative of the survival of whatever is humane in humanity:

> At the same time, such a shift in fundamental prospects for governance is a sufficiently plausible outcome as to make the struggle to achieve it the only responsible basis for positive citizenship at this stage of history. Whether ours is an axial moment of normative restructuring of collective and individual life cannot yet be determined, but such possibilities inherent in the present situation provide us with the best and most realistic basis of hope about how to work toward human betterment, as understood and applied in many separate ways around the world. (Ibid.: 254–5)

This is clearly a framework within which the *transformative* or cosmopolitan dimension of conflict resolution comes into prominence. The challenge centres on a non-violent transformation of present deep asymmetries and unequal relations, that can only be achieved through a holistic conception of structural peacebuilding (economic and political), and an inclusive understanding of cultural peacebuilding that reaches down to the discursive and institutional continuities that perpetuate direct, structural and cultural violence. It is a noble project and would represent a full realization of the deep logic inherent in all conflict resolution values and principles. Even if not attainable in the foreseeable future, to those it inspires it already defines the preferred direction of the arrow of history and thereby informs all contributory conflict resolution undertakings – including even the much more modest holding operations of *conflict containment* that aim to limit the spread of violent conflict and protect the space within which settlement and transformation may eventually be able to operate.

We illustrate this with reference to the possible future evolution of world politics in three key areas: international law, international intervention and the role of the United Nations (see table 16.3).

Table 16.3 International law, international intervention and the United Nations

Aspect	International law	Intervention	United Nations
System	Great power diktat	Intervention (A) (realist)	International organization as tool of great power politics
Society	International law as limited mutual adjustment of state interests	Non-intervention (pluralist)	United Nations as forum for interstate accommodation
Community	International law as instrument of progressive change	Intervention (B) (solidarist; internationalist)	United Nations as repository for genuine cosmopolitan norms; legitimizer for international action

International Law

Uncompromising realists, who continue to interpret world affairs solely in terms of an international system of states, dismiss international law as irrelevant at best and follow Kennan in his scorn for 'the legalistic-moralistic approach to international relations' (1984). Others, following Morgenthau, may acknowledge state compliance in practice with most of the rules of international law, but think that this is no more than a 'self-enforcement' of what in any case simply reflects complementary state interests (1973; see also Barker, 2000: 70–6). Neo-realists do not even discuss international law, and a quasi-realist such as Bobbitt (2002) does not include it as a topic in the index of his 900-page book. He sees international law as a discredited and bankrupt aspect of the passing age of the nation-state, unsuited to the challenges of the dawning era of the market-state (2002: 716, 805, 813, 821).

Those writing in the peace research and conflict resolution field generally take a radically different view. They turn either to 'institutionalist' theorists of the international society of states or to 'liberal' theorists of international community for an understanding of international law within which conflict resolution can operate (Barker, 2000: 76–82).[1]

Here, at the intersection of international relations and international law, Jackson defines international society as 'still predominantly pluralist in its normative framework' (2000: 122–9), so that international law protects the integrity of community within state boundaries, but does not yet extend to determining how international society as a whole should 'act collectively in regard to common goals' (ibid.: 127). This is consonant with the conflict containment and conflict settlement dimensions of conflict resolution.

For Falk (1995), on the other hand, the imagined reality of world community presupposes that state sovereignty would provide 'no exemption from the obligations of international law', drawn as these obligations would be 'as impartially as possible' from the procedures of international institutions such as the UN, or guided by quasi-democratic transnational bodies such as citizen's associations (ibid.: 101–3). Here it is conflict transformation that moves centre stage. One of the most fruitful recent developments in this area comes from the constructivist idea that, although international rules may initially arise from a convergence of state interest, once these international legal rules are normalized and internalized, they subsequently alter the nature of state interest and even of state identity (Koh, 1997; Byers, 1999; Barker, 2000: 82–94, quoting Arend, 1998):

> [A] legal system such as the international legal system does more than simply create expectations and promote stability. It also fulfils the essentially social function of transforming applications of power into legal obligation, of turning 'is' into 'ought'. (Byers, 1999: 6)

This is an admirable encapsulation of the kind of structural and cultural metamorphosis that conflict transformation aims to achieve.

International Intervention

This topic was introduced in chapter 13, so we need only make a few comments here with reference to table 16.3. What we label 'Intervention (A)' – the intervention of more powerful states in less powerful states in pursuit of national interest – is precisely characteristic of the realist world of international anarchy. This is extended by quasi-realists into the use of intervention by 'coalitions of the willing' to forestall emerging threats along the lines envisaged in the September 2002 US National Security Strategy Report (NSSR). This contrasts dramatically with the fundamental international society norm of non-intervention, seen to be constitutive because without it such a society could not exist. And this contrasts again with 'Intervention (B)' – intervention sanctioned by the international community to uphold the solidarist norms of international law (including humanitarian law as well as collective security). According to the principle of mutuality, this implies holding the powerful accountable to cosmopolitan principles as well as others, and addressing the conflicts at the global as well as at the local levels.

Conflict resolution research is torn between these last two positions. Its practitioners recognize the force of the pluralist argument that the non-intervention norm is an essential bulwark against hegemonic intervention, and that to breach it in favour of Intervention (B) may open the floodgate to Intervention (A). But they also feel the moral power of the solidarist argument that to insist on non-intervention and stand back in the face of tyranny, barbarity and state collapse is to hand control to the unscrupulous and abdicate those very values that constitute a humane international community in the first place. We can readily understand why conflict resolution is pulled in both directions. This represents an as yet unresolved clash between settlement and transformation principles within the international society/international community heartland where those principles mainly apply. But there is agreement in rejecting quasi-realist arguments that envisage 'public goods' essential to the society of states being upheld by its most powerful members unconstrained by questions of international law and legitimacy. And, as argued in chapter 8, there is agreement that, once an international intervention purporting to be in the name of the international community has taken place, however controversial, then internationally endorsed conflict resolution principles acceptable to the host population should govern the reconstruction and withdrawal process.

The United Nations

Finally, what of the United Nations and other international institutions and organizations? Neither a realist world nor a radically revolutionary world has much time for the UN. Bobbitt (2002) certainly gives it short shrift, with very few mentions and those mainly derogatory. He sees the UN as one of the 'discredited multinational institutions of the nation-state', incapable of responding effectively to the new challenges of the era of the market-state, and if anything more likely to be used 'as a way of frustrating action in order to control the acts of its strongest member, the United States' (2002: 821). Instead, he looks to coalition-building and cooperation among allies to deliver the collective goods (shared intelligence, surveillance information, missile and cyber defences) needed to 'forestall peer competition and defeat international terrorism'. This is as far as the scope for conflict resolution goes. It is dwarfed by the fight against international terrorism, which Bobbitt sees as a struggle with a non-territorial 'virtual state' (indeed, a form of market-state) (ibid.: 820). In this way, as with Huntington and his substitution of clashing civilizations for competing states, quasi-realists project traditional realist understandings into the future, albeit no longer posited on the persistence of the traditional nation-state. Conflict resolution is drastically sidelined in these scenarios, together with the UN.

In contrast with all of this, we have seen throughout this book how most of those in the field of conflict resolution and transformation, while as aware as any of its shortcomings, nevertheless see the UN as a manifestation of clear progress having been made over the last fifty years from a conflict resolution perspective, and as central to aspirations for further progress in future. We saw in chapters 2 and 5 how, after each convulsion in western-global politics over the past five hundred years, a new system has emerged. The UN system is the first to have evolved into a truly global society of states, as the central process of decolonization quadrupled its membership from some fifty to some two hundred. This has been an epoch-making event, and another example of a surprising transformation in global norms hardly suspected by some of the UN's founders.

Indeed, it is possible to see the conflict containment, conflict settlement and conflict transformation dimensions of conflict resolution as all previsaged in the overlapping UN systems. Conflict containment principles are clearly recognizable in the development of UN peacekeeping, and the way in which it links the UN Charter Chapter VII enforcement provisions to wider processes of positive peacebuilding (see chapters 6 and 8). Conflict settlement principles are central to UN Charter Chapter VI provisions on the peaceful settlement of disputes, with mechanisms ranging from fact-finding and good offices, through to conciliation, mediation and negotiation, and on to arbitration (see chapter 7). There is also Chapter VIII, where regional arrangements are encouraged to play active roles in furthering these aims. Conflict transformation principles on structural and cultural peacebuilding do not have a section to themselves in the UN Charter, but are foreshadowed in UN Charter clauses on equal development and human rights, and are strongly present in the emphasis on conflict prevention that culminated in the 1990s (see chapter 5).

In short, most of those engaged in conflict resolution and transformation hope that, far from being seen to have failed comprehensively in the post-Cold War world as both realists and some Marxists contend, and therefore being sidelined (realists) or replaced (Marxists), the United Nations may, on the contrary, continue to evolve as the only genuinely global political institution capable of delivering authoritative endorsement of fundamental international values, and of conferring legitimacy on the most difficult international undertakings. It has this legitimacy as the institutional embodiment of the first truly global society of states. Those who work in the conflict resolution field are well aware that the UN remains a hybrid organization, reflecting the coexisting aspects of the international collectivity: at the same time an instrument manipulated by the great powers, a forum for the mutual accommodation of state interests, and a repository of cosmopolitan values (see table 16.3). They understand that in the key relationship between the military/economic power of the United States and the legitimacy power of the UN lie the twin dangers of the USA either side-lining the UN or integrating it into its own global strategy. They know that the UN food-for-oil programme in Iraq, for example, was scandalously subject to abuse, and that UN operations such as those in Cambodia, Somalia, Bosnia and Liberia were marred by 'sex, drugs and corruption' (Cain et al., 2004). They understand why, like all statespersons, the UN Secretary-General has to adapt to the existing dispositions of political power, while at the same time trying to preserve and promote the cosmopolitan values inherent in the organization. But many of them are encouraged that, despite all this, and without its own military threat power or independent economic exchange power, the UN still retains its unique reservoir of legitimacy or integrative power. These are precisely the resources in the end most valued in conflict transformation – like those long-range gravitational forces that are easily overwhelmed over short distances, but eventually prevail over greater ones. That is why most of those engaged in conflict resolution see the United Nations as the essential institutional global framework for the realization of conflict resolution goals.

Conflict Resolution: The Next Generation

We conclude by reminding readers of the work of the first three generations of contributors to conflict resolution and conflict transformation as described in chapter 2, and of the fourth generation that has been the subject of the rest of this book. What is the main task for the next generation – generation five (see table 16.4)?

In chapter 2, under *precursors*, we concentrated on the generation between the world wars in the 1920s and 1930s. We suggested that many contributory streams from the inter-war period would feed into the formal inauguration of the field after World War II. At higher levels of conflict we noted how international relations, as a distinct discipline area initiated in the 1920s, at first shared many goals and characteristics with what came to be called conflict resolution in the

Table 16.4 Conflict resolution: five generations

Generation 1	Precursors	1925–1945
Generation 2	Founders	1945–1965
Generation 3	Consolidators	1965–1985
Generation 4	Reconstructors	1985–2005
Generation 5	Universalizers	2005–

next generation, and how it was the takeover of IR by realists in the 1930s and 1940s that created much of the conceptual space later occupied by conflict resolution. In this sense revulsion against the mass carnage of World War I launched the impetus that finally led to the creation of the conflict resolution enterprise.

The next generation, the *founders*, will always hold a special position of influence in the conflict resolution field. This was the time in the immediate aftermath of World War II when the distinctive features of the field were defined and exemplified. We have suggested that seven characteristics in particular marked it out and continue to make it distinctive from other areas of study (Rogers and Ramsbotham, 1999; Woodhouse, 1999). The new formal conflict resolution enterprise was to be multidisciplinary, multilevel and transcultural; it was to focus on the challenge of non-violent conflict transformation; it was to be both analytic and normative; it was to be both theoretic and applied; and it was to incorporate a range of approaches and methodologies in which statistical analysis would inform responses ranging across the 'objectivist'   (rational   actor/bargaining),   'subjectivist' (communications/problem-solving), 'structuralist' (institution-building) and 'transformative' (dialogical and discursive) spectrum. In this way a major challenge was laid down to the deterrence-based security arrangements that held sway during the Cold War period.

The third generation of *consolidators*, continuing to labour under the constraints of the Cold War, achieved three main things. First, they elaborated and filled in what had up until then been lacunae in the field, ranging from clearer conceptualization of the deeper levels of cultural and structural peacebuilding, through more cogent comparative study of peacemaking (negotiation, mediation, problem-solving), and on to engagement with the challenge of various aspects of peacekeeping. At the heart of this was analysis of the sources of prevailing patterns of intractable conflict, deep-rooted conflict and protracted social conflict. The second main achievement was to begin a constructive dialogue with decision-makers on both sides of the iron curtain, so that, building on existing diplomatic expertise, conflict resolution approaches could begin to contribute to a strengthening of periods of détente and softening of periods of renewed confrontation. The third main achievement was to encourage the geographical spread of conflict resolution centres and organizations throughout the world. In this way the enterprise enhanced its international credentials and attained the critical mass required to make a significant contribution when the Cold War unexpectedly came to an end, ushering in the main challenges for the next generation.

With the advent of Mikhail Gorbachev in the Soviet Union in 1985 the geopolitical landscape suddenly changed. This initiated the period

that forms the main topic of this book, the work of the fourth generation of post-Cold War conflict resolvers, whom we have called *reconstructors*. As conflict resolution became better known and more widely
invoked by aid and development workers, governments, international
organizations and journalists, its increased prominence exposed it to
raised expectations and sharper criticism. This book has attempted to
trace the way in which the field has responded. Emphasis has been
placed on greater sophistication in understanding how to bring to
bear and coordinate appropriate approaches at different stages of
conflict – contingency and complementarity – and how to dovetail
peacekeeping, peacemaking and peacebuilding resources. There has
been better awareness of the importance of integrating grassroots,
middle-level and elite support in conflict transformation, as well as
overcoming gender and culture blindness. At the same time those
working in the conflict resolution field, like others, have had to grap-
ple with the question of how to respond to spoilers, criminals and
those who rely on terrorist methods. Great efforts have been made to
think through the conflict resolution implications of the use of military force. And direct critiques of the conflict resolution field from a
number of realists, political economists and critical theorists have
been listened to and, it is hoped, constructively learned from.

So, what is the task for the future fifth generation? We suggest the
title *universalizers*, because in our view it is the 'culture question' that
is, in the end, the decisive one, lying as it does at the heart of the enterprise of cosmopolitan conflict resolution. As we look ahead to the next
twenty years, we see the number one priority as ensuring that conflict
resolution is indeed truly international, as its founders intended. If
the central goal of transforming potential violence into non-violent
change is not shared cross-culturally, then there is no international,
let alone cosmopolitan, conflict resolution field. We hope that the
next generation will come from all parts of the world, and will draw
from their own cultures in pushing forward shared human understanding of the costs of failure to manage conflict non-violently and of
the benefits to be gained by strengthening non-violent conflict resolution capacity within and between societies.

The work of the fifth generation will take place in a world that is
changing rapidly, most especially under the impact of global information communications technology (ICT). It has been a constant concern
of peace researchers and peace activists throughout the modern era
that new scientific and technological knowledge has frequently been
appropriated to advance the military power of states and also the
lethality and efficiency of military systems in general. In the early
years of the twenty-first century the same phenomenon seems to be
about to repeat itself as the massive information processing capacity of

new information and communication technologies is applied to the revolution in military affairs, where precision-guided and automated weapons systems threaten a new era of automated war. The field of peace and conflict studies is also being radically affected by the impact of ICT in such a way that traditional distinctions between national, international and local levels of activity are being eroded and the basis for a global partnership for peacebuilding is being constructed. The Internet opens up a uniquely global or cosmopolitan space which peacemakers can use as a potent tool and environment within which to educate, advocate and problem-solve. The challenge to transform and develop the communications revolution as a technology for peace is one that will be a key priority in the years ahead (Reynolds Levy, 2004).

In this chapter we have referred to the daunting task of cosmopolitan conflict resolution in relation to three possible future alternatives: a revival of the Hobbesian anarchy, a new quasi-realist dispensation, or a neo-Marxist world in which liberal governance is co-opted to serve the interests of global capital. For the first of these to materialize, instead of the wealth of the few spreading and lifting the many out of destitution, the existing islands of prosperity would shrink relative to an expanding sea of poverty as population differentials swamped the potential for wealth generation and distribution. For the second, quasi-realist future to predominate, the threats from a combination of international terror and weapons of mass destruction would be joined by a revived militarized geopolitical great-power rivalry, as current US hegemony comes to be challenged by other countries, acting either singly or in strategic alliances. For the third, neo-Marxist alternative to prevail, current attempts to foster liberal governance would continue to be commandeered by global capital to police the unruly perimeters and reshape dependent societies in the image of the capitalists, unless and until a revolt of the dispossessed destroyed the system. Or there is the grim Foucauldian version of this scenario in which hegemonic interests continue to manifest themselves in terms of power-knowledge through networks of transnational transactions, so that the piecemeal resistances that continually emerge on the margins either remain there, or are themselves co-opted to serve new hegemonic interests.

The genuinely emancipatory cosmopolitan future to which in the end the conflict resolution enterprise belongs, does not accept the ineluctability of any of these three alternative futures – although recognizing their cogency. Instead, based on its analysis of the roots and dynamics of contemporary and possible future conflict, it argues that a steady enhancement of local through to global capacity to transform actually or potentially violent conflict into non-violent processes of change is desirable, necessary – and possible. Central here is the idea of cosmopolitan citizens acting across frontiers to find ways to address both local and global conflict formations non-violently.

We end by repeating that conflict resolution – containment, settlement and transformation – is not an enterprise that simply reinforces the status quo to the advantage of the haves and to the disadvantage of the have-nots. Nor does it make 'noble savage' assumptions about human nature, or ignore the potency of exclusionist ideologies, or close its eyes to the realities of resource conflicts or interstate power struggles. On the contrary, conflict resolution is founded on the idea that the sources of violence, and the identity and nature of its promoters and perpetrators, must be understood if they are to be combated. It knows all too well that in many situations the odds are stacked against it, and that it will take great skill and steadfastness and patience to overcome them. It accepts that conflict is an essential part of social change and that conflictants will have different interests and perceptions, but insists that conflicts be pursued in a way that recognizes the humanity of those with whom we find ourselves in conflict.

In the end, therefore, it is an awareness of shared humanity that underpins the global enterprise of cosmopolitan conflict resolution. And the task of the next generation of workers in the field is to push forward the widening of the circle of recognition towards the culminating point when it is acknowledged in all parts of the world – particularly by young people – that subordinate identities, whether of family, clan, ethnic group, nation, state, class, gender, culture or religion, do not cancel out the deepest identity of all – humanity – even in the most intense political conflicts.

Notes

Chapter 1 Introduction to Conflict Resolution: Concepts and Definitions

1 The OSCE created new institutions for conflict management such as the High Commissioner on National Minorities (HCNM) and the Office for Democratic Institutions and Human Rights (ODIHR). The OAU set up its 1993 Mechanism for Conflict Prevention, Management and Resolution (MCPMR).

2 In attempting to distinguish conflict resolution from conflict transformation, for example, Lederach (2003) characterizes the former as content-centred rather than relationship-centred, aimed at immediate agreement rather than long-term process, and committed only to de-escalation rather than also including escalation to pursue constructive change (p. 33). We see this as a misleading caricature – in fact reminiscent of the way Burton (1990) characterized 'dispute settlement' when he was trying to define conflict resolution in terms similar to Lederach's conflict transformation.

3 As shown, for example, in the titles and/or contents of: Floyer Acland (1995); Mitchell and Banks (1996); Fisher (1997); Kriesberg (1998); Jeong (1999); Deutsch and Coleman, eds (2000); Hauss (2001); Wallensteen (2002b); Cheldelin et al. (2003).

4 This can be seen in the different ways conflict is defined. For example, most social scientists define conflict in behavioural terms, as here: there is conflict 'whenever incompatible activities occur' and 'an action that is incompatible with another action prevents, obstructs, interferes, injures or in some way makes the latter less likely to be effective' (Deutsch, 1973: 10). But some define conflict in cognitive terms, as here: 'A social conflict exists when two or more parties believe they have incompatible objectives' (Kriesberg, 1982: 17).

5 Fisher and Keashly's 1991 complementarity and contingency model of third party intervention related escalation/de-escalation phases such as segregation, polarization and violence to intervention strategies such as conciliation, mediation and peacekeeping.

6 Technically, where one party's gain is the other's loss we should refer to *constant-sum* conflicts, and where both can lose or both can gain, to *non-constant-sum*. However, the zero-sum and non-zero-sum language has passed into general usage, although it is less precise.

7 This has not been the end of the story. Further competitions have been held with slight variations in the conditions, allowing for the possibilities that players might make mistakes in detecting another player's move. Here a population of Tit-for-Tat players do badly, because after making a mistake they get locked into mutual defection, and a somewhat nicer strategy, called 'Generous', which forgives the first defection and then retaliates, outperforms

332

Tit-for-Tat. Generous in turn allows even nicer strategies to spread, reaching at the limit the ultra-nice 'Always Cooperate', which, however, can then be invaded by the ultra-nasty 'Always Defect'. If the players are allowed to remember the outcomes of previous moves, other strategies do well, especially one called 'Simpleton', which sticks to the same strategy if it did well last time and changes if it did badly.

Chapter 2   Conflict Resolution: Origins, Foundations and Development of the Field

1 Sorokin was a professor of sociology in Russia, but left for the USA in 1922 following a dispute with Lenin. He founded the Department of Sociology at Harvard in 1930 and the third volume of his four-volume *Social and Cultural Dynamics*, published in the late 1930s, contained an analysis of war including a statistical survey of warfare since the sixth century BC. Both Wright and Richardson referred to Sorokin's work, but he had a limited influence otherwise. Richardson was born into a prominent Quaker family in Newcastle in the north of England in 1881. He worked for the Meteorological Office, but served from 1913 to the end of the war with the Friends' Ambulance Unit in France. His experience in the war, his background in science and mathematics and his growing interest in the new field of psychology all combined to lead him to research into the causes of war. He took a second degree in psychology in the late 1920s and he spent much time in the 1930s developing his arms race model. During the Second World War he decided to retire from his post as Principal of Paisley Technical College in order to devote his time to his peace research. He compiled a catalogue of all conflicts he could find information on since 1820 and by the middle of the 1940s he had collated his various studies, which were not published, however, until after his death, when Quincy Wright (with whom Richardson had entered into correspondence in his later years) and other academics succeeded in having them issued posthumously in two volumes (*Arms and Insecurity* and *Statistics of Deadly Quarrels*) in 1960. Philip Quincy Wright (1890–1970) was a professor of political science at the University of Chicago from 1923, becoming professor of international law from 1931. He produced his monumental *A Study of War* after sixteen years of comprehensive research, which was initiated in 1926.
2 The first publication from the *UN Intellectual History Project* at the Ralph Bunche Institute, University of New York, is Emmerij et al. (2001). Forthcoming volumes include MacFarlane and Khong on human security, and Jain on women and gender.
3 *Essays in Peace Research*, published in six volumes between 1977 and 1988, and *Papers in English*, published in seven volumes in 1980, represent the main body of Galtung's thinking. Good synthetic statements by Galtung about his general view of the scope and priorities for peace research appear in 'Twenty-five years of peace research: ten challenges and some responses' (1985). *Peace by Peaceful Means* (1996) and the timely and critical assessment of Galtung by Peter Lawler (1995) provide the most up-to-date accounts.
4 See, for example, Boulding (1977), and Galtung's reply (1987).
5 The best general account of Quaker mediation remains Yarrow (1978). See also the work of other Quakers who have worked in the Quaker tradition or who applied and developed Curle's approach: Curle (1981); Bailey (1985); Williams and Williams (1994); McConnell (1995).

Chapter 3   Statistics of Deadly Quarrels

1 This research was regularly updated: see Vasquez (1987) for a useful review. For a more comprehensive idea of the range of empirical data available during the Cold War, see Cioffi-Revilla (1990).

2 A comparison of conflict datasets reveals discrepancies both in criteria for inclusion and in reliable figures for what are often chaotic and politically contested war zones. Despite considerable effort we have found no way of definitively reconciling these discrepancies, so that this list represents a series of compromises between competing datasets. For comparisons of different datasets, see Gleditsch et al. (2002) and Marshall (2002).

3 One of the problems here is defining regions in the first place. Geographical regions do not always coincide with the most important political groupings (for example, Arab North Africa is often included in the Middle East), some countries are difficult to 'place' (is Turkey in the Middle East? is Greece in the Balkans? is Afghanistan in Central or South Asia?), and sub-regions often emerge as the most significant loci for analysis (the Caucasus, the Greater Horn of Africa).

4 For example, Chazan et al.'s list of 'types of domestic political conflict' in Africa is organized in terms of whether they are (a) elite, (b) factional, (c) communal, (d) mass, or (e) popular (1992: 189–210).

5 For example, Holsti (1991: 306–34).

6 For example, Oliver Furley groups 29 conflict causes suggested by Timour Dmitrichev into four somewhat confusing categories: (a) military causes, (b) political/international causes, (c) political/domestic causes, (d) persecution causes (Furley, ed., 1995: 3–4).

7 For example, Mitchell (1991: 25) contrasts 'internal regime wars' which involve 'struggles over the control of a polity's state apparatus and the form of underlying economic and social systems', with 'ethnonational conflicts' which involve 'struggles to defend – and promote – identity on behalf of ethnolinguistic or ethnoreligious communities'; while Rothman (1992: 38) distinguishes between 'interest-based intra-state conflicts', and 'needs-based communal conflicts'. We class Gurr's ethnonationalist wars as identity-secession conflicts.

8 Gurr distinguishes seven types of politically active communal group (national peoples, regional autonomists, communal contenders, indigenous peoples, militant sects, ethnoclasses, dominant minorities) which have four 'general orientations to, and demands on, the state' which may lead to conflict: access, autonomy, exit and control (1995: 3–5). All of these can be distinguished from the 'irredentist' claims of one state on territory beyond its borders on the basis of identity (e.g. Pakistan's claims in Kashmir), which would be classed as a form of interstate conflict.

9 Whether it is possible any longer to distinguish between terrorism and international crime is controversial. Some commentators blur or merge them, as seen in terms such as 'economic terrorism' or 'criminal terrorism'. Others insist on a distinction, such as Phil Williams, editor of the journal *Transnational Organised Crime*, who acknowledges 'an organised crime-terrorism nexus', but argues that:

> the distinction between terrorist and criminal organisations should not be blurred. They still have different objectives – political change in the former case and the accumulation of wealth in the latter. These divergent aims and priorities represent a potential source of tension between them. Co-operation is still more likely to be fragmented and temporary than systematic and long-term. (p. 75)

10 Wehr suggested that what was necessary in conflict mapping was: (1) a short summary description (one page maximum), (2) a conflict history, (3) conflict context (geographical boundaries, political structures, communications networks, etc.), (4) conflict parties (primary, secondary, interested third parties) including power relations (symmetrical or asymmetrical), main goals, potential for coalitions, (5) conflict issues (facts-based, values-based, interests-based, non-realistic), (6) conflict dynamics (precipitating events, issue emergence, polarization, spiralling, stereotyping), (7) alternative routes to a solution of the problem(s), (8) conflict regulation or resolution potential (internal limiting factors, external limiting factors, interested or neutral third parties, techniques of conflict management). Wehr's conflict mapping guide was to be applicable to 'the full range of conflict types from interpersonal to international levels'.

Chapter 4   Understanding Contemporary Conflict

1 For example, the 'seven main approaches' listed by Paul Wehr in terms of the central propositions: that conflict is innate in social animals; that it is generated by the nature of societies and the way they are structured; that it is dysfunctional in social systems and a symptom of pathological strain; that it is functional in social systems and necessary for social development; that it is an inevitable feature of competing state interests in conditions of international anarchy; that it is a result of misperception, miscalculation and poor communication; that it is a natural process common to all societies (1979: 1–8). Each of these will carry its own implications for conflict resolution.

2 Needless to say, most theories escape such neat classification. For example, twentieth-century realist theories of interstate war have tended to combine explanations in terms of the international anarchy (contextual) and the security dilemma (relational), whereas classical realists emphasized 'fallen' human nature (internal). Frustration-aggression theories, on the other hand, have usually combined scarce resources (contextual) and a tendency to aggression in some/all individuals or societies when frustrated (internal).

3 For example, compare five well-supported interpretations of the Cold War: the orthodox western view that the Cold War was caused by Soviet aggression, the revisionist view that attributed it to the global ambitions of capitalist imperialism, the neo-realist view that interpreted it in terms of normal inter-power rivalry in a bipolar world, the neo-liberal view that saw it as a dangerous dynamic generated by mutual worst-case security preoccupations, and the 'radical' view that it was an 'imaginary war' generated by the interest of elites on either side to maintain control within their own blocs (Kaldor, 1991).

4 The same is true of the Bosnian conflict, where the common outside view that this was a three-way squabble between Croat, Serb and Muslim factions was passionately rejected, albeit on very different grounds, by most of those directly involved.

5 As Holsti himself notes, the incidence of interstate war per year per state decreased from 0.035 for the period 1918–41 to 0.005 for the period 1945–95, although this is to some extent offset by the fact that the average number of states rose from 30 to 140 in the two periods (1996: 24).

6 For example, Richardson compared the frequency, duration and costs of wars between dyads of states with such variables as alliance groupings, geographical proximity, population and culture. Since then a flood of material has been produced: see Luard (1986); Levy (1989); Midlarsky, ed. (1989); Holsti (1991); Vasquez (1993).

7   Although many, including major contributors like David Singer (1996), see progress still being made, some commentators conclude that the overall results of attempts at statistical analysis of interstate conflict have been disappointing. After a careful survey of some of the main hypotheses, for example, Holsti finds that '[i]n a significant proportion of the systemic studies of war, there is no verdict' (1991: 5), while for Dougherty and Pfalzgraff, '[u]p to the present time, the statistical techniques have produced no startling surprises, and few conclusive or unambiguous results' (1990: 347). Many of the claimed positive 'external' correlations have been challenged, such as whether rigid alliance systems produce war (Singer and Small, 1968), or whether bipolar or multipolar balances of power are more stable (Waltz, 1979), or at what point in a transition of power between a rising and falling hegemon war is most likely (Organski, 1958), or whether arms races increase the probability of war (Wallace, 1977). The same is true of 'internal' correlations, such as those said to support the theory that 'lateral pressure' from population and economic growth breeds war (Choucri and North, 1975), or that democracies do not fight wars. In an elaborate study of 236 variables relating to internal attributes of 82 nations, Rummel found no significant quantitative correlation with foreign conflict behaviour (1970). In addition, some of the more generally accepted conclusions seem rather obvious, such as that great powers fight more wars, or that alliance membership increases the chance that a state will become involved in war if its partner does.

8   As with almost all classical or neo-classical approaches in the security field, however, the theory has been substantially adapted in the 1990s in an attempt to account for the wider range of determinants now seen to be relevant (Buzan et al., 1997). In particular: the emphasis on the military and political sectors has been expanded to include environmental, economic and societal sectors (introducing the concept of cross-sectoral 'heterogeneous' security complexes); local causes are seen to have global effects and vice versa; states are no longer regarded as necessarily the main referents with 'societal security' introduced as a major theme (1997: ch. 6); and 'microregions' are recognized as subunits within the boundaries of a state. The concept of security itself is taken to be intersubjective and socially constructed (1997, ch. 2). It remains to be seen whether greater sophistication has been bought at the expense of conceptual clarity and predictive power.

9   For example, the Tigris (Iran, Iraq, Syria, Turkey), the Jordan (Israel, Jordan, Saudi Arabia, Syria) and the Nile (Burundi, Democratic Republic of the Congo (Zaire), Egypt, Eritrea, Ethiopia, Kenya, Rwanda, Sudan, Tanzania, Uganda).

10 For example, most major armed conflicts are found in countries low down on the UN Development Program's annual *Human Development Index* (which measures education, health and standard of living) or the World Bank's *World Development Report* – only one country (Colombia) in PIOOM's 1996 list of high-intensity conflicts was among the top fifty countries in the UNDP *Human Development Index* for that year, whereas seven were amongst the lowest twenty-five (Jongman and Schmid, 1997). Similar conclusions are included in the UN High Level Panel Report *A More Secure World* (2004).

Chapter 5   Preventing Violent Conflict

1   This is a narrower definition than that of Boutros-Ghali, who included under the rubric of conflict prevention measures taken to forestall violence, to limit the spread of violence, and to prevent the recurrence of violence after a

settlement (Boutros-Ghali, 1992). Michael Lund confines his definition of preventive diplomacy to preventing peaceable disputes from escalating into violence by 'action taken in vulnerable places and times to avoid the threat or use of armed force' (1996: 37). His definition is somewhat narrower than ours as it focuses on actions rather than other categories of preventors.

2 As Suganami points out, explanation is a more rigorous requirement than prediction (1996). We may note that one event follows another in a regular sequence: but this does not *explain* the second event. Ancient Chinese astronomers found a correspondence between supernovae and social disasters, but in the absence of any adequate explanation we are now inclined to dismiss their observations. More interestingly, the Chinese detected a link between unusual animal behaviour and subsequent earthquakes. Contemporary naturalists suspect that some animals may be able to sense earth tremors below the level of human sensitivity – we can accept an *explanation* linking the animal behaviour and the earthquake, through the tremors that induce them both.

3 Of course, there remain important major powers that are not tied in to the dominant political and economic institutions (e.g. China), governments that perceive their interests as threatened by the dominant system and which are willing to fight against it (Iraq under Saddam Hussein), and many minor states in the global periphery that are less interlocked into interdependent relationships with each other than they are with the major capital and trading systems of the centre.

Chapter 6   Containing Violent Conflict: Peacekeeping

1 This material can be accessed at <www.econ.worldbank.org/programs/conflict>.

2 We are grateful to Peter Langille whose comments on this chapter were of great help in refining our thinking and analysis.

3 On such proposals, see for example Johansen (1990).

4 For early pioneer efforts in this respect, see Frye (1957) and Clark and Sohn (1966). The literature on enhanced UN capability (including rapid reaction and standing forces) is now well developed. For proposals and efforts to develop some form of permanent UN capability in the early 1990s, see Johansen (1990); Carver (1993); Urquhart (1993); Conetta and Knight (1995); Cox and Legault (1995); Kaysens and Rathjens (1996); Schwartzberg (1997); Rosenblatt and Thompson (1998); Langille (2000, 2000b); Mendlovitz and Fousek (2000); Heidenrich (2001).

Chapter 7   Ending Violent Conflict: Peacemaking

1 Even major international wars may be episodes in long-term violent conflicts: about half of the international conflicts that occurred between 1816 and 1992 were the result of 'enduring rivalries' between rivals who constituted only 5 per cent of the dyads in conflict; civil conflicts too may have an episodic character.

2 In his study of 91 civil wars in the period 1945–92, Licklider (1995) finds 57 that had ended; of these, 14 ended in negotiation and the other 43 in military victory. Heraclides (1998), in a study of the endings of 70 separatist armed conflicts of the period 1945–96, found outright victory by the incumbent state in 16 cases, outright victory by the separatist movement in 5 cases, some form

of accommodation in 18 cases – of which two broke down – ongoing violence in 29 cases and an unresolved or frozen conflict in 8 cases.

3 The study of the means by which internal and mixed internal-international conflicts terminate is still relatively new, and we cannot cite many systematic studies of the field. There is agreement that there are no simple patterns in why civil wars end (Licklider, ed., 1993; King, 1997). Licklider suggests that in order to reach an ending it is necessary to obtain political change in the losing side, if there is one, or otherwise on both sides; that both sides must see the military situation as unstable and unlikely to improve; that the weaker side should not be helped by an external government; that 'quiet mediation' and 'mediation with muscle' can both facilitate endings (Licklider, ed., 1993).

4 Although such massive changes are difficult for agents to bring about deliberately, they illustrate the links between conflict resolution and the wider issues of international governance, international economic and political relationships, and the international, regional and economic orders.

5 Curle makes this personal change the basis for his theory of peacemaking: see Curle (1971, 1986).

6 Fisher and Keashly (1991) suggested that conflict resolution attempts should be appropriate to the stage of a conflict, and argued for a 'contingency approach', in which the attempt suited the conflict stage; for example, conciliation at an early stage where communications are poor, consultation when the conflict has escalated and relationships are breaking down, arbitration or power mediation when hostility is under way, and peacekeeping when the parties are attemping to destroy one another (Keashly and Fisher, 1996: 244–9). Webb argues that the case of Yugoslavia demonstrates that the type of sequencing and coordination Fisher and Keashly urge is unattainable in international conflicts, and that their model is too formulaic and schematic, but he accepts the case for the complementarity of a variety of third-party methods (Webb et al., 1996).

7 Although, arguably, responsibility for the failures lies mainly with the major states (Parsons, 1995).

8 For reviews of the UN's post-Cold War role as a conflict manager, see Berridge (1991) and Parsons (1995). For an account of its recent work, see Findlay (1996).

9 The UN has not been able to impose settlements (Parsons, 1995). Boutros Boutros-Ghali retracted his advocacy of coercive peacemaking one year after making it (Boutros-Ghali, 1992, 1993).

10 The South Tyrol settlement is a good example of such a process. The initial agreement of 1946, that South Tyrol should be Italian but autonomous, was interpreted to the disfavour of the German speakers by including a large Italian-speaking province in the area defined as having autonomy. This led to a period of tension crowned by bomb explosions in the 1960s, but then a series of de-escalatory steps led towards an interim settlement in 1969. A joint study commission was set up and after lengthy negotiations agreement was reached on a sequence of steps which would provide full autonomy and cultural and linguistic rights to the German speakers. It was not until 1992 that both sides agreed that the implementation of measures was complete (Alcock, 1970, 1994).

11 There is also an increasing process of learning between peace processes. For example, parties from Northern Ireland visited South Africa in June 1997 and returned with ideas that helped to overcome the hurdle of decommissioning as a precondition to negotiations.

12 The account here rests heavily on Zartman's account of the negotiations (1995).
13 In 1984 Hendrik van der Merwe, a conflict researcher and director of the Centre for Intergroup Studies in Cape Town, had pioneered contacts with the ANC leadership in Lusaka, with the help of the newspaper editor Piet Muller. Others were also active, for example the Foundation for International Conciliation, which engaged in a facilitated mediation over features of a constitution that might be widely acceptable in 1985–6 (see Miall, 1992: 78–80).

Chapter 8 Post-War Reconstruction

1 The relevant literature varies in the sub-set of intervention, reconstruction and withdrawal operations covered. Some spotlight peace implementation operations (Crocker et al., eds, 1996; Hampson, 1996; Stedman et al., eds, 2002). Others concern UN peace operations (Bertram, 1995; Ratner, 1995; Durch, ed., 1996; Ginifer, ed., 1997; Durch et al., 2003). Others again are broader studies of how civil wars end (Licklider, 1993; Doyle and Sambanis, 2000), or of various forms of 'post-conflict' peacebuilding (Lake, ed., 1990; Kumar, ed., 1997; Griffiths, ed., 1998; Cousens and Kumar, eds, 2000; Reychler and Paffenholz, eds, 2001; Lund, 2003; Woodward, 2003; Paris, 2004). All of these are in turn distinct from the parallel literature on humanitarian intervention which includes a different dataset: 1991 Iraq, 1990–6 Liberia, 1992–5 Bosnia, 1992–3 Somalia (Unified Task Force), 1994 Rwanda (Operation Turquoise) and 1999 Kosovo (Ramsbotham and Woodhouse, 1996; Wheeler, 2000; Chesterman, 2001; Holzgrefe and Keohane, eds, 2003).
2 The disastrous unravelling of the post 1994–6 IRW operation in Haiti by early 2004 does not contradict this conclusion: up to and beyond the June 1995 elections, phase one of the mission was generally seen to have been successfully completed.
3 Naomi Klein, *Guardian*, 18 April 2005.
4 With his usual perspicacity, Clausewitz himself was well aware of this – in the sentence immediately following his famous observation that war is simply 'a continuation of political intercourse, with the addition of other means', he adds that the 'main lines along which military events progress, and to which they are restricted, are political lines that continue throughout the war into the subsequent peace' (Clausewitz, 1832/1976: 75).

Chapter 10 Reconciliation

1 Conflict managers have an inclusive approach; a goal of reconciliation; a pragmatic focus; an emphasis on process; a recognition of particular norms and cultures of the societies in conflict; an assumption of moral equivalence; the idea that conflict resolution is negotiable and that outside actors should be politically neutral. Democratizers have an exclusive approach; a goal of justice; a principled focus; an emphasis on outcomes; an insistence on universal norms endorsed by the international community; an insistence on moral accountability; the conviction that justice is not negotiable and that outside actors cannot be morally neutral (Baker, 1996: 567).
2 The TRC distinguished four kinds of truth: factual or forensic truth, personal or narrative truth, social or dialogical truth, and healing and restorative truth (Boraine, 2000: 151–3).

Chapter 11   Terror and Global Justice

1 In the US National Security Strategy Report of 20 September 2002, Theme 4 reaffirmed the long-standing priority in US foreign policy to 'promote the development of free and open societies on every continent. . . . In keeping with our heritage and principles, we do not use our strength to push for unilateral advantage. We seek to create a balance of power that favours human freedom.'

2 The Takfiris (named after their claim to the right to declare other Muslims apostates) are decribed as 'the most radical' of the Wahhabi-Salafists (Wahhabis in Saudi Arabia, Salafis – from *Salaf* meaning 'past' – outside Saudi Arabia) (Olivetti, 2001: 19, 42).

Chapter 12   Gender in Conflict Resolution

1 We are grateful to Sarah Perrigo whose lectures to the Bradford MA class in Conflict Resolution brought this classification to our attention and who, as a longstanding advocate of the importance of gender analysis, helped to develop our thinking on these issues.

Chapter 14   Dialogue, Discourse and Disagreement

1 'Statements of positions' are 'phrases that record what each side is actually saying' (the disagreement), whereas interests are 'needs and concerns that lie below the surface' (Fisher et al., 1994: 39).

2 The programme of the Community Relations Council in Northern Ireland has included: *mutual understanding work* ('to increase dialogue and reduce ignorance, suspicion and prejudice'), *anti-sectarian and anti-intimidation work* ('to transfer improved understanding into structural changes'), *cultural traditions work* ('to affirm and develop cultural confidence that is not exclusive'), *political options work* ('to facilitate political discussion within and between communities, including developing agreed principles of justice and rights') and *conflict resolution work* ('to develop skills and knowledge which will increase possibilities for greater social and political cooperation') (Fitzduff, 1989).

3 Of the alternatives, the 'formalist' paradigm focuses on the study of 'ourselves (and others)' and is seen to be rooted in the confidence of positivist universalism, the 'historical' paradigm focuses on 'others (and ourselves)' and recalls the 'methodological hermeneutics' of Schleiermacher and Dilthey, and the 'comparative methods and theory' paradigm studies 'how we ought to study others and ourselves'.

Chapter 15   Culture, Religion and Conflict Resolution

1 Mead's four-page 1940 essay 'Warfare is only an invention – not a biological necessity' has been talismanic here – taken up, for example, by UNESCO in 1950, and repeated in the 1986 'Seville Statement on Violence' that challenged as 'scientifically incorrect' the idea that war was an evolutionary predisposition in human beings (Seville Statement on Violence, 1989).

2 Galtung distinguishes between world cosmologies, where a cosmology is defined as 'collectively held subconscious ideas about what constitutes normal and natural reality', held by the major Occidental, Oriental and Indic civilizations, where the Occident includes Judaic, Christian and Islamic

traditions, the Orient includes Buddhist, Sinic and Nipponic traditions, and the Indic (Hindu) constitutes the 'vast in-between, whether seen as cross-roads or cradle of the other two' (1996: 211).

3 Avruch is thinking here of examples such as Edward Hall's (1976) distinction between 'high-context' and 'low-context' cultures, or of Blake and Mouton's (1964) 'managerial grid' along the lines illustrated in chapter 1 (figure 1.4) when applied to different cultures.

4 We are indebted to our colleague, Rhys Kelly, for invaluable insights on this topic.

Chapter 16   Future Directions: Towards Cosmopolitan Conflict Resolution

1 Institutionalism ranges from the minimalist conception of regime theorists (Krasner, 1983), for whom international law is hardly more substantial than it was for Morgenthau, through to more substantial concepts akin to those of the 'English School' (Keohane, 1989). Liberal theorists see individuals rather than states as the fundamental subjects of international as of domestic law. Barker (2000; ch. 3) offers a lucid account.

References

Aall, P. 1996: Nongovernmental organisations and peacemaking. In Crocker and Hampson, eds, 433–42.

Abi-Ezzi, K. 2005: *Peacemaking Strategies in the Israeli-Palestinian Conflict: A Re-evaluation*. London: Routledge.

Abu Nimer, 2003: *Nonviolence and Peacebuilding in Islam*. Florida: University Press of Florida.

Ackermann, A. 2003: The idea and practice of conflict prevention. *Journal of Peace Research*, 40(3), 339–47.

Adelman, H. and Suhrke, A. 1996: Early warning and conflict management. In B. Jones, *Study of the Project on International Response to Conflict and Genocide: Lessons from the Rwanda Experience*. York University: Centre for Refugee Studies.

Adeyemi, A. 1997: Post-armistice violence: the upsurge of crime after armed Conflicts – African examples. Paper presented at ISPAC International Conference on 'Violent Crime and Conflicts', Courmayer, Italy, October.

Afshar, H., ed., 1997: *Women and Empowerment*. London: Routledge.

Agger, I. 1995: *Theory and Practice of Psycho-Social Projects Under War Conditions in Bosnia-Herzegovina and Croatia*. Zagreb: ECHO/ECTF.

Aggestam, K. 1999: *Reframing and Resolving Conflict: Israeli-Palestinian Negotiations 1988–1998*. Lund: Lund University Press; Lund Political Studies 108.

Agha, H. and Mulley, R. 2001: Camp David: the tragedy of errors. *New York Review of Books*, 48(13), 9 August.

Akashi, Y. 1994: The challenge of peacekeeping in Cambodia. *International Peacekeeping*, 1(2), 204–15.

AKUF (Arbeitsgemeinschaft Kriegsursachenforschung) 2002: *Das Kriegsgeschehen 2002 im Uberblick [Overview of wars in 2002]*. Hamburg: AKUF

Albin, C. 1997: Negotiating intractable conflicts: on the future of Jerusalem. *Cooperation and Conflict*, 32(1), 29–77.

Albin, C. 2001: *Justice and Fairness in International Negotiation*. Cambridge: Cambridge University Press.

Alcock, A. E. 1970: *A History of the South Tyrol Question*. London: Michael Joseph.

Alcock, A. 1994: South Tyrol. In Miall H., ed., 46–55.

Alden, C. 1995: Swords into ploughshares? The United Nations and demilitarization in Mozambique. *International Peacekeeping*, 2(2), 175–93.

Althusser, L. 1970: Ideology and the state. In Althusser, *Collected Essays*. New York and London: Monthly Review Press, 1971.

Anderson, B. 1983: *Imagined Communities*. London: Verso.

Anderson, M. 1996: *Do No Harm: Supporting Local Capacities for Peace Through Aid*. Cambridge, Mass: Development for Collaborative Action.

Anderson, M. 1996b: Humanitarian NGOs in confict intervention. In Crocker and Hampson, eds, 343–54.

Anderson, M. 1999: *Do No Harm: How Aid Can Support Peace – or War*. Boulder, Col.: Lynne Rienner.

Anderson, M. and Woodrow, P. 1989: *Rising from the Ashes: Development Strategies in Times of Disaster*. Boulder, Col.: Westview and UNESCO Presses.

Annan, K. 1997: *Renewal Amid Transition: Annual Report on the Work of the Organization*. New York: United Nations.

Annan, K. 1997b: *Renewing the United Nations: A Program for Reform*, Report of the UN Secretary-General, UN Doc. A/51/950 (July).

Annan, K. 1997c: UN Secretary-General's reform announcement: part II measures and proposals, 16 July. *Conflict Resolution Monitor 2*. Bradford: Department of Peace Studies, 34–6.

Annan, K. 1998: *Address*. Ditchley Park, UK, 26 June.

Annan, K. 1999: Report of the Secretary-General to the Security Council on the protection of civilians in armed conflict. S/1999/957 (8 September).

Anstee, M. 1993: Angola: the forgotten tragedy, a test case for UN peacekeeping. *International Relations*, 11(6).

Anstee, M. 1996: *Orphan of the Cold War: The Inside Story of the Collapse of the Angolan Peace Process 1992–93*. Basingstoke: Macmillan.

Appleby, R. 2000: *The Ambivalence of the Sacred: Religion, Violence and Reconciliation*. Lanham, Md: Rowman and Littlefield.

Arend, D. 1998: Do legal rules matter? International law and international politics. *Virginia Journal of International Law*, 38.

Armstrong, K. 2001: *The Battle for God: Fundamentalism in Christianity, Judaism, and Islam*. London: Harper Collins.

Ashford, O. 1985: *Prophet – or Professor? The Life and Work of Lewis Fry Richardson*. Bristol: Adam Hilger.

Ashmore, R., Jussim, L. and Wilder, D., eds, 2001: *Social Identity, Intergroup Conflict and Conflict Reduction*. Oxford: Oxford University Press.

Askandar, K. 1997: ASEAN as a conflict management organization. PhD thesis. Bradford University.

Asmal, K., Asmal, L. and Roberts, R. 1996: *Reconciliation Through Truth: A Reckoning of Apartheid's Criminal Governance*. Capetown: Mayibuye Books.

Aspen Institute 1997: *Conflict Prevention: Strategies to Sustain Peace in the Post-Cold War World*. Aspen, Col.: The Aspen Institute.

Augsburger, D. 1991: *Intercultural Mediation*. Philadelphia: Westminster Press.

Augsburger, D. 1992: *Conflict Mediation Across Cultures*. Louisville, Ky: Westminster/John Knox Press.

Austin, A. 2004: Early warning and the field: a cargo cult science? In Austin et al., eds.

Austin A., Fischer, M., and Ropers, N., eds, 2004: *Transforming Ethnopolitical Conflict: the Berghof Handbook*. Berlin: VS Verlag für Sozialwissenschaften.

Avruch, K. 1998: *Culture and Conflict Resolution*. Washington, DC: United States Institute of Peace.

Avruch, K., and Black, P. 1987: A generic theory of conflict resolution: a critique. *Negotiation Journal*, 3(1), 87–96, 99–100.

Avruch, K. and Black, P. 1991: The culture question and conflict resolution. *Peace and Change*, 16(1), 22–45.

Avruch, K., Black, P. and Scimecca, J. 1991: *Conflict Resolution: Cross Cultural Perspectives*. Westport, Conn.: Greenwood Press.

Axelrod, R. 1984: *The Evolution of Cooperation*. New York: Basic Books.

Axelrod, R. and Keohane, R. 1986: Achieving co-operation under anarchy. In K. Oye, ed., *Co-operation under Anarchy*. Princeton, NJ: Princeton University Press.

Ayoob, M. 1995: *The Third World Security Predicament: State Making, Regional Conflict, and the International System*. Boulder, Col.: Lynne Rienner.

Ayoob, M. 1996: State making, state breaking, and state failure. In Crocker and Hampson, eds, 37–52.

Azar, E. 1979: Peace amidst development. *International Interactions*, 6(2), 203–40.

Azar, E. 1986: Protracted international conflicts: ten propositions. In Azar and Burton, 28–39.

Azar, E. 1990: *The Management of Protracted Social Conflict: Theory and Cases*. Aldershot: Dartmouth.

Azar, E. 1991: The analysis and management of protracted social conflict. In Volkan et al., eds, 93–120.

Azar, E. and Burton, J. 1986: *International Conflict Resolution: Theory and Practice*. Sussex: Wheatsheaf.

Azar, E. and Cohen, S. 1981: The transition from war to peace between Israel and Egypt. *Journal of Conflict Resolution*, 7(4), 317–36.

Bailey, S. 1982: *How Wars End: The United Nations and the Termination of Armed Conflict 1946–64*, 2 vols. Oxford: Clarendon Press.

Bailey, S. 1985: Non-official mediation in disputes: reflections on Quaker experience. *International Affairs*, 61(2), 205–22.

Baker, P. 1996: Conflict resolution versus democratic governance: divergent paths to peace. In Crocker and Hampson, eds, 563–72.

Baker, P. 2001: Conflict resolution versus democratic governance. In Crocker et al., eds, 753–64.

Bakwesegha, C. 1997: The role of the Organisation of African Unity in conflict prevention, management, and resolution in the context of the political evolution of Africa. *African Journal on Conflict Prevention, Management and Resolution*, 1(1), 4–22.

Ball, N. 1996: The challenge of rebuilding war-torn societies. In Crocker and Hampson, eds, 607–22.

Ball, N. 1997: Demobilizing and reintegrating soldiers: lessons from Africa. In Kumar, ed., 85–106.

Ball, N. 2001: The challenge of rebuilding war-torn societies. In Crocker et al., eds, 719–36.

Ball, N. and Halevy, T. 1996: *Making Peace Work: The Role of the International Development Community*. Washington, DC: Overseas Development Council, Policy Essay 18.

Bandura, A. 1973: *Aggression: A Social Learning Analysis*. Englewood Cliffs, NJ: Prentice-Hall.

Banks, M., ed., 1984: *Conflict in World Society*. Brighton: Harvester.

Barber, B. 1984: *Strong Democracy*. Berkeley: University of California Press.

Barber, B. 2001: *Jihad vs. McWorld*. New York: Ballantine.

Barker, J. 2000: *International Law and International Relations*. London: Continuum.

Barkow, J., Cosmides, L. and Tooby, J., eds, 1992: *The Adapted Mind: Evolutionary Psychology and the Generation of Culture*. New York: Oxford University Press.

Bauwens, W. and Reychler, L., eds, 1994: *The Art of Conflict Prevention*. London: Brassey's.

Beilin, Y. 1999: *Touching Peace: From the Oslo Accord to a Final Agreement*. London: Weidenfeld & Nicolson.

Bellamy, A. and Williams, P., eds, 2004: *Peace operations and global order*. *International Peacekeeping*, 11(1). Special issue.

Bellamy, A., Williams, O. and Griffin, S. 2004: *Understanding Peacekeeping*, Cambridge: Polity.

Bendahmane, D., ed., 1987: *Conflict Resolution: Track Two Diplomacy*. Washington, DC: Foreign Services Institute, US Department of State.

Benedict, R. 1934: *Patterns of Culture*. New York: Houghton Mifflin.

Benhabib, S. 1986: *Critique, Norm and Utopia: A Study of the Foundations of Critical Theory*. New York: Columbia University Press.

Benhabib, S. 1992: *Situating the Self: Gender, Community and Postmodernism in Contemporary Ethics*. Cambridge: Polity Press.

Bennett, C. 1995: *Yugoslavia's Bloody Collapse: Causes, Course and Consequences*. London: Hurst.

Bercovitch, J., ed., 1991: International mediation. *Journal of Peace Research*, 28(1). Special issue.

Bercovitch, J., ed., 1996: *Resolving International Conflicts: The Theory and Practice of Mediation*. Boulder, Col.: Lynne Rienner.

Bercovitch, J. and Rubin, J., eds, 1992: *Mediation in International Relations: Multiple Approaches to Conflict Management*. London: Macmillan.

Bercovitch, J., Anagnoson, J. T. and Wille, D. L. 1991: Some conceptual issues and empirical trends in the study of successful mediation in international relations. *Journal of Peace Research*, 28(1), 7–17.

Berdal, M. 1996: Disarmament and demobilisation after civil wars. Adelphi Paper 303. Oxford University Press, for International Institute of Strategic Studies.

Berdal, M. and Keen, D. 1998: Violence and economic agendas in civil wars: some policy implications. *Millennium*, 26(3), 795–818.

Berdal, M. and Malone, D., eds, 2000: *Greed and Grievance: Economic Agendas in Civil Wars*. Boulder, Col.: Lynne Rienner.

Berger, P. 1999: *The Desecularization of the World: Resurgent Religion and World Politics*. Washington, DC: Eardmans.

Berhane-Selassie, T. 1994: African women in conflict resolution. *Counter Focus*, 120, 1–3.

Berman, M. and Johnson, J., eds, 1977: *Unofficial Diplomats*. New York: Colombia University Press.

Berman, P. 2003: *Terror and Liberalism*. New York: W. W. Norton.

Bermant, G., Kelman, H. and Warwick, D., eds, 1978: *The Ethics of Social Intervention*. New York: Halsted Press.

Bernath, C. and Nyce, S. 2002: A peacekeeping success: lessons learned from UNAMSIL. In Langholtz et al., eds, 119–42.

Berridge, G. 1991: *Return to the UN*. London: Macmillan.

Berridge, G. 1995: *Diplomacy: Theory and Practice*. New York: Prentice Hall.

Bertram, E. 1995: Reinventing governments: the promise and perils of United Nations Peacebuilding. *Journal of Conflict Resolution*, 39(3), 387–418.

Betts, R. 1994: The delusions of impartial intervention. *Foreign Affairs*, 73(6), 20–33.

Bew, P. and Gillespie, G. 1996: *The Northern Ireland Peace Process, 1993–96: A Chronology*. London: Serif.

Bhaskar, R. 1989: *The Possibility of Naturalism*. Hemel Hempstead: Harvester.

Black, R. and Coser, K., eds, 1999: *The End of the Refugee Cycle? Refugee Repatriation and Reconstruction*. New York: Berghahn Books.

Blake, P. and Mouton, J. 1964: *The Managerial Grid*. Houston: Gulf Publishing.

Blake, P., Shephard, H. and Mouton, J. 1963: *Managing Intergroup Conflict in Industry*. Houston: Gulf Publishing.

Bloed, A.1993: *The Conference on Security and Cooperation in Europe: Analysis and Basic Documents, 1972–1993*. Boston: Dordrecht.

Bloomfield, D. 1997: *Peacemaking Strategies in Northern Ireland: Building Complementarity in Conflict Management Theory*. London: Macmillan.

Bloomfield, L. and Leiss, A. 1969: *Controlling Small Wars: A Strategy for the 1970s*. New York: Knopf.

Bloomfield, L. and Moulton A. 1997: *Managing International Conflict: From Theory to Policy*. New York: St Martin's Press.

Bobbitt, P. 2002: *The Shield of Achilles: War, Peace and the Course of History*. London: Allen Lane.

Booth, K. and Dunne, T., eds, 2002: *Worlds in Collision: Terror and the Future of Global Order*. Houndmills: Palgrave.

Boraine, A. 2000: Truth and reconciliation in South Africa: the third way. In Rotberg and Thompson, eds, 141–57.

Boraine, A., Levy, J. and Scheffer, R., eds, 1997: *Dealing with the Past: Truth and Reconciliation in South Africa*. Cape Town: IDASA.

Boulding, E. 1976: *The Underside of History: A View of Women Through Time*. Boulder Col.: Westview.

Boulding, E. 1990: *Building a Global Civic Culture: Education for an Interdependent World*. Syracuse: Syracuse University Press.

Boulding, E. 1991: Peacemaking as an evolutionary capacity: reflections on the work of Teilhard de Chardin, Martin Buber and Jane Addams. In Woodhouse, ed., 289–302.

Boulding, E. 1994: *Women's Movements for Social Change: Social Feminism and Equity Feminism*, based on her address to the International Sociological Association, Bielefeld, Germany: reproduced by the Women's International League for Peace and Freedom at <www.wilpf.int.ch/> publications.

Boulding, E. 2000: *Cultures of Peace: The Hidden Side of History*. Syracuse, NY: Syracuse University Press.

Boulding, E. 2001: A vision thing. *Peace Matters*. Peace Pledge Union, 34 (Summer).

Boulding, K. 1961: *Perspectives on the Economics of Peace*. New York: Institute for International Orders.

Boulding, K. 1962: *Conflict and Defense*. New York: Harper and Row.

Boulding, K. 1977: Twelve friendly quarrels with Johan Galtung. *Journal of Peace Research*, 14(1), 75–86.

Boulding, K. 1978: Future directions in conflict and peace studies. *Journal of Conflict Resolution*, 22(2), 342–54.

Boulding, K. 1989: *Three Faces of Power*. Newbury Park, Calif.: Sage.

Boutros-Ghali, B. 1992: *Agenda For Peace: Preventive Diplomacy, Peacemaking and Peacekeeping*. Report of the UN Secretary-General, A/47/277-S/24111 (June).

Boutros-Ghali, B. 1993: An agenda for peace: one year later. *Orbis*, 37(3), 323–32.

Boutros-Ghali, B. 1994: *General Assembly Report of the Secretary-General on the Work of the Organization*. New York: United Nations.

Boutros-Ghali, B. 1995: *Supplement to An Agenda for Peace: Position Paper of the Secretary General on the Occasion of the Fiftieth Anniversary of the United Nations*. New York: United Nations.

Boutros-Ghali, B. 1995b: *An Agenda for Development: Report of the Secretary-General*. New York: United Nations.

Boutwell, J., Klare, M. and Reed, L., eds, 1995: *Lethal Commerce: The Global Trade in Small Arms and Light Weapons*. Cambridge, Mass.: American Academy of Arts and Sciences.

Boyce, J. 2002: *Investing in Peace: Aid and Conditionality After Civil Wars*. London: IISS. Adelphi Paper No. 351.

Bracher, K. 1973: *The German Dictatorship: The Origins, Structure and Consequences of National Socialism*, trans. J. Steinberg. London: Penguin.

Bracken, P. and Petty, C., eds, 1998: *Rethinking the Trauma of War*. London: Save the Children/Free Association Books.

Brahimi Report 2000: *Report of the Panel on United Nations Peace Operations*. UN Doc. A/55/305-S/2000/809 (August).

Brauwens, W. and Reychler, L. 1994: *The Art of Conflict Prevention*. London: Brassey's.

Bringe, T. 1993: We are all neighbours. Film. *Disappearing World*. London: Granada TV.

Brinton, C. 1938: *The Anatomy of Revolution*. New York: W. W. Norton.

Britton, R. 2002: The eleventh of September massacre. In Covington et al., eds, 31–3.

Broome, B. 1993: Managing differences in conflict resolution: the role of relational empathy. In Sandole and van der Merwe, eds, 97–111.

Brown, M., ed., 1993: *Ethnic Conflict and International Security*. Princeton: Princeton University Press.

Brown, M., ed., 1996: *The International Dimensions of Internal Conflict*. Cambridge, Mass: MIT Press.

Brownlie, I. 1973: Thoughts on kind-hearted gunmen. In R. Lillich, ed., *Humanitarian Intervention and the United Nations*. Chartlottesville: University of Virginia Press, 139–48.

Brundtland, H. 1987: *Our Common Future*. Oxford: Oxford University Press for the World Commission on Environment and Development.

Brzoska, M. 2004: 'New Wars' discourse in Germany. *Journal of Peace Research*, 41(1), 107–17.

Bull, H. 1977: *The Anarchical Society: A Study of Order in World Politics*. London: Macmillan.

Bull, H. and Watson, A. 1984: *The Expansion of International Society*. Oxford: Clarendon Press.

Burr, V. 1995: *An Introduction to Social Constructionism*. London: Routledge.

Burton, J. 1968: *Systems, States, Diplomacy and Rules*. London: Macmillan.

Burton, J. 1969: *Conflict and Communication: The Use of Controlled Communication in International Relations*. London: Macmillan.

Burton, J. 1972: *World Society*. London: Macmillan.

Burton, J. 1979: *Deviance, Terrorism and War*. New York: St Martins Press.

Burton, J. 1984: *Global Conflict: The Domestic Sources of International Crisis*. Brighton: Wheatsheaf.

Burton, J. 1987: *Resolving Deep-Rooted Conflict: A Handbook*. Lanham, Md.: Univeristy Press of America.

Burton, J. 1990: *Conflict: Resolution and Provention* (vol. 1 of the Conflict Series). London: Macmillan.

Burton, J., ed., 1990: *Conflict: Human Needs Theory* (vol. 2 of the Conflict Series). London: Macmillan.

Burton, J. 1997: *Violence Explained*. Manchester: Manchester University Press.

Burton, J. 2001: Peace begins at home. *International Journal of Peace Studies*, 6(1), 3–10.

Burton, J. and Dukes, F., eds, 1990: *Conflict: Readings in Management and Resolution* (vol. 3 of the Conflict Series). London: Macmillan.

Burton, J. and Dukes, F., 1990b: *Conflict: Practices in Management, Settlement and Resolution* (vol. 4 of the Conflict Series). London: Macmillan.

Bury, J. 1932: *The Idea of Progress*. New York: Dover Publications.

Bush, K. 1995: Towards a balanced approach to rebuilding war-torn societies. *Canadian Foreign Policy*, 3(3), 49–69.

Bush, K. 1998: *A Measure of Peace: Peace and Conflict Impact Assessment (PCIA) of Development Projects in Conflict Zones*. Ottawa: International Development Research Council.

Buzan, B. 1991: *People, States and Fear: An Agenda for International Security Studies in the Post-Cold War Era*. 2nd edn. Boulder, Col.: Lynne Rienner.

Buzan, B., Waever, O. and de Wilde, J. 1997: *Security: A New Framework for Analysis*. Boulder, Col.: Lynne Rienner.

Byers, M. 1999: *Custom, Power and the Power of Rules: International Relations and Customary International Law*. Cambridge: Cambridge University Press.

Byrne, B. 1996: Towards a gendered understanding of conflict. *IDS Bulletin*, 27(3), 31–40.

Cahill, K., ed., 1996: *Preventive Diplomacy: Stopping Wars Before They Start*. New York: Basic Books.

Cain, K., Postlewait, H. and Thompson, A. 2004: *Emergency Sex and Other Desperate Measures: A True Story from Hell on Earth*. Miramax.

Cairns, E. 1997: *A Safer Future: Reducing the Human Costs of War*. Oxford: Oxfam Publications.

Call, C. and Barnett, M. 1999: Looking for a few good cops: peacekeeping, peace-building and UN Civilian Police. *International Peacekeeping*, 6(4), 43–68.

Canada Report, 1995: *Towards a Rapid Reaction Capability for the United Nations*. Ottawa: Department of Foreign Affairs.

Carnegie Commission on Preventing Deadly Conflict 1997: *Preventing Deadly Conflict*. Washington, DC: Carnegie Corporation of New York.

Carnegie Endowment for International Peace 1996: *Unfinished Peace: Report of the International Commission on the Balkans*. Washington, DC: Carnegie Institute.

Carter Center 1995: *State of World Conflict Report*. Atlanta, Ga.: International Negotiation Network.

Carter, J. 1992: The real cost of war. *Security Dialogue*, 23(4), 21–4.

Carver, R. 1993: A UN volunteer military force: four views. *The New York Review of Books*, XL(12), 24 June.

Cash, J. 1996: *Identity, Ideology and Conflict*. Cambridge: Cambridge University Press.

Chagnon, N. 1983: *Yanomamo: The Fierce People*. 3rd edn. New York: Holt, Rinehart and Winston.

Chalmers, M. 2004: *Spending to Save: An Analysis of the Cost Effectiveness of Conflict Prevention versus Intervention after the Onset of Violent Conflict*. Synthesis Report, Centre for International Cooperation and Security, Department of Peace Studies, University of Bradford.

Chandler, D. 2001: The people-centred approach to peace operations: the new UN agenda. *International Peacekeeping*, 8(1), Spring, 1–19.

Chandler, D. 2004: The responsibility to protect? imposing the liberal peace. In Bellamy and Williams, eds, 59–81.

Charters, D., ed., 1994: *Peacekeeping and the Challenge of Civil Conflict Resolution*. New Brunswick: Centre for Conflict Studies: University of New Brunswick.

Chatterjee, D. and Scheid, D., eds, 2003: *Ethics and Foreign Intervention*. Cambridge: Cambridge University Press.

Chayes, A. and Raach, G. 1995: *Peace Operations: Developing the American Strategy*. Washington, DC: National Defense University Press, Institute for National Strategic Studies.

Chazan, N., Mortimer, R., Ravenhill, J. and Rothchild, D. 1992: *Politics and Society in Contemporary Africa*. Boulder, Col.: Lynne Rienner.

Cheldelin, S., Druckman, D. and Fast, L., eds, 2003: *Conflict: From Analysis to Intervention*. London: Continuum.

Chester, G. and Rigby, A., eds, 1986: *Articles of Peace*. Bridport: Prism Press.

Chesterman, S. 2001: *Just War or Just Peace? Humanitarian Intervention and International Law*. Oxford: Oxford University Press.

Choucri, N. and North, R. 1975: *Nations in Conflict: National Growth and International Violence*. San Francisco: Freeman.

Christie, D., Wagner, R. and Winter, D., eds, 2001: *Peace, Conflict and Violence: Peace Psychology for the Twenty-First Century*. New Jersey: Prentice-Hall.

Chubin, S. 1993: The South and the New World Order. *Washington Quarterly*, 16(4), 87–107.

Cillers, J., ed., 1995: *Dismissed: Demobilization and Reintegration of Former Combatants in Africa*. Pretoria: Institute of Defence Policy.

Cioffi-Revilla, C. 1990: *The Scientific Measurement of International Conflict: Handbook of Datasets on Crises and Wars 1495–1988*. Boulder, Col.: Lynne Rienner.

Clapham, C. 1996: *Africa in the International System: The Politics of State Survival*. Cambridge: Cambridge University Press.

Clapham, C. 1996b: Rwanda: the perils of peace-making. *Journal of Peace Research*, 35(2), 193–210.

Clark, G. and Sohn, L. B. 1966: *World Peace Through World Law: Two Alternative Plans*. 3rd edn. Cambridge, Mass.: Harvard University Press.

Clark, H. 2000: *Civil Resistance in Kosovo*. London: Pluto.

Clark, I. 1997: *Globalization and Fragmentation: International Relations in the Twentieth Century*. Oxford: Oxford University Press.

Clausewitz, C. von 1832/1976: *On War*, trans. and ed. M. Howard, M. Paret and P. Paret. Princeton, NJ: Princeton University Press.

Clements, K. and Ward, W., eds, 1994: *Building International Community: Cooperating for Peace Case Studies*. St Leonards, NSW: Allen and Unwin Australia.

Cleves, P., Colletta, N. and Sambanis, N. 2002: Addressing conflict: emerging policy at the World Bank. In Hampson and Malone, eds, 321–55.

Cockell, J. 1998: Peacebuilding and human security. In Wallensteen, ed.

Cohen, J. 1999: *Conflict Prevention in the OSCE: An Assessment of Capacities*. The Hague: Clingendael Institute.

Cohen, R. 1990: *Culture and Conflict in Egyptian-Israeli Relations: A Dialogue of the Deaf*. Bloomington: Indiana University Press.

Cohen, R. 1991: *Negotiating Across Cultures: Communication Obstacles in International Diplomacy*. Washington, DC: United States Institute of Peace.

Cohen, R. 1994: Pacific unions: a reappraisal of the theory that democracies do not go to war with each other. *Review of International Studies*, 20(3), 207–23.

Cohen, R. 1996: Cultural aspects of international mediation. In Bercovitch, ed., 107–28.

Coleman, J. 1957: *Community Conflict*. New York: Free Press.

Collier, P. 1994: Demobilization and insecurity: a study in the economics of the transition from war to peace. *Journal of International Development*, 6(3), 343–52.

Collier, P. 2000: Doing well out of war: an economic perspective. In Berdal and Malone, eds, 91–111.

Collier, P. 2001: Economic causes of civil conflict and their implications for policy. In Crocker et al., eds, 143–62.

Collier, P. and Hoeffler, A. 1998: On economic causes of civil war. *Oxford Economic Papers*, 50, 563–73.

Collier, P. and Hoeffler, A. 2001: Greed and grievance in civil war. World Bank Development Research Group.

Collier, P., Elliot, V., Håvard, H., Hoeffler, A., Reynal-Querol, M. and Sambanis, N. 2003: *Breaking the Conflict Trap: Civil War and Development Policy*. Oxford: World Bank/Oxford University Press.

Commission on Global Governance 1995: *Our Global Neighbourhood*. New York: Oxford University Press.

Conetta, C. and Knight, C. 1995: *Vital Force: A Proposal for the Overhaul of the UN Peace Operations System and for the Creation of a UN Legion*. Cambridge, Mass.: Commonwealth Institute.

Conflict Management Group 1993: *Methods and Strategies in Conflict Prevention: Report of an Expert Consultation in Connection with the Activities of the CSCE High Commissioner on National Minorities*. Cambridge, Mass.: Conflict Management Group.

Coogan, T. 1995: *The Troubles: Ireland's Ordeal 1966–1995 and the Search for Peace*. London: Hutchinson.

Cook, R. 2000: International intervention in humanitarian crisis. Written answer to parliamentary question, 31 January, British Embassy Press Release.

Cook, R. 2002: Guiding humanitarian intervention. Speech to American Bar Association, 19 July. Available at <http://www.fco.gov.uk>.

Cooper, N. 2001: Conflict goods: the challenge for peacekeeping and conflict prevention. *International Peacekeeping*, 8(3), 21–38.

Corbin, J. 1994: *Gaza First: The Secret Norway Channel to Peace Between Israel and the PLO*. London: Bloomsbury.

Coser, L. 1956: *The Functions of Social Conflict*. New York: Free Press.

Cousens, E., Kumar, C. with Werminster, K., eds, 2000: *Peacebuilding as Politics: Cultivating Peace in Fragile Societies*. Boulder: Lynne Rienner.

Covington, C., Williams, C., Arundale, J. and Knox, J., eds, 2002: *Terrorism and War: Unconscious Dynamics of Political Violence*. London: Karnac.

Coward, H. and Smith, G., eds, 2004: *Religion and Peacebuilding*. New York: State University of New York Press.

Cox, D. and Legault, A., eds, 1995: *UN Rapid Reaction Capabilities: Requirements and Prospects*. Cornwallis: The Pearson Peacekeeping Press.

Cox, M. 1997: The IRA ceasefire and the end of the Cold War. *International Affairs*, 73(4), 671–93.

Cox, R. 1981: Social forces, states and world orders: beyond international relations theory. *Millenium*, 10(2).

Cox, R. 1996: *Approaches to World Order*. Cambridge: Cambridge University Press.

Cranna, M., ed., 1994: *The True Cost of Conflict*. London: Earthscan, for Safer World.

Creative Associates 1997: *Preventing and Mitigating Violent Conflicts*. Washington, DC: Creative Associates International Inc.

Crocker, C. and Hampson, F. 1996: Making peace settlements work. *Foreign Policy*, 104 (Fall), 54–71.

Crocker, C. and Hampson, F., eds, 1996: *Managing Global Chaos: Sources of and Responses to International Conflict*. Washington, DC: United States Institute of Peace Press.

Crocker, C., Hampson, F. and Aall, P., eds, 1999: *Herding Cats: Multiparty Mediation in a Complex World*. Washington, DC: United States Institute of Peace.

Crocker, C., Hampson, F. and Aall, P., eds, 2001: *Turbulent Peace: The Challenges of Managing International Conflict*. Washington, DC: United States Institute of Peace.

Crocker, D. 2000: Truth commissions, transitional justice, and civil society. In Rotberg and Thompson, eds, 99–121.

Curle, A. 1971: *Making Peace*. London: Tavistock.

Curle, A. 1973: *Education for Liberation*. London: Tavistock.

Curle, A. 1981: *True Justice: Quaker Peacemakers and Peacemaking*. London: Swarthmore.

Curle, A. 1986: *In the Middle: Non-Official Mediation in Violent Situations*. Oxford: Berg.

Curle, A. 1990: *Tools for Transformation: A Personal Study*. Stroud: Hawthorne Press.

Curle, A. 1994: New challenges for citizen peacemaking. *Medicine and War*, 10(2), 96–105.

Curle, A. 1995: *Another Way: Positive Response to Contemporary Conflict*. Oxford: John Carpenter.

Curle, A. 1999: *To Tame the Hydra: Undermining the Cultures of Violence*. Charlbury, Oxford: John Carpenter.

Dahl, R. 1989: *Democracy and Its Critics*. Newhaven: Yale University Press.

Dahl, R. 2000: *On Democracy*. Newhaven: Yale University Press.

Dahlitz, J., ed., 1999: *Peaceful Resolution of Major International Disputes*. New York: United Nations.

Dahrendorf, R. 1957: Towards a theory of social conflict. *Journal of Conflict Resolution*, 2(2), 170–83.

Danchev, A. and Keohane, R., eds, 1994: *International Perspectives on the Gulf Conflict 1990–91*. Houndmills: Macmillan.

Darby, J. 1998: *Scorpions in a Bottle: Conflicting Cultures in Northern Ireland*. London: Minority Rights Publications.

Davies, J. and Gurr, T., eds, 1998: *Preventive Measures: Building Risk Assessment and Crisis Early Warning Systems*. Lanham, Md.: Rowman and Littlefield.

Davies, J., Harff, B. and Speca, A. 1997: *Dynamic Data for Conflict Early Warning: Synergy in Early Warning*. Toronto: Prevention/Early Warning Unit, Centre for International and Security Studies.

Davies, N. 1996: *Europe: a History*. Oxford: Oxford University Press.

Davis, M., Dietrich, W., Scholdan, B. and Sepp, D., eds, 2004: *International Intervention in the Post-Cold War World: Moral Responsibility and Power Politics*. Armonk, NY: M. E. Sharpe.

Dawkins, R. 1989: *The Selfish Gene*. Oxford: Oxford University Press.

Dawkins, R. 1998: *Unweaving the Rainbow: Science, Decision and the Appetite for Wonder*. Boston: Houghton Mifflin.

de Cuellar, P., Choue, J. and Choue Y.-S. 1999: *World Encyclopaedia of Peace*, 4. New York: Oceana Publications.

de Nevers, R. 1993: Democratization and ethnic conflict. In Brown, ed., 61–78.

de Reuck, A. 1984: The logic of conflict: its origin, development and resolution. In Banks, ed., 96–111.

de Reuck, A. and Knight, J., eds, 1966: *Conflict in Society*. London: CIBA Foundation.

de Soto, A. and del Castillo, G. 1994: Obstacles to peacebuilding. *Foreign Policy* (Spring): 69–83.

de Waal, F. 1989: *Peacemaking Among Primates*. Cambridge Mass.: Harvard University Press.

de Waal, F. 1998: *Chimpanzee Politics: Power and Sex Among the Apes*. Baltimore: Johns Hopkins University Press.

de Wilde, J. 1991: *Saved From Oblivion: Interdependence Theory in the First Half of the Twentieth Century*. Aldershot: Dartmouth.

Dedring, J. 1994: Early warning and the United Nations. *Journal of Ethno-Political Development*, 4(1), 98–104.

Department For International Development 2002: *Conducting Conflict Impact Assessments: Guidance Notes*. London: DFID.

Des Forges, A. 1996: Making noise effectively: lessons from the Rwanda catastrophe. In Rotberg, ed., 213–32.

Deutsch, K. 1954: *Political Community at the International Level: Problems of Definition and Measurement*. Garden City, NY: Doubleday.

Deutsch, K. 1957: *Political Community and the North Atlantic Area*. Princeton, NJ: Princeton University Press.

Deutsch, M. 1949: A theory of cooperation and conflict. *Human Relations*, 2, 129–52.

Deutsch, M. 1973: *The Resolution of Conflict: Constructive and Destructive Processes*. New Haven: Yale University Press.

Deutsch, M. 1990: Sixty years of conflict. *International Journal of Conflict Management*, 1(3): 237–63.

Deutsch, M. and Coleman, P., eds, 2000: *The Handbook of Conflict Resolution: Theory and Practice*. San Francisco: Jossey Bass.

Diamond, L. and MacDonald, J. 1996: *Multi-Track Diplomacy: A Systems Approach to Peace*. Washington, DC: Kumarian Press.

Dollard, J., Doob, L., Miller, N., Mowrer, O. and Sears, R. 1939: *Frustration and Aggression*. New Haven: Yale University Press.

Doob, L., ed., 1970: *Resolving Conflict in Africa: The Fermeda Workshop*. New Haven: Yale University Press.

Dougherty, J. and Pfalzgraff, R. 1990: *Contending Theories of International Relations*. New York: Harper and Row.

Downs, G. and Stedman, S. 2002: Evaluation issues in peace implementation. In Stedman et al., eds, 43–69.

Doyle, M. 1986: Liberalism and world politics. *American Political Science Review*, 80, 1151–69.

Doyle, M. 1995: *UN Peacekeeping in Cambodia: UNTAC's Civil Mandate*. Boulder, Col.: Lynne Rienner.

Doyle, M. 1999: A liberal view: preserving and expanding the liberal pacific union. In Paul and Hall, eds, 41–66.

Doyle, M. and Sambanis, N. 2000: International peacebuilding: a theoretical and quantitative analysis. *American Political Science Review*, 94(4), 779–801.

Drakulic, S. 1994: *Balkan Express*. London: Harper.

Drower, G. 1995: *John Hume: Man of Peace*. London: Vista.

Druckman, D., ed., 1977: *Negotiations: Social-Psychological Perspectives*. Beverly Hills, Calif.: Sage.

Druckman, D. 1986: Four cases of conflict management: lessons learned. In Behdamane, D. and MacDonald, J., eds, *Perspectives on Negotiation: Four Case Studies and Interpretations*. Washington, DC: Centre for the Study of Foreign Affairs, Foreign Service Institute, US Department of State, 263–88.

Druckman, D. and Green, J. 1995: Playing two games: internal negotiations in the Philippines. In Zartman, ed., 1995b, 299–331.

Dudouet, V. 2005: Nonviolence and conflict resolution: towards complementarity. PhD thesis. Department of Peace Studies, University of Bradford.

Duffey, T. 1998: *Culture, Conflict Resolution and Peacekeeping*. PhD thesis. Bradford: Department of Peace Studies, University of Bradford.

Duffield, M. 1994: The political economy of internal war. In Macrae and Zwi, eds, 50–69.

Duffield, M. 1997: Evaluating conflict resolution: contexts, models and methodology. In Sorbo et al., eds, 79–112.

Duffield, M. 2001: *Global Governance and the New Wars: The Merging of Development and Security*. London: Zed Books.

Dugan, M. 1996: A nested theory of conflict. *Women in Leadership*, 1(1), 9–20.

Dukes, F. 1993: Public conflict resolution: a transformative approach. *Negotiation Journal*, 9(1).

Dukes, F. 1996: *Resolving Public Conflict: Transforming Community and Governance*. Manchester: Manchester University Press.

Dukes, F., Priscolish, M. and Stephens, J. 2000: *Reaching for Higher Ground in Conflict Resolution*. San Francisco: Jossey-Bass.

Dunn, D. 1995: Articulating an alternative: the contribution of John Burton. *Review of International Studies*, 21, 197–208.

Durch, W., ed., 1993: *The Evolution of UN Peacekeeping*. Basingstoke: Macmillan.

Durch, W., ed., 1996: *UN Peacekeeping, American Policy and the Uncivil Wars of the 1990s*. Basingstoke: Palgrave.

Durch, W. J., Holt, V. K., Earle, C. R. and Shanahan, M. K. 2003: *The Brahimi Report and the Future of UN Peace Operations*. Washington, DC: Stimson Center.

Elshtain, J.-B., ed., 1992: *Just War Theory*. Oxford: Blackwell.

Emmerij, L., Jolly, R. and Weiss, T. 2001: *Ahead of the Curve? UN Ideas and Global Challenges*. Bloomington: University of Indiana Press.

Encarnacion, T., McCartney, C. and Rosas, C. 1990: The impact of concerned parties on the resolution of disputes. In Lindgren et al., eds, 42–96.

Enloe, C. 1988: *Does Khaki Become You? The Militarization of Women's Lives*. London: Pandora.

Enloe, C. 1993: *The Morning After: Sexual Politics at the End of the Cold War*. Berkeley: University of California Press.

Enloe, C. 2000: *Maneuvers: The International Politics of Militarizing Women's Lives*. Berkeley: University of California Press.

Eriksson, M. 1996: *The International Response to Conflict and Genocide: Lessons from the Rwanda Experience*. Copenhagen: Steering Committee of Joint Evaluation of Emergency Assistance to Rwanda.

Eriksson, M., ed., 2002: *States in Armed Conflict*. Uppsala: Uppsala Publishing House.

Eriksson, M., Wallensteen, P. and Sollenberg, M. 2003: Armed conflict, 1989–2002. *Journal of Peace Research*, 40(5), 593–607.

Esman, J. 2004: *An Introduction to Ethnic Conflict*. Cambridge: Polity.

Esty, D., Goldstone, J. A., Gurr, T. R., Surko, P. T. and Unger, A. N. 1998: The state failure project: early warning research for US foreign policy planning. In Davies and Gurr, eds., 27–38.

Etzioni, A., 1964: On self-encapsulating conflicts. *Journal of Conflict Resolution*, 8(3), 242–55.

European Platform for Conflict Prevention and Transformation 1998: *Prevention and Management of Violent Conflict: An International Directory*. Utrecht: European Platform for Conflict Prevention and Transformation.

Evans, G. 1993: *Cooperating for Peace: The Global Agenda for the 1990s and Beyond*. Victoria: Allen and Unwin.

Evans, G. 1994: Peacekeeping in Cambodia: lessons learned. *NATO Review*, 42(4), 24–7.

Falk, R. 1985: A new paradigm for international legal studies: prospects and proposals. In R. Falk, F. Kratochwil and S. H. Mendlovitz, eds, *International Law: A Contemporary Perspective*. Boulder, Col.: Westview, 651–702.

Falk, 1995: *On Humane Governance: Toward a New Global Politics*. Cambridge: Polity.

Falkenmark, M. 1990: Global water issues confronting humanity. *Journal of Peace Research*, 27(2), 177–90.

Farah, A. 1993: *The Roots of Reconciliation*. London: Action Aid.

Fearon, J. 2004: Why do some civil wars last so much longer than others? *Journal of Peace Research*, 41(3), 303–20.

Fein, H. 1990: Explanations of genocide. *Current Sociology*, 38(1), 32–50.

Feldman, N. 2003: *After Jihad: America and the Struggle for Islamic Democracy*. Basking Ridge, NJ: Farrar, Strauss and Giroux.

Fetherston, B. 1994: *Towards a Theory of United Nations Peacekeeping*. London: Macmillan/St Martin's.

Fetherston, B. 1995: UN peacekeepers and cultures of violence. *Cultural Survival Quarterly* (Spring), 19–23.

Fetherston, B. 1998: Transformative peacebuilding: peace studies in Croatia. Paper presented at the International Studies Association Annual Convention, Minneapolis (March).

Fetherston, B., Ramsbotham, O. and Woodhouse, T. 1994: UNPROFOR: some observations from a conflict resolution perspective. *International Peacekeeping*, 1(2), 179–203.

FFI (Norwegian Defence Research Establishment) 2000: *Why Terrorism Occurs: A Survey of Theories and Hypotheses on Causes of Terrorism*, Report No. 02769.

FFI (Norwegian Defence Research Establishment) 2000b: *Violence, Political Terrorism and Organised Crime: Security Policy Challenges of Non State Actors' Use of Violence*, Report No. 06444.

Findlay, T. 1995: *Cambodia: The Legacy and Lessons of UNTAC*. Oxford: Oxford University Press for SIPRI.

Findlay, T. 1996: Armed conflict prevention, management and resolution. In *SIPRI Yearbook 1996: Armaments, Disarmament and International Security*. Stockholm: Stockholm International Peace Research Institute.

Fisher, G. 1980: *International Negotiation: a cross-cultural perspective*. Chicago: Intercultural Press.

Fisher, R. 1990: *The Social Psychology of Intergroup and International Conflict*. New York: Springer-Verlag.

Fisher, R. 1997: *Interactive Conflict Resolution*. Syracuse, New York: Syracuse University Press.

Fisher, R. and Keashly, L. 1991: The potential complementarity of mediation and consultation within a contingency model of third party intervention. *Journal of Peace Research*, 28(1), 29–42.

Fisher R., Kopelman, E. and Schneider, K. 1994: *Beyond Machiavelli: Tools for Coping with Conflict*. Cambridge, Mass.: Harvard University Press.

Fisher, R. and Ury, W. 1981: *Getting to Yes*. Boston: Houghton Mifflin.

Fisher, S., Ludin, J., Williams, S. and Dekha, I. 2000: *Working With Conflict*. London: Zed Books.

Fitzduff, M. 1989: *A Typology of Community Relations Work and Contextual Necessities*. Belfast: Community Relations Council.

Floyer Acland A. 1995: *Resolving Disputes Without Going to Court*. London: Century Business Books.

Follett, M. 1942: *Dynamic Administration: The Collected Papers of Mary Parker Follett*, ed. H. Metcalf and L. Urwick. New York: Harper.

Forsythe, D. 1977: *Humanitarian Politics: the International Committee of the Red Cross*. Baltimore: Johns Hopkins University Press.

Fortna, V. 1993: United Nations Transition Assistance Group. In Durch, ed., 59–70.

Foucault, M. 1972: *The Archaeology of Knowledge*. London: Tavistock.

Foundation on Inter-Ethnic Relations 1996: *Bibliography of Works on the OSCE High Commissioner on National Minorities*. The Hague: Foundation on Inter Ethnic Relations.

Francis, D. 1994: Power and conflict resolution. In International Alert, *Conflict Resolution Training in the North Caucasus, Georgia and the South of Russia*. London: International Alert, 11–20 April.

Francis, D. 2002: *People, Peace and Power: Conflict Transformation in Action*. London: Pluto.

Franck, T. 2003: Interpretation and change in the law of humanitarian intervention. In Holzgrefe and Keohane, eds, 204–31.

Freire, P. 1970/2000: *Pedagogy of the Oppressed*. New York: Continuum.

Fry, D. and Bjorkqvist, K., eds, 1997: *Cultural Variation in Conflict Resolution: Alternatives to Violence*. Mahwah, NJ: Lawrence Erlbaum Associates.

Frye, W. R. 1957: *A United Nations Peace Force*. New York: Oceana Publications.

Furley, O., ed., 1995: *Conflict in Africa*. London: I. B. Tauris.

Gadamer, H. 1960/1975: *Truth and Method*. New York: Seabury Press.

Galama, A. and van Tongeren, P. 2002: *Towards Better Peacebuilding Practice. On Lessons Learned, Evaluation Practices and Aid and Conflict*. Utrecht: European Centre for Conflict Prevention.

Galtung, J. 1959: Pacifism from a sociological point of view. *Journal of Peace Research*.

Galtung, J. 1969: Conflict as a way of life. In H. Freeman, ed., *Progress in Mental Health*. London: Churchill.

Galtung, J. 1975: Three approaches to peace: peacekeeping, peacemaking and peacebuiding. In *Peace, War and Defence: Essays in Peace Research*, vol. 2, 282–304. Copenhagen: Christian Ejlers.

Galtung, J. 1977–88: *Essays in Peace Research*. 6 vols. Copenhagen: Christian Ejlers.

Galtung, J. 1980: *Papers in English*. 7 vols. Oslo: Peace Research Institute Oslo (also see a comprehensive bibliography of Galtung's publications at <www.transcend.org>).

Galtung, J. 1984: *There are Alternatives! Four Roads to Peace and Security*. Nottingham: Spokesman.

Galtung, J. 1985: Twenty-five years of peace research: ten challenges and some responses. *Journal of Peace Research*, 22(2).

Galtung, J. 1987: Only one friendly quarrel with Kenneth Boulding. *Journal of Peace Research*, 24(2), 199–203.

Galtung, J. 1989: *Solving Conflicts: A Peace Research Perspective*. Honolulu: University of Hawaii Press.

Galtung, J. 1990: Cultural violence. *Journal of Peace Research*, 27(3), 291–305.

Galtung, J. 1996: *Peace by Peaceful Means: Peace and Conflict, Development and Civilization*. London: Sage.

Galtung, J. 2004: *Transcend and Transform: An Introduction to Conflict Work*, London: Pluto.

Galtung, J. and Jacobsen, C. (with contributions by Brand-Jacobsen, K. and Tschudi, F.), 2000: *Searching for Peace: the Road to TRANSCEND*. London: Pluto Press.

Gantzel, K. and Schwinghammer, T. 2000: *Warfare Since the Second World War*. London: Transaction Publishers.

Gastrow, P. 1995: *Bargaining for Peace: South Africa and the National Peace Accord*. Washington, DC: US Institute of Peace.

GCPP 2003: *The Global Conflict Prevention Pool: A Joint UK Government Approach to Reducing Conflict*. London: FCO.

Geller, D. and Singer, D. 1998: *Nations at War: A Scientific Study of International Conflict*. Cambridge: Cambridge University Press.

Giddens, A. 1987: *The Nation State and Violence*. Berkeley: University of California Press.

Ginifer, J., ed., 1997: *Beyond the Emergency: Development Within UN Peace Missions*. London: Frank Cass.

Glasl, F. 1982: The process of conflict escalation and roles of third parties. In G. B. J. Bomers and R. B. Peterson, eds, *Conflict Management and Industrial Relations*. The Hague: Kluwer Nijhoff Publishing.

Glazer, N. 1983: *Ethnic Dilemmas 1964–1982*. Cambridge, Mass.: Harvard University Press.

Gleditsch, N. and Hegre, H. 1997: Democracy and peace, three levels of analysis. *Journal of Conflict Resolution*, 41, 283–310.

Gleditsch, N., Wallensteen, P., Eriksson, M., Sollenberg, M. and Strand, H. 2002: Armed conflict 1946–2001. *Journal of Peace Research*, 39(5), 615–37.

Gleick, P. 1995: Water and conflict: fresh water resources and international security. In Lynn-Jones and Miller, eds, 84–117.

Goldstone, R. 1997: War crimes: a question of will. *The World Today* 53(4): 106–8.

Goldstone, R. 2000: *For Humanity: Reflections of a War Crimes Investigator*. New Haven: Yale University Press.

Goodall, J. 1986: *The Chimpanzees of Gombe: Patterns of Behaviour*. Cambridge, Mass.: Harvard University Press.

Goodwin-Gill, G. 1994: *Free and Fair Elections in International Law*. Geneva: Inter-Parliamentary Union.

Goodwin-Gill, G. and Cohn, I. 1994: *Child Soldiers: The Role of Children in Armed Conflicts*. Oxford: Clarendon Press.

Gopin, M. 2000: *Between Eden and Armageddon: The Future of World Religions, Violence and Peacemaking*. Oxford: Oxford University Press.

Grant, J. 1992: *The State of the World's Children*. New York: UNICEF.

Gray, C. 2002: World politics as usual after September 11: realism vindicated. In Booth and Dunne, eds, 226–34.

Graybill, L. 1998: South Africa's Truth and Reconciliation Commission: ethical and theological perspectives. *Ethics and International Affairs*, 12, 43–62.

Gregory, S. 2004: The failed prescriptions of violence. *Yorkshire Post*, 22 September.

Grenier, Y. and Daudelin, J. 1995: Foreign assistance and the market-place of peacemaking: lessons from El Salvador. *International Peacekeeping*, 2(3), 350–64.

Griffiths, A., ed., 1998: *Building Peace and Democracy in Post-Conflict Societies*. Halifax: Dalhousie University.

Grugel, J. 2002: *Democratization: A Critical Introduction*. Houndmills: Palgrave.

Gulliver, P. 1979: *Disputes and Negotiations: A Cross-Cultural Perspective*. New York: Academic Press.

Gurr, T. 1970: *Why Men Rebel*. Princeton, NJ: Princeton University Press.

Gurr, T. 1993: *Minorities at Risk: A Global View of Ethnopolitical Conflict*. Washington, DC: US Institute of Peace.

Gurr, T. 1995: Transforming ethnopolitical conflicts: exit, autonomy or access? In Rupesinghe, ed., 1–30.

Gurr, T. 1996: Minorities, nationalists and ethnopolitical conflict. In Crocker and Hampson, eds, 53–78.

Gurr, T. 1998: Strategies of accommodation in plural societies. Paper given at the International Studies Association Conference, Minneapolis, USA, March.

Gurr, T. 2000: *Peoples Versus States: Minorities at Risk in the New Century*. Washington, DC: US Institute for Peace.

Gurr, T. and Harff, B. 1994: *Ethnic Conflict in World Politics*. Boulder, Col.: Westview Press.

Gurr, T. and Harff B. 1996: *Early Warning of Communal Conflicts and Genocide: Linking Empirical Research to International Responses*. Tokyo: United Nations University.

Gurr, T., Marshall, M. and Khosla, D. 2001: *Peace and Conflict 2001: A Global Survey of Armed Conflicts, Self-Determination Movements, and Democracy*. University of Maryland: Center for International Development and Conflict Management.

Gutman, A. and Thompson, D. 2000: The moral foundations of truth commissions. In Rotberg and Thompson, eds, 22–44.

Haass, R. 1990: *Conflicts Unending: The United States and Regional Disputes*. New Haven: Yale University Press.

Habermas, J. 1982: A reply to my critics. In J. Thompson and D. Held, eds, *Habermas: Critical Debates*. London: Macmillan.

Habermas, J. 1984: *Reason and the Rationalization of Society*, vol. 1 of *The Theory of Communicative Action* (2 vols), tr. T. McCarthy. Cambridge: Polity. (First published in 1981 as *Theorie des kommunikativen Handelns*. Frankfurt: Surhkamp Verlag.)

Habermas, J. 1992: *Postmetaphysical Thinking*. Cambridge, Mass.: MIT Press.

Haleem, H., Ramsbotham, O., Risaluddin, S. and Wicker, B. 1998: *The Crescent and the Cross: Muslim and Christian Approaches to War and Peace*. Houndmills: Macmillan.

Hall, E. 1976: *Beyond Culture*. New York: Anchor Books.

Hall, L., ed., 1993: *Negotiation: Strategies for Mutual Gain*. London: Sage.

Halliday, F. 2002: *Two Hours that Shook the World: September 11, 2001: Causes and Consequences*. London: Sage Books.

Hampson, F. 1996: *Nurturing Peace: Why Peace Settlements Succeed or Fail*. Washington, DC: US Institute of Peace.

Hampson, F. 1996b: Why orphaned peace settlements are more prone to failure. In Crocker and Hampson, eds, 533–50.

Hampson, F. 1997: Third-party roles in the termination of intercommunal conflict. *Millennium*, 26(3), 727–50.

Hampson, F. and Malone, D., eds, 2002: *From Reaction to Conflict Prevention: Opportunities for the UN System*. London and Boulder: Lynne Rienner.

Hannum, H. 1990: *Autonomy, Sovereignty and Self-Determination: The Accommodation of Conflicting Rights*. Philadelphia: University of Pennsylvania Press.

Hansen, A. 1997: Political legitimacy, confidence-building and the Dayton Peace Agreement. *International Peacekeeping*, 4(2), 74–90.

Hansen, W., Ramsbotham, O. and Woodhouse, T. 2004: Hawks and doves: peacekeeping and conflict resolution. In Austin et al., eds, 295–320.

Harding, J. 1994: *Small Wars, Small Mercies: Journeys in Africa's Disputed Nations*. London: Penguin.

Harris, N. 2003, *The Return of Cosmopolitan Capital: Globalisation, the State and War*. London: I. B. Tauris.

Harris, P. and Reilly, B., eds, 1998: *Democracy and Deep-rooted Conflict: Options for Negotiators*. Stockholm: Institute for Democracy and Electoral Assistance (IDEA).

Harvey, R. 2003: *The Fall of Apartheid: The Inside Story from Smuts to Mbeki*. Basingstoke: Palgrave.

Hauss, C. 2001: *International Conflict Resolution*. London: Continuum.

Hegre, H. 2004: The duration and termination of civil war. *Journal of Peace Research*, 41(3), 243–52.

Hegre, H., Ellingsen, T., Gates, S. and Gleditsch, N. 2001: Towards a democratic civil peace? Democracy, political change and civil war 1816–1992. *American Political Science Review*, 95(1), 33–48.

Heidenrich, J. G. 2001: *How to Prevent Genocide: A Guide for Policymakers, Scholars and the Concerned Citizen*. Westport: Praeger.

Heininger, J. 1994: *Peacekeeping in Transition: The United Nations in Cambodia*: New York: Twentieth Century Press.

Held, D. 1995: *Democracy and the Global Order: From the Modern State to Cosmopolitan Governance*. Cambridge: Polity.

Held, D. 2004: *Global Covenant: The Social Democratic Alternative to the Washington Consensus*. Cambridge: Polity.

Held, D., McGrew, A., Goldblatt, D. and Perraton, J. 1999: *Global Transformations*. Cambridge: Polity.

Heldt, B., ed., 1992: *States in Armed Conflict 1990–91*. Uppsala: Uppsala University.

Helman, G. and Ratner, S. 1992–3: Saving failed states. *Foreign Policy* 89 (winter): 3–30.

Henderson, E. and Singer J. D., 2000: Civil War in the post-colonial world, 1946–92. *Journal of Peace Research*, 37, 275–99.

Heraclides, A. 1998: The ending of unending conflicts: separatist wars. *Millennium*, 26(3), 679–708.

Hewstone, N. and Brown, R., eds, 1986: *Contact and Conflict in Intergroup Encounters*. Oxford: Blackwell.

Hill, S. and Rothchild, D. 1996: The contagion of political conflict in Africa and the world. *Journal of Conflict Resolution*, 30(4), 716–35.

Hinsley, F. 1963: *Power and the Pursuit of Peace*. Cambridge: Cambridge University Press.

Hinsley, F. 1987: Peace and war in modern times. In R. Väyrynen, ed., *The Quest for Peace: Transcending Collective Violence and War Among Societies, Cultures and States*. London: Sage.

Hoffman, M. 1987: Critical theory and the inter-paradigm debate. *Millennium*, 16(2), 234–62.

Hoffman, M. 2004: Peace and conflict impact assessment methodology. In Austin, ed., 171–91.

Hoffmann, B. 1998: *Inside Terrorism*. New York: Columbia University Press.

Holbrooke, R. 1999: *To End a War*. New York: The Modern Library.

Holliday, D. and Stanley, W. 1993: Building the peace: preliminary lessons from El Salvador. *Journal of International Affairs*, 46(2), 415–38.

Hollis, M. and Lukes, S., eds, 1982: *Rationality and Relativism*. Oxford: Blackwell.

Holm, T. and Eide, E., eds, 2000: *Peacebuilding and Police Reform*. London: Frank Cass.

Holsti, K. 1991: *Peace and War: Armed Conflicts and International Order 1648–1989*. Cambridge: Cambridge University Press.

Holsti, K. 1992: Governance without government: polyarchy in nineteenth century European international politics. In J. Rosenau and E. Czempiel, eds, *Governance Without Government: Order and Change in World Politics*. Cambridge: Cambridge University Press.

Holsti, K. 1996: *The State, War, and the State of War*. Cambridge: Cambridge University Press.

Holt, D. 1994: United Nations Angola Verification Mission II. In Clements and Ward, eds, 302–10.

Holzgrefe, J. and Keohane, R., eds, 2003: *Humanitarian Intervention: Ethical, Legal and Political Dilemmas*. Cambridge: Cambridge University Press.

Homer-Dixon, T. 1991: On the threshold: environmental changes as causes of acute conflict. *International Security*, 16(2), 7–16.

Homer-Dixon, T. 1994: Environmental scarcities and violent conflict: evidence from cases. *International Security*, 19(1), 5–40.

Homer-Dixon, T. 1995: On the threshold: environmental changes as causes of acute conflict. In Lynn-Jones and Miller, eds, 43–83.

Hopmann, P. 2001. Disintegrating states: separating without violence. In Zartman, ed., 113–64.

Horowitz, D. 1985: *Ethnic Groups in Conflict*. Berkeley: University of California Press.

Horowitz, D. 1991: Making moderation pay: the comparative politics of ethnic conflict management. In Montville, ed., 451–75.

Horowitz, D. 1993: Democracy in divided societies. *Journal of Democracy*, 4(4), 18–38.

Howard, M. 1976: *War in European History*. London: Oxford University Press.

Howard, M. 1983: *The Causes of War and Other Essays*. Cambridge, Mass: Harvard University Press.

Howard, M. 2000: *The Invention of Peace. Reflections on War and International Order*. London: Profile Books.

Human Rights Watch 1995: *Slaughter Among Neighbours: The Political Origins of Communal Violence*. New Haven: Yale University Press.

Hume, C. 1994: *Ending Mozambique's War: The Role of Mediation and Good Offices*. Washington, DC: US Institute of Peace.

Huntington, S. 1991: *The Third Wave: Democratization in the Late Twentieth Century*. Norman: University of Oklahoma Press.

Huntington, S. 1996: *The Clash of Civilizations and the Remaking of World Order*. New York: Simon and Schuster.

Ikle, F. 1971: *Every War Must End*. New York: University of Columbia Press.

Independent Working Group on the Future of the United Nations 1995: *The United Nations In Its Second Half-Century* (a project supported by Yale University and the Ford Foundation).

International Alert 1996: *Resource Pack for Conflict Transformation*. London: International Alert.

International Commission on Intervention and State Sovereignty (ICISS) 2001: *The Responsibility to Protect*. Ottawa, Canada: International Development Research Centre.

International Commission on the Balkans 1996: *Unfinished Peace: Report of the International Commission on the Balkans*. Washington, DC: Brookings Institution.

International Crisis Group 2002: *Middle East End-Game: Getting To A Comprehensive Arab-Israeli Peace Settlement*. Washington, DC: International Crisis Group, 16 July.

International Federation of Red Cross and Red Crescent Societies (IFRCRCS) 1996: *World Disasters Report 1996*. Oxford: Oxford University Press.

International Institute of Strategic Studies (IISS) 1997: Chart of armed conflict. In IISS, *Military Balance*. London: IISS.

International Institute of Strategic Studies (IISS) 2004: *Military Survey*. London: IISS.

International Peace Academy (IPA) 2001: *Executive Summary, Refashioning the Dialogue: Regional Perspectives on the Brahimi Report on UN Peace Operations*. London: IPA, March.

Irani, G. 1999: Islamic mediation techniques for Middle East conflicts. *MERIA Journal*, 3(2).

Jabri, V., ed., 1990: *Mediating Conflict: Decision-Making and Western Intervention in Namibia*. Manchester: Manchester University Press.

Jabri, V. 1996: *Discourses on Violence: Conflict Analysis Reconsidered*. Manchester: Manchester University Press.

Jackson, R. 1990: *Quasi-states, Sovereignty, International Relations and the Third World*. Cambridge: Cambridge University Press.

Jackson, R. 2000: *The Global Covenant: Human Conduct in a World of States*. Oxford: Oxford University Press.

Jain, D. (forthcoming): *Women Enrich the UN and Development*. University of Indiana Press.

Janis, I. 1973: *Victims of Groupthink*. Boston, Mass.: Houghton Mifflin.

Janning, J. and Brusis, M. 1997: *Exploring Futures for Kosovo: Kosovo Albanians and Serbs in Dialogue*. Munich: Research Group on European Affairs.

Jaster, R. 1990: The 1988 Peace Accords and the future of South-Western Africa. *Adelphi Papers*. London: IISS.

Jean, F., ed., 1993: *Life, Death and Aid: The Medecins sans Frontières Report on World Crisis Intervention*. London: Routledge.

Jegen, M. E. 1996: *Sign of Hope*. Uppsala: Life and Peace Institute.

Jentleson, B., ed., 1999: *Opportunities Missed, Opportunities Seized: Preventive Diplomacy in the Post-Cold War World*. Carnegie Commission on Preventing Deadly Conflict. New York: Rowman and Littlefield.

Jentleson, B. 1999: Preventive diplomacy and ethnic conflict: possible, difficult, necessary. In Jentleson, ed.

Jeong, H.-W., ed., 1999: *Conflict Resolution: Dynamics, Process and Structure*. Aldershot: Ashgate.

Jervis, R. 1976: *Perception and Misperception in International Politics*. Princeton: Princeton University Press.

Jervis, R. 1982: Security regimes. *International Organization*, 36(2), 357–78.

Johansen, R. C. 1990: UN peacekeeping: the changing utility of military force. *Third World Quarterly*, 12 April, 53–70.

Jones, B. 2002: The challenges of strategic coordination. In Stedman et al., eds, 89–115.

Jones, D. 1999: *Cosmopolitan Mediation? Conflict Resolution and the Oslo Accords*. Manchester: Manchester University Press.

Jongman, A. and Schmid, A. 1996: Contemporary armed conflicts – a brief survey. In van Tongeren, ed., 25–9.

Jongman, A. and Schmid, A. 1997: *Mapping Violent Conflicts and Human Rights Violations in the mid-1990s*. London: Leiden University.

Juergensmeyer, M. 2000: *Terror in the Mind of God: The Global Rise of Religious Violence*. Berkeley: University of California Press.

Jung, D., Schlichte, K. and Siegelberg, J. 1996: Ongoing wars and their explanation. In van de Goor et al., eds, 50–66.

Kacowicz, A. 1995: Explaining zones of peace: democracies as satisfied powers? *Journal of Conflict Resolution*, 32(3): 265–76.

Kagan, D. 1995: *On the Origins of War*. New York: Doubleday.

Kaldor, M. 1991: *The Imaginary War: Understanding the East–West Conflict*. London: Blackwell.

Kaldor, M. 1999/2001: *New and Old Wars: Organized Violence in a Global Era*. Cambridge: Polity.

Kaldor, M. 2003: *Global Civil Society*. Cambridge: Polity.

Kaldor, M. and Vashee, B., eds, 1997: *New Wars: Restructuring the Global Military Sector*. London: Pinter.

Kapila, M. and Wermester, K. 2002: Development and conflict: new approaches in the United Kingdom. In Hampson and Malone, eds.

Kaplan, R. 1994: The coming anarchy. *Atlantic Monthly*, 273 (Feb), 44–76.

Karl, T. 1992: El Salvador's negotiated revolution. *Foreign Affairs* (Spring), 147–64.

Karp, A. 1994: The arms trade revolution: the major impact of small arms. *Washington Quarterly*, 17(4), 65–77.

Kaufmann, C. 1996: Possible and impossible solutions to ethnic civil wars. *International Security*, 20(4), 136–75.

Kaysens, C. and Rathjens, G. 1996: *Peace Operations by the United Nations: The Case for a Volunteer UN Military Force*. Cambridge, Mass.: Committee on International Security Studies.

Keashly, L. and Fisher, R. 1996: A contingency perspective on conflict interventions: theoretical and practical considerations. In Bercovitch, ed., 235–61.

Keegan, J. 1993: *A History of Warfare*. New York: Alfred A. Knopf.

Keen, D. 1995: *The Benefits of Famine*. Princeton, NJ: Princeton University Press.

Keen, D. 1998: *The Economic Function of Violence in Civil Wars*. Adelphi Paper 320. London: IISS.

Kelly, G. 1955: *A Theory of Personality: The Psychology of Personal Constructs*. New York: W. W. Norton.

Kelly, R. 2002: Liberating Memory. PhD thesis. University of Bradford.

Kelman, H. 1992: Informal mediation by the scholar/practitioner. In Bercovitch and Rubin, eds, 191–237.

Kelman, H. 1996: The interactive problem-solving approach. In Crocker and Hampson, eds, 500–20.

Kelman, H. 1997: Social-psychological dimensions of international conflict. In Zartman and Rasmussen, eds, 191–237.

Kelman, H. 1999: Transforming the relationship between former enemies: a social-psychological analysis. In Rothstein, ed., 193–205.

Kelman, H. and Cohen, S. 1976: The problem-solving workshop: a social-psychological contribution to the resolution of international conflicts. *Journal of Peace Research*, 13(2), 79–90.

Kemp, W., 2001: *Quiet Diplomacy in Action: The OSCE High Commissioner on National Minorities*. The Hague: Kluwer Law International.

Kennan, G. 1984: *American Diplomacy*. Chicago: University of Chicago Press.

Kennedy, P. 1993: *Preparing for the Twenty First Century*. London: Harper Collins.

Keohane, R. 1989: *International Institutions and State Power: Essays in International Relations Theory*. Boulder, Col.: Westview Press.

Keohane, R. and Nye, J. 1986: *Power and Interdependence*. Harvard: Harper Collins.

Kerman, C. 1974: *Creative Tension: The Life and Thought of Kenneth Boulding*. Ann Arbor: Michigan.

Keukeleire, S. 1994: The European Community and conflict management. In Bauwens and Reychler, eds, 137–79.

Khrychikov, S. and Miall, H. 2002: Conflict prevention in Estonia. *Security Dialogue*, 33(2), 19–208.

Kim, S. and Russett, B. 1996: The new politics of voting alignments in the United Nations General Assembly. *International Organization*, 50, 629–52.

King, C. 1997: *Ending Civil Wars*. Adelphi Paper 308. Oxford: Oxford University Press for the IISS.

Kingma, K. 1997: Demobilization of combatants after civil wars in Africa and their reintegration into civilian life. *Policy Sciences*, 30(3), 51–165.

Kingma, K. 2001: Demobilizing and reintegrating former combatants. In Reychler and Paffenholz, eds, 405–15.

Kinloch, S. 1996: Utopian or pragmatic? A UN permanent military volunteer force. *International Peacekeeping*, 3(4), 166–90.

Kiss, E. 2000: Moral ambition within and beyond political constraints: reflections on restorative justice. In Rotberg and Thompson, eds, 68–98.

Koh, H. 1997: Why do nations obey international law? *Yale Law Journal*, 2599.

Kouchner, B. 2001: A first-hand perspective from Kosovo (quoted Alexander Ramsbotham). *UN and Conflict Monitor*. London: United Nations Association.

Krasner, S. 1983: *International Regimes*. Ithaca: Cornell University Press.

Krause, K. 1996: Armaments and conflict: the causes and consequences of 'military development'. In van de Goor et al., eds, 173–96.

Kreimer, A., Eriksson, J., Muscat, R., Arnold, M. and Scott, C. 1998: *The World Bank's Experience With Post-Conflict Reconstruction*. Washington, DC: World Bank.

Kressell, K. and Pruitt, D., eds, 1989: *Mediation Research*. San Francisco: Jossey-Bass.

Kriesberg, L. 1973: *The Sociology of Social Conflicts*. Englewood Cliffs, NJ: Prentice-Hall.

Kriesberg, L. 1982: *Social Conflicts*. Englewood Cliffs, NJ: Prentice-Hall.

Kriesberg, L. 1991: Conflict resolution applications to peace studies. *Peace and Change* 16(4): 400–17.

Kriesberg, L. 1992: *International Conflict Resolution*. New Haven, Conn.: Yale University Press.

Kriesberg, L. 1992b: *De-Escalation and Transformation of International Conflict*. New Haven, Conn.: Yale University Press.

Kriesberg, L. 1997: The development of the conflict resolution field. In Zartman and Rasmussen, eds, 51–77.

Kriesberg, L. 1998: *Constructive Conflicts: From Escalation to Resolution*. Lanham: Rowman & Littlefield.

Kriesberg, L. 1998b: Reconciliation: conceptual and empirical issues. Paper given at the International Studies Association Annual Convention, Minneapolis, March.

Kriesberg, L. 2001: Mediation and the transformation of the Israeli-Palestinian conflict. *Journal of Peace Research*, 38(3), 373–92.

Kriesberg, L., Northrup, A. and Thorson, S., eds, 1989: *Intractable Conflicts and Their Transformation*. Syracuse, NY: Syracuse University Press.

Kritz, N., ed., 1995: *Transitional Justice: How Emerging Democracies Reckon with Former Regimes*. Vol. 1: *General Considerations*. Washington, DC: US Institute of Peace.

Kritz, N. 1996: The rule of law in the postconflict phase: building a stable peace. In Crocker and Hampson, eds, 587–606.

Krska, V. 1997: Peacekeeping in Angola (UNAVEM I and II). *International Peacekeeping*, 4(1), 75–97.

Kumar, K., ed., 1997: *Rebuilding Societies After Civil War: Critical Roles for International Assistance*. Boulder, Col.: Lynne Rienner.

Kumar, K., ed., 1998: *Postconflict Elections, Democratization and International Assistance*. Boulder, Col.: Lynne Rienner.

Kung, H. and Kuschel, K.-J., eds, 1993: *A Global Ethic: The Declaration of the Parliament of the World's Religions*. New York: Continuum.

Kuttab, J. 1988: The pitfalls of dialogue. *Journal of Palestine Studies*, 17(2), 84–108.

Kymlicka, W. 1995: *The Rights of Minority Cultures*. Oxford: Oxford University Press.

Lake, A., ed., 1990: *After the Wars: Reconstruction in Afghanistan, Indochina, Central America, South Africa and the Horn of Africa*. New Brunswick, NJ: Transaction Publishers.

Lake, D. and Rothchild, D. 1996: Containing fear: the origins and management of ethnic conflict. *International Security*, 21(2), 41–75.

Lake, D. and Rothchild, D., eds, 1997: *The International Spread and Management of Ethnic Conflict*. Princeton: Princeton University Press.

Lang, A., ed., 2003: *Just Intervention*. Washington, DC: Georgetown University Press.

Langholtz, H., Kondoch, B. and Wells, A., eds, 2002: *The Yearbook of International Peacekeeping Operation*. Vol. 8. Leiden/Boston: Martinus Nijhoff.

Langille, H. P. 2000: Conflict prevention: options for rapid deployment and UN standing forces. In Woodhouse and Ramsbotham, eds, 219–53.

Langille H. P. 2000b: *Renewing Partnerships For The Prevention Of Armed Conflict: Options to Enhance Rapid Deployment and Initiate a UN Standing Emergency Capability*. Ottawa: Canadian Centre for Foreign Policy Development.

Langille H. P. 2002: *Bridging the Commitment-Capacity Gap: Existing Arrangements and Options for Enhancing UN Rapid Deployment Capabilities*. Wayne, NJ: Centre for UN Reform Education.

Langille, H. P., Faille, M., Hammond, J. and Hughes, C. 1995: A preliminary blueprint of long-term options for enhancing a United Nations rapid reaction capability. In D. Cox and A. Legault, eds, *UN Rapid Reaction Capabilities: Requirements and Prospects*. Cornwallis: The Pearson Peacekeeping Press.

Laqueur, W. 1999: *The New Terrorism: Fanaticism and the Arms of Mass Destruction*. Oxford: Oxford University Press.

Laqueur, W. 2004: *No End to War: Terrorism in the Twenty-First Century*. New York: Continuum.

Large, J. 1997: *The War Next Door: A Study of Second Track Intervention During the War in ex-Yugoslavia*. Stroud: Hawthorn Press.

Larsen, K., ed., 1993: *Conflict and Social Psychology*. London: Sage (PRIO).

Last, D. 1997: *Theory, Doctrine, and Practice of Conflict De-Escalation in Peacekeeping Operations*. Nova Scotia: Lester B. Pearson Canadian International Peacekeeping Training Centre.

Last, D. 2000: Organising for effective peacebuilding. In Woodhouse and Ramsbotham, eds, 80–96.

Laue, J. 1981: Conflict intervention. In E. Olsen and M. Micklin, eds, *Handbook of Applied Sociology*. New York: Praeger.

Laue, J. 1990: The emergence and institutionalisation of third-party roles in conflict. In Burton and Dukes, eds, 256–72.

Laue, J. and Cormick, C. 1978: The ethics of intervention in community disputes. In Bermant et al., eds, 205–32.

Lawler, P. 1995: *A Question of Values: Johan Galtung's Peace Research*. Boulder, Col.: Lynne Reinner.

Leatherman, J., DeMars, W., Gaffney, P. and Väyrynen, R. 1999: *Breaking Cycles of Violence: Conflict Prevention in Instrastate Crises*. West Hartford, Conn.: Kumarian Press.

Lederach, J. 1994: *Building Peace: Sustainable Reconciliation in Divided Societies*. Tokyo: United Nations University Press.

Lederach, J. 1995: *Preparing for Peace: Conflict Transformation Across Cultures*. New York: Syracuse University Press.

Lederach, J. 1995b: Conflict transformation in protracted internal conflicts: the case for a comprehensive framework. In Rupesinghe, ed., 201–22.

Lederach, J. 1997: *Building Peace: Sustainable Reconciliation In Divided Societies*. Washington, DC: United States Institute of Peace.

Lederach, J. 1999: *The Journey Toward Reconciliation*. Scottdale, Pa.: Herald Press.

Lederach, J. 2001: Civil society and reconciliation. In Crocker et al., eds, 841–54.

Lederach, J. 2003: *The Little Book of Conflict Transformation*. Intercourse, Pa.: Good Books.

Lederach, J. and Jenner, J. 2002: *A Handbook of International Peacebuilding: Into the Eye of the Storm*. Indianapolis, Ind.: Jossey Bass Wiley.

Lederach, J. and Wehr, P. 1991: Mediating conflict in Central America. *Journal of Peace Research* 28(1), 85–98.

Leitenberg, M. 2003: Deaths in wars and conflicts between 1945 and 2000. Cornell University Peace Studies Program Occasional Paper #29. <www.cissm. umd.edu/documents/deaths%20wars%20conflicts.pdf>.

Lentz 1955: *Towards a Science of Peace*. New York: Bookman Associates.

LeVine 1961: Anthropology and the study of conflict: an introduction. *Journal of Conflict Resolution*, 5(1), 5–15.

Levy, J. 1989: The causes of war: a review of theories and evidence. In Tetlock et al., 209–333.

Levy, J. 1996: Contending theories of international conflict: a levels-of-analysis approach. In Crocker and Hampson, eds, 3–24.

Lewer, N. 1999: International non-governmental organisations and peacebuilding: perspectives from peace studies and conflict resolution. Working Paper 3, Centre for Conflict Resolution, Department of Peace Studies, University of Bradford.

Lewer, N. and Schofield, S. 1997: *Non-Lethal Weapons: A Fatal Attraction? Military Strategies and Technologies for 21st Century Conflict*. London: Zed Books.

Lewin, K. 1948: *Resolving Social Conflicts*. New York: Harper and Brothers.

Lewis, B. 2002: *What Went Wrong? The Clash Between Islam and Modernity in the Middle East*. London: Weidenfeld and Nicolson.

Lichbach, M. 1989: An evaluation of 'does economic inequality breed conflict?' studies. *World Politics*, 41(4), 431–71.

Licklider, R., ed., 1993: *Stopping the Killing: How Civil Wars End*. New York: New York University Press.

Licklider, R. 1995: The consequences of negotiated settlements in civil wars 1945–1993. *American Political Science Review*, 89(3), 681–90.

Lijphart, A. 1968: *The Politics of Accommodation: Pluralism and Democracy in the Netherlands*. Berkeley: University of California Press.

Lijphart, A. 1977: *Democracy in Plural Societies*. New Haven, Conn.: Yale University Press.

Lijphart, A. 1995: Self-determination versus pre-determination of ethnic minorities in power-sharing systems. In W. Kymlicka, ed., *The Rights of Minority Cultures*. Oxford: Oxford University Press, 275–87.

Lillich, R. 1967: Forcible self-help by states to protect human rights. *Iowa Law Review*, 53, 325–51.

Lindgren, G., Wallensteen, G. and Nordquist, K., eds, 1990: *Issues in Third World Conflict Resolution*. Uppsala: Department of Peace and Conflict Research.

Linklater, A. 1998: *The Transformation of Political Community*. Cambridge: Polity.

Lizee, P. 1994: Peacekeeping, peacebuilding and the challenge of conflict resolution in Cambodia. In Charters, ed., 135–48.

Llamazares, M. and Reynolds, R. 2003: NGOs and peacebuilding in Kosovo. Working Paper 13, Centre for Conflict Resolution, Department of Peace Studies, University of Bradford.

Londregan, J. and Poole, K. 1990: Poverty, the coup trap and the seizure of executive power. *World Politics*, 42(2), 151–83.

Lorenz, K. 1966: *On Aggression* (original title: *The so-called Evil: Towards the Natural History of Aggression*). New York: Harcourt, Brace and World.

Love, M. 1995: *Peacebuilding Through Reconciliation in Northern Ireland*. Aldershot: Avebury.

Luard, E. 1986: *War in International Society: A Study in International Sociology*. London: I. B. Tauris.

Lund, M. 1995: Underrating Preventive Diplomacy. *Foreign Affairs* (July/August), 160–3.

Lund, M. 1996: *Preventing Violent Conflicts*. Washington, DC: US Institute of Peace.

Lund, M. 1999: Preventive diplomacy for Macedonia, 1992–1996: containment becomes nation-building. In Jentleson, ed., ch. 8.

Lund, M. 2003: *What Kind of Peace is Being Built: Taking Stock of Post Conflict Peacebuilding and Charting Future Directions*. Ottawa: International Development Research Agency.

Lund, M. and Rasamoelina, G., eds, 2000: *The Impact of Conflict Prevention Policy. Cases Measures, Assessments*. Part I, *Frontiers of Knowledge: What is Effective in Conflict Prevention?* Baden Baden: Nomos Verlagsgesellschaft Publishers/European Union Conflict Prevention Network, Stiftung Wissenschaft und Politik, Ebenhausen, Germany.

Luttwak, E. 1999: Give war a chance. *Foreign Affairs*, 78(4).

Lynch, C. 2002: Implementing peace settlements: multiple motivations, factionalism and implementation design. PhD thesis. Dublin City University.

Lynn-Jones, S. and Miller, S., eds, 1995: *Global Dangers*. Cambridge, Mass: MIT Press.

MacDonald, J. and Bendahmane, D., eds, 1987: *Conflict Resolution: Two Track Diplomacy*. Washington, DC: Center for the Study of Foreign Affairs.

MacFarlane, S. and Khong, Y. (forthcoming): *Human Security and the UN: A Critical History*. University of Indiana Press.

Mack, A. 1985: *Peace Research in the 1980s*. Canberra: Australian National University.

Mack, A. 2003: Plus ça change. *Security Dialogue*, 34(3), 363–7.

Mackinlay, J., ed., 1996: *A Guide to Peace Support Operations*. Providence, RI: Brown University, Thomas J. Watson Jr. Institute for International Studies.

Macrae, J. and Zwi, A., eds, 1994: *War and Hunger: Rethinking International Responses to Complex Emergencies*. London: Zed Books for Save the Children Fund (UK).

Madden, J. 1994: *Namibia: A Lesson for Success*. In Clement and Ward, eds, 255–60.

Magas, B. 1993: *The Destruction of Yugoslavia: Tracing the Break-Up 1980–92*. London: Verso.

Mak, T. 1995: The case against an International War Crimes Tribunal for former Yugoslavia. *International Peacekeeping*, 2(4), 536–63.

Malaquias, A. 1996: The UN in Mozambique and Angola: lessons learned. *International Peacekeeping*, 3(2), 87–103.

Mani, R. 2002: *Beyond Retribution: Seeking Justice in the Shadows of War*. Cambridge: Polity.

Mansbach, R. and Vasquez, J. 1981: *In Search of Theory: A New Paradigm for Global Politics*. New York: Columbia University Press.

Mansfield, E. and Snyder, J. 1995: Democratization and the danger of war. *International Security*, 20(1), 5–38.

Mansfield, E. and Snyder, J. 2001: Democratic transitions and war. In Crocker et al., eds, 113–26.

Marshall, D. 2000: Women in war and peace: grassroots peacebuilding. *Peaceworks*, 34 (August). US Institute of Peace.

Marshall, M. 2002: Measuring the societal impact of war. In Hampson and Malone, eds, 63–104.

Marshall, M. and Gurr, T. 2003: *Peace and Conflict 2003: A Global Survey of Armed Conflicts, Self-Determination Movements, and Democracy*. College Park, Md.: Center for International Development and Conflict Management.

Martin, G. 2003: *Understanding Terrorism: Challenges, Perspectives, and Issues*. London: Sage.

Martin, M. 1994: *Cambodia: A Shattered Society*. Los Angeles: University of California Press.

Maslow, H. 1954: *Motivation and Personality*. New York: Harper Bros.

Maxwell, J. and Maxwell, D. 1989: Male and female mediation styles and their effectiveness. Paper presented at the National Conference on Peacemaking and Conflict Resolution, Montreal, February/March.

Mayall, J., ed., 1996: *The New Interventionism 1991–94: United Nations Experience in Cambodia, former Yugoslavia and Somalia*. Cambridge: Cambridge University Press.

Maynard, K. 1997: Rebuilding community: psychosocial healing, reintegration and reconciliation at grassroots level. In Kumar, ed., 203–26.

McCalin, M. 1995: *The Reintegration of Young Ex-Combatants into Civilian Life: A Report to the International Labour Office*. Geneva: ILO.

McConnell, J. 1995: *Mindful Mediation: A Handbook for Buddhist Peacemakers*. Bangkok: Buddhist Research Institute.

McCoubrey, H. and White, N. 1995: *International Organizations and Civil Wars*. Aldershot: Dartmouth.

McGarry, J. and O'Leary, B., eds, 1993: *The Politics of Ethnic Conflict Regulation*. London: Routledge.

McGarry, J. and O'Leary, B. 1995: *Explaining Northern Ireland: Broken Images*. Oxford: Oxford University Press.

McKay, S. and Mazurana, D. 2004: *Where are the Girls? Girls in Fighting Forces in Northern Uganda, Sierra Leone, and Mozambique. Their Lives Before and After War*. Canada: International Center for Human Rights and Democratic Development.

Mead, M. 1940: Warfare is only an invention – not a biological necessity. *Asia*, 40, 402–5.

Mearsheimer, J. 1990: Back to the future: instability in Europe after the Cold War. *International Security*, 15(1) (Summer), 5–56.

Medlicott 1956: *Bismarck, Gladstone and the Concert of Europe*. London: Athlone Press.

Mendlovitz, S. and Fousek, J. 2000: A UN constabulary to enforce the law on genocide and crimes against humanity. In N. Reimer, ed., *Protection Against Genocide: Mission Impossible?* London: Praeger, 105–22.

Menold, J. 2004: Evaluation and impact assessment of peacebuilding projects: understanding the impact of external assistance on peace and conflict. MA thesis. University of Bradford, Department of Peace Studies.

Meron, T. 1993: The case for war crimes trials in Yugoslavia. *Foreign Affairs*, 72(3), 122–35.

Messer, E., Cohen, M. and D'Costa, J. 1998: Food from peace: breaking the links between conflict and hunger. Food, Agriculture, and the Environment Discussion Paper 24. Washington: International Food Policy Research Centre, <www.ifpri.org/2020/dp/dp24.pdf>.

Mertus, J. 1999: *Kosovo: How Myths and Truths Started a War*. Berkeley: University of California Press.

Miall, H. 1991: *New Conflicts in Europe: Prevention and Resolution*. Vol. 10. Oxford: Oxford Research Group Current Decisions Report.

Miall, H. 1992: *The Peacemakers: Peaceful Settlement of Disputes Since 1945*. London: Macmillan.

Miall, H., ed., 1994: *Minority Rights in Europe*. London: Pinter/Royal Institute of International Affairs.

Miall, H. 1995: *Albania: Development and Conflict*. London: International Alert.

Miall, H. 1997: The OSCE role in Albania: a success for conflict prevention? *Helsinki Monitor*, 8(4), 74–85.

Miall, H. 2000: Preventing potential conflicts: assessing the impact of light and deep conflict prevention in Central and Eastern Europe and the Balkans. In Lund and Rasamoelina, eds, 23–45.

Miall, H. 2003: Global governance and conflict prevention. In F. Cochrane, R. Duffy and J. Selby, eds, *Global Governance, Conflict and Resistance*. Houndmills: Palgrave, 59–77.

Miall, H. 2004: Conflict transformation: a multi-dimensional task. In Austin et al., eds, 67–90.

Mickey, R. and Albion, A. 1993: Ethnic relations in the Republic of Macedonia. In I. Cuthbertson and J. Liebowitz, eds, *Minorities: The New Europe's Old Issue*. Prague: Institute for East-West Studies.

Midlarsky, M., ed., 1989: *Handbook of War Studies*. Boston: Unwin Hyman.

Migdal, J. 1988: *Strong Societies and Weak States: State–Society Relations and State Capabilities in the Third World*. Princeton, NJ: Princeton University Press.

Millennium Report of the Secretary General to the United Nations, 2000: *We the Peoples: The Role of the United Nations in the Twenty First Century*. New York: Department of Public Information.

Ministry of Defence (Netherlands) 1995: *A UN Rapid Deployment Brigade: A Preliminary Study*. The Hague: Ministry of Defence of the Netherlands.

Minow, M. 1998: *Between Vengeance and Forgiveness: Facing History After Genocide and Mass Violence*. Boston: Beacon Press.

Minow, M. 2000: The hope for healing: what can truth commissions do? In Rotberg and Thompson, eds, 235–60.

Mitchell, C. 1981: *The Structure of International Conflict*. London: Macmillan.

Mitchell, C. 1991: Classifying conflicts: asymmetry and resolution. *Annals of the American Academy of Political and Social Science*, 518, 23–38.

Mitchell, C. 1993: Problem-solving exercises and theories of conflict resolution. In Sandole and van der Merwe, eds, 78–94.

Mitchell, C. 1995: *Cutting Losses: Reflections on Appropriate Timing*. Fairfax, Va.: George Mason University.

Mitchell, C. 1999: The anatomy of de-escalation. In Jeong, ed., 37–58.

Mitchell, C. 2000: *Gestures of Conciliation: Factors Contributing to Successful Olive Branches*. Basingstoke: Macmillan.

Mitchell, C. and Banks, M. 1996: *Handbook of Conflict Resolution: The Analytical Problem-Solving Approach*. London: Pinter/Cassell.

Mitchell, C. and Webb, K., eds, 1988: *New Approaches to International Mediation*. Westport, Conn.: Greenwood Press.

Mitchell, G. 1999: *Making Peace*. New York: Alfred Kopf.

Mitchell, P. 1995: Party competition in an ethnic dual party system. *Ethnic and Racial Studies*, 18(4), 773–93.

Mitchell, S., Gates, S. and Hegre, H. 1999: Evolution in democracy-war dynamics. *Journal of Conflict Resolution*, 43(6), 771–92.

Mitchels, B. 2003: Trauma, therapy and conflict. PhD thesis. University of Bradford.

Mitrany, D. 1943: *A Working Peace System: An Argument for the Functional Development of International Organization*. New York: Oxford University Press.

Mekenkamp, M. et al., eds, 2002: *Searching for Peace in Central and South Asia: An Overview of Conflict Prevention and Peacebuilding*. Boulder: Lynne Rienner.

Montagu, A., ed., 1978: *Learning Non-Aggression: The Experience of Non-Literate Societies*. New York: Oxford University Press.

Montgomery, T. 1995: *Revolution in El Salvador: From Civil Strife to Civil Peace*. Boulder, Col.: Westview Press.

Montville, J., ed., 1991: *Conflict and Peacemaking in Multiethnic Societies*. New York: Lexington Books.

Montville, J. 1993: The healing function in political conflict resolution. In Sandole and van der Merwe, eds, 112–28.

Moore, C. 1986: *The Mediation Process: Practical Strategies for Resolving Conflict*. San Francisco: Jossey-Bass.

Moore, J. 1972: *Law and the Indo-China War*. Princeton: Princeton University Press.

Moore, J., ed., 1974: *Law and Civil War in the Modern World*. Baltimore: Johns Hopkins University Press.

Moore, J. 1974: Towards an applied theory for the regulation of intervention. In Moore, ed., 3–37.

Morgenthau, H. 1973: *Politics Among Nations: The Struggle for Power and Peace*. 5th revised edn. New York: Kopf.

Morris, B. 2002: Camp David and after: an exchange: 1. An interview with Ehud Barak. *New York Review of Books*, 40(10), June 13.

Moseley, A. and Norman, R., eds, 2002: *Human Rights and Military Intervention*. Aldershot: Ashgate.

Msabaha, I. 1995: Mozambique's murderous rebellion. In Zartman, ed., 204–30.

Mueller, J. 1989: *Retreat from Doomsday: The Obsolescence of Major War*. New York: Basic Books.

Munck, R. 1986: *The Difficult Dialogue: Marxism and Nationalism*. London: Zed Books.

Munkler, H. 2005: *The New Wars*. Cambridge: Polity.

Muravchik, J. 1996: *Promoting Peace through Democracy*. In Crocker and Hampson, eds, 573–86.

Newman, E. 2004: The 'New Wars' debate: a historical perspective is needed. *Security Dialogue*, 35(2).

Newman, S. 1991: Does modernization breed ethnic conflict? *World Politics*, 43(3), 451–78.

Nhat Hanh, T. 1988: *Being Peace*. Berkeley: Parallax Press.

Nordstrom, C. 1992: The backyard front. In Nordstrom and Martin, eds, 260–74.

Nordstrom, C. 1994: *Warzones: Cultures of Violence, Militarisation and Peace*. Canberra: Australian National University, Peace Research Centre.

Nordstrom, C. 1995: Contested identities, essentially contested powers. In Rupesinghe, ed., 93–111.

Nordstrom, C. 1997: *Girls and Warzones: Troubling Questions*. Uppsala: Life and Peace Institute.

Nordstrom, C. and Martin, J., eds, 1992: *The Paths to Domination, Resistance and Terror*. Berkeley: University of California Press.

Northrup, T. 1989: The dynamic of identity in personal and social conflict. In Kriesberg et al., eds, 35–82.

Norwegian Refugee Council Global IDP Project (2004): *Internal Displacement: A Global Overview of Trends and Developments in 2003*. <www.idpproject.org>.

Nye, J. 1993: *Understanding International Conflicts: An Introduction to Theory and History*. New York: Harper Collins.

Nye, J. 2002: *The Paradox of American Power: Why the World's Only Superpower Can't Go It Alone*. Oxford: Oxford University Press.

O'Flaherty, M. and Gisvold, G., eds, 1998: *Post War Protection of Human Rights in Bosnia and Herzegovina*. Boston: Martinus Nijhoff.

O'Leary, B. and McGarry, J. 1996: *The Politics of Antagonism: Understanding Northern Ireland*. London: Athlone.

O'Loughlin, J. 2004: The political geography of conflict: Civil wars in the hegemonic shadow. In C. Flint, ed., *The Geography of War and Peace*. New York: Oxford University Press.

Oliveti, V. 2001: *Terror's Source: The Ideology of Wahhabi-Salafism and its Consequences*. Birmingham: Amadeus Books.

Organski, A. 1958: *World Politics*. New York: Knopf.

Osgood, C. 1962: *An Alternative to War or Surrender*. Urbana: Urbana University Press.

Ottaway, M. 1995: Eritrea and Ethiopia: negotiations in a transitional conflict. In Zatman, ed., 103–19.

Ottaway, M. 2003: *Democracy Challenged: The Rise of Semi-Authoritarianism*, Washington, DC: Carnegie Endowment for International Peace.

Outram, Q. 1997: 'It's terminal either way': an analysis of armed conflict in Liberia 1989–1996. *Review of African Political Economy*, 73, 355–71.

Pankhurst, D. 1998: Issues of justice and reconciliation in complex political emergencies. Paper given at the British International Studies Association annual conference, Leeds, December.

Pankhurst, D. and Pearce, J. 1997: Engendering the analysis of conflict: perspectives from the South. In Afshar, ed., 155–63.

Parekh, B. 2002: Terrorism or intercultural dialogue. In Booth and Dunne, eds, 270–83.

Paris, R. 1997: Peacebuilding and the limits of liberal internationalism. *International Security*, 22(2), 54–89.

Paris, R. 2001: Wilson's ghost: the faulty assumptions of postconflict peacebuilding. In Crocker et al., eds, 765–84.

Paris, R. 2003: Peacekeeping and the constraints of global culture. *European Journal of International Relations*, 9(3), 441–73.

Paris, R. 2004: *At War's End: Building Peace After Civil Conflict*. Cambridge: Cambridge University Press.

Parker, M. 1996: The mental health of war-damaged populations. *War and Rural Development in Africa*, 27(3), 77–85.

Parsons, A. 1995: *From Cold War to Hot Peace: UN Interventions 1947–1995*. London: Penguin.

Paul, T. and Hall, J., eds, 1999: *International Order and the Future of World Politics*. Oxford: Oxford University Press.

Peace Direct 2004: *Unarmed Heroes: The Courage to Go Beyond Violence*. London: Clairview.

Peang-Meth, A. 1991: Understanding the Khmer: sociological-cultural observations. *Asian Survey*, 30(5), 442–55.

Pearce, J. 1986: *Promised Land: Peasant Rebellion in Chalatenango, El Salvador*. London: Latin American Bureau.

Peck, C. 1993: *Preventive Diplomacy: A Perspective for the 1990s*. New York: Ralph Bunche Institute on the United Nations.

Peck, C. 1998: *Sustainable Peace: The Role of the UN and Regional Organizations in Preventing Conflict*. Lanham, NJ: Rowman and Littlefield.

Peirce, C. 1958: *The Collected Papers of C. S. Peirce*. Vol. 5. Cambridge, Mass.: Harvard University Press.

Peou, S. 2003: The United Nations, peacekeeping, and collective human security: from *An Agenda for Peace* to the Brahimi Report. *International Peacekeeping*, 9(2), Summer, 51–68.

Perrigo, S. 1991: Feminism and peace. In Woodhouse, ed., 303–22.

Pettifer, J. 1992: The new Macedonian question. *International Affairs*, 68(3), 475–85.

Petty, C. and Campbell, S. 1996: *Re-Thinking the Trauma of War*. London: Save the Children Conference Report.

Pillar, Paul R. 1983: *Negotiating Peace: War Termination as a Bargaining Process*. Princeton: Princeton University Press.

Pinker, S. 2002: *The Blank Slate*. London: Penguin.

Ploughshares Project 1995: *Armed Conflicts Report 1995*. Waterloo, Ontario: Institute of Peace and Conflict Studies.

Poehlman-Doumbouy, S. and Hill, F. 2001: Women and peace in the United Nations. *New Routes: A Journal of Peace Research and Action* (Life and Peace Institute, Sweden), 6(3).

Pogge, T. 2002: *World Poverty and Human Rights: Cosmopolitan Responsibilities and Reforms*. Cambridge: Polity.

Porter, N. 1996: *Rethinking Unionism: An Alternative Vision for Northern Ireland*. Belfast: Blackstaff.

Posen, B.P. 1993: The security dilemma and ethnic conflict. In Brown, ed., 103–24.

Post, J., Ruby, K. and Shaw, E. 2002: The radical group in context: (1) an integrated framework for the analysis of group risk for terrorism; (2) identification of critical elements in the analysis of risk for terrorism by radical group type. *Studies in Conflict and Terrorism*, 25, 73–126. London: Taylor and Francis.

Potter, D., Goldblatt, D., Kiloh, M. and Lewis, P., eds, 1997: *Democratization*. Cambridge: Polity.

Poulton, H. 1995: *Who are the Macedonians?* London: Hurst and Co.

Prasso, S. 1995: Cambodia a three billion dollar boondoggle. *Bulletin of the Atomic Scientists*, 51(2), 36–40.

Prendergast, J. and Smock, D. 1996: *NGOs and the Peace Process in Angola*. Washington, DC: US Institute of Peace.

Pruitt, D. 1981: *Negotiation Behaviour*. New York: Academic Press.

Pruitt, D. and Carnevale, P. 1993: *Negotiation in Social Conflict*. Pacific Grove, Calif.: Brooks/Cole.

Pruitt, D. and Rubin, J. 1986: *Social Conflict: Escalation, Stalemate and Settlement*. New York: Random House.

Prunier, G. 1995: *The Rwanda Crisis: History of a Genocide 1959–1994*. London: Hurst and Company.

Pugh, M. 1995: Peacebuilding as developmentalism: concepts from disaster research. *Contemporary Security Policy*, 16(3), 320–46.

Pugh, M. 2004: 'Peacekeeping and Critical Theory', *International Peacekeeping*, 11(1), 56–82.

Pugh, M. 2000: *Regeneration of War-Torn Societies*. Basingstoke: Macmillan.

Rabin, Y. 1996: *The Rabin Memoirs*. 2nd edn. Bnei Brak: Steimatzky.

Raiffa, H. 1982: *The Art and Science of Negotiation*. Cambridge, Mass.: Harvard University Press.

Raknerud, A. and Hegre, H. 1997: The hazard of war: reassessing the evidence for the democratic peace. *Journal of Peace Research*, 34, 385–404.

Ramsbotham, O. 1997: Humanitarian intervention 1990–5: a need to reconceptualize? *Review of International Studies*, 23, 445–67.

Ramsbotham, O. 1998: Islam, Christianity and forcible humanitarian intervention. *Ethics and International Affairs*, 12, 81–102.

Ramsbotham, O. 2004: Intervention, reconstruction and withdrawal operations 1989–2004. Paper presented at Wilton Park conference on post-war reconstruction, December.

Ramsbotham, O. 2004b: Radical disagreement: a new challenge for conflict resolution. Paper presented at British International Studies Association Conference, Warwick, December.

Ramsbotham, O. 2005: Cicero's challenge: from just war to just intervention. Paper presented at Iserlohn Conference, Germany, October.

Ramsbotham, O. 2005b: Taking radical disagreement seriously: implications for the theory and practice of conflict resolution. Paper presented at the Political Studies Association Conference, Leeds, April.

Ramsbotham, O. (forthcoming) *Radical Disagreement*.

Ramsbotham, O. and Woodhouse, T. 1996: *Humanitarian Intervention in Contemporary Conflict*. Cambridge: Polity.

Ramsbotham, O. and Woodhouse, T. 1999: Options for the development of codes of conduct for conflict resolution. Paper presented at Codes of Conduct Conference, Soesterberg, Netherlands, April.

Ramsbotham, O. and Woodhouse, T. 1999b: *Encyclopedia of International Peacekeeping Operations*. Santa Barbara: ABC-CLIO.

Randle, M., ed., 2002: *Challenge to Nonviolence*. Bradford: University of Bradford.

Rapoport, A. 1967: *Fights, Games and Debates*. Ann Arbor: University of Michigan Press.

Rapoport, A. 1971: Various conceptions of peace research. *Peace Research Society (International) Papers* XIX, 91–106.

Rapoport, A. 1989: *The Origins of Violence*. New York: Paragon House.

Rapoport, A. 1992: *Peace: An Idea Whose Time Has Come*. Ann Arbor: University of Michigan Press.

Rapoport, A. and Chammah, A. 1965: *The Prisoner's Dilemma: A Study in Conflict and Cooperation*. Ann Arbor: University of Michigan Press.

Rasmussen, D., ed., 1990: *Universalism vs. Communitarianism: Contemporary Debates in Ethics*. Cambridge, Mass.: MIT Press.

Rasmussen, J., Lewis, J. and Zartman, W., eds, 1997: *Peacemaking in International Conflict: Method and Techniques*. Washington, DC: United States Institute of Peace.

Rasmussen, M. V. 2003: *The West, Civil Society and the Construction of Peace*. Basingstoke: Palgrave.

Ratner, S. 1995: *The New UN Peacekeeping: Building Peace in Lands of Conflict After the Cold War*. Palgrave: Basingsoke.

Rawls, J. 1993: *Political Liberalism*. New York: Columbia University Press.

Rawls, J. 1999: *The Law of Peoples*. Cambridge, Mass.: Harvard University Press.

Reimann, C. 1999: *The Field of Conflict Management: Why Does Gender Matter?* Bonn: AFB-Texte, Nr 4/99, Information Unit Peace Research.

Reimann, C. 2002: *All You Need is Love – and What About Gender? Engendering Burton's Human Needs Theory*. Working Paper 10. Bradford: Centre for Conflict Resolution, Department of Peace Studies, University of Bradford.

Renner, M. 2002: *The Anatomy of Resource Wars*. Worldwatch Institute: Worldwatch Paper No. 162.

Reno, W. 1999: *Warlord Politics and African States*. Boulder, Col.: Lynne Rienner.

Reychler, L. and Paffenholz, T., eds, 2001: *Peacebuilding: A Field Guide*. Boulder, Col.: Lynne Rienner.

Reynal-Querol, M. 2002: Ethnicity, political systems and civil wars. *Journal of Conflict Resolution*, 46(1), 29–54.

Reynolds Levy, L. and Wessels, L. 2001: Developing an online learning strategy for conflict resolution training. Centre for Conflict Resolution Working Paper. University of Bradford, Department of Peace Studies, May.

Reynolds Levy, L. 2004: The Internet and Post Conflict Peacebuilding. PhD thesis. Department of Peace Studies, University of Bradford.

Rice, E. 1988: *Wars of the Third Kind: Conflict in Underdeveloped Countries*. Berkeley: University of California Press.

Richardson, L. 1960: *Arms and Insecurity*. Pittsburgh, Pa.: Boxwood Press.

Richardson, L. 1960b: *Statistics of Deadly Quarrels*. Pittsburgh, Pa.: Boxwood Press.

Rieff, D. 1994: The illusions of peacekeeping. *World Policy Journal*, 11(3), 1–18.

Rigby, A. 2001: *Justice and Reconciliation: After the Violence*. Boulder, Col.: Lynne Rienner.

Roberts, A. 1990: Law, lawyers and nuclear weapons. *Review of International Studies*, 16(1).

Robertson, G. 1999: *Crimes Against Humanity: The Struggle for Global Justice*. London: Penguin.

Rogers, C. 1980: *A Way of Being*. Boston: Houghton Mifflin.

Rogers, P. 2000: *Losing Control: Global Security in the Twenty-first Century*. London: Pluto.

Rogers, P. and Dando, M. 1992: *A Violent Peace: Global Security after the Cold War*. London: Brasseys.

Rogers, P. and Ramsbotham, O. 1999: Peace research – past and future. *Political Studies*.

Rose, H. and Rose, S., eds, 2001: *Alas Poor Darwin: Arguments Against Evolutionary Psychology*. London: Vintage.

Rosecrance, R. 1986: *The Rise of the Trading State: Commerce and Conquest in the Modern World*. New York: Basic Books.

Rosenblat, L. and Thompson, L. 1998: The door of opportunity: creating a permanent peacekeeping force. *World Policy Journal* (spring), 36–42.

Ross, M. 1993: *The Culture of Conflict: Interpretations and Interests in Comparative Perspective*. New Haven: Yale University Press.

Rotberg, R., ed., 1996: *Vigilance and Vengeance: NGOs Preventing Ethnic Conflict in Divided Societies*. Washington, DC: Brookings Institution.

Rotberg, R. 2000: Truth commissions and the provision of truth, justice, and reconciliation. In Rotberg and Thompson, eds, 3–21.

Rotberg, R. 2004: *When States Fail: Causes and Consequences*. Princeton, NJ: Princeton University Press.

Rotberg, R. and Thompson, D., eds, 2000: *Truth v. Justice: The Morality of Truth Commissions*. Princeton, NJ: Princeton University Press.

Rothman, J. 1992: *From Confrontation to Cooperation: Resolving Ethnic and Regional Conflict*. Newbury Park, Calif.: Sage.

Rothstein, R., ed., 1999: *After the Peace: Resistance and Reconciliation*. Boulder, Col.: Lynne Rienner.

Rouhana, N. and Korper, S. 1996: Dealing with dilemmas posed by power asymmetry in intergroup conflict. *Negotiation Journal*, 12(4).

Ruane, J. and Todd, J. 1996: *The Dynamics of Conflict in Northern Ireland*. Cambridge: Cambridge University Press.

Rubin, B. 1994: *Revolution Until Victory? The Politics and History of the PLO*. Cambridge, Mass.: Harvard University Press.

Rubin, B. 1996: *Towards Comprehensive Peace in Southeast Europe: Conflict Prevention in the Southern Balkans*. Report of the South Balkans Working Group of the Council on Foreign Relations Center for Preventive Action. New York: Twentieth-Century Fund.

Rufin, J. 1993: The paradoxes of armed protection. In Jean, ed., 11–23.

Rule, J. 1988: *Theories of Civil Violence*. Berkeley: University of California Press.

Rummel, R. J. 1970: *Applied Factor Analysis*. Evanston, Ill.: Northwestern University Press.

Rummel, R. 1996: *Common Foreign and Security Policy and Conflict Prevention*. London: Saferworld and International Alert.

Rupesinghe, K., ed., 1995: *Conflict Transformation*. London: Macmillan.

Rupesinghe, K. 1996: *General Principles of Multi-Track Diplomacy*. London: International Alert.

Rupesinghe, K. 1996b: Teaching the elephant to dance: developing a new agenda at the UN. In Y. Sakomoto, ed., *Global Transformation: Challenges to the State System*. Tokyo: United Nations University.

Russett, B. 1993: *Grasping the Democratic Peace: Principles for a Post-Cold War World*. Princeton, NJ: Princeton University Press.

Russett, B., Bruce, M. and Oneal, J. 2001: *Triangulating Peace: Democracy, Interdependence, and International Organizations*. New York: W. W. Norton.

Ryan, S. 1990: *Ethnic Conflict and International Relations*. Brookfield, VT: Dartmouth.

Saferworld, 1996: *Angola: Conflict Resolution and Peace-Building*. London: Saferworld.

Sahnoun, M. 1994: *Somalia: The Missed Opportunities*. Washington, DC: US Institute of Peace.

Said, E. 1995: *Peace and its Discontents*. London: Vintage.

Said, E. 2000: *The End of the Peace Process: Oslo and After*. London: Granta.

Salem, P. 1993: In theory: a critique of western conflict resolution from a non-western perspective. *Negotiation Journal*, 9(4), 361–9.

Salem, P., ed., 1997: *Conflict Resolution in the Arab World: Selected Essays*. New York: American University of Beirut.

Sandole, D. 1999: *Capturing the Complexity of Conflict: Dealing with Violent Ethnic Conflicts of the Post-Cold War Era*. London: Pinter.

Sandole, D. and Sandole-Saroste, I. 1987: *Conflict Management and Problem Solving: Interpersonal to International Applications*. Manchester: Manchester University Press.

Sandole, D. and van der Merwe, H., eds, 1993: *Conflict Resolution Theory and Practice: Integration and Application*. Manchester: Manchester University Press.

Saunders, H. 1999: *A Public Peace Process: Sustained Dialogue to Transform Racial and Ethnic Conflicts*. New York: Palgrave.

Schelling. T. 1960: *The Strategy of Conflict*. Cambridge, Mass.: Harvard University Press.

Schmeidl, S. and Adelman, H., eds, 1997: *Synergy in Early Warning: Conference Proceedings*. Toronto: Centre for International and Security Studies, York University.

Schmid, A. 1997: Early warning of violent conflicts. In P. Schmid, ed., *Violent Crime and Conflicts*. Milan: ISPAC (International Scientific and Professional Advisory Council of the United Nations Crime Prevention and Criminal Justice Programme).

Schmid, A. and Jongman, A. 1988: *Political Terrorism: A New Guide to Actors, Authors, Concepts, Data Bases, Theories and Literature*. Amsterdam: Transactions Books.

Schmid, H. 1968: Peace research and politics. *Journal of Peace Research*, 5(3), 217–32.

Schnabel, A. and Carment, D., eds, 2004: *Conflict Prevention From Rhetoric to Reality: Organizations and Institutions*, vol. 1. Lanham: Lexington Books.

Schnabel, A. and Carment, D., eds, 2004b: *Conflict Prevention From Rhetoric to Reality: Opportunities and Innovations*, vol. 2. Lanham: Lexington Books.

Schöpflin, G. 1994: *Politics in Eastern Europe*. London: Blackwell.

Schuett, O. 1997: The International War Crimes Tribunal for the Former Yugoslavia and the Dayton Peace Agreement: peace versus justice? *International Peacekeeping*, 4(2), 91–114.

Schwartzberg, J. E. 1997: A new perspective on peacekeeping: lessons from Bosnia and elsewhere. *Global Governance*, 3(1), 1–15.

Serbe, G., Macrae, J. and Wohlgemuth, L. 1997: *NGOs in Conflict: An Evaluation of International Alert*. Fantoft-Bergen, Norway: Christian Michelsen Institute.

Seville Statement on Violence, reprinted in Groebel, J., Hinde, J. and Hinde, R., eds, 1989: *Aggression and War: Their Biological and Social Bases*. Cambridge: Cambridge University Press, xxiii–xvi.

Shadid, A. 2002: *The Legacy of the Prophet: Despots, Democrats, and the New Politics of Islam*. Boulder, Col.: Westview Press.

Shain, Y. and Linz, J. 1995: *Between States: Interim Governments and Democratic Transitions*. Cambridge: Cambridge University Press.

Shamir, J. and Shikaki, K. 2002: Determinants of reconciliation and compromise among Israelis and Palestinians. *Journal of Peace Research*, 39(2), 185–202.

Sharp, G. 1973: *The Politics of Nonviolent Action*. Boston: Porter Sargent.

Sharp, J. 1997/8: Dayton Report card. *International Security*, 22(3), 101–37.

Shaw, M. 2000: *War and Genocide*. Cambridge: Polity.

Shaw, M. 2000b: *Theory of the Global State: Globality as an Unfinished Revolution*. Cambridge: Cambridge University Press.

Shawcross, W. 1994: *Cambodia's New Deal*. Washington, DC: Carnegie Endowment for International Peace.

Shear, J. 1996: Bosnia's post-Dayton traumas. *Foreign Policy*, 104 (Fall), 87–101.

Shearer, 1997: Exploring the limits of consent: conflict resolution in Sierra Leone. *Millennium Journal of International Studies*, 26(3), 845–60.

Sherif, M. 1966: *In Common Predicament: Social Psychology, Intergroup Conflict and Cooperation*. Boston: Houghton Mifflin.

Sherman, F. 1987: Pathway to Peace: The United Nations and the Road to Nowhere. Unpublished dissertation. Pennsylvania State University.

Shlaim, A. 1995: *War and Peace in the Middle East: A Concise History*. London: Penguin.

Shlaim, A. 2000: *The Iron Wall: Israel and the Arab World*. London: Allen Lane.

Siccama, J. G. 1996: *Conflict Prevention and Early Warning in the Political Practice of International Organizations*. The Hague: Netherlands Institute of International Relations, Clingendael Institute.

Simmel, G. 1902: The number of members as determining the sociological form of the group. *American Journal of Sociology*, 8, 158–96.

Singer, D. 1996: Armed conflict in the former colonial regions: from classification to explanation. In van de Goor et al., eds, 35–49.

Singer, D. and Small, M. 1968: Alliance aggregation and the onset of war 1815–1945. In Singer, ed., *Quantitative International Politics: Insights and Evidence*. New York: Free Press, 247–86.

Singer, D. and Small, M. 1972: *The Wages of War, 1816–1965: A Statistical Handbook*. New York: Wiley.

SIPRI Yearbook: 1997. Oxford: Oxford University Press for SIPRI.

Sisk, T. 1997: *Power Sharing and International Mediation in Ethnic Conflicts*. Washington, DC: US Institute of Peace.

Sisk, T. and Reynolds, A., eds, 1998: *Elections and Conflict Management in Africa*. Washington, DC: US Institute of Peace.

Sites, P. 1990: Needs as analogues of emotions. In Burton, ed., 7–33.

Skaar, E. 1999: Truth commissions, trials – or nothing? Policy options in democratic transitions. *Third World Quarterly*, 20, 1109–28.

Skjelsbaek, K. 1991: The UN Secretary General and the Mediation of International Disputes. *Journal of Peace Research*, 28(1), 99–115.

Slim H. 1997: *Doing the Right Thing: Relief Agencies, Moral Dilemmas and Moral Responsibility in Political Emergencies and War*. Uppsala: Nordiska Afrikainstitutet, Atudies on Emergencies and Disaster Relief, No. 6.

Slye, R. 2000: Amnesty, truth and reconciliation: reflections on the South African amnesty process. In Rotberg and Thompson, eds, 170–88.

Small Arms Survey 2002: *Small Arms Survey 2002*. Oxford: Oxford University Press.

Smith, A. 1986: *The Ethnic Origins of Nations*. Oxford: Blackwell.

Smith, A. 1995: *Nations and Nationalism in a Global Era*. Cambridge: Polity.

Smith, A. 2003: From democracy to conflict: the UN's search for peace and security. *Security Dialogue*, 34(3), 357–62.

Smith, C. 2004: *Palestine and the Arab-Israeli Conflict*. 5th edn. Boston, Ma.: St Martin's Press.

Smith, J. 1995: *Stopping Wars: Defining the Obstacles to Cease-fire*. Boulder, Col.: Westview Press.

Snow, D. 1996: *Uncivil Wars: International Security and the New Internal Conflicts*. Boulder, Col.: Lynne Rienner.

Snyder, J. 2000: *From Voting to Violence: Democratization and Nationalist Conflict*. New York: W. W. Norton.

Sollom, R. and Kew, D. 1996: *Humanitarian Assistance and Conflict Prevention in Burund*. In Rotberg, ed., 235–59.

Solomon, R. 1997: The global information revolution and international conflict management. Overview presentation to the conference on Virtual Diplomacy, Washington, DC, US Peace Institute, April.

Sorenson and Wood, eds, 2004: *The Politics of Peacekeeping in the Post Cold War Era*. London: Taylor and Francis.

Sorokin, P. 1937: *Social and Cultural Dynamics*. New York: American Book.

South Commission, 1990: *The Challenge to the South*. Oxford: Oxford University Press.

Sponsel, L. 1996: The natural history of peace: the positive view of human nature and its potential. In T. Gregor, ed., *A Natural History of Peace*. Nashville, Tenn.: Vanderbilt University Press.

Stamato, L. 1992: Voice, place and process: research on gender, negotiation and conflict resolution. *Mediation Quarterly*, 9(4), 375–86.

Stavenhagen, R. 1996: *Ethnic Conflicts and the Nation-State*. Houndmills: Macmillan.

Steans, J. 1998: *Gender and International Relations*, Cambridge: Polity.

Stedman, S. 1991: *Peacemaking in Civil War: International Mediation in Zimbabwe, 1974–1980*. Boulder, Col.: Lynne Reinner.

Stedman, S. 1995: Alchemy for a new world order: overselling 'preventive diplomacy'. *Foreign Affairs*, 74 (May/June), 14–20.

Stedman, S. 1997: Spoiler problems in peace processes. *International Security*, 22(2), 5–53.

Stedman, S., Rothchild, D. and Cousens, E., eds, 2002: *Ending Civil Wars: The Implementation of Peace Agreements*. Boulder, Col.: Lynne Rienner, IPA/CISAC.

Stein, B., Cuny, F. and Reed, R., eds, 1995: *Refugee Repatriation During Conflict: A New Conventional Wisdom*. Dallas: Center for the Study of Societies in Crisis.

Stern, J. 2003: *Terrorism in the Name of God: Why Religious Militants Kill*. New York: Harper Collins.

Stewart, F. 2002: Horizontal inequalities as a source of conflict. In Hampson and Malone, eds.

Stewart, F. and Fitzgerald, V. 2001: *War and Underdevelopment*. Oxford: Oxford University Press.

Stewart, J., ed., 1986: *Bridges Not Walls: A Book About Interpersonal Communication*. New York: McGraw-Hill.

Stewart, J. and Thomas, M. 1986: Dialogic listening: sculpting mutual meanings. In Stewart, ed., 192–210.

Stewart, R. 1993: *Broken Lives: A Personal View of the Bosnian Conflict*. London: Harper Collins.

Stiehm, J. 1995: Men and women in peacekeeping: a research note. *International Peacekeeping*, 2(4), 564–9.

Stromseth, J. 2003: Rethinking humanitarian intervention: the case for incremental change. In Holzgrefe and Keohane, eds, 232–72.

Stuart, D. 1994: United Nations involvement in the peace process in El Salvador. In Clements and Ward, eds, 261–72.

Suganami, H. 1996: *On the Causes of War*. Oxford: Clarendon Press.

Sullivan, J. 1994: How peace came to El Salvador. *Orbis*, 38(1), 83–98.

Summerfield, D. 1996: *The Impact of War and Atrocity on Civilian Populations: Basic Principles for NGO Interventions and a Critique of Psychosocial Trauma Projects*. London: Overseas Development Institute.

Sumner, W. G. 1906: *Folkways*. Boston: Ginn.

Susskind, L. 1987: *Breaking the Impasse: Consensual Approaches to Resolving Public Disputes*. New York: Basic Books.

Swing, W. 2003: The role of MONUC in the DRC's peace process. *Conflict Trends*, 4, 25–9.

Tajfel, H., ed., 1978: *Differentiation Between Social Groups: Studies in the Social Psychology of Intergroup Relations*. European Monographs in Social Psychology, No. 14. London: Academic Press.

Taylor, A. and Miller, J., eds, 1994: *Conflict and Gender*. Cresskill, NJ: Hampton Press.

Tetlock, P., Husbands, J., Jervis, R., Stern, P. and Tilly, C., eds, 1989: *Behaviour, Society and Nuclear War*. Oxford: Oxford University Press.

Thakur, R. 2001: Research note: Cambodia, East Timor and the Brahimi Report. *International Peacekeeping*, 8(3), Autumn.

Tilly, C. 1978: *From Mobilization to Revolution*. Reading, Mass.: Addison-Wesley.

Tooby, J. and Cosmides, L. 1992: Psychological foundations of culture. In Barkow et al., eds.

Touval, S. 1985: *The Peace Brokers; Mediators in the Arab-Israeli Conflict, 1948–1979*. Princeton: Princeton University Press.

Touval, S. 1992: The study of conflict resolution: is there unity in diversity? *Negotiation Journal*, 8(2): 147–52.

Touval, S. 1994: Why the UN fails. *Foreign Affairs*, 73(5): 44–57.

Touval, S. and Zartman, W., eds, 1985: *International Mediation: Theory and Practice*. Boulder, Col.: Westview Press.

Trachtenberg, M. 1993: Intervention in historical pespective. In L. Reed and

C. Kaysen, eds, *Emerging Norms of Justified Intervention*. Cambridge, Mass.: American Academy of Arts and Sciences, 15–36.

Travers, D. 1993: The use of Article 99 of the Charter by the Secretary-General, in House of Commons Foreign Affairs Committee, *Third Report*, Session 1992–3, vol. II, HC235-II, 336–57.

Turnbull, C. 1978: The politics of non-aggression. In Montagu, ed., 161–221.

Tutu, D. 1999: *No Future Without Forgiveness*. London: Rider.

Twiss, S. 1993: Curricular perspectives in comparative religious ethics: a critical examination of four paradigms. *Annual of the Society of Christian Ethics*, 249–69.

Ugglas, M. 1994: Conditions for successful preventive diplomacy. In S. Carlsson, ed., *The Challenge of Preventive Diplomacy: The Experience of the CSCE*. Stockholm: Ministry of Foreign Affairs, Norstedts Tryckeri AB.

UK Ministry of Defence 2004: *The Military Contribution to Peace Support Operations* (JWP 3.50), 2nd edn. Shrivenham, UK: Joint Doctrine and Concepts Centre.

UNDP 1996: *Human Development Index 1996*. New York: United Nations Development Program.

UNHCR 1995: *The State of the World's Refugees*. Oxford: Oxford University Press.

UNHCR 2004: *Global Refugee Trends: Overview of Refugee Populations, New Arrivals, Durable Solutions, Asylum-Seekers and Other Persons Of Concern to UNHCR*. 15 June 2004. Geneva: UNHCR Population Data Unit, <www.unhcr.ch/ statistics>.

UNIDR 1996: *Managing Arms in Peace Processes: The Issues*. Geneva: UN Institute for Disarmament Research.

United Nations 1992: *Report of the Secretary-General on the United Nations Observer Mission in El Salvador*. New York: UN Department of Public Information.

United Nations 1993: *The Truth Commission Report: From Madness to Hope, The 12-Year War in El Salvador*. New York: UN Department of Public Information.

United Nations 1994: *Report of the Secretary-General on the UN Observer Mission in El Salvador*. New York: UN Department of Public Information.

United Nations 1995: *The United Nations and El Salvador, 1990–1995*. New York: UN Department of Public Information.

United Nations 1996: *The Blue Helmets: A Review of United Nations Peace-Keeping*. New York: UN Department of Public Information.

United Nations 1996b: *Report of the Secretary-General on the United Nations Angola Verification Mission (UNAVEM III), 27 June 1996*. New York: UN Department of Public Information.

United Nations 1996c: *The United Nations and Rwanda, 1993–1996*. New York: UN Department of Public Information.

United Nations 1999: *Report of the Independent Inquiry into the Actions of the United Nations During the 1994 Genocide in Rwanda*. New York: United Nations, S/1999/1257.

United Nations 1999b: *The Fall of Srebrenica. Report of the Secretary-General to the UN General Assembly*. New York: United Nations, A/54/549.

United Nations 2000: *We The Peoples: The Role of the United Nations in the Twenty-First Century*. Millennial Report of the Secretary-General. New York: UN Department of Public Information.

United Nations 2001: *The Prevention of Armed Conflict: Report of the Secretary-General*. New York: United Nations, A/55/985–S/2002/574.

United Nations 2002: *Secretary-General's Statement to the Security Council*. New York: UN Department of Public Information

United Nations Development Programme, 2002: *Human Development Report 2002: Deepening Democracy in a Fragmented World, Overview*. New York: UNDP.

United Nations High-Level Panel 2004: *A More Secure World: Our Shared Responsibility. Report of the High-Level Panel on Threats, Challenges and Change*. New York: United Nations.

United Nations Policy Working Group on the UN and Terrorism (UNPWG) 2003: New York: United Nations, S/AC.40/2003/SM.1/2; 26/2/03. <www.un.org/Docs/sc/committees/1373/documentation.html>.

United Nations Security Council 1992: *Second Special Report of the Secretary-General on the United Nations Transitional Authority in Cambodia*. New York: UN Department of Public Information.

United Nations Security Council 2002: *On Women, Peace and Security*. SCR 7551, 28 October.

UNRISD 1995: *Rebuilding War-Torn Societies*. Geneva: UN Research Institute for Social Development.

Urquhart, B. 1993: A UN volunteer military force. *New York Review of Books*, 40(11), 10 June, 3–4.

Urquhart, B. 1995: Prospects for a UN rapid response capability. In D. Cox and A. Legault, eds, *UN Rapid Reaction Capabilities: Requirements and Prospects*. Cornwallis: The Pearson Peacekeeping Press.

US Department of Defense 1998: *Hidden Killers 1998: The Global Landmine Crisis*. Washington, DC: US Department of State.

US Department of State 2002: *Patterns of Global Terrorism*. Washington, DC: Department of State, Bureau of Public Affairs (Office of the Coordinator for Counterterrorism) (published annually, <www.state.gov/>).

Utting, P. 1994: *Between Hope and Insecurity: The Social Consequences of the Cambodian Peace Process*. Geneva: UNRISD.

Van Crefeld, M. 1991: *The Transformation of War*. New York: The Free Press.

Van Crefeld, M. 2000: *The Rise and Decline of the State*. Cambridge: Cambridge University Press.

van de Goor, L., Rupesinghe, K. and Sciarone, P., eds, 1996: *Between Development and Destruction: An Enquiry into the Causes of Conflict in Post-Colonial States*. New York: St Martin's Press.

van den Dungen, P. 1996: Initiatives for the pursuit and institutionalisation of peace research. In L. Broadhead, ed., *Issues in Peace Research*. Department of Peace Studies, University of Bradford, 5–32.

van den Dungen, P. and Wittner, L. 2003: Peace history: an introduction. *Journal of Peace Research: Special Issue on Peace History*, 40(54), 363–75.

van der Merwe, H. 1989: *Pursuing Justice and Peace in South Africa*. London: Routledge.

van der Stoel, M. 1994: The role of the CSCE High Commissioner on National Minorities in CSCE preventive diplomacy. In S. Carlson, ed., *The Challenge of Preventive Diplomacy*. Stockholm: Ministry for Foreign Affairs.

van Evera, S. 1994: Hypotheses on nationalism and war. *International Security*, 18(4), 5–39.

van Tongeren, P. 1996: *Prevention and Management of Conflicts: An International Directory*. The Hague: Dutch Centre for Conflict Prevention.

van Tongeren, P., van de Veen, H. and Verhoeven, J., eds, 2002: *Searching for Peace in Europe and Eurasia: An Overview of Conflict Prevention and Peacebuilding Activities.* Boulder, Col.: Lynne Rienner.

Van Walraven, K. and van der Vlugt, J. 1996: *Conflict Prevention and Early Warning in the Political Practice of International Organizations.* The Hague: Clingendael Institute.

Vasquez, J. 1987: The steps to war: toward a scientific explanation of correlates of war findings. *World Politics,* 40 (October), 108–45.

Vasquez, J. 1993: *The War Puzzle.* Cambridge: Cambridge University Press.

Vasquez, J. 1995: Why global conflict resolution is possible: meeting the challenge of the new world order. In Vasquez et al., eds, 131–53.

Vasquez, J., Johnson, J. and Stamato, L., eds, 1995: *Beyond Confrontation: Learning Conflict Resolution in the Post-Cold War Era.* Ann Arbor: University of Michigan Press.

Vassall-Adams, G. 1994: *Rwanda: An Agenda for International Action.* Oxford: Oxfam.

Vattel, E. de 1758/1964: *The Law of Nations or the Principles of Natural Law Applied to the Conduct and to the Affairs of Nations and of Sovereigns.* Dobbs Ferry, NY: Oceana Publications.

Väyrynen, R. 1984: Regional conflict formations: an intractable problem of international relations. *Journal of Peace Research,* 21(4), 337–59.

Väyrynen, R., ed., 1991: *New Directions in Conflict Theory: Conflict Resolution and Conflict Transformation.* London: Sage.

Väyrynen, T. 2004: Gender and UN peace operations: the confines of modernity. In Bellamy and Williams, eds, 125–42.

Vickers, J. 1993: *Women and War.* London: Zed Press.

Vickers, M. 1995: *The Albanians, A Modern History.* London: I. B. Tauris.

Vickers, M. 1998: *Between Serb and Albanian: A History of Kosovo.* London: Hurst.

Vickers, M. and Pettifer, J. 1997: *From Anarchy to a Balkan Identity.* London: Hurst and Co.

Villa-Vincenzio, C. and Verwoerd, W. 2000: Constructing a report: writing up the 'truth'. In Rotberg and Thompson, eds.

Vives, A. 1994: *No Democracy Without Money: The Road to Peace in Mozambique.* London: Catholic Institute for International Relations.

Volkan, J., Montville, J. and Julius, D., eds, 1990: *The Psychodynamics of International Relationships,* vol. 2. Lexington, Mass.: D. C. Heath.

Volkan, V. and Harris, M. 1993: Vaccinating the political process: a second psychopolitical analysis of relationships between Russia and the Baltic states. *Mind and Human Interaction,* 4(4), 169–90.

von Hippel, K. 2002: The roots of terrorism: probing the myths. *Political Quarterly,* 73, Supplement 1, August, 25–39.

Waldmeier, P. 1998: *Anatomy of a Miracle: The End of Apartheid and the Birth of the New South Africa.* London: Penguin.

Wallace, M. 1977: Arms races and escalation: some new evidence. *Journal of Conflict Resolution,* 23, 3–16.

Wallensteen, P. 1984: Universalism vs. particularism: on the limits of major power order. *Journal of Peace Research,* 21(3), 243–57.

Wallensteen, P., ed., 1988: *Peace Research: Achievements and Challenges.* Boulder/London: Westview Press.

Wallensteen P., ed., 1998: *Preventing Violent Conflicts: Past Record and Future Challenges.* Uppsala: Uppsala University Department of Peace and Conflict Research.

Wallensteen, P. 2002: Reassessing recent conflicts: direct vs. structural prevention. In Hampson and Malone, eds.

Wallensteen, P. 2002b: *Understanding Conflict Resolution*. London: Sage.

Wallensteen, P. and Axell, K. 1995: Armed conflict at the end of the Cold War, 1989–93. *Journal of Peace Research*, 30(3), 331–46.

Wallensteen, P. and Sollenberg, M. 1996: After the Cold War: emerging patterns of armed conflicts. *Journal of Peace Research*, 32(3), 345–60.

Wallensteen, P. and Sollenberg, M. 1997: Armed conflicts, conflict termination and peace agreements 1989–96. *Journal of Peace Research*, 34(3), 339–58.

Wallensteen, P. and Sollenberg, M. 2001: Armed conflict, 1989–2000. *Journal of Peace Research*, 38(5), 629–44.

Wallerstein, I. 1979: *The Capitalist World Economy*. Cambridge: Cambridge University Press.

Walton, R. and McKersie, R. 1965: *A Behavioral Theory of Labor Negotiations: An Analysis of a Social Interaction System*. New York: McGraw-Hill.

Waltz, K. 1959: *Man, the State and War*. New York: Columbia University Press.

Waltz, K. 1979: *Theory of International Politics*. Reading, Mass.: Addison-Wesley.

Waltz, K. 2002: The continuity of international politics. In Booth and Dunne, eds, 348–53.

Walzer, M., ed., 1995: *Towards a Global Civil Society*. Oxford: Berghahn Books.

Ward, M. D. and Gleditsch, K. S. 1998: Democratizing for Peace. *American Political Science Review*, 92 (March), 51–62.

Wardlow, G. 1982: *Political Terrorism, Tactics and Counter-Measures*. Cambridge: Cambridge University Press.

Webb, K., Koutrakou, V. and Walters, M. 1996: The Yugoslavian conflict, European mediation and the contingency model: a critical perspective. In Bercovitch, ed., 171–89.

Weber, T. 1999: Gandhi, deep ecology, peace research and Buddhist economics. *Journal of Peace Research*, 36(3), 349–61.

Weber, T. 2001: Gandhian philosophy, conflict resolution theory, and practical approaches to negotiation. *Journal of Peace Research*, 38(4), 493–513.

Wehr, P. 1979: *Conflict Regulation*. Boulder, Col.: Westview Press.

Wehr, P. and Lederach, J. 1996: Mediating conflict in Central America. In Bercovitch, ed., 55–74.

Weiss, T. and Collins, C. 1996: *Humanitarian Challenges and Intervention: World Politics and the Dilemmas of Help*. Boulder, Col.: Westview Press.

Wheeler, N. 2000: *Saving Strangers: Humanitarian Intervention in International Society*. Oxford: Oxford University Press.

White, N. 1993: *Keeping the Peace: The United Nations and the Maintenance of International Peace and Security*. Manchester: Manchester University Press, Melland Schill Monographs in International Law.

Whitman, J. and Pocock, D., eds, 1996: *After Rwanda: The Co-ordination of United Nations Humanitarian Asssistance*. London: Macmillan.

Whittaker, D. 1999: *Conflict and Reconciliation in the Contemporary World*. London: Routledge.

Whittaker, D., ed., 2001: *The Terrorism Reader*. New York: Routledge.

Whyte, J. 1990: *Interpreting Northern Ireland*. Oxford: Clarendon Press.

Wider Peacekeeping 1995: British Army Field Manual, vol. 5. London: HMSO.

Wight, M. 1977: *Systems of States*, ed. H. Bull. Leicester: Leicester University Press.

Wilkinson, P. 1996: *Peace Support Operations*. London: Joint Warfare Publication 3.01.

Wilkinson, P. 2000: Peace support under fire: lessons from Sierra Leone. *International Security Information Service*, Briefing No. 2, June.

Williams, D. and Young, T. 1994: Governance, the World Bank and liberal theory. *Policy Studies*, 42.

Williams, M. 1998: *Civil–Military Relations and Peacekeeping*. London: IISS, Adelphi Paper 321.

Williams, P. 1998: Terrorism and organized crime: convergence, nexus or transformation? In G. Jervas, ed., *FOA Report on Terrorism*. Stockholm: FOA, 69–91.

Williams, S. and Williams, S. 1994: *Being in the Middle by Being at the Edge: Quaker Experience of Non-Official Political Mediation*. London: Quaker Peace and Service.

Wilson, E. 1975/2000: *Sociobiology: The New Synthesis*. Cambridge, Mass.: Harvard University Press.

Wilson, E. 1998: *Consilience: The Unity of Knowledge*. New York: Kopf.

Wilton Park Conference 2003: *Transforming War Economies*. Report of the 725th Wilton Park Conference, in association with the International Peace Academy, New York, October.

Wimmer, A., Goldstone, R. J., Horowitz, D. L., Joras, U. and Schetter, C., eds, 2004: *Facing Ethnic Conflicts: Towards a New Realism*. Lanham: Rowman & Littlefield.

Woodhouse, T. 1986: To live our lives so as to take away the occasion for war: some observations on the peaceful economy. In Chester and Rigby, eds, 70–89.

Woodhouse, T., ed., 1991: *Peacemaking in a Troubled World*. Oxford: Berg.

Woodhouse, T. 1999: Peacebuilding from below. In J. Perez de Cuellar and Yong Seek Choue, eds, *World Encyclopaedia of Peace*, vol. 4. New York: Oceana Publications, 293–6.

Woodhouse, T. 1999b: *International Conflict Resolution: Some Critiques and a Response*. Bradford: Centre for Conflict Resolution, Working Paper 1, Department of Peace Studies, University of Bradford.

Woodhouse, T. and Ramsbotham, O. 1996: *Peacekeeping: Terra Incognita – Here be Dragons – Peacekeeping and Conflict Resolution in Contemporary Conflict: Some Relationships Considered*. University of Ulster: INCORE/United Nations University.

Woodhouse, T. and Ramsbotham, O., eds, 2000: *Peacekeeping and Conflict Resolution*. London: Frank Cass.

Woodhouse, T. and Ramsbotham, O. 2003: Conflict prevention and the democratic peace: conflict, democracy and terror. Policy paper prepared for IDEA, Stockholm.

Woodhouse, T. and Ramsbotham, O. 2005: Cosmopolitan peacekeeping and the globalization of security. *International Peacekeeping*, 12(2), 139–56.

Woodward, S. 1995: *Balkan Tragedy: Chaos and Dissolution After the Cold War*. Washington, DC: The Brookings Institution.

Woodward, S. 2003: *On War and Peacebuilding: Unfinished Legacy of the 1990s*. New York: City University of New York.

World Bank, 1998: *Post-Conflict Reconstruction: The Role of the World Bank*. Washington, DC: World Bank.

World Bank, 2003: *The Role of the World Bank in Conflict and Development: An Evolving Agenda*. At <www.lnweb18.worldbank.org/ESSD/sdvext.nsf/67ByDocName/ AboutUS) >.

World Bank, 2003b: *The World Bank in Conflict Prevention and Reconstruction: Issue Brief.* At <www.lnweb18.worldbank.org/ESSD/sdvext.nsf/67ByDocName/AboutUS) >.

Wright, Q. 1942: *A Study of War.* Chicago: University of Chicago Press.

Yarrow, C. H. 1978: *Quaker Experiences in International Conciliation.* New Haven, Conn: Yale University Press.

Young, O. 1967: *The Intermediaries: Third Parties in International Crises.* Princeton: Princeton University Press.

Zaagman, R. and Thorburn, J. 1997: *The Role of the High Commissioner on National Minorities in OSCE Conflict Prevention.* The Hague: Foundation on Inter-Ethnic Relations.

Zartman, W., ed., 1978: *The Negotiation Process: Theories and Applications.* Beverley Hills, Calif.: Sage.

Zartman, W. 1985: *Ripe for Resolution: Conflict and Intervention in Africa.* New York: Oxford University Press.

Zartman, W. 1995: Negotiating the South African Conflict. In Zartman, ed., 1995b.

Zartman, W., ed., 1995: *Collapsed States: The Disintegration and Restoration of Legitimate Authority.* Boulder, Col.: Lynne Rienner.

Zartman, W., ed., 1995b: *Elusive Peace: Negotiating an End to Civil Wars.* Washington, DC: Brookings Institution.

Zartman, W. 1997: Toward the resolution of international conflicts. In Zartman and Rasmussen, eds, 3–22.

Zartman, W. 2000: Mediating conflicts of need, greed and creed. *Orbis*, 24(2), 255–66.

Zartman, W., ed., 2000: *Traditional Cures for Modern Conflict: African Conflict 'Medicine'.* Boulder, Col.: Lynne Rienner.

Zartman, W., ed., 2001: *Preventive Negotiation.* Lanham, Md.: Rowman and Littlefield.

Zartman, W. and Berman, M. 1982: *The Practical Negotiator.* New Haven, Conn.: Yale University Press.

Zartman, W. and Rasmussen, J., eds, 1997: *Peacemaking in International Conflict: Methods and Techniques.* Washington, DC: United States Institute of Peace Press.

Zartman, W. and Rubin, J. 1996: *Power and Asymmetry in International Negotiations.* Laxenburg, Austria: International Institute of Applied Systems Analysis.

Index